# COMPARATIVE ADVANTAGE AND GROWTH

GP90 01093

# COMPARATIVE ADVANTAGE AND GROWTH

**Trade and Development in Theory and Practice**

**H. D. Evans**

St. Martin's Press

New York

First published in the United States of America in 1989

Printed in Great Britain

ISBN 0-312-00955-0

**Library of Congress Cataloging-in-Publication Data**

Evans, H. David (Henry David)
  Comparative Advantage and Growth
  Includes bibliographies and index.
  Contents: v.  1. Comparative advantage and growth
  1. Commerce.  2. Economic development.
3. Comparative advantage (Commerce)  I. Title.
HF1008.E83 1989    382    87-16370
ISBN 0-312-00955-0 ( v. 1.)

To Barbara, Ben and Simon, and
in memory of Jessica

# CONTENTS

# PREFACE

The early formulation of the ideas behind this study arose from a conference on *Alternative Perspectives on Trade and Development* and a series of seminars and workshops held at the IDS during the 1970s. During that time, I felt an uneasy tension between the precision of the Sraffian approach to trade theory and the vision of the Fundamentalist school of the Marxian tradition. More recently, I have found a more satisfactory resolution of a number of theoretical issues in the new school of analytical or 'rational choice' Marxism.

I am acutely aware that in writing yet another book on such a wide-ranging topic, I will not do justice to any part of the story. The trade specialist will notice the numerous gaps in the analysis, whilst those in development studies are bound to complain that the theoretical treatment is far too technical and economistic. My only defence is that, in spite of the long gestation period in producing this study, there is still no single source which attempts to draw together the core elements of the trade, growth and development literature in quite the way I have done. I have tried to pay attention to both the consistency and usefulness of the trade models in relation to the theoretical and empirical compromises which must be made when choosing models which attempt to capture some strategic aspects and stylised facts about world trading relationships. Specialisation within the trade and growth literature all too often produces technical brilliance without attention being given to some of the stylised facts. This book is written in the hope that others will also find the particular fusion of alternative perspectives I have offered useful.

My debts to colleagues, friends and family are many. Diane

Elson, Arghiri Emmanual and Robin Murray had an important influence on the early formulation of the ideas and have been very supportive of the project throughout. Lyn Mainwaring and Ian Steedman have been a constant source of advice, comment and encouragement, and I have benefited greatly from discussions with Rob Eastwood, John Roemer and Alasdair Smith. Revisions to the manuscript have indirectly benefited from the comments and criticisms of early drafts of my chapter on 'Alternative Perspectives on Trade and Development' in H. B. Chenery and T. N. Srinivasan (eds) (1989) *Handbook of Development Economics*, Amsterdam: North-Holland. I have had close personal support and advice from many colleagues at the IDS, particularly from Robert Cassen, Carlos Fortin, Raphie Kaplinsky, Michael Lipton and Adrian Wood, and from Jerzy Osiatynski who was a Visiting Fellow at the IDS during 1983/4. The IDS secretarial and administrative staff have cheerfully put up with numerous drafts and reformulations whilst working under considerable pressure, particularly Marion Huxley who did an excellent job in putting the whole manuscript into the word processor. I was also very fortunate in having Pauline Cherry to do the graphical work, Jonathan Perraton and Haris Gazdar to help check the manuscript, and Haris Gazdar to prepare the index. Responsibility for the remaining errors of commission and omission is, of course, mine.

To Edward Elgar, former managing editor of Wheatsheaf Press, and Peter Johns, senior commissioning editor of Harvester Wheatsheaf, I have special thanks for their belief in the project and patience throughout innumerable delays in the preparation of the manuscript as the form and shape of the study changed. Most of all, without the loving support of my wife Barbara Einhorn, and my children Ben and Simon, the entire project would never have been completed.

David Evans, 1989

# GLOSSARY OF SYMBOLS

In this glossary, the main notational conventions used throughout the work are set out. It does not include occasional modification in the text. There is some duplication of the symbols used where this can be done without confusion.

*Indexes*

m       number of countries
n        number of commodities (or industries)
q        number of primary non-produced inputs

*Parameters*

a        intermediate input-output coefficients
A       matrix of intermediate input-output coefficients
b        fixed capital services coefficients
B       matrix of fixed capital coefficients $b_{ij}$
$\lambda$        primary non-produced input coefficients
$\Lambda$       matrix of primary non-produced input coefficients $\lambda_{ij}$
$\ell$        labour input coefficient or vector of labour input coefficients
r        resource services input coefficient or vector of resource service input coefficients
d        depreciation
$\eta$        pure price elasticity of demand or elasticity of offer curve
$\sigma$        marginal propensity to consume
$\varepsilon$        elasticity of demand for imports
$\Delta$       elasticity of demand for imports less 1

| | |
|---|---|
| $\Psi$ | primary non-produced input share |
| $\theta$ | cost share |
| $\chi$ | income share; also expenditure share |
| $\phi$ | trade share |
| $\alpha$ | elasticity of substitution in production; also used as a parameter of the total cost function or as a shift parameter |
| $\beta$ | parameter of cost function |
| $\tau$ | efficiency paramter in production function |
| $\delta$ | parameter related to the elasticity of substitution; also the rate of pure time preference |
| $t$ | tariff or trade tax (subsidy if $-$ve); occasionally used as subscript to indicate transport costs; also for time period |

*Variables and functional operators*

| | |
|---|---|
| $C, c$ | consumption and consumption per worker; also net output and net output per worker |
| $D$ | demand |
| $S, s$ | supply; also savings and propensity to save; also as subscript to indicate stationary state |
| $I, i$ | investment and investment per worker |
| $E, e$ | exports and exports per worker |
| $M, m$ | imports and imports per worker; $m$ also a scalar related to the balance of payments surplus or deficit |
| $K, k$ | value of the capital stock and capital output ratio; also $k$ used as country superscript |
| $X, x$ | gross output and gross output per worker; $X$ also used for intermediate input flow |
| $Y, y$ | total income and income per worker |
| $L$ | demand for labour |
| $R$ | demand for resource services |
| $V$ | demand for generalised primary non-produced input services or primary non-produced input embodiment |
| $\bar{L}$ | supply of labour measuring the capacity of labour to deliver labour power |
| $\bar{R}$ | supply of resource measuring the capacity of the resource to deliver resource services |
| $\bar{V}$ | supply of generalised primary non-produced inputs |

| | |
|---|---|
| $p$ | commodity prices |
| $w$ | wage rate |
| $\varrho$ | rate of profit |
| $\pi$ | resource rent per unit of resource |
| $z$ | Rental/wage or $\pi/w$ ratio |
| $g$ | rate of growth of output or income |
| $G$ | $(1 + g)$ |
| $n$ | rate of growth of workforce or the rate of growth of population |
| $\mu$ | degree of unionisation |
| $v$ | price of generalised primary non-produced inputs |
| $W$ | total wages; also total wealth |
| $\Pi$ | total rent |
| $P$ | total profit; also $(1 + \varrho)$ |
| $\lambda$ | Lagrangean multiplier; also ratio of employment $L^2/L^1$ |
| $U$ | utility; also stochastic error term |
| $-$ | indicates variable given or exogenous |
| $\hat{}$ | change of a variable or, occasionally, diagonal matrix |
| $'$ | partial derivative or, occasionally, transpose of a matrix |
| $\dagger$ | indicates direct and indirect input coefficients |
| $\cdot$ | rate of change of variable per unit of time, or the time derivative of a variable |

# 1 · ALTERNATIVE PERSPECTIVES ON TRADE AND DEVELOPMENT

## 1.1 THE QUESTIONS TO BE ANSWERED

A book on trade and development must address some of the basic theoretical and policy questions to be answered in the field. Elsewhere I have suggested the following five questions (Evans, 1989):

1. What is the role of trade in the process of economic development?
2. What patterns of international exchange best serve the objectives of developing countries?
3. What are the consequences of various instruments used by developed and developing countries aimed at achieving the desired pattern of trade?
4. Are the classical and neo-classical theories of international trade suitable for application to the situation of developing countries?
5. How is trade related to class relationships and to inequalities of income and power, both within and between developed and developing countries?

Broadly speaking, this book draws on four strands of thought on trade and development, namely classical, neo-classical, Marxian and structuralist-institutionalist (see Bardhan (1988) for a broader discussion of those schools). Whilst this book has something to say about all of these questions, the main questions addressed are (1)–(4), with emphasis on question (4).

There are no agreed maps for navigating between the shoals of the contending methodologies and assumptions used in the major schools which have been drawn on in this book. All too often, when neither theory nor empirical evidence are decisive, legitimate differences in judgement can become caught up with different values and welfare weights. The differences between the major schools are often narrower than perceived and the particular fusion I have offered has been strongly influenced by the new school of analytical Marxism (see Roemer, 1986).

## 1.2 SMITH, RICARDO, MARX AND MODERN TRADE THEORY

There is a strong tradition within trade theory to regard movements on given production and consumption possibilities frontiers as providing the most important insights into the sources of gains from trade. Such a procedure often overlooks the historically radical consequences of the effects of the opening of foreign trade.[1]

In Smith's view, a trade-induced division of labour is the main underlying condition for modern economic growth. Abstracting from the new institution which gave birth to this division of labour, the factory, Adam Smith's argument was implicitly based on economies of scale. Another aspect is the 'vent for surplus' argument for the opening of trade developed by Smith and elaborated by Myint (1958) which suggests that, in the absence of trade, the economy may be operating inside its production possibilities frontier.

The opening of trade therefore may lead to two types of irreversible changes: the realisation of scale economies and the utilisation of previously under-utilised resources.[2] Smithian trade-induced growth is 'trade as the engine of growth' *par excellence.*

The formalisation of the theory of comparative advantage by Torrens and Ricardo treated the opening of trade in a much more abstract fashion, using the autarky construct to define relative prices in the pre-trade position and therefore the possibility of gainful trade. The great strength of the formal analysis of comparative advantage is that it makes more precise some of the consequences of the opening of trade and the characteristics of a trading equilibrium. In classical Ricardian theory, the preconditions for the establishment of each trading unit were taken for granted – for example, the development of a capitalist national economy with complete internal mobility of factors and complete external immobility of factors. It is worth recalling that this procedure does not necessarily conform with the historical conditions under which national economies were formed, as emphasised by the Marxian tradition and also noted by Williams (1929).

The central message of Williams' critique of classical trade theory was that the development of the world economy went hand in hand with the development of the national economy. This meant that the international mobility of commodities and factors was far greater than their mobility within national economies at an early stage of their development, thus undermining the assumed dichotomy between national mobility and international immobility of capital and labour. Williams was right for the analysis of the opening of trade. It is possible to take part of his critique on board, either through the analysis of interregional as well as international trade, as in Ohlin (1933), or by modelling of imperfect mobility, as in Harris and Todaro (1970). In practice, trade theory is mainly used for the analysis of changes in a with-trade equilibrium position rather than for historical analysis of the opening and development of trading relationships.

The units of analysis and property relations assumed to be in place in the formal trade models rest uneasily alongside the real historical entities. The trading units referred to as 'England', 'America', 'North', 'South' or 'Tropics' are to be interpreted as trading units with stylised structural characteristics and prop-erty relations which bear a rough relationship to the real his-torical entities, or groups of countries, referred to. For example, 'America' as discovered by Columbus refers to both North and South America. Here, it could equally refer to a South American country such as Argentina exporting beef, or a North American country such as the USA exporting wheat. This caveat should be borne in mind when using formal trade models to understand the interrelations between trade, growth and development.

The Marxian tradition is ambivalent about the role of formal models of trade, notwithstanding Marx's own application of Ricardian theory when discussing his counter-tendencies for the rate of profit to fall.[3] This is reflected in the voluminous Marxian literature on imperialism, the expansion of capitalism as a social system.[4] Yet Murray (1978, page 18) argues that 'any general

**Table 1.1**   Historical rates of growth (1820–1985); arithmetic averages for 16 countries.

| | Average annual change (%) | |
|---|---|---|
| | GDP | Exports |
| 1820–70 | 2.2[a] | 4.0[b] |
| 1870–1913 | 2.5 | 3.9 |
| 1913–50 | 1.9 | 1.0 |
| 1950–73 | 4.9 | 8.6 |
| 1973–9 | 2.5 | 4.8 |
| 1979–85 | 1.9 | 3.5 |

[a] Average for 13 countries.
[b] Average for 10 countries.
Source: Maddison (1982, Table 4.9) and World Bank (1987, Fig. 3.2).

theory of imperialism should be able to explain the motive for expansion, the timing of expansion, the forms of expansion and the mechanisms of expansion (of capitalism internationally)'. It would seem that the application of trade theory, by clarifying the economic motives and the economic analysis, might help to answer these questions.

In spite of the strong empirical association between periods of rapid growth of trade and the rate of growth of GDP over a long historical period, shown in Table 1.1, there is much ambiguity on this issue in the Marxian and structuralist-institutionalist literature on trade and development. With the exception of the period between 1870 and 1912, the association between trade and growth is positive. However, the statistical relationship says nothing about the direction of causality, which can only be established with the help of a theoretical model.

The theoretical models of trade and growth favoured by the Marxian and structuralist-institutionalist schools often fail to take into account resource endowments as one of the determinants of comparative advantage and growth. A central feature of this book is to suggest that a useful starting point is the two-commodity circulating capital model with two primary non-produced inputs. The analysis of comparative advantage and growth presented allows a role for both produced means of production and resource-based trade whilst leaving open the possible institutional determination of one of the factor prices. It can also be used as the starting point for comparative dynamic analysis. The choice of a model depends on a judgement about the best way to capture some strategic elements of the problem under analysis. The consequences of excluded factors and simplifying approximations must inevitably be left to more informal theorising and judgement.

For the most part, standard maximising behaviour has been assumed throughout this book. The usual analysis of the potential gains from trade uses either community indifference curves or revealed preference analysis.[5] Indifference curves have not generally been shown in the diagrams but standard utility functions have been used in the formal analysis in the appendices. One deviation from the standard welfare analysis is the exploration of the consequences of incorporating wealth as a direct argument in the utility function in the discussion of the intertemporal gains from trade in Chapters 5 and 6. Where judgements are made on income distribution, they have been made explicit.

## 1.3 TRADE AND DEVELOPMENT STRATEGY AND THE ROLE OF THE STATE

Few would argue with the proposition that trade policy implications must derive from an overall development strategy and the overall context of the development process including the role of the state.

There is a widespread consensus which recognises the importance of the state in the development process. A reflection of this can be found in the attention given to this issue in recent World Bank *World Development Reports*. However, there is less agreement on which aspects are most important – its class base, its administrative capacity, or its modes of intervention. Nor is there agreement on the most appropriate methods of analysis.

It is widely held that Britain, which up to the middle of the nineteenth century was the only industrial power, achieved the transition to modern economic growth without extensive state intervention except in the formation of economic rights. Nevertheless, this has not been the case for 'latecomers' such as Germany, the USA, Japan, and most recently the newly industrialising countries or NICs. The most well-known late eighteenth century and nineteenth century argument in favour of pervasive state intervention in the process of industrialisation and the development of a modern nation state are the infant industry and infant nation arguments (Hamilton, 1791; List, 1885). More recently, Gerschenkron (1966), in analysing the industrialisation experience of the European countries (particularly Germany and Russia) in the last century, argued that the more backward the economy, the greater was the part played by the state and other institutions in initiating and promoting industrial development. This view of the state as the main initiator of modern economic growth differs qualitatively from that of most neo-classical and Marxist perspectives.

State intervention from a neo-classical perspective is analysed in the context of market failure and the operation of interest group politics (see, for example, Bhagwati, 1982; Bates, 1981, 1983; Little, 1982; Olsen, 1982; Srinivasan, 1986). That is, in the presence of distortions and imperfections in commodity and factor markets, corrective policies are required for an efficient allocation of resources and the realisation of comparative advantage. It is sometimes implicitly concluded that it may be in the national interest for the state to have sufficient centralised power to operate against interest groups which distort the operation of the market. This contradiction may go some way to account for the relative lack of concern of neo-classical commentators over the association of phases of economic 'liberalisation' or the freeing of markets with authoritarian governments and the curtailment of political rights in many developing countries. This ignores the historical association of the evolution of economic rights being required as a pre-requisite for the development of civil society and a democratic political process to check the exercise of arbitrary power (see, for example, World Bank, 1987, Box 4.2). Indeed, one of the factors inhibiting market-oriented economic reform and participation in world trade in the socialist countries is the slow progress in making the required political reforms.

I have argued in Evans (1989) that question (5), the systematic consideration of class, inequality and power, can be brought to bear on trade and development issues without loss of analytical rigour. Class is an important factor in the analysis of distribution and inequality, in relations of domination required for the maintenance of property relations, in the economic effects of domination at the point of production both between countries and within them. It also needs to be considered in any analysis of the developmental state. In all of these ways, class has direct and indirect implications for the analysis of trade and development. These considerations partly influenced the choice of models discussed in this book, particularly in Chapters 6 and 7, the discussion of normative trade theory and institutions in Chapter 8, and the empirical evidence on the relationship between efficiency and growth discussed in Chapter 9. There is nothing intrinsic in the view of the state, class, power, values or policy concerns addressed in this book which cannot be accommodated by the standard theory of trade policy discussed by Bliss (1989). The general principle of the standard theory, that the best forms of policy intervention are those which tackle inefficiency directly, applies. However, there is less agreement when it is argued that the ranking of policy instruments is influenced by the institutional context in which they are deployed.

## 1.4   SOME EXCLUDED CONSIDERATIONS

In the discussion of distribution and inequality, relations of exploitation and domination have not been included in the formal economic analysis. To some extent, these have been taken up elsewhere, but there remains much to be done in this area. Exclusion of the analysis of exploitation is not of particular importance since, in the international context, the embodied labour proxy as an indicator of exploitation breaks down (see Evans, 1989, Section 3). The formal analysis of the microeconomics of domination at the point of production, discussed in Evans (1989, Section 4), was excluded on the grounds of space. Informally, work in this area is used in justifying the Ricardo–Marx–Lewis distribution closure discussed in Chapter 6, and in the interpretation of empirical results in the relationship between price efficiency and growth discussed in Chapter 9.

Another set of exclusions are the new theories of trade with economies of scale and imperfect competition, surveyed by Greenaway and Milner (1987). There is widespread disagreement on the importance of the new theories of trade with imperfect competition for developing countries (see, for example, Srinivasan, 1987). Where the new theories provide arguments for interventionist trade and industrialisation policies, they have been included in the discussion of normative trade policy and institutions discussed in Chapter 8. Ultimately, my defence of these and other exclusions from this book reflects my desire to focus on the core trade and development theories which must inevitably carry the burden of explanation of comparative advantage and growth for developing countries.

## 1.5   THE ORGANISATION OF THE BOOK

The Ricardian tradition and some of its modern extensions and applications which can be found in the development literature is discussed in Chapters 2 and 3. The dominant neo-classical view of the Ricardian theory of comparative advantage is based on a timeless version of the static Ricardian model. It is argued that a more useful interpretation of Ricardo can be based on an open economy version of his model of a growing economy in which time plays an essential role. Chapters 4 and 5 develop the modern neo-classical or Heckscher–Ohlin–Samuelson (H–O–S) theory of comparative advantage. Chapter 4 deals with the basic elements of the static H–O–S theory and some complications arising from the addition of more countries, commodities and factors, from the inclusion of intermediate inputs, from scale economies and from the explicit inclusion of transport costs. Particular attention is paid to the popular but overworked Jones–Samuelson specific factors model which is usually used to illustrate the link between Ricardo, Ohlin and the modern literature. Chapter 5 develops some of the basic propositions about trade and growth in a comparative static and dynamic framework, concluding with a preliminary discussion of the modification to the analysis when wealth is explicitly included in the utility function. In these chapters, some of the important debates in the literature are referred to only in so far as the application of some of the basic propositions developed are strongly influenced by choice of model or behavioural assumptions.

The positive contributions of the neo-Ricardian literature on trade and growth are discussed in Chapter 6. Considerable attention is then paid to developing a circulating capital model with labour and a resource in which time is essential, providing a link between Ricardo, Ohlin and the modern neo-classical and neo-Ricardian theories. The circulating capital model is also the form of the neo-classical trade model used in empirical tests. The discussion of the intertemporal gains from trade examine some of the consequences of including wealth in the utility function. An analytical Marxian perspective on trade and development is developed in Chapter 7 through an application of the circulating capital model to the historical analysis of nineteenth-century trade between England and America. Some of the key stylised facts about this trade, particularly in relation to the role of institutional determinants of one of the factor prices in determining the pattern of trade and potential factor movements, are consistent with the model used. This model is further developed for the analysis of terms of trade and other issues relating to trade between developed and developing economies. Special consideration is given to North–South and South–South trade when the skill endowments rather than resource endowments play a central role in determining comparative advantage and growth.

In Chapter 8, two aspects central to the formulation of trade and development strategies are discussed. First, the basic elements of normative trade theory are summarised. Second, the preliminary remarks made on the role of the state in Section 1.3 are developed in relation to the most important instruments of trade policy.

The empirical findings in some of the areas of major concern in the literature on trade and growth are examined in the first part of Chapter 9. These include the empirical testing of theories of comparative advantage, the relationship between trade and growth, the long-run terms of trade between developed and developing countries, the fallacy of composition, and the relationship between trade policy regimes and non-market contributions to growth performance. The final section of Chapter 9 draws together some of the implications of the findings of the chapter on alternative trade and development strategies.

## NOTES

1. For the historical effects of opening Africa to the world economy see Sender and Smith (1986).
2. Establishing the role of trade in the 'vent for surplus' is a difficult task. It requires the identification of particular institutional features or of domestic preferences which give rise to the under-utilisation of resources, which will vary from case to case. S. Smith (1976) discusses some of the pitfalls which arise from the hasty application of the vent for surplus model to the Nigerian colonial experience.
3. For a discussion of some of the analytical difficulties in using classical Marxian value theory for economic analysis, see Steedman (1977), Morishima and Catephores (1978) and Roemer (1981, 1982). Recent contributions to the Marxian value debate include Elson (ed.) (1979), Fine and Harris (1979), Roemer (ed.) (1986) and Steedman (ed.) (1981).
4. For an excellent survey of Marxian theories of imperialism, see Brewer (1980).
5. See, for example, Little (1960) and Dobb (1969) on the problems involved in deriving community indifference curves. Michaely (1977, Chapter 1) provides a good introduction to the use of revealed preferences in trade theory.

# 2 · RICARDO'S BRILLIANT RUN

## 2.1 THE RICARDIAN VISION

There is much common ground between the issues discussed in classical political economy and the contemporary development debate. Ricardo is of particular interest in this context because two of his major themes were the theory of growth and the theory of trade.

In part, Ricardo's analysis of growth was concerned with the struggle for power in England between a progressive and modernising manufacturing capitalist class and a reactionary landed gentry living mainly on rents from agricultural land. Without the import of corn and the export of manufactures, profit and the accumulation of capital would be limited by a growing rent on land. Ricardo identified with the interests of manufacturing and commercial capital, particularly in the debates over the future of the Corn Laws at the end of the Napoleonic Wars.[1] The removal of the Corn Laws would allow the import of cheaper foreign corn and lower the cost of bread, thus removing an immediate cause for discontent among the working class, and simultaneously improving the profitability of capital. It would lower rent in the short run, helping to break the power of the landed gentry over the rising influence of industrial capital, and releasing wage labour for employment in the faster-growing export sectors producing manufactures. Free trade would provide the basis for the expansion of industrial capital without the shackles of diminishing returns from land and a long-run redistribution of income to the landed class.

The economic pessimism of his dynamic model of the closed

economy, constrained by the availability of land and the conflict of interest between landlords and capitalists, was tempered by his optimistic view of accumulation and growth under free trade.[2]

The essence of the above economic analysis can be readily captured by the simple Ricardian models discussed in Sections 2.2 and 3.5. It is not surprising then to find that the Ricardian framework has inspired much of the contemporary trade and growth literature discussed throughout this book. The discussion starts here with the Ricardian theory of comparative advantage in the context of a two-sector two-country or 2 × 2 model of the world economy.

## 2.2    RICARDO'S THEORY OF COMPARATIVE ADVANTAGE

### 2.2.1    The static model

The analytical relationship between distribution, growth and trade set out above was never put together explicitly by Ricardo. He based his exposition of the principle of comparative advantage[3] on a static model of trade between England and Portugal in which neither capital nor land was required for production. All class, distribution, growth and conflict issues were eliminated and free trade was associated with a harmony of interests.[4] In his example, both England and Portugal could produce both cloth and wine using only labour. He assumed that labour was perfectly mobile between cloth and wine production in each country, that labour was required in fixed proportions to produce each commodity, that there were constant returns to scale, that there were no externalities and that there was perfect competition. Furthermore, he assumed that each country could exist independently in autarky prior to the opening of trade. With the opening of trade, competitive producers in each country responded to opportunities for trade in cloth and wine by exploiting any pre-trade differences in the relative costs of producing cloth and wine. With no transport costs and no labour mobility between each country, the final equilibrium price ratio could lie anywhere between the autarky relative cost ratios for England and Portugal, the so-called Ricardian limbo region. The usual textbook treatment of the Ricardian model is completed by specifying the demand side of the model. It is then possible to determine the equilibrium price ratio within the limbo region, the quantities of cloth and wine traded, and the distribution of the gains from trade between England and Portugal.

### 2.2.2  A simple dynamic model: single country

The above static model can be transformed into a dynamic model in simple reproduction[5] by explicitly introducing the role of time in production, as is done in Ricardo's model of growth, and by dividing the economic agents into a class of capitalists who own all of the stock of capital, and workers who only sell their labour power.[6] In this case, it makes more sense to switch the illustrative example from the static context of cloth and wine production in England and Portugal to the dynamic context of manufactures and food production in England and America. In the simple dynamic model, the wage-good food must be explicitly identified and the capital stock is made up entirely of the wage fund of food. For simplicity, it is assumed that both manufactures and food require the same period of production, say one year, and that labour power can only be set to work in the production process if it is given its annual wage in advance by the employing capitalist class. If the subsistence wage is given in terms of food,[7] then the remaining product over and above wages can be paid out as profit to the capitalists who advance the wage fund capital over the period of production.

Throughout this book, unless explicitly stated otherwise, the following assumptions are made for all models:

1. Perfect competition.
2. Constant returns to scale.
3. Standard utility behaviour.
4. Domestic factor mobility and international factor immobility.
5. No fixed capital.
6. No joint production.
7. No externalities.

The equilibrium price and quantity conditions which must be satisfied by a single country in autarky to ensure that simple reproduction takes place, ignoring for the moment the growth and demand sides of the model, can be specified by two sets of inequalities as follows:

*Nominal price relations, closed economy*

$$\begin{array}{cc} \text{wages and profits} & \text{price} \\ w\ell_1(1 + \varrho) \;\geqq\; & p_1 \\ w\ell_2(1 + \varrho) \;\geqq\; & p_2 \end{array} \qquad (2.1)$$

*Quantity relations (factor usage), closed economy*

$$\begin{array}{cc} \text{labour use} & \text{wage fund limit} \\ \ell_1 X_1 + \ell_2 X_2 \;\leqq\; & \bar{K}/\bar{w} \end{array} \qquad (2.2)$$

$$\begin{array}{c} \text{reproduction of wage fund} \\ C_2 \geqq \bar{K} \end{array} \qquad (2.3)$$

*Non-negativity constraints*

$$w \geqq 0, \quad \varrho \geqq 0, \quad p_1 \geqq 0, \quad p_2 \geqq 0, \quad X_1 \geqq 0, \quad X_2 \geqq 0$$

The parameters and variables are as follows:

$\ell_1$, $\ell_2$ are fixed labour input coefficients defined for a standard working day
$p_1$, $p_2$ are commodity prices
$w$, $\varrho$ are money wages and the rate of profit
$X_1$, $X_2$ are commodity outputs
$\bar{L}$ is the total labour available
$\bar{K}$ is the wage fund measured in terms of commodity 2
$\bar{w}$ is the subsistence wage measured in terms of commodity 2.

In words, inequalities (2.1) simply state that excess profits can be no greater than zero. Inequalities (2.2 and 2.3) state that labour used must be no more than the employment limit given by the size of the wages fund divided by the subsistence wage, and that the wage fund or capital stock must be at least replaced. Inequality (2.3) implies that workers consume only the wage good $X_2$. The non-negativity constraints ensure that economically meaningless negative values are eliminated from the set of possible wages, profits, prices and output levels.

When capitalists maximise profits, when workers are prepared to offer their labour power for the standard working day at the subsistence wage and when both commodities are produced, equation (2.1) will hold as an equality. Dividing the first equation by the second we obtain the relationship between the labour coefficients and relative prices or:

$$(\ell_1/\ell_2) = (p_1/p_2) \qquad (2.4)$$

This is the simple Ricardian and also the Marxian case in which prices are proportional to the labour values. The maximum rate of profit can be found by dividing the maximum surplus product by the wage fund, both measured in terms of food. The maximum surplus product is obtained when wages are at their subsistence levels. By substituting the subsistence wage $\bar{w}$ *for* $w/p_2$ in (2.1), the reader can easily check that the equilibrium rate of profit under autarky is given by

$$\varrho_{max} = (1 - \bar{w}\ell_2)/\bar{w}\ell_2 \qquad (2.5)$$

The Ricardian autarky model can be illustrated diagrammatically. The production possibilities frontier can be derived from (2.2) by setting each output $X_1$ and $X_2$, respectively, equal to zero. The maximum output of $X_1$ and $X_2$ which can be produced is equal to $\bar{K}/\ell_1\bar{w}$ and $\bar{K}/\ell_2\bar{w}$, respectively, given by $OB$ and $OA$, respectively, in Fig. 2.1. The reader can readily check that the slope of the production possibilities frontier $AB$ in Fig. 2.1 is equal to minus the labour time ratio $-(\ell_1/\ell_2)$ and is also equal to minus the relative price ratio $-(p_1/p_2)$ from (2.4).

The equilibrium requirement that the wage fund or capital stock be reproduced implies that the output of the wage good is equal to or greater than the initial wage fund. In Fig. 2.1, $OO'$ is equal to the wage fund $\bar{K}$ and the solution must be on or above the line through $O'D$. Thus the feasible set of production points under autarky for a single country will be given by the set of points bounded by $O'AB'$ shown in Fig. 2.1. Optimising behaviour of the capitalists and workers will ensure that the final equilibrium production and consumption points will lie on the line $AB'$. Given that workers consume the entire wage fund (equal to $OO'$), capitalists can consume anywhere along $AB'$ so that the final autarky production and consumption point could be at a point such as $E$. Given the assumptions of constant returns to scale, fixed proportions and a single non-produced input labour, all prices are independent of the composition of final outputs and

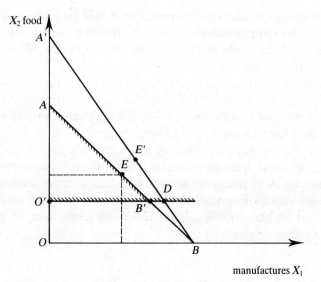

**Fig. 2.1**   The Ricardian single-country trade model.

the choice of the consumption point has no effect on autarky prices.[8]

Suppose now that the opportunity to trade is opened up at fixed world prices. That is, the economy is small enough to be a price taker on world markets. If the world price ratio is different from the autarky price ratio, then profit maximisation and the given offer of labour power will lead to the country specialising in production and exporting one of the two commodities, importing its requirements of the other. At the given subsistence wage, workers will not gain from the opportunity of trade but capitalists will, experiencing an increased rate of profit when the wage-good food is imported.

In terms of Fig. 2.1, suppose that the price of manufactures relative to food is greater on the world market than under autarky, or $(p_1/p_2)^* > (p_1/p_2)^a$ where the asterisk indicates world prices and an autarky price. The slope of world price line passing through the domestic production point $E$ is greater than the slope of the autarky price line given by production possibilities frontier $AB$.

In this case, it is more profitable for capitalists to reallocate their capital and employ labour in the production of additional manufactures. Eventually, all production will be specialised in the production of manufactures at point $B$ in Fig. 2.1. The opportunity to trade at world prices permits consumption to take place at those points on the consumption possibilities frontier $BA'$ (whose slope is given by the world price ratio – $(p_1/p_2)^*$ which satisfy the capital reproduction constraint. Final consumption at any point on $DA'$, such as $E'$, satisfies the equilibrium requirements. A final with-trade consumption point such as $E'$ leaves workers with the same subsistence wage and allows capitalists to consume more of both commodities than at the autarky consumption point $E$. With-trade consumption at $E'$ is superior to autarky consumption at $E$ in terms of the Pareto criterion. Any consumption point on the with-trade consumption possibilities frontier above $O'D$ potentially improves capitalists' welfare compared with the autarky point $E$. A stronger statement about the gains from trade requires an explicit choice of the welfare criterion and assumptions by which the potential gains from trade are realised.[9]

The effects of the opening of trade on the equilibrium rate of profit can be found by dividing the inequalities (2.1) by the price of the wage-good food, $p_2$, and setting the real wage equal to the subsistence wage or $(w/p_2) = \bar{w}$. Thus, using the assumption that the price of manufactures in terms of food is greater on the world market than under autarky or $(p_1/p_2)^* > (p_1/p_2)^a$ and substituting into the first of the inequalities, it follows that specialisation in the production and export of manufactured goods will raise the rate of profit and $\varrho^*_{max} > \varrho^a_{max}$. When the price of manufactured goods in terms of corn is equal to or less on the world market than under autarky or $(p_1/p_2)^* \leqq (p_1/p_1)^a$, food will be produced. In this case, it can be readily seen from the second inequality in (2.1) and (2.5) above that the maximal rate of profit will be independent of the terms of trade and the rate of profit will be unchanged by the opening of trade. Only when imported commodities enter into the wage bundle will the rate of profit increase with the opening of trade.[10]

The growth characteristics of the model have no bearing on the analysis of the pattern of trade and can be easily described when the Ricardian assumptions are made. At any time it is the wage-fund capital stock which constrains the level of activity. The Malthusian population mechanism ensures that there is a perfectly elastic supply of labour in the long run at the subsistence wage and the rate of growth of the workforce automatically adjusts to the rate of growth of the capital stock. If all investment is made out of profits and if the capitalists' propensity to save is fixed, then the long-run steady state rate of growth, satisfying the equilibrium condition that savings equals investment, will be determined. These ideas are expressed in the following equations:

$$S = s_c \varrho \bar{K}, \quad I = g\bar{K} \quad \text{and} \quad g = s_c \varrho \quad (2.6)$$

where $S$ is total savings, $s_c$ is the capitalists' propensity to save, $I$ is total investment, $g$ is the rate of growth, and all other variables are as previously described. Thus, the subsistence wage and the technical characteristics of production of the wage good determine the rate of profit, as shown in equation (2.5). Given the long-run equilibrium rate of profit and the capitalists' propensity to save, the long-run steady state growth rate is determined. To the extent that the wage good is imported, the rate of profit and the rate of growth will both increase with the opening of trade.

In the simple dynamic model, there is no interaction between growth, profit and distribution, and the determinants of the pattern of trade. The growth characteristics of the model do affect the equilibrium conditions and the distribution of the gains from trade when a second country is introduced. This aspect is considered in Section 3.5.

The autarky price ratios in the Ricardian model are determined by the relative labour values or costs independently of the demand side. As is already clear from the discussion on the opening of trade, the final with-trade price ratios will coincide with the autarky price ratios by chance. The role of demand in the determination of the world price ratios, first noted by Mill (1844), is made clear in the analysis of a simple world economy in which two countries have the possibility of entering trade.

### 2.2.3   A simple dynamic model: two countries

The analysis of trade between two countries requires the specification of the behaviour of the second country. Each variable and parameter in (2.1) to (2.3) is given a country superscript $k = 1, 2$ for countries 1 and 2, or England and America, respectively. Each country differs in the subsistence wage, the labour cost

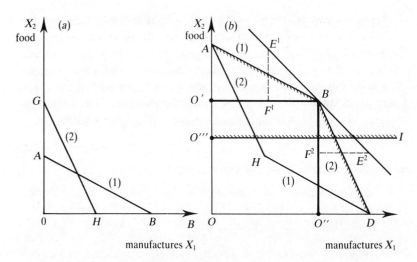

**Fig. 2.2**   The 2 × 2 Ricardo–Mill model of the world economy.

ratios, the stock of capital and in the demand conditions. The production possibilities frontier and the autarky equilibrium for country 2 follows on exactly the same lines as for country 1, which is then aggregated to form the two-country 'world' production possibilities frontier and the associated autarky and trading equilibrium in the initial period as shown in Fig. 2.2.

The production possibility frontiers for countries 1 and 2 are shown in Fig. 2.2(a) by the lines $AB$ and $GH$. Country 1 (England) has the lower relative cost of producing manufactures and will produce and export commodity 1 (manufactures) in exchange for commodity 2 (food), which is produced and exported by country 2 (America). The individual production possibility frontiers are then aggregated as shown in Fig. 2.2(b). The world economy is completely specialised in the production of commodity 2 (food) at point $A$ in Fig. 2.2(b). This point on the world production possibilities frontier is found by the sum of the maximum possible production of commodity 2 (food) for each country in Fig. 2.2(a) or $(OA + OG)$. Similarly, complete specialisation in commodity 1 (manufactures) at point $D$ in Fig. 2.2(b) is given by $(OH + OB)$ from Fig. 2.2(a). The points of incomplete specialisation in the world economy at $B$ and $H$ in Fig. 2.2(b) can be found by linear aggregation from Fig. 2.2(a) or by $(OB + OG)$ and $(OA + OH)$, respectively. The linear segments $AB$ and $HD$ in Fig.

2.2(b) correspond to the production possibilities frontier for country 1 (England), whilst the segments $AH$ and $BD$ correspond to the production possibilities frontier for country 2 (America). When both countries are producing somewhere on their respective production possibilities frontiers ($AB$ and $GH$ in Fig. 2.2(a)), the world economy is producing within the region bounded by $ABDH$. The maximal world output frontier is given by the locus of points joining $A$, $B$ and $D$.

### 2.2.4   Gains from trade for the world

For any world terms of trade within the Ricardian limbo region defined by the autarky price ratios for country 2 (America) and country 1 (England), respectively, or

$$(\ell_1^2/\ell_2^2) \geqq (p_1/p_2)^* \geqq (\ell_1^1/\ell_2^1) \tag{2.7}$$

there is the possibility of a gain from trade for one or both countries. The world terms of trade line $E^1BE^2$ satisfies the equilibrium price conditions for both countries separately and for the world economy as a whole. The world production and consumption is at $B$, and world production of commodity 2, food, satisfies the minimum requirements to reproduce the wage fund, given by $OO'''$. Redefining the origins for individual countries 1 and 2 as $O'$ and $O''$ respectively, gains from trade can be illustrated using Fig. 2.2(b). Country 1 (England) consumes at $E^1$, exporting $F^1B$ of commodity 1 (manufactures) in return for $F^1E^1$ of commodity 2 (food). Country 2 (America) consumes at $E^2$, exporting $BF^2$ of commodity 2 (food) in exchange for $F^2E^2$ of commodity 1 (manufactures).

Rotation of the terms of trade line $E^1BE^2$ traces the locus of all consumption points for countries 1 and 2. When switches in production to $A$ or $D$ are taken into account, the reciprocal demand or offer curves for each country can be constructed.[11] The equilibrium terms of trade in the Ricardian system at a point in time are therefore governed by reciprocal demands or some other mechanism such as the relative bargaining power of the two countries in trade. The labour costs or labour values serve only to specify the limits within which the equilibrium terms of trade can move.

## 2.2.5    The pattern of trade

In the Ricardian model, relative labour input ratios or the technical conditions in production determine the pattern of trade and the limits to the final equilibrium terms of trade. Relative labour costs per unit can therefore be said to determine comparative advantage in the Ricardian sense. Simple manipulation of inequalities (2.7) yields a ranking of commodities according to comparative advantage.

By assumption, the labour productivity ratios for each good in the two countries are strictly unequal. Thus, dropping the price term and multiplying both sides of (2.7) by $(\ell_2^1/\ell_1^2)$ yields:

$$(\ell_1^1/\ell_1^2) < (\ell_2^1/\ell_2^2) \tag{2.7a}$$

The comparison of labour productivities for each commodity in turn in both countries gives the ranking of commodities according to comparative advantage, so that country 1 (England) has a comparative advantage in producing commodity 1 (manufactures) and country 2 (America) has a comparative advantage in producing commodity 2 (food).

## 2.2.6    Specialisation and the international distribution of the gains from trade

One of the corollaries of the simple Ricardian model of trade is that, for countries of a similar size and similar consumer preferences, there will be a tendency towards complete specialisation in production, provided there are differences in production techniques causing a divergence in their pre-trade price ratios. In Fig. 2.2(b), it can be seen that there are four possible points of complete specialisation of which three will be possible equilibrium outputs, namely at $A$, $B$ and $D$. If the model is restricted to require that both commodities are produced in the world economy, then only one point of complete specialisation, $B$, will be relevant. Other possible equilibrium positions lie on the line segments between $A$ and $B$, and between $B$ and $D$. These will be points of incomplete specialisation for one country, with complete specialisation for the other. When the final equilibrium point is at $B$, there will be complete specialisation. It follows

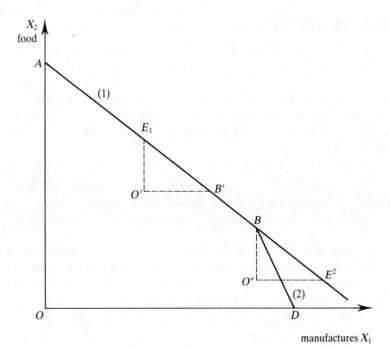

**Fig. 2.3**   Distribution of the gains from trade between large and small countries in the Ricardian case.

that the international distribution of the gains from trade will be governed entirely by the final terms of trade within the Ricardian limbo region, whether it is reciprocal demand, the outcome of relative bargaining strength, or some other mechanism which determines the equilibrium position. If one of the trading nations is economically very large compared with its trading partners, such as England in the nineteenth century compared with America, it is more likely that there will be incomplete specialisation for the large country. In this case, shown in Fig. 2.3 with only two countries, the international terms of trade will be governed by the internal or autarky terms of trade of the large country and will have nothing to do with reciprocal demand or bargaining power.

In Fig. 2.3, country 1 (England) is large relative to country 2 (America). The international consumption bundle chosen is at an equilibrium point such as $B'$ on the world production possibilities frontier $AE^1B'BD$, rather than at point $B$ where both countries are completely specialised. The equilibrium positions for both countries are assumed to be consistent with the reproduction of the capital stocks (not shown). Country 1's (England's) autarky terms of trade will determine the international terms of trade for production anywhere along $AB$ so that $(\ell_1^1/\ell_2^1) = (p_1/p_2)^*$. When world production is at $B'$, $O'B'$ of commodity 1 is exported (imported) from country 1(2) and $O'E^1$ is imported (exported) from country 2(1). All of the gains from trade accrue to country 2 (America) when its pre-trade production techniques are different from the incompletely-specialised country 1 (England).

This conclusion will be modified somewhat for many countries and many commodities, as explained in the next section.


## 2.3    SOME EXTENSIONS TO THE RICARDIAN SYSTEM

The extensions to the Ricardian system considered in this section owe much to the development of linear programming and its application to the understanding and solution of optimising problems in economics. It is useful to consider these developments because they confront the empirical assumptions of the simplest Ricardian model and provide a useful bridge to the neo-classical, neo-Ricardian and Marxian models considered in the subsequent chapters of this book.


### 2.3.1    Many countries and many commodities

Any application of the Ricardian model must take into account the fact that there are many countries and many commodities in the world economy. Whereas the number of countries ($m$) in the world economy is less than 200, the number of commodities ($n$) produced is to be numbered in thousands or tens of thousands, depending on the narrowness of the definition of specific technical conditions in production which is used to define each commodity.[12] Industrial classification which produces fewer commodities than countries in the world economy, as is often necessary in empirical work involving either a single country or a small number of countries, deals with aggregate production coefficients which are not suitable for the purposes of theoretical analysis. The observations made here are therefore only for cases in which the number of commodities is greater than the number of countries, or $n > m$.

With two countries and $n$ commodities, two-dimensional geometry fails since the world production possibilities frontier is now defined in $n$ dimensional space. However, some comparisons can be made using the $2 \times 2$ case shown in Fig. 2.2(b) and the $2 \times 3$ case shown in Fig. 2.4. In the discussion which follows, it makes no difference whether the production possibilities frontier is constrained by the size of the wages fund (given a fixed wage), or by the size of the workforce as in the modern neoclassical discussion of these issues.

Figure 2.4 is constructed on exactly the same basis as Fig. 2.2(b), under the assumption that $\ell_1^1/\ell_1^2 < \ell_2^1/\ell_2^2 < \ell_3^1/\ell_3^2$. Thus, in the commodity 1–commodity 2 or $X_1X_2$ plane, the world production possibilities frontier is made up of two line segments $AB$ and $BC$, corresponding to the frontiers for country 2 and country 1, respectively, as indicated in the diagram. Similarly, the line segments $CD$ and $DE$, and $EF$ and $FA$, make up the frontier in $X_2X_3$ and $X_3X_1$ planes, respectively. The individual country production possibilities frontiers associated with each line segment are also marked. The diagram is completed by joining $DF$ and $BF$ to yield a final world production possibilities surface made up of three planes $ABF$, $BCDF$ and $DEF$. Notice that the surface $BCDF$ is a parallelogram, since the trade-off along $DF$ and $CB$ is for country 1 switching between commodity 1 and commodity 2 production, and for country 2 switching between commodity 2 and commodity 3 production along $CD$ and $BF$. It is now a straightforward matter to establish all the possible patterns of trade associated with the example.

In Table 2.1, the eleven possible optimal patterns of specialisation associated with the world production possibilities frontier shown in Fig. 2.4 are spelt out when there are no limits placed on the model by the requirement that the wages-fund be reproduced. Notice that the first six patterns of specialisation involve one or more commodities not being produced and are therefore of less interest than the five cases with production of all three commodities. Of these, only two involve complete specialisation of production of each commodity in one country (*commodity specialisation*); the remaining three cases involve the incomplete specialisation of one commodity in two countries. From the point

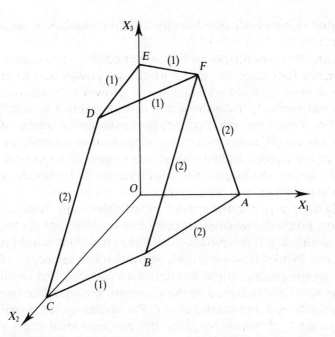

**Fig. 2.4**   The 2 × 3 Ricardian model of the world economy.

**Table 2.1**   Optimal country patterns of specialisation in the 2 × 3 Ricardian model.

| Specialisation associated with | A | B | C | D | E | F | ABF | BCDF | DEF | DF | BF |
|---|---|---|---|---|---|---|---|---|---|---|---|
| commodity 1 | 1&2 | 1 | – | – | – | 1 | 1&2 | 1 | 1 | 1 | 1 |
| commodity 2 | – | 2 | 1&2 | 1 | – | – | 2 | 1&2 | 1 | 1 | 2 |
| commodity 3 | – | – | – | 2 | 1&2 | 2 | 2 | 2 | 1&2 | 2 | 2 |

of view of the *country*, four cases will involve one country completely specialised in producing only one commodity and the remaining case involves both countries incompletely specialised in producing two commodities.

It was shown in Section 2.2.5 that in the 2 × 2 case, the two commodities could be ranked in order of comparative advantage as in inequality (2.7a). By pairwise grouping of the commodities associated with each possible pattern of specialisation, the argument can be readily extended to the 2 × 3 and 2 × $n$ cases to produce a chain of comparative advantage

$$\ell_1^1/\ell_1^2 \leqq \ell_2^1/\ell_2^2 \leqq \ell_3^1/\ell_3^2 \ldots \leqq \ell_n^1/\ell_n^2 \tag{2.8}$$

The commodity subscript is expanded to $n$ and the ordering of each commodity is arbitrarily selected according to the comparative advantage ranking. In this case, demand conditions will determine which commodities are intermediate in the ranking. Thus, in the 2 × 3 case shown in Fig. 2.4 and Table 2.1, for the five cases in which all three commodities are produced, country 1 will always produce and export commodity 1 and country 2 will always produce and export commodity 3, whilst the location of commodity 2 and the pattern of commodity 2 trade is indeterminate. For further discussion, see Appendix 2.1.

It is not possible to determine with any accuracy what will happen to the number of possible cases of commodity or country specialisation as $n$ increases, but it will generally be the case that the number of possible equilibrium positions with one country completely specialised will not increase. Thus, increasing the number of commodities will increase the number of cases involving incomplete commodity and country specialisation, provided the two countries are of a similar size. Of course, if one is large and the other small, it will be more likely that the small country will specialise in the production of fewer commodities than the larger country. In contrast, increasing the number of countries will tend to increase the number of both commodity and country specialisations.

On the basis of the previous discussion, it is possible to make some intuitive guesses about the extent of commodity and country specialisation, recalling that the order of magnitude of countries $m$ will be at most 200, and the number of commodities $n$ will be at least 7,000. If the countries are of a similar size, it is clear that incomplete country and commodity specialisations will be the rule rather than the exception. This will be true even in the Ricardian case of fixed proportions, constant returns to scale and only labour as the primary non-produced input. When country size is taken into account, noting that there are many high- and low-income countries which are small relative to the major industrial and large developing countries, the Ricardian model predicts a high degree of incomplete commodity and country specialisation for the major economies of the world economy. Only for the larger number of very small countries will the tendency towards country specialisation become manifest. This result is in contrast with much discussion of the Ricardian model, which often emphasises the strong assumptions that produce complete specialisation in the textbook case.[13]

### 2.3.2 Additional general and specific factors

It is possible to introduce any number of additional factors, such as land or fixed industry specific inputs, into the production process. These can be of a general type used in every industry, or specific inputs required in only one industry, or a subset of industries. The relaxation of the assumption of a single primary factor, labour, fundamentally alters the character of the Ricardian theory of comparative advantage since labour cost ratios are no longer the proximate basis for trade. For simplicity, the assumption of fixed proportions and constant returns to scale is retained.

In the single country, two-commodity case, such fixed endowments can be introduced using inequalities of the form:

$$\lambda_{i1}X_1 + \lambda_{i2}X_2 \leqq V_i \tag{2.9}$$

where the factor input coefficient is $\lambda_{ij}$ and the supply of the $i$th factor is $\bar{V}_i$; $i = 1, 2 \ldots q$, $j = 1, 2$ and $q$ is the number of factor inputs. When both $\lambda_{i1}, \lambda_{i2} > 0$, the associated primary input will be a general one, being required for the production of both commodities. If $\lambda_{i1} > 0$ and $\lambda_{i2} = 0$ or $\lambda_{i1} = 0$ and $\lambda_{i2} > 0$, the primary input will be specific to the production of commodities 1 and 2, respectively. When $i = 1$ and $\lambda_{11}, \lambda_{12} > 0$, the inequality (2.9) reduces to the original case of a single factor input, labour, with $\lambda_{11} = \ell_1$, $\lambda_{12} = \ell_2$ and $\bar{V}_1 = \bar{K}/\bar{w}$, as shown in inequality (2.2).

The additional primary non-produced inputs will command a rent. Thus, the original production possibilities frontier $AB$ in Fig. 2.1 is modified in Fig. 2.5 for the case of two general factors inputs, $\bar{V}_1$ and $\bar{V}_3$, and one industry specific input, $\bar{V}_2$.

If the first general input is labour so that $\bar{V}_1 = \bar{L}$ as in the standard neo-classical representation of the static Ricardian model,

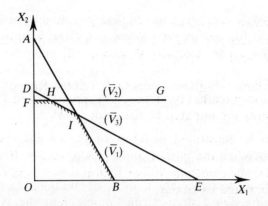

**Fig. 2.5**  The single-country Ricardian model with additional primary factors.

then $AB$ in Fig. 2.5 is the labour supply constraint. The slope of the line $AB$ will be given by the labour input ratios or $-\lambda_{11}/\lambda_{12}$. This corresponds to the simple dynamic Ricardian model discussion in Section 2.2.2 and in Fig. 2.1. The second general input $\bar{V}_3$ could be taken to represent either a second category of skilled labour, or a resource, used in both industries. A specific resource used only in industry 2 is represented by $\bar{V}_2$. Thus, the production possibilities frontier is given by $FHIB$ in Fig. 2.5. The slope of each segment of the production possibilities frontier will be given by $-\lambda_{i1}/\lambda_{i2}$.

The pricing implications of the introduction of additional factor inputs follow easily. Suppose for simplicity that all income is imputed as rent. Consider then the following five possible equilibrium commodity price ratios.

*Case 1.*  When $p_1/p_2 = 0$, only the constraint involving the specific resource $\bar{V}_2$ is binding. All income is imputed to the specific resource $\bar{V}_2$ and rent on all other resources is equal to zero.

*Case 2.*  When $0 > -(p_1/p_2) > -(\lambda_{31}/\lambda_{32})$, the constraints involving $\bar{V}_2$ and $\bar{V}_3$ will be binding. Rent is imputed to resources $\bar{V}_2$ and $\bar{V}_3$; resource $\bar{V}_1$ is free.

*Case 3.*  When $-(p_1/p_2) = -(\lambda_{31}/\lambda_{32})$, only the constraint involving $\bar{V}_3$ is binding. Rent is imputed to $\lambda_3$; resources $\lambda_1$ and $\lambda_2$ are free.

*Case 4.* When $-(\lambda_{31}/\lambda_{32}) > -(p_1/p_2) > -(\lambda_{11}/\lambda_{12})$, the constraints involving $\bar{V}_1$ and $\bar{V}_3$ are binding. Rent is inputed to resources $\bar{V}_1$ and $\bar{V}_3$; resource $\bar{V}_2$ is free.

*Case 5.* When $-(p_1/p_2) \leqq -(\lambda_{11}/\lambda_{12})$, only the constraint involving labour (resource $\bar{V}_1$) is binding. Resources $\bar{V}_2$ and $\bar{V}_3$ are free and all returns are imputed to the resource $\bar{V}_1$.

Case 5 can be illustrated in terms of the original example in Section 2.1. When the rate of profit is zero or $\varrho = 0$, and when there is a labour constraint rather than a wages fund constraint, all rent is imputed to labour.

The addition of a second country to the analysis is straightforward and need not be illustrated diagrammatically. From the point of view of the single country, up to two factor inputs will attract a non-zero rent.[14] More generally, it can be seen intuitively that the full employment of additional factor inputs will depend on there being more commodities included. If there are $n$ commodities and $q$ factor inputs, then for $n < q$, up to $n$ of the factor inputs will be fully employed and attract a non-zero price. When $n \geqq q$, it is possible (but not necessary) for all of the primary inputs to be fully employed.

How far should disaggregation be taken on the input side? One could number many hundreds of thousands of specific resources and factors.[15] However, apart from the irreducible qualities of nature and historical endowments of such non-reproducibles as works of art, there are few productive inputs which are non-reproducible and specific in the long run. In fact, it is an open question as to whether labour (or labour embodied in the wages fund) should be treated as a produced rather than a factor or non-produced input. The rule of thumb which suggests that labour should be treated as a primary non-produced input, but physical capital as produced means of production, is roughly confirmed by Brody (1970). He estimates that the number of years of production in a modern industrial economy, such as Hungary or the USA, required to reproduce physical capital (including infrastructure) is about three to four years, whilst ten years of output is required to reproduce the labour force. However, for present purposes, it is sufficient to note that technical and institutional differentiation is central to the Ricardian theory of comparative advantage. The role of additional factor inputs in determining such differentiation, apart from the irreducible qualities of nature, is secondary. It will therefore be convenient to think that the number of commodities exceeds the number of factors in the long run by a large order of magnitude and $n > q$. To the extent that a relatively small number of primary non-produced factor inputs may be included, the tendency towards incomplete specialisation already noted for the case where the number of commodities exceeds the number of countries or $n > m$ will be reinforced.

### 2.3.3   Generalised intermediate inputs

Produced inputs used directly in the production process such as seed for food production were assumed away in the opening exposition of the Ricardian model considered in Section 2.2. Attention was focused on the role of seed advanced for the period of production as an intermediate input used indirectly in the production process in the wages fund. In this section, the polar opposite assumption is made, namely that there is no wage fund, but produced inputs used directly in production are required. For simplicity, output is assumed to be constrained by the supply of labour $\bar{L}$ as in the previous section. The direct intermediate input–output coefficients are given by $a_{ij}$ for $i, j = 1, 2$, where $a_{ij}$ refers to the input of commodity $i$ required for the production of one unit of commodity $j$ for the period of production, taken as one year.

With intermediate inputs, the gross output frontier is given by the full employment of labour constraint as shown by $AB$ in Fig. 2.6.

Intermediate input–output usage is taken into account through the material balance conditions which require that at least enough output of each commodity is available to satisfy intermediate input usage and net output usage. Thus:

$$C_1 + a_{11}X_1 + a_{12}X_2 \leqq X_1$$
$$C_2 + a_{21}X_1 + a_{22}X_2 \leqq X_2 \qquad (2.10)$$

where $C_1$ and $C_2$ are the net outputs.

The net output frontier can be derived by replacing inequalities with equalities and substituting the material balance condition

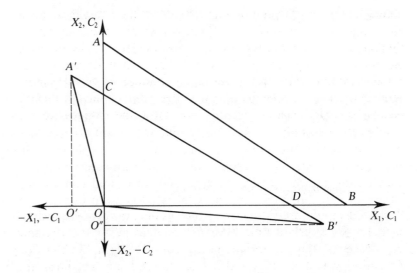

**Fig. 2.6**  Intermediate inputs in the Ricardian two-commodity, single-country case.

(2.10) into the supply constraint (2.9) for the case when there is only a single primary non-produced input, labour. Setting the employment limit equal to the labour supply $\bar{L}$, and applying the condition that the economy must be productive as shown in Appendix 2.2, it is derived by constructing the rays $OA'$ and $OB'$ in Fig. 2.6.

When trade is possible, the production of each commodity can be considered in isolation since the intermediate input requirements of the other commodity can be imported. Thus, when a unit of commodity 1 is produced, the net amount available after commodity 1 inputs into commodity 1 have been considered will be given by $(1 - a_{11})$. Commodity 2 inputs imported for a unit of commodity 1 production will be given by $-a_{21}$. The imported input requirements are shown in the negative quadrant since no domestic resources are required to produce them. Thus, the ray $OB'$ in Fig. 2.6 represents the combinations of net outputs of commodity 1 and commodity 2 inputs into commodity 1 for any given level of gross output of commodity 1.

The maximum gross output of commodity 1 possible, given the supply of labour, is given by $X_1 = \bar{L}/\ell_1$. The maximum net output of commodity 1, is given by $C_1 = X_1(1 - a_{11}) = \bar{L}(1 - a_{11})/\ell_1$, shown in Fig. 2.6 by the horizontal line $O''B'$. The imported input requirements of commodity 2 are given by $X_1 a_{21} = \bar{L} a_{21}/\ell_1$, the distance $OO''$ shown in Fig. 2.6 and the ray $OB'$ has a slope given by $-a_{21}/(1 - a_{11})$.

The combinations of net output of commodity 2 and the imported input requirements of commodity 1, are shown in Fig. 2.6 by the ray $OA'$. The maximum net output of commodity 2 is given by the distance $O'A'$. The complete net output frontier is given by joining the extreme points $A'B'$, and the slope of the net output frontier can be found in a straightforward manner by substituting for the various vertical and horizontal components shown in Fig. 2.6. Thus, the slope of $A'B'$ is given by

$$-(O'A' + OO'')/(O'O + O''B')$$

$$= -(\ell_1(1 - a_{22}) + \ell_2 a_{21})/(\ell_2(1 - a_{11}) + \ell_1 a_{12}) \quad (2.11)$$

which is the same as derived in equation (A2.2.5) in Appendix 2.2. When no trade is possible, the relevant combinations of maximal net output which can be produced are given by the points on the net output frontier which lie on the positive quadrant, $CD$. As discussed in Appendix 2.2, the condition that the economy is productive is equivalent, in the two-commodity case, to the requirement that there must be points on the net output frontier which lie in the positive quadrant.

The implications of the introduction of intermediate inputs are profound. Within the neo-classical tradition the main observation had been that, because the net output frontier has extreme points $A'$ and $B'$ in the NW and SE quadrants when trade is introduced, the possibility of gains from trade is enhanced; specialised production will be at $A'(B')$ rather than $C(D)$ and the consumption possibilities frontiers will lie further to the northeast. This occurs because, if produced inputs $a_{ij}$ can now be obtained through trade, gains from trade arise from the benefits of specialisation in produced inputs as well as final consumption commodities. Moreover, in 1986 intermediate inputs accounted for around two-thirds of the world's merchandise trade – 20 per cent for raw materials (including fuels) and 44 per cent for intermediates.[16] On the pricing side, the main neo-classical observation has been to use the $a_{ij}$ coefficients to take into account protection of intermediate inputs in assessing the resource re-allocation effects of tariff structures which affect both intermediate and final commodities, or the concept of effective protection. This will be taken up again in Section 5.4

In addition to the above, the neo-Ricardian and Marxian traditions have emphasised the role of intermediate inputs as circulating capital. Thus, if the produced means of production are regarded as circulating capital advanced by capitalists in the production process, then the equilibrium price conditions (2.1) will have to be modified to:

$$(w\ell_1 + p_1 a_{11} + p_2 a_{21})(1 + \varrho) \geqq p_1$$

$$(w\ell_2 + p_1 a_{12} + p_2 a_{22})(1 + \varrho) \geqq p_2 \qquad (2.12)$$

where both intermediate inputs are advanced by capitalists for the whole period of production, thereby attracting the charge of $\varrho$, the rate of profit on capital advanced. It is clear from the inspection of inequality (2.12) that the equilibrium commodity price ratio will be a non-linear function involving both the technical coefficients of production and the rate of profit $\varrho$ as shown in Appendix 2.2. This means that, for $\varrho > 0$, the no-trade price ratio will no longer be given by the slope of the net output frontier $A'B'$. The full implications of the interpretation of intermediate inputs as circulating capital will be taken up in Chapters 6 and 7 on neo-Ricardian and neo-Marxian trade theory.

### 2.3.4   Transport costs and non-traded commodities

The abstraction from distance so far is at variance with the obvious existence of transport costs and their possible influence on the pattern of trade. In order to illustrate the effects of distance, consider first the opposite extreme, where transport costs are such that, over the range of relative price changes considered, some commodities never enter into trade. Examples of such commodities are numerous, particularly for service activities where the act of personal or productive consumption cannot be separated from production itself.

Consider the introduction of a non-traded commodity into a single-country three-commodity Ricardian model in which the third commodity has such high transport costs that it is always non-traded. For given world prices and wages, the choice be-

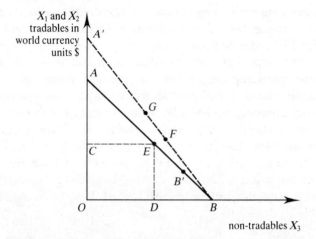

Fig. 2.7   Non-tradables in the single-country Ricardian model.

tween outputs $X_1$ and $X_2$ as the export commodity will be determined in exactly the same way as before. There will be complete specialisation and one of the inequalities (2.1) will be satisfied as an equality while the remaining commodity will be unprofitable to produce. On the consumption side, the tradable commodities can be aggregated into a single composite commodity, provided world prices remain fixed.[17] Thus it is possible to reduce the dimensions of the analysis to consider a single composite tradable commodity and a non-tradable commodity in the case of a single country which is a price taker on the world market. The resultant equilibrium can be illustrated in the usual two-dimensional manner, making the assumption that output is constrained by the supply of labour $\bar{L}$.

In Fig. 2.7, the output of the tradables sector is measured in terms of world currency units at the given prices $\bar{p}_1$ and $\bar{p}_2$. If the country specialises in the production of commodity 1, then for a given labour supply the maximum total output of tradables when the non-tradable output of commodity 3 is equal to zero will be given by $OA = \bar{p}_1\bar{L}/\ell_1$. Similarly, if all labour is allocated to non-tradable production, the maximal output of commodity 3 will be given by $OB = \bar{L}/\ell_3$. Thus, the production possibilities frontier $AEB'B$ in Fig. 2.7 can be drawn with a slope $OA/OB = -(\bar{p}_1\bar{L}/\ell_1)/(\bar{L}/\ell_3) = -\bar{p}_1\ell_3/\ell_1$ and the price of the non-tradable commodity 3 in terms of world currency units is given by $p_3/\bar{p}_1 =$

$-\ell_3/\ell_1$. If the point $E$ is the chosen final consumption point, the production of tradables $DE$ will exactly match the consumption of tradables and there will be balance of payments equilibrium. Similarly, the output of the non-tradable commodity $CE$ will exactly match consumption.

In the discussion of the Ricardian model so far, the exchange rate between domestic and world currency units has played no analytical role. This is only true as long as there are no non-traded commodities. The inclusion of a non-tradable commodity in the model described above leads to a result of fundamental importance: the price of the non-tradable commodity 3 in terms of world currency units measures the real exchange rate, or the non-tradable/tradable price ratio. The importance of this result will become apparent when changes are introduced which shift the real exchange rate.

The analytical importance of the non-tradable commodity can be illustrated by considering the impact of a technical change in the production of one of the tradable commodities. Say there is a dramatic fall in the labour input requirements for commodity 2, so that the new labour coefficient $\ell_2^* < \ell_2$. If the rise in labour productivity is such that the marginal revenue product from commodity 2 production now exceeds that of commodity 1 production, or $\bar{p}_2/\ell_2^* > \bar{p}_1/\ell_1$, commodity 2 will be exported and commodity 1 production will cease altogether.

The new production possibilities frontier is shown by $A'GFB$ in Fig. 2.7. On account of the improvement in labour productivity in one of the tradables, the real wage measured in terms of both tradables will rise. This will be reflected in a rise in the price of the non-traded commodity 3 or an appreciation of the real exchange rate as the price of the non-tradable adjusts to a higher real wage measured in terms of tradables.[18] The new production and consumption point will be at $G$ if the substitution effects in consumption arising from the technical change are more powerful than the income effects and the output of non-tradables falls. Conversely, if the income effects are sufficiently strong, the new consumption and production point will be at $F$ and the output of non-tradables will rise. Thus, commodity 1 might be a traditional export and commodity 2 a new method of producing the traditional export, such as plantation methods. Alternatively, a new discovery might take place, which transforms commodity 2 production from import competing to exporting commodity, such as a new mineral deposit. In both cases, the effects on the rest of the economy are the same. There will be a sharp decline in the fortunes of the traditional export industry and the emergence of new exported commodities with an increase in the price of non-tradables, which will have uncertain effects on non-tradable outputs. Historically, this phenomenon has always been a feature of radical changes in the way in which particular nations, regions or social formations are inserted into the world economy.

In modern parlance, such dramatic changes in the fortunes of traded commodities are often referred to as the Dutch disease after the effects of North Sea gas discoveries on the Dutch economy in the 1960s. Thus, a new discovery of a mineral resource such as oil or gas has similar effects on the production possibilities frontier for tradables to the improvement in productivity analysed above. However, since the only resource included in the analysis so far is labour, it is not an interesting framework for considering such resource-change effects, and the analysis will have to wait until Section 5.5.

The above analysis treated transport costs as either zero or infinity. It is not easy to give graphic illustration of the consequences of transport costs for in-between cases. For a small peripheral country, world prices will be given at the point of sale or purchase in the principal central markets and the relevant border prices for importing and exporting will require the addition or subtraction of transport costs. Thus, in the three-commodity Ricardian case, if $\bar{p}_1$, $\bar{p}_2$ and $\bar{p}_3$ are the given world prices at principal markets, if transport costs measured in terms of foreign exchange are given by $a'_1$, $a'_2$ and $a'_3$, and if the prices of each commodity when exported or imported are $p_i^e$ and $p_i^m$ respectively, for $i = 1, 2, 3$ the relevant domestic border prices for our small peripheral economy will be:

$$p_1^e = \bar{p}_1 - a'_1$$
$$p_1^m = \bar{p}_1 + a'_1$$
$$p_2^e = \bar{p}_2 - a'_2$$
$$p_2^m = \bar{p}_2 + a'_2$$
$$p_3^e = \bar{p}_3 - a'_3$$
$$p_3^m = \bar{p}_3 + a'_3 \tag{2.13}$$

Suppose that commodity 3 is an importable in the principal central markets and that transport costs 3 are initially very large so that commodity 3 is non-traded in the small peripheral home economy. Commodities 1 and 2 are exported and imported, respectively. If transport costs for commodity 3, equal to $a_3^t$, decline radically, for example through the introduction of refrigeration for the transport of perishable food products such as meat, commodity 3 might well shift from being effectively a non-traded commodity to being an exportable commodity. The effects on such an economy will be similar to those described above for a radical rise in labour productivity in the import competing industry. Exports of the traditional export commodity 1 will decline and will possibly become non-tradable or even an importable whilst commodity 3 production will dramatically increase. Whilst such a result has been forced in order to make the point, it is evidently unwise both theoretically and historically to assume that transport costs have no effects on the pattern of trade. This point and some further complications will be taken up again in Section 4.3.4.

This account of the Ricardian derivation of the principle of comparative advantage demonstrates its generality: it is *the* starting point for *all* analysis of trade flows. Although Ricardo's own demonstration (and later neo-classical accounts) was essentially static, it is a simple matter to integrate it with growth models. Thus it can be seen that the principle is compatible with a class analysis of the economy. The principle is not confined to the standard textbook results derived from strong assumptions, and can readily accommodate a many commodity-many country world. Where appropriate, the role of demand patterns and/or international bargaining power can be brought to bear on the analysis.

## APPENDIX 2.1   THE JONES INEQUALITY AND THE ASSIGNMENT PROBLEM[19]

The elegant simplicity of the Ricardian model makes it possible to examine comparative advantage in more general terms than in Sections 2.2.2 or 2.2.3 of the text.

In Fig. 2.2(b), the world production possibilities frontier is shown for the 2 × 2 case. There are three efficient points of complete specialisation on the frontier, points $A$, $B$ and $C$, and one inefficient point $H$. In order to develop the argument, consider the two points $B$ and $H$. The common characteristic of these points is that there is complete specialisation, but the pattern of trade is reversed at each point. Thus, both the specialisation at $B$ and $H$ may be said to belong to the same class of assignments where one country is assigned to the production of each commodity.

Consider the efficient point $B$. When production takes place at $B$, it must be true that the price of commodity 1 is given by cost conditions in country 1, and the price of commodity 2 by the cost conditions in country 2. Thus:

$$w^1 \ell_1^1 = p_1$$
$$w^2 \ell_2^2 = p_2 \qquad \text{(A2.1.1)}$$

Similarly, by assumption, specialisation at point $H$ on the second assignment of commodities to countries is inefficient, so it must be true that:

$$w^1 \ell_2^1 \geqq p_2$$
$$w^1 \ell_1^2 \geqq p_1 \qquad \text{(A2.1.2)}$$

If we multiply both sides of the equalities (A2.2.1) and the inequalities (A2.1.2), we find that:

$$w^1 w^2 \ell_1^1 \ell_2^2 = p_1 p_2 \leqq w^1 w^2 \ell_2^1 \ell_1^2$$

and $\qquad \qquad \ell_1^1/\ell_1^2 \leqq \ell_2^1/\ell_2^2 \qquad \text{(A2.1.3)}$

This is none other than a rewritten form of our expression for the Ricardian limbo region in equation (2.7) in the text, or the Jones inequality (see Chipman, 1965a, page 508).

Jones (1961) generalises the argument for the $n \times n$ case before suggesting a way of dealing with the $m \times n$ case where $m$ is the number of countries and $n$ is the number of commodities. As has already been noted in the text, the $n \times n$ case is not very interesting since any realistic specification of the relation between different commodities produced and countries in the real world suggests that $n > m$. For present purposes, it seems more useful to explore the $2 \times 3$ and $2 \times n$ cases before making a brief observation about the $m \times n$ case where $n > m$.

**Table A2.1.1**   Possible assignments in the 2 × 3 Ricardian case.

| | Assignments | | | |
| | A | B | C | D |
|---|---|---|---|---|
| commodity 1 | country 1 | country 2 | country 1&2 | country 1&2 |
| commodity 2 | country 2 | country 1 | country 1 | country 2 |
| commodity 3 | country 1&2 | country 1&2 | country 2 | country 1 |

Suppose that for two different sets of prices, $p$ and $p^*$, the patterns of specialisation or assignments designated $A$ and $C$ are optimal. Consider also two other assignments in the same class of assignments as $A$ and $C$ designated $B$ and $D$, respectively, as shown in Table A2.1.1.

In assignments $A$ and $B$, commodities 1 and 2 each have one country assigned to them and commodity 3 has both countries assigned. Similarly, in assignments from $C$ and $D$, commodities 2 and 3 each have a country assigned to them and commodity 1 has both countries assigned. Now consider the assignments $A$ and $B$, $C$ and $D$ pair-wise. Since by assumption $A$ is optimal for one term of trade and $C$ is optimal for another, it follows that:

| $A$ | $B$ | $C$ | $D$ |
|---|---|---|---|
| $w^1\ell_1^1 = p_1$ | $w^2\ell_1^2 \geqq p_1$ | $w^1\ell_1^1 = p_1^*$ | $w^1\ell_1^1 = p_1^*$ |
| $w^2\ell_2^2 = p_2$ | $w^1\ell_2^1 \geqq p_2$ | $w^2\ell_1^2 = p_1^*$ | $w^2\ell_1^2 = p_1^*$ |
| $w^1\ell_3^1 = p_3$ | $w^1\ell_3^1 = p_3$ | $w^1\ell_2^1 = p_2^*$ | $w^2\ell_2^2 \geqq p_2^*$ |
| $w^2\ell_3^2 = p_3$ | $w^2\ell_3^2 = p_3$ | $w^2\ell_3^2 = p_3^*$ | $w^1\ell_3^1 \geqq p_3^*$ |

Take first the equations and inequalities for assignments $A$ and $B$. Multiplying the right- and left-hand sides together gives:

$$w^1w^2w^1w^2\ell_1^1\ell_2^2\ell_3^1\ell_3^2 = p_1p_2p_3p_3 \leqq w^2w^1w^1w^2\ell_1^2\ell_2^1\ell_3^1\ell_3^2 \quad (A2.1.4)$$

which simplifies to:

$$\ell_1^1/\ell_1^2 \leqq \ell_2^1/\ell_2^2 \quad (A2.1.5)$$

Consider now the equations and inequalities for assignments $C$ and $D$. Multiply the left- and right-hand sides of the equation and inequalities as before to yield:

$$w^1w^2w^1w^2\ell_2^1\ell_3^2\ell_2^1\ell_3^2 = p_1^*p_1^*p_2^*p_3^* \leqq w^1w^2w^2w^1\ell_1^1\ell_1^2\ell_2^2\ell_3^1$$

**Table A2.1.2**  Possible assignments in the 2 × $n$ Ricardian case.

| | Assignments | | | |
|---|---|---|---|---|
| | $A$ | $B$ | $C$ | $D$ |
| commodity 1 | country 1 | country 2 | | |
| commodity 2 | country 2 | country 1 | | |
| commodities 3,4...$n$ | countries 1&2 | countries 1&2 | | |
| commodities 1,4,5...$n$ | | | countries 1&2 | countries 1&2 |
| commodity 2 | | | country 1 | country 2 |
| commodity 3 | | | country 2 | country 1 |

which simplifies to:

$$\ell_2^1/\ell_2^2 \leqq \ell_3^1/\ell_3^2 \qquad (A2.1.6)$$

Putting (A2.1.5) and (A2.1.6) together gives:

$$\ell_1^1/\ell_1^2 \leqq \ell_2^1/\ell_2^2 \leqq \ell_3^1/\ell_3^2 \qquad (A2.1.7)$$

which is none other than the first three terms of inequality (2.8) of the text. Thus, commodities can be ranked in order of comparative advantage, with country 1 showing its greatest comparative advantage in commodities 1, 2 and 3 in that order.

The above argument easily generalises to the 2 × $n$ case. The numbering of the commodities is quite arbitrary. Consider two classes of assignments, the first where countries 1 or 2 are assigned to commodities 1 or 2 and no countries are assigned to commodities 3, 4 ... $n$ and the second where no countries are assigned to commodities 1, 4, 5 ... $n$ and countries 1 or 2 are assigned to commodities 2 or 3. These are shown in Table A2.1.2 as assignments $A$, $B$, $C$ and $D$.

By obvious extension of the argument for the 2 × 3 case, it follows that for comparisons of $A$ and $B$, $C$ and $D$, respectively, for two different sets of prices, with $A$ and $C$, respectively, assumed to be the optimal assignments, inequalities (A2.1.5) and (A2.1.6) can also be shown to hold. If other pairs of assignments are considered, then by appropriate choice of numbering:

$$\ell_1^1/\ell_1^2 \leqq \ell_2^1/\ell_2^2 \leqq \ldots \leqq \ell_n^1/\ell_n^2 \qquad (A2.1.8)$$

This is none other than inequality (2.8) of the text.

When there are only two countries, bilateral comparisons at

different terms of trade can be made and the commodities ranked in order of comparative advantage. However, when we have $n$ commodities and $m$ countries with $n > m$, multilateral comparisons must be made and there is no simple or unique ordering of commodities according to the countries with the strongest and weakest comparative advantage. It is only posible to observe that in this case there will be incomplete specialisation and that the pattern of trade with be governed by multilateral comparisons in which the labour coefficients and the pattern of demand will interact to determine the final equilibrium.

## APPENDIX 2.2    THE NET OUTPUT FRONTIER WITH INTERMEDIATE INPUTS

Using matrix notation, the net output constraints (2.10) and the labour use constraint (2.2) can be rewritten as:

$$[C] + [A][X] \leqq [X] \qquad (A2.2.1)$$

$$[\ell][X] \leqq \bar{L} \qquad (A2.2.2)$$

where $[C]$ and $[X]$ are $(n \times 1)$ vectors of net outputs and gross outputs, respectively, $[A]$ is an $(n \times n)$ matrix of input–output coefficients $a_{ij}$, and $[\ell]$ is a $(1 \times n)$ sector of labour input coefficients. Notice that the labour usage constraint (2.2) has been re-written to reflect the switch from the wage fund as the limit on labour use to labour supply, corresponding to the discussion in Section 2.3.3 of the text. Alternatively, the net output frontier can be defined for $\bar{L} = 1$ so that the frontier is expressed per unit of labour employed, independently of the level of employment and the determination of the level of activity. Setting (A2.2.1) and (A2.2.2) as equalities and substituting (A2.2.1) into (A2.2.2) yields

$$[\ell^{+}][C] = \bar{L} \qquad (A2.2.3)$$

where $[\ell^{+}] = [\ell][I - A]^{-1}$, a $(1 \times n)$ vector of direct and indirect labour input coefficients. For $[C] \geqq 0$ and $n = 2$, the net output constraint in the positive quadrant may be plotted as in Fig. 2.6 in the text. If net outputs can be negative for all except one commodity, as will be the case with foreign trade, the full production possibilities frontier $A'CDB'$ in Fig. 2.6 can be drawn. Here, $O'A' = \bar{L}(1 - a_{22})/\ell_2$ and $O''B' = \bar{L}(1 - a_{11})/\ell_1$.

In the two-commodity case the requirement that the economy be productive in the absence of trade so that at least some points on the net output frontier be in the positive quadrant can be expressed as a condition that the slope of the ray $OA'$ be greater than the slope of the ray $OB'$ or

$$(1 - a_{22})(1 - a_{11}) \geqq a_{21}a_{12} \qquad (2.2.4)$$

This is known as the Hawkins–Simon condition. In the many commodity case, this generalises into the requirement that the input–output matrix has at least one semi-positive definite eigen vector associated with a positive eigen root (see Dorfman, Samuelson and Solow (1958) and Brody (1970) for further discussion).

The slope of the net output frontier can be found by totally differentiating (A2.2.3) and setting $d\bar{L} = 0$ to yield:

$$dC_2/dC_1 = - \ell_1^\dagger/\ell_2^\dagger$$

$$= - \frac{\ell_1(1 - a_{22}) + \ell_2 a_{21}}{\ell_1 a_{12} + \ell_2(1 - a_{11})} \qquad (A2.2.5)$$

The reader can verify this with the aid of Fig. 2.6 by noting that:

$$\text{slope } A'B' = - \frac{\bar{L}(1 - a_{22})/\ell_2 + \bar{L}a_{21}/\ell_1}{\bar{L}a_{12}/\ell_2 + \bar{L}(1 - a_{11})/\ell_1}$$

$$= - \frac{\ell_1(1 - a_{22}) + \ell_2 a_{21}}{\ell_1 a_{12} + \ell_2(1 - a_{11})}$$

As noted in the text, the slope of the net output frontier will not, in general, be the same as the autarky price ratio when there are intermediate inputs and $\varrho > 0$. Relation (2.12) in the text can be rewritten as:

$$w\ell_1(1 + \varrho) = p_1(1 - a_{11}(1 + \varrho)) - p_2 a_{21}(1 + \varrho)$$

$$w\ell_2(1 + \varrho) = -p_1 a_{12}(1 + \varrho) + p_2(1 - a_{22}(1 + \varrho))$$

$$\text{or} \quad w(1 + \varrho)[\ell] = [p][I - A(1 + \varrho)] \qquad (A2.2.6)$$

where $[p]$ is a $(1 \times n)$ vector of prices. Thus, the autarky price ratio in the two-commodity case will be:

$$-(p_1/p_2) = - \frac{\ell_1(1 - a_{22}(1 + \varrho)) + \ell_2 a_{21}(1 + \varrho)}{\ell_1 a_{12}(1 + \varrho) + \ell_2(1 - a_{11}(1 + \varrho))}$$

or    $$[p] = w(1 + \varrho)[\ell][I - A(1 + \varrho)]^{-1} \qquad (A2.2.7)$$

Note that the autarky price ratio is now dependent upon the rate of profit $\varrho$. When $\varrho = 0$, (A2.2.7) reduces to (A2.2.5), the slope of the net output frontier. The full implications of this modification to the Ricardian model will be taken up in Chapter 6.

## NOTES

1.  That Ricardo became a large landowner in later life is not neces-sarily indicative of a conflict of interest here (see Halevy, 1928, page 341 and Deane, 1978, page 63). In the very long run, there is no conflict of interest between manufacturers and landlords. As shown in Section 3.5, the absolute amount of rent will be the same in the long-run stationary state regardless of the level of protection. If relative wealth of landowners and manufacturers counts, an ele-ment of conflict of interest emerges. Insofar as the elimination of the protection of corn raises either profits or wages (or both) in the short or medium term, there will be an additional source of conflict of interest between landowners and manufacturers.
2.  See Halevy (1928, part III, Ch. 1) for a discussion of the contradic-tion in Ricardo's work between the natural harmony of interest and economic optimism, and the emphasis on conflict of interest be-tween landlords and the rest of society and his economic pessim-ism. He suggests that Ricardo, the parliamentary orator, was more favourably inclined to the language of optimism than Ricardo the theoretical writer. The natural harmony of interest emerges most clearly in his static model of trade discussed in Section 2.2.1. In the dynamic open model of trade discussed in Section 3.5, the short- and medium-run optimism of free trade gives way to long-run pessimism when diminishing returns reasserts itself for the world economy as a whole.
3.  There was close interaction between Torrens and Ricardo in the discovery of the principle of comparative advantage with the main credit going to Torrens. See Chipman (1965a, pages 481–2).
4.  See, for example, Ricardo (1817, page 133).
5.  Simple reproduction means that the economy exactly reproduces the starting stock of capital by the end of each period of produc-tion, that there is no tendency for capitalists to reallocate their wage-fund capital between the two sectors, or for workers to move between the two sectors. In the Marxian tradition, simple repro-duction also implies that all of the social, political and institutional arrangements in the given society are reproduced over time.

6. The formal treatment of the closed and open Ricardian growth models has been developed by Pasinetti (1960), Findlay (1974) and Burgstaller (1986). In the discussion here, attention is confined to steady state solutions in a comparative dynamic context.

7. Ricardo's theory of subsistence wages was based on the Malthusian law of population growth in which the supply of labour (population growth) and the demand for labour (employment) were regulated through the price of labour (wages). It included both biological and social determination of the subsistence wage and population growth. See Ricardo (1817, Ch. 1 and Ch. 5), Kaldor (1955, page 85, footnote 1), Metcalfe and Steedman (1973) and Steedman (1982).

8. That is, Samuelson's well-known non-substitution theorem holds. See Samuelson (1951) and Section 2.3.4.

9. Contrary to Ricardo's optimistic view that free trade would bring gains to all, in general there will be losers as well as gainers. Standard analysis of the gains from trade assumes that there has been a welfare improvement when there are potential gains from trade, even if the losers are not compensated. Generally speaking, I think it is important to make any judgements on the welfare weights explicit wherever possible.

10. For a more detailed analysis, see Metcalfe and Steedman (1973).

11. For a simple derivation of offer curves, see Caves and Jones (1981, pages 49–51).

12. Two approaches can be taken to establishing a lower bound on the number of commodities $n$ which enter trade. First, the Standard International Trade Classification or SITC has 1,024 basic entries (UN, 1975, page vii). Depending on the narrowness of the definition, it is not difficult to imagine ten or even 100 further subdivisions of each basic category. Alternatively, the International Standard Industrial Classification or ISIC defines about 12,000 basic *activities* rather than commodities (UN, 1971, page iv). If one supposed that each activity produced at least one technologically separable commodity, then the bench-mark is for $n \simeq 12,000$. Of these, approximately 7,000 are associated with mainly tradable agricultural, mining and manufacturing categories and 5,000 with mainly non-tradable utilities, construction and service activities. It therefore seems quite appropriate to assume that the number of commodities is greater than the number of countries or $n > m$ by a very large order of magnitude.

13. See, for example, Caves and Jones (1981, pages 88–9).

14. The possibility that more than two constraints could pass through one of the points on the production possibilities frontier is ruled out by assumption.

15. It is not possible to put a bench-mark upper or lower bound on the size of $q$. For example, taking human skills as a disaggregation of one set of primary non-produced factors, the International Standard Classification of Occupations (ISCO) lists 1,506 basic categor-

ies (ILO, 1969, page 2, page 5). However, there is no obvious reason why this could not be disaggregated further, quite apart from the specification of different types of land. The suggestion in the text that it is convenient to think of $n > q$ by a large order of magnitude is based on the observation that none of the major theories of comparative advantage refer to a highly disaggregated set of non-reproducible inputs. Therefore the inclusion of a limited set of disaggregated non-reproducible inputs does not alter the general rule that there will be incomplete specialisation in the simplest models of comparative advantage.

16.  Raw materials are defined as primary products less food. Intermediates are defined as iron and steel, chemicals, other semi-manufactures, and engineering products less road motor vehicles less household appliances (see GATT, 1986–7).

17.  For an introduction to the aggregation of commodities into a composite commodity, see Henderson and Quandt (1980, pages 48–9). The original definition of the aggregation conditions required for the formation of a composite commodity is due to Hicks (1946, pages 312–13).

18.  This follows because, at unchanged prices for tradables, the real wage can be measured in terms of either tradable commodity. Thus, in the original situation, the money wage is given by $w = \bar{p}_1/\ell_1 = \bar{p}_2/\ell_2$, when profits are zero. With technical change in industry 2, the new money wage payable in industry 2 will be given by $w^* = \bar{p}_2/\ell_2^*$ and $w^* > w$ since $\ell_2^* < \ell_2$. Since world prices remain unchanged, the real wage must also increase when measured in terms of either tradable commodity. The price of non-tradables after the change will be give by $p_3^* = \bar{p}_2\ell_3/\ell_2^* > \bar{p}_1\ell_3/\ell_1 = p_3$ and the price of non-tradables in terms of foreign exchange has risen.

19.  For a slightly different elementary exposition of the assignment problem, see Caves and Jones (1981, supplement to Ch. 5, pages 501–7). A more advanced treatment can be found in Chipman (1965a, pages 507–9), Jones (1961), McKenzie (1954b) and Whitin (1953).

# 3 · RICARDIAN APPLICATIONS AND PERSPECTIVES

## 3.1 INTRODUCTORY REMARKS

The discussion so far has centred on some of the analytical aspects of Ricardo's theory of comparative advantage. Further insight can be obtained by looking at Ricardo in the light of his predecessors, both in relation to the aspects of their work which he took up, and those which he did not pursue. Some of these are examined in Section 3.2. Arguably, Arthur Lewis has made the most important applications of the Ricardian framework to modern trade and development issues. These are discussed in Sections 3.3 and 3.4. A fuller perspective on the Ricardian theory of trade and growth is offered in Section 3.5. The chapter closes by reviewing the Ricardian contribution in the light of the neoclassical revolution in Section 3.6.

## 3.2 RICARDO AND HIS PRECURSORS

### 3.2.1 The mercantilists and the physiocrats

The classic attack on the mercantilists' policy of restricting trade was made by Adam Smith in Book IV of *The Wealth of Nations* (Smith, 1776). Ricardo provided the definitive classical restatement of these criticisms using a coherent labour theory of value, together with a framework for the analysis of the effects of government restriction on prices, profitability and growth. This left out any account of the mercantilists' views on the essential role of the state in the development process independent of its role in influencing market prices. A wider view of the mercantilist discourse reveals a strong legal component in the discussion of how to set up the machinery of government for an emerging nation state and for the active intervention of the state as an agent in the development process.[1]

The most strenuous and consistent nineteenth-century objections to Ricardo's abstraction from the role of the state came from List (1885), whose views influenced the protectionist trade policies of the emerging German and American states. These views have echoes in the Marxian and structuralist-institutionalist traditions. For example, Bukharin (1972) attempted to develop a conceptual framework for the analysis of the nation state in the world economy, and Sideri (1970) looked at trade and power in an historical and contemporary context. Another contemporary argument for the role of the state in the development process outside of its role in influencing market prices can be found in Gerschenkron (1966). However, the standard abstraction from these issues is retained until the discussion of normative trade theory and the institutions of trade policy in Chapter 8.

Ricardo, in line with other classical political economists, identified in labour *the* source of surplus product. The mercantilists were rightly criticised by the classical political economists for their identification of *the* source of surplus product in exchange, just as the French physiocrats were criticised for their identification of agriculture as *the* source of surplus product. The idea that labour is *the* source of surplus product, still retained by the fundamentalist Marxian tradition, is not useful. As noted in Section 2.3.3, the equilibrium conditions for an economy using intermediate inputs require that the intermediate inputs themselves are productive of surplus product as well as labour. What matters is the relative importance of different sources of surplus product in theory, in history, and in the contemporary period.

Another important aspect of physiocratic thought was their representation of the social circuit of the economic system, the advance of corn at the end of one harvest for the reproduction of the next cycle and its return with the following harvest. This idea was reflected by Ricardo in his model of growth. The simple dynamic model discussed in the previous chapter also captures this idea with the advance of the wages fund at the beginning of the productive cycle yielding a return at the end of the cycle.

### 3.2.2    Trade theory in the light of Smith and Ricardo

There is a strong tendency within trade theory to regard movements around given production and consumption possibilities frontiers as providing the most important insights into the sources of gains from trade. Such a procedure understates the often radical nature of the effects of the opening of foreign trade historically. In this regard, the Ricardian tradition is very different from Adam Smith's starting point.

In Smith's view, a trade-induced division of labour is the main underlying condition for modern economic growth, an argument which was implicitly based on economics of scale. Little formal attention is paid to economies of scale in this book except in Section 4.3, although it is relevant when discussing trade policy issues and when interpreting the empirical relationship between trade and growth in Chapters 8 and 9.

Another aspect is the 'vent for surplus' argument for the opening of trade elaborated by Myint (1958). This suggests that in the pre-trade position the economy may be operating inside the production possibilities frontier such as described in Fig. 2.1. This may arise because of a highly inelastic demand for domestic consumption requirements, or through a high degree of internal immobility of domestic resources. Such a possibility has an obvious basis in standard Keynesian analysis, or in the contemporary discussion of the effects of import compression on aggregate demand.

Whereas the relationship between trade and capacity utilisation must be identified empirically on a case by case basis, the point that the opening of trade may not be well described by shifts along the production possibilities frontier is of general importance. This was in fact the central message of Williams (1929). His critique of classical trade theory was that the development of the world economy went hand in hand with the development of the national economy, a similar point to that made by Bukharin (1972) in a different context. Historically, there was in fact far more international mobility of commodities and factors than with national economies at an early stage of their development. This undermines the assumed dichotomy between national mobility and international immobility of capital and labour in the classical theory of comparative advantage. The opening of trade, or major changes in trading relationships, may therefore lead to irreversible changes in scale economies and in the utilisation of resources through changes in factor mobility and in demand. Such trade-induced growth is 'trade as the engine of growth' *par excellence*.

In practice, trade theory is applied to the analysis of the with-trade equilibrium position rather than the opening of trade. This is well exemplified by the applications of the simple Ricardian model in the next two sections.

## 3.3 TRADE AND SURPLUS LABOUR

It has long been recognised that one of the key characteristics of developing countries is the underemployment and unemployment of labour (see Lewis, 1954, 1972; Kalecki, 1960; and Marglin, 1976). More recently, the re-emergence of mass unemployment in the central capitalistic economies has brought the Marxian and Keynesian problematic (see Godfrey, 1985) back into focus. Thus, any useful model of trade and growth must allow for the consequences of underemployed and/or unemployed labour at an institutionally determined real wage.

In the classical Ricardian model discussed in the previous chapter, it was the Malthusian population principle that ensured long-run full employment at an institutionally given subsistence wage. This is not a credible mechanism to determine the long-run balance between the supply and demand for labour at a given real wage. For developing countries, Lewis argues that the marginal productivity of labour is zero within the non-capitalist subsistence sector of the economy, or at least lower than that obtainable in the capitalist sectors of the economy, whereas the opportunity cost for such labour to leave the subsistence sector is given by the average product of labour in the subsistence sector. Small holdings practising subsistence agriculture may employ family labour even when its marginal product falls below the wage. Economic transactions may not be separate from social ties and obligations. Further, when a member of the family leaves the plot to work for an industrial wage, failure to distinguish between the product of labour and other owned resources such as capital and land means that the opportunity cost of such labour is set at

**Table 3.1**   Lewis surplus labour example. Source: Lewis (1954, p. 185).

|  |  | Food | Manufactures |
|---|---|---|---|
| country 1: (capitalistic) | average output/labour ratio $1/\ell_i^1$ (average) | 3 | 3 |
|  | marginal output/labour ratio $1/\ell_i^1$ (marginal) | 3 | 3 |
| country 2: (dual economy) | average output/labour ratio $1/\ell_i^2$ (average) | 2 | 1 |
|  | marginal output/labour ratio $1/\ell_i^2$ (marginal) | 0 | 1 |

the *average* rather than the *marginal* subsistence product. This surplus labour model constrasts with the Myint (1958, page 28) version of the vent for surplus argument discussed in the previous section. The latter model is about the transfer of peasant economic units *en bloc* to new land, rather than surplus labour supplied by labour dislodged from peasant production for employment in the capitalistic sector. In the case of the developed capitalist economies, Lewis usually assumed full employment at a market clearing wage. Alternatively, the employment of labour can be determined by the size of the initial wage fund, and an institutionally fixed wage and the excess supply of labour might be considered to be a part of the reserve army of labour as in the Marxian case. Either assumption can be deployed in the models considered below. A fuller discussion of models of unemployment in developed capitalist economies is left until Section 6.2.

Some of the essential implications of the Lewis surplus labour argument for developing countries are captured in two static Ricardian trade models (Lewis, 1954, 1969). First, he contrasts the classical framework for the Law of Comparative Costs, which holds for a fully employed capitalist economy with a surplus labour or dual economy, as shown in Table 3.1.

In Table 3.1, it is assumed for the capitalistic country 1 that the average and marginal output/labour ratios are the same. This implies constant returns to scale and an autarky price ratio $(p_1^1/p_2^1)^a = 1$. The production possibilities frontier for the capitalistic country shown by $AB$ in Fig. 3.1(a) for an arbitrarily chosen total wages fund which ensures that all labour can be fully employed at an endogenously determined real wage is the same as in Fig. 2.1.

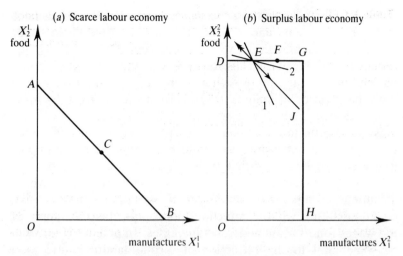

**Fig. 3.1**   The static Ricardian $2 \times 2$ model with Lewis-type surplus labour.

Country 2 with a dual economy is radically different. In manufactures, it is assumed that average and marginal output/labour
ratios are the same, so that there is constant returns to scale.
However, in the subsistence food producing sector, it is assumed
that there is a fixed food output given by $OD$ in Fig. 3.1(b) and a
marginal productivity of labour of zero. The maximum output of
manfacturers is constrained by the number of workers available
for employment in the capitalistic sector of the economy. The
withdrawal of labour from the subsistence food sector to work in
the manufacturing sector can be accomplished without any decline in the output of food along $DEFG$ in Fig. 3.1(b) and the
complete production possibilities frontier is given by $DEFGH$.

The surplus labour argument modifies the equilibrium price
condition (2.1) in a simple way. As before, it is assumed that
competitive prices in the capitalistic sector are formed by wage
costs and profit earned on the wages fund. However, in the
subsistence sector, there is no profit earned on the initial stocks
of food and all returns are imputed to labour. Thus, the equilibrium price conditions will be:

$$w\ell_1(1 + \varrho) \geqq p_1$$
$$w\ell_2 \geqq p_2 \qquad (3.1)$$

If the initial stocks of food are divided between the subsistence sector requirements and a wage fund for the capitalistic sector and if the manufacturing wage is determined by the average product of labour in the subsistence sector, the initial equilibrium output could be at a point such as $E$ in Fig. 3.1(b). At this point, the relative price of manufactures to food will be given by $p_1/p_2$ = $\ell_1(1 + \varrho)/\ell_2$, which will be greater than the competitive capitalist price ratio in the absence of surplus labour which is simply $\ell_1/\ell_2$. It is the latter price ratio which governs the social opportunity cost of labour, rather than the average cost of labour in subsistence production. Of course, this is an extreme case where an unlimited amount of labour can be withdrawn from subsistence agriculture without affecting food output, as the supply of the wages fund for manufactures increases. In practice, there will be some limit to the extraction of surplus labour before food production will begin to decline such as indicated by point $F$, modifying the production possibilities frontier to $DEFH$ (not drawn). Also, there may be changes in subsistence agriculture which accompany the extraction of surplus or underemployed labour and of additional food supplies for manufacturing workers (Marglin, 1976, pages 15–16).

The full impact of this departure from the Ricardian case can be seen with the opening of trade. Suppose that the capitalist country 1 remains incompletely specialised and the world price ratio is given by the autarky prices in country 1. The consumption possibilities frontier in country 2 will be given by the world price line $EJ$ in Fig. 3.1(b). In the dual-economy country 2, three possibilities emerge, depending on the ratio of the world price of manufactures and food, and the domestic price ratios with and without prices governed by the social opportunity cost of labour. When both domestic price ratios are greater than the world price ratio, or:

$$\ell_1(1 + \varrho)/\ell_2 > \ell_1/\ell_2 > (p_1/p_2)^*$$

the dual economy country will correctly export food in return for manufactures. When both domestic price ratios are less than the world price ratio, or:

$$(p_1/p_2)^* > \ell_1(1 + \varrho)/\ell_2 > \ell_1/\ell_2$$

then the dual economy will correctly export manufactures in

return for food. However, when the world price ratio lies in between the two domestic price ratios, or:

$$\ell_1(1 + \varrho)/\ell_2 > (p_1/p_2)^* > (\ell_1/\ell_2)$$

then the dual economy will export food in return for manufactures when in fact it should export manufactures in return for food. This case is illustrated in Fig. 3.1(b).

As long as the amounts of food and manufactures traded are small relative to total production, the subsistence wage in terms of food will remain unchanged with the opening of trade. The ratio of the prices of manufactures and food under conditions of surplus labour, $\ell_1(1 + \varrho)/\ell_2$, is shown by line 1, passing through $E$. The social opportunity cost of labour, $\ell_1/\ell_2$, is reflected by line 2. It is clear that there are potential gains from trade if the economy moves in the direction ≫ on the consumption possibilities frontier $EJ$. With surplus labour pricing, the economy incorrectly trades in the direction > on $EJ$. In the neighbourhood of $E$ any movement in the direction marked > on $EJ$ would lead to potential loss from free trade since the consumption point will be inside the production possibilities frontier. Obviously, if such exports of food were continued to any extent, the subsistence wage in terms of food would be undermined in the longer run as the food availability per person declined and the relative price of manufactures rose. With the de-accumulation of wages fund capital employed in manufactures over time, the production point $E$ would shift to the left on $DEFG$ (not drawn), and the with-trade consumption possibilities frontier $EJ$ will shift downwards.

It would be more socially desirable for country 2 to export manufactures in exchange for food, moving in the direction marked ≫ on the consumption possibilities frontier $EJ$, accumulating wages fund capital in manufactures and shifting the production point $E$ to the right. This would have the advantage of augumenting subsistence food supplies through external trade, reflecting the underlying social opportunity costs in the surplus labour economy.

The second extension of the static Ricardian model is designed to explain the terms of trade between tropical products and manufactures (Lewis, 1969, pages 17–22). The static analysis is developed here and the comparative statics of terms of trade changes is left until the next section. The key change in the

**Table 3.2**    Lewis Tropical terms of trade example. Source: Lewis (1969, p. 18).

|  |  | Manufactures $X^1_1$ | Food $X^1_2$ and $X^2_2$ | Commercials $X^2_3$ |
|---|---|---|---|---|
| country 1 | average and marginal output/labour ratios $1/\ell^1_i$ | 3 | 3 | – |
| country 2 | average and marginal output/labour ratios $1/\ell^2_i$ | – | 1 | 1 |

model presented above is the introduction of a third tradable commodity. Suppose that country 1 is the developed capitalist country producing food and manufactures whilst country 2 is a dual economy producing both food in the subsistence sector and a commercial cash-crop or capitalistically-organised export sector.

Lewis's numerical example is based on the productivities shown in Table 3.2. It is clear from Table 3.2 that the surplus labour side of the dual economy has been suppressed. To further simplify the argument, the rate of profit $\varrho$ is set equal to zero in both countries. The conditions of the supply of food, manufactures and 'commercials' will be governed by the Ricardian transformation frontier constrained either by the availability of food for productive workers in the capitalistic and dual economies (the wages fund) as before, or by the supply of wage labour.

If it is assumed that food is a homogeneous tradable commodity, then the relative price of manufactures and commercials will be governed by the productivity of manufactures in relation to food, and of commercials in relation to food. This can be seen from the world production possibilities frontier in three-dimensional space shown in Fig. 3.2.

For the sake of argument, it is assumed that both country 1 and country 2 can employ a labour force of 10 units at a market-clearing wage. Thus, if both countries allocate all their employable labour to food production, world food output will be 40 units or $OD$. If country 2 now switches from 10 units of food production to 10 units of commercials production, the segment $DE$ of the world production possibilities frontier is defined. Further reduc-

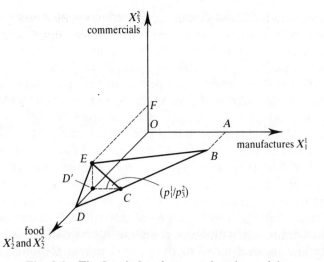

**Fig. 3.2** The Lewis 2 × 3 terms of trade model.

tion of food output in the world economy will not increase commercials output; the segment $EF$ will therefore define the world production possibilities frontier for a single period with increasing unemployment in country 1 as food production is reduced. Similarly, if $D$ is taken as the initial point, a reduction of food output in country 1 will allow manufactures output to expand along the segment $DCB$. Once $B$ is reached, producing 10 units of food and 30 units of manufactures, further expansion of manufactures cannot be achieved by reducing food output in country 2; $AB$ therefore defines a further segment of the production possibilities frontier. With country 1 and country 2 both specialising in manufactures and commercials, the points $A$ and $F$ will be on the production possibilities frontier. There can be no reallocation of labour between manufactures and commericals with a zero food output so there are no other points on the production possibilities frontier in the $X_1^1 - X_3^2$ plane. Joining the points $EB$ completes the production possibilities frontier. Full employment of the relevant productive stocks in both countries is achieved on the surface of the production possibilities frontier bounded by $BCDE$, shown with solid lines. It is now possible to illustrate the determination of the terms of trade when both countries are incompletely specialised.

Consider the level of world food output, given by $OD$, produced in country 1 and country 2. A reduction of 1 unit of food production in country 2 will allow the production of 1 unit of commericals and a reduction of 1 unit of food production in country 1 will allow manufactures output to expand by 1 unit. From the point of view of the world economy, the valuation of 1 unit of commercials is the same as 1 unit of manufactures in terms of food and the relative price is given by $(p_1^1/p_3^2) = 1$. Similarly, the exchange ratio between manufactures and commercials is equal to 1 on all points on the surface $BCDE$. Further, the 10 units of labour in country 1 will receive three times the wage as in country 2, measured in terms of food. In other words, the factoral terms of trade will be 3. Thus, in contrast to the $2 \times 2$ Ricardian model in which reciprocal demand will determine the terms of trade when there is complete specialisation, the commodity and factoral terms of trade are supply-determined in the special Lewis case. With additional assumptions about the bias in technical change in countries 1 and 2, respectively, hypotheses can be generated regarding the terms of trade between manufactures and commercials. The comparative statics of both models are examined in the next section.

## 3.4   SOME COMPARATIVE STATIC RESULTS

The formal determination of the equilibrium terms of trade was implicit in the Ricardo–Mill model of the world economy discussed in Section 2.2. The equilibrium terms of trade was determined such that balance of payments equilibrium was achieved. The stability of the equilibrium depends on the elasticities of the implied reciprocal demand curves. Depending on the amount of time implicitly allowed for the equilibrium adjustment process to take, the analysis can refer to the short, medium or long run.

The import demand functions for each country can be written as a function of relative prices and income, with country 1 importing commodity 2 and country 2 importing commodity 1, as:

$$M_2^1 = M_2^1(p_2/p_1, Y^1) = M_2^1(1/p, Y^1)$$
$$M_1^2 = M_1^2(p_1/p_2, Y^2) = M_1^2(p, Y^2) \tag{3.2}$$

where $M_i^k$ is the import of commodity $i$ into country $k$, $Y^k$ is real income in each country and $(p_1/p_2) = p$; $i,k = 1,2$. Excess demand in the world economy measured in terms of commodity 2 will therefore be given by the difference between the import demand functions, both measured in terms of commodity 2, or $M_2^1 - M_1^2(p_1/p_2)$. Market stability requires that changes in world excess demand as prices change converges, so that a rise in the price of commodity 1 relative to commodity 2 leads to a rise in the imports of commodity 2 into country 1 and a fall in the imports of commodity 1 into country 2. Formally, the stability condition requires that

$$d(M_2^1 - M_1^2(p_1/p_2))/d(p_1/p_2) > 0 \qquad (3.3)$$

In terms of the elasticities of demand, (3.3) is equivalent to the standard Marshall–Lerner condition:

$$\Delta \equiv \eta^1 + \eta^2 + \sigma^1 + \sigma^2 + \varepsilon_s^1 + \varepsilon_s^2 - 1 > 0 \qquad (3.4)$$

where $\eta^1$ and $\eta^2$ are the absolute values of the pure substitution effect in demand, $\sigma^1$ and $\sigma^2$ are the marginal propensities to import, $\varepsilon_s^1$ and $\varepsilon_s^2$ are the elasticities of supply for import competing production, and $\Delta$ is defined by equation (3.4). In the $2 \times 2$ Ricardo–Mill model with complete specialisation, there is no price-responsive import-competing production and the elasticity of supply of import competing production is zero, or $\varepsilon_s^1 = \varepsilon_s^2 = 0$. For a derivation of the Marshall–Lerner condition (3.4) and the comparative statics which follows, see Appendix 3.1.

The comparative static properties of the Ricardo–Mill model can be derived from the total differentiation of the balance of payments condition. This condition can be written as:

$$M_2^1 - M_1^2(p_1/p_2) = 0 \qquad (3.5)$$

Totally diffentiating the balance of payments condition (3.5) and finding expressions for the underlying changes in consumption and trade yield the desired expressions for changes in the terms of trade and incomes resulting for some exogenous shift in outputs:

$$\hat{p} = (p_1/\hat{p}_2) = \frac{-\sigma^1 \cdot dX_1^1 + \sigma^2 \cdot dX_2^2}{M_2^1 \cdot \Delta} \cdot \frac{p_1}{p_2} \qquad (3.6)$$

$$dY^1 = \frac{(\Delta - \sigma^1)dX_1^1 + \sigma^2 dX_2^2}{\Delta} \cdot \frac{p_1}{p_2}$$

$$dY^2 = \frac{\sigma^1 dX_1^1 + (\Delta - (p_1/p_2)\sigma^2)dX_2^2}{\Delta} \tag{3.7}$$

where the $\hat{}$ refers to the change of a variable or $\hat{p} = dp/p$, $dY^1$ and $dY^2$ are indexes of real income changes and all other variables and parameters are as previously defined. (Equation (3.6) is from equation (A3.1.16) and equations (3.7) is from equations (A3.1.17).)

The comparative static results may now be summarised. Provided the Marshall–Lerner condition holds and $\Delta > 0$, an expansion of output by one country relative to the other, whether due to productivity change or the growth of its workforce, will lead to a deterioration of its terms of trade. An extreme example of this would be where the developing country 2 attempts to grow faster than the developed country 1, roughly expressed by setting the output change in country 1 equal to zero, or $dX_1^1 = 0$, and the output change in country 2 greater than zero, or $dX_2^2 > 0$. It follows immediately from equation (3.6) that in this case the terms of trade move against the developing country and $(p_1\hat{/}p_2) > 0$. What is now a commonplace argument was rather more striking when first elaborated by Mill (1844). However, it need not cause great concern provided the productivity changes underlying such an expansion of output are not entirely competed away by the declining terms of trade in the long run, the problem of 'damnifying' trade or immiserising growth first noticed by Edgeworth (1894). This problem can be illustrated if the workforce is constant in both countries but a productivity change in the developing country 2 is greater than zero and $dX_2^2 > 0$. Incomes will expand in the developed country 1 provided the Marshall–Lerner condition is satisfied, or $\Delta > 0$. However, incomes will only rise in the developing country 2 if, in addition, a more stringent condition holds, namely $(\Delta - (p_1/p_2) \cdot \sigma^2) > 0$. This may not hold if the Marshall–Lerner condition is satisfied, but the price and income elasticities of demand for imports into the developed country are low and the income elasticity of demand for imports into the developing country is high, or $\eta^1$, $\eta^2$ and $\sigma^1$ are small but $\sigma^2$ is large.

In the Lewis tropical terms of trade model, there is incomplete specialisation and the Marshall–Lerner condition always holds, since there is a perfectly elastic supply of import-competing production in both countries. The comparative static results of changes in labour productivities analysed in detail in Appendix 3.1 can be summarised as follows:

*Commodity or net-barter terms of trade*

$$\ell_1^1 - \ell_2^1 = \hat{p}_1$$

$$\ell_3^2 - \ell_2^2 = \hat{p}_3 \qquad (3.8)$$

where the $\ell$s and the $\hat{p}$s refer to changes in the labour/output ratios and in commodity prices relative to food. The manufactures/food terms of trade will be governed by a comparison of the changes in labour productivity in manufactures and food in the developed countries. Similarly, the commercials/food terms of trade will be governed by the comparison of labour productivities in commercials and food production in developing countries.

*Real wages in terms of food*

$$-\ell_2^1 = \hat{w}^1$$

$$-\ell_2^2 = \hat{w}^2 \qquad (3.9)$$

where the $\hat{w}$s refer to real wages measures in terms of food. Thus, the real wage movements in developed temperate and developing tropical countries depend entirely on the changes in labour productivity in temperate and tropical food production.

*Income effects*

$$\chi_{e_1}^1(\ell_1^1 - \ell_2^1) - \chi_{m_3}^1(\ell_3^2 - \ell_2^2) - \chi_{x_1}^1\ell_1^1 - \chi_{x_2}^1\ell_2^1 + \hat{L}^1 = \hat{Y}^1$$

$$-\chi_{m_1}^2(\ell_1^1 - \ell_2^1) + \chi_{e_3}^2(\ell_3^2 - \ell_2^2) - \chi_{x_2}^2\ell_2^2 - \chi_{x_3}^2\ell_3^2 + \hat{L}^2 = \hat{Y}^2$$

$$(3.10)$$

where the $\hat{L}$s and $\hat{Y}$s refer to changes in the workforce and real income, and the $\chi$s refer to various shares of commodities, exports and imports in total income. (Equations (3.8) are from equations (A3.1.20), equations (3.9) are from (A3.1.19) and equations (3.10) are from equation (A3.1.30).) It can be seen

**Table 3.3**   Lewis terms of trade model with stylised facts.

| | Labour productivity changes | Price effects | Wage effects in terms of food | Income effects in terms of food |
|---|---|---|---|---|
| $X_1^1$ manufactures | $-\ell_1^1 < -\ell_2^1$ | $\hat{p}_1 > 0$ | $\hat{w}^1 = -\ell_2^1$ | $\hat{Y}^1 = \chi_{e_1}^1(\ell_1^1 - \ell_2^1)$ |
| $X_2^1, X_2^2$ food | $-\ell_2^1 > -\ell_2^2$ | $\hat{p}_2 = 0$ | $\hat{w}^2 = 0$ | $-\chi_{m_3}^1\ell_3^2 - \chi_{x_1}^1\ell_1^1 - \chi_{x_2}^1\ell_2^1$ |
| $X_3^2$ commercials | $-\ell_3^2 > 0$ | $\hat{p}_3 < 0$ | | $\hat{Y}^2 = -\chi_{m_1}^2(\ell_1^1 - \ell_2^1)$ |
| | | | | $-\ell_3^2(\chi_{x_3}^2 - \chi_{e_3}^2)$ |

from equation (3.10) that the final income changes in the developed and developing country depend on the productivity changes in each sector, net of terms of trade gains or losses on imports or exports, plus the overall change in the workforce employed. It is readily apparent that a commercials/manufactures terms of trade movement against the developing country will only translate into an absolute income loss if a large share of commercials production is exported and if manufactures form a large component of imports.

These results can be further simplified by imposing some of Lewis's 'stylised facts' on the analysis. First, it is assumed that the rate of growth of labour productivity in food in the developed temperate country is greater than in the developing tropical country or $-\ell_2^1 > -\ell_2^2$; for simplicity, it may be assumed that there is no labour productivity change in tropical food production in the developing country and $\ell_2^2 = 0$. Second, it is assumed that the rate of growth of labour productivity in commercials in the developing country is also low but is greater than in tropical food production, or $-\ell_3^2 > -\ell_2^2$. Third, it is assumed that manufactures labour productivity growth is less than in temperate food production, or $-\ell_1^1 < -\ell_2^1$. The effects of these labour productivity growth assumptions on prices, wages and incomes are summarised in Table 3.3.

The results follow easily from the assumptions of the model. The commodity manufactures/commercials terms of trade move against the developing country. On account of the higher rate of growth of labour productivity in temperate compared with tropical food, there is a widening wage differential between developed and developing countries. The presumption is that the developed/

developing country income differential will also increase, unless food production is a very small proportion of developed and developing country output and the improvement in temperate food productivity is very large. This result serves as a useful reminder that the commodity terms of trade effects must be interpreted with care. Such effects do not refer to the aggregate country terms of trade effects since one or other country exports food. The real income effects can still be positive for developing countries in spite of adverse terms of trade movements. It is even possible for developed/developing country income differentials to lower when there are adverse terms of trade movements.

The two Lewis models stand in strong contrast with each other. The first model emphasises the relationship between a capitalistic sector and a non-capitalist subsistence sector within a national economy. Demand plays a central role in determining the internal commodity terms of trade as in the Ricardo–Mill model considered at the beginning of this section. The international terms of trade model is the mirror opposite, with both the demand side and the dual economy aspects suppressed. The two sides of the analysis are put together in Section 7.3.

## 3.5   DIMINISHING RETURNS IN AGRICULTURE

The applications of Ricardian theory to trade and development issues discussed in the previous two sections do not explicitly take into account the effects of natural resource constraints. Such constraints will affect the pattern of trade, the rate of profit and growth, the terms of trade and so on. In the context of rapidly changing patterns of developing country trade, for example, the rapidly rising share of manufactures in developing country exports, it is important that choice of trade model allows for this possibility. The addition of agricultural land as a specific primary resource into the dynamic model introduced in Section 2.2 dramatically transforms that model and the range of results which can be obtained, providing a useful bridge to the neo-classical models discussed in subsequent chapters.

The rate of growth of the supply of the agricultural resource adjusted for technical improvements will now determine the long-run steady state rate of profit when the supply of labour is perfectly elastic at the subsistence wage. Following Ricardo's pessimism on this score, and to simplify the exposition, it is assumed that the rate of growth of the effective supply of land and the rate of profit is zero in the long run.

A 'snapshot' of the economy, before the long-run rate of profit is driven down to zero by diminishing returns to the agricultural resource, can be readily described by modifying the equilibrium conditions (2.1) to (2.3) and (2.6). Thus, retaining all of the simplifying assumptions set out in Sections 2.2.1 and 2.2.2 and focusing on the equalities which obtain when there is incomplete specialisation, the non-steady state equilibrium (excluding the demand conditions) can be described by the following relations:

*Nominal price relations, closed economy*

$$\text{wages, profits and rent} \qquad \text{price}$$
$$w\ell_1(1 + \varrho) \quad = \quad p_1$$
$$w\ell_2(1 + \varrho) + \pi r_2 \quad = \quad p_2 \qquad (3.11)$$

*Quantity relations (factor usage), closed economy*

$$\text{labour use} \qquad \text{wage fund limit}$$
$$\ell_1 X_1 + \ell_2 X_2 = \qquad \bar{K}/\bar{w}$$
$$r_2 X_2 = \qquad \bar{R}$$
$$X_2 \gtreqqless \qquad \bar{K} \qquad (3.12)$$

*Marginal productivity of labour*

$$MPL_1 = 1/\ell_1$$
$$MPL_2 = \alpha - \beta L_2 \qquad (3.13)$$

*Optimising conditions in production*

$$MPL_1 \cdot p_1 = w(1 + \varrho)$$
$$MPL_2 \cdot p_2 = w(1 + \varrho) \qquad (3.14)$$

*Rate of growth of capital stock*
$$g = s_c \varrho \qquad (3.15)$$

All the parameters and variables are as previously described, plus:

$r_2$            is the resource/output ratio in agricultural pro-
                duction (sector 2)
$\pi$            is the rent on the agricultural resource
$\bar{R}$        is the available stock of the agricultural re-
                source
$MPL_1, MPL_2$   are the marginal products of labour in manu-
                facturing (sector 1) and agriculture (sector 2)
$L_2$            is the amount of labour employed in agriculture
                (sector 2)
$\alpha, \beta$  are parameters defining the diminishing mar-
                ginal productivity of labour applied to a fixed
                amount of the agricultural resource.

The nominal price equations (3.11) state that unit costs must be equal to the price of the output. The first two quantity equations in (3.12) state that all of the wage fund is used up during the period of production, and that all of the agricultural resource is used in food production. The reproduction constraint, the inequality in (3.12), says that food output must be at least as great as that required to reproduce the wage fund. The particular linear form of the constant returns to scale production function is shown in equations (3.13). The optimising conditions shown in equations (3.14) are derived from the profit maximising condition that the marginal revenue product of labour in producing each commodity must be equal to the wage rate marked up by the rate of profit. Finally, the macro equilibrium conditions between savings and investment described in equation (2.6) are summarised in the relationship between growth and savings, shown in equation (3.15).

The modified production possibilities frontier for a given 'snapshot' equilibrium is shown in Fig. 3.3. When all labour is employed in manufactures, output $B$ is obtained. In the absence of food production, none of the agricultural resource is used and rent will be zero. When labour is moved to food production, increasing amounts of manufactures must be foregone as a result of the diminishing returns to labour applied to agricultural land given by equation (3.13). The production possibilities frontier will therefore be concave to the origin and the maximum amount of food obtainable when all labour is allocated to food production is given by $OA$. The slope of the production possibilities frontier

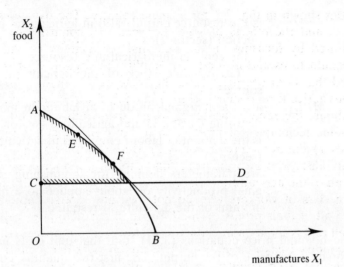

**Fig. 3.3**   Trade in manufactured goods and food with diminishing returns in food production.

will be given by the ratio of the marginal productivities of labour in manufactures and food, respectively. Thus at a 'snapshot' equilibrium production point such as $E$, the optimising conditions (3.14) ensure that the price ratio will be equal to the inverse of the marginal productivity ratios. If point $E$ is also the autarky equilibrium consumption point, which satisfies the constraint on the initial endowment of capital shown by the line $CD$, then the autarky price ratio will be given by $(MPL_2/MPL_1)^a = (p_1/p_2)^a$ where $a$ is for autarky.

Suppose that the possibility of trade is introduced at higher relative prices for manufactures or for world prices $(p_1/p_2)^* > (p_1/p_2)^a$. The country will switch some production from food to manufactures, exporting manufactures in exchange for food. There will be incomplete specialisation with production at $F$. The consumption of profit and rent will be to the left of $F$ on the consumption possibilities frontier passing through $F$. Similarly, if world prices are such that $(p_1/p_2)^* < (p_1/p_2)^a$, the country will find it profitable to export food in exchange for manufactures.

The elimination of the tendency towards complete specialisation in the Ricardian 2 × 2 model of trade by the introduction of diminishing returns in agriculture is highlighted by the snapshot device which was used to construct the production possibilities frontier shown in Fig. 3.3 for a single country. The dynamics of growth and the effects of trade between two countries can be illustrated by focusing on the marginal productivity conditions in manufactures and in food. To simplify the argument, it is assumed that both countries have the same quantities of a homogenous agricultural resource of the same fertility, the same quality of labour, the same subsistence wages spent only on food and the same techniques of production in both manufactures (commodity 1) and in food (commodity 2). Both countries have a class of capitalists who own the wage-fund capital, a rentier class who own all of the agricultural resource used only in food production, and a class of workers who do not own any assets. Capitalists spend all of their profits on food for the accumulation of capital and all rent is spent on manufactures. However, it is now assumed that country 1 has a larger wage-fund capital stock than country 2.

Consider each country under autarky. The linear marginal product of labour functions for food production in each country, $MPL_2^1$ and $MPL_2^2$ in Figs 3.4(a) and (b), respectively, will have the same positions and slopes since each country has the same quantities of the homogeneous agricultural resource. The same subsistence wage in each country, measured in terms of food, is shown by the distance $O^1D^1$ and $O^2D^2$ in Fig. 3.4(a) and (b), respectively. Since country 1 has the larger wage-fund capital stock than country 2, and since workers and capitalists consume only food and rentiers consume only manufactures, it must be true that capitalist-farmers in country 1 will employ more labour than in country 2 under autarky. Employment in food production in each country is shown by $O^1N^1$ and $O^2N^2$ in Fig. 3.4(a) and (b), respectively, and $O^1N^1 > O^2N^2$. Total food production will therefore be given by the area under the marginal product curves, $O^1A^1F^1N^1$ and $O^2A^2F^2N^2$ for countries 1 and 2, respectively. The optimising conditions in production (3.14) imply that rent at the intensive margin will be equal to zero. The marginal product of labour in food production for each country is therefore divided between wages and profits, shown by $N^1G^1$ and $G^1F^1$, respectively, for country 1 by $N^2G^2$ and $G^2F^2$, respectively, for country 2. By assumption, capitalist farmers in country 1 employ more labour than in country 2, but face the same technical condition in production, pay the same wage, and rent the same amount of land. It must therefore be the case that the marginal product of labour in food production is lower in country 1 than in country 2, and consequently the rate of profit received by capitalist farmers must be lower in country 1 than in country 2, as shown by the ratios $G^1F^1/N^1G^1$ and $G^2F^2/N^2G^2$ for each country, respectively.

Consider now the manufacturing sector in each country. For the rate of profit to be the same as in food production, the marginal product of labour in manufactures in terms of food must be the same as in food production. Thus, from the optimising conditions (3.14), the relationship between the marginal productivities and the autarky price ratios in each country will be given by:

$$MPL_2^1 = (p_1/p_2)_a^1 \cdot MPL_1^1$$

and $$MPL_2^2 = (p_1/p_2)_a^2 \cdot MPL_1^2 \qquad (3.16)$$

By assumption, manufactures have the same constant returns to scale techniques in each country using fixed proportions of labour, so that $MPL_1^1 = MPL_1^2 = 1/\ell_1$. Further, it has already been established that the marginal product of labour in food production is lower in country 1 than in country 2, so that $MPL_2^1 < MPL_2^2$. Therefore it must be the case that the autarky price of food in country 1 is greater than in country 2, or $(p_1/p_2)_a^1 < (p_1/p_2)_a^2$.

In terms of Figs 3.4(a) and (b), the marginal product of labour in manufactures in each country, measured in terms of food, is given by the distances $N^1F^1$ and $N^2F^2$, respectively. The level of employment in manufactures can also be shown by the distances $N^1N'^1$ and $N^2N'^2$ for country 1 and country 2, respectively. Since the total stock of capital is higher in country 1 than in country 2, and since manufactures are consumed out of rent, it must be the case that manufacturing employment is higher in country 1 than in country 2 and $N^1N'^1 > N^2N'^2$. This completes the description of the autarky position in each country prior to either growth or the opening of trade. Consider first what happens when each country grows without the opening of trade.

In the initial position described in Figs 3.4(a) and (b), investment can take place out of profits, thus expanding the wage fund and increasing employment in the next period. The increased demand for food will increase employment in food production, and the process can continue until the marginal product of labour

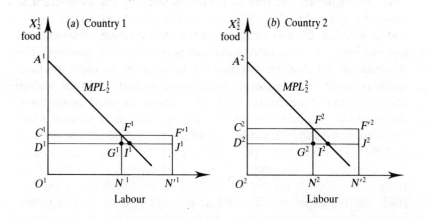

**Fig. 3.4** The Ricardian two-sector, two-country model of trade and growth.

in food production is driven down to $I^1$ and $I^2$ in each country, respectively. At this point, the stationary state equilibrium is reached. Since the marginal product of labour in manufactures is constant in manufactures but declining in food, the accumulation process drives the terms of trade in favour of food and $(p_1/p_2)$ falls over time. Further, since country 2 has a lower capital stock initially compared with country 1, the stationary state will take longer to reach. However, given the initial assumptions and no technical change, both countries will grow till they reach the same levels of output and employment.

If the opportunity for trade is opened up at the end of the initial period of production, and if the terms of trade are somewhere between the autarky price ratios so that $(p_1/p_2)_a^1 < (p_1/p_2)^* < (p_1/p_2)_a^2$, country 1 will find it profitable to export manufactures in exchange for food exported from country 2. Country 1 will not need to employ so much of its workforce in food production, so that the marginal productivity of labour in food production also rises. With more labour employed in food production in country 2, the marginal product of labour will fall. These changes in the allocation of labour will raise profits in country 1 and lower them in country 2. With accumulation and trade, both countries will end up in a stationary-state equilibrium, but it will now take longer to reach the stationary state in country 1; the opposite will be true for country 2.[2]

The dynamic Ricardian model with diminishing returns in food production gives a much richer set of results than the simpler dynamic model described in Section 2.2. It makes clear Ricardo's findings on the consequences of the corn laws in England during and after the Napoleonic wars. Protection of food production limits the possibilities of trade. Compared with free trade, the protection of food lowers the rate of profit and the rate of growth and therefore limits the potential size of the manufacturing sector. Conversely, the expansion of manufactures through free trade will only be limited by the extent to which the terms of trade turn against manufactures, and the extent to which the supply of labour is less than perfectly elastic in the long run, leading to a rise in wages as accumulation takes place.

## 3.6   RICARDO IN THE LIGHT OF THE NEO-CLASSICAL REVOLUTION

The central points of neo-classical criticism of the Ricardian theory of comparative advantage, discussed in Section 2.3, were the tendency towards complete specialisation and the exogenous specification of differences in labour productivity between countries. These criticisms take on a very different light when viewed in the context of a many-commodity and many-country world, and of his dynamic theory of growth.[3] It was noted that in Section 2.3.1 that, with many countries and many commodities, the tendency towards complete specialisation which characterises the static Ricardian model is lessened. With the introduction of an agricultural resource such as land, the tendency towards complete specialisation is further lowered, but this result is of greater theoretical than empirical interest. The importance of the inclusion of land in the dynamic model of growth is that the initial endowments of productive stocks now play a central role in determining comparative advantage and the pattern of trade. Thus, it is the higher endowment of capital compared with land which gives country 1 its comparative advantage in the production of manufactures compared with country 2 when everything else is the same. Labour productivity differences in food production in each country can arise because of different factor endowments, as well as from differences in the available techniques of production. It is apparent that there is a much greater richness and diversity of results which can be obtained from within the Ricardian tradition than is often concluded by neo-classical economists. The strengths and limits of the static Ricardian model and simple dynamic model are well illustrated by the contrast between the supply-side considerations which influence North–South terms of trade in the Lewis model, with incomplete specialisation, and the demand side influences, which operate when there is complete specialisation and the terms of trade lie within the Ricardian limbo region. In both the static and the simple dynamic models, there is little scope for an interaction between supply- and demand-side influences on the pattern of trade and the terms of trade. The dynamic Ricardian model with land included, considered in the previous section, begins to close the gap between pure supply-side models and pure demand-side models by providing a more general treatment of the influence of the supply of productive factors in determining comparative advantage and the pattern of trade. These considerations are taken up within the context of neo-classical theories of comparative advantage, discussed in the next two chapters.

## APPENDIX 3.1  THE MARSHALL–LERNER CONDITION AND SOME COMPARATIVE STATICS[4]

The stability condition (3.3) in the text can be re-written as:

$$-\hat{M}_2^1/(1/\hat{p}) - \hat{M}_1^2/\hat{p} - 1 > 0$$

or $$\varepsilon_m^1 + \varepsilon_m^2 - 1 > 0 \qquad (\text{A3.1.1})$$

where the $\hat{\ }$ notation refers to the rate of change of a variable, such as $dM_2^1/M_2^1 = \hat{M}_2^1$ or $dp/p = \hat{p}$ where $p = (p_1/p_2)$ and $\varepsilon_m^1$ and $\varepsilon_m^2$ are the absolute values of the elasticities of demand for imports in countries 1 and 2, respectively. Note that $\hat{p} = -1/\hat{p}$. Writing $C_i^k$ for total consumption of commodity $i$ in country $k$ and $Y^k$ as total income in country $k$, the import demand function

(3.2) for country 1 importing commodity 2 and country 2 importing commodity 1 may be broken into its component parts as follows:

$$M_2^1 = C_2^1(1/p, Y^1) - X_2^1(1/p)$$

$$M_1^2 = C_1^2(p, Y^2) - X_1^2(p) \tag{A3.1.2}$$

Totally differentiating (A3.1.2) and simplifying a little yields:

$$dM_2^1 = - \frac{\partial C_2^1}{\partial(1/p)} \cdot \frac{dp}{p^2} + \frac{\partial C_2^1}{\partial Y^1} \cdot dY^1 + \frac{\partial X_2^1}{\partial(1/p)} \cdot \frac{dp}{p^2}$$

$$dM_1^2 = \frac{\partial C_1^2}{\partial p} \cdot dp + \frac{\partial C_1^2}{\partial Y^2} \cdot dY^2 - \frac{\partial X_1^2}{\partial p} \cdot dp \tag{A3.1.3}$$

To complete the derivation of the Marshall–Lerner condition, an expression for $dY^1$ and $dY^2$ is required. The mathematical argument is simplified by following the utility approach, and the aggregate social welfare function for each country may be written as:

$$U^1 = U^1(C_1^1, C_2^1)$$

$$U^2 = U^2(C_1^2, C_2^2) \tag{A3.1.4}$$

Totally differentiating the social welfare function yields:

$$dU^1 = \frac{\partial U^1}{\partial C_1^1} \cdot dC_1^1 + \frac{\partial U^1}{\partial C_2^1} \cdot dC_2^1$$

$$dU^2 = \frac{\partial U^1}{\partial C_1^2} \cdot dC_1^2 + \frac{\partial U^2}{\partial C_2^2} \cdot dC_2^2 \tag{A3.1.5}$$

Dividing through by $\partial U^1/\partial C_2^1$ and $\partial U^2/\partial C_2^2$, and noting the optimising conditions in consumption which imply that:

$$\frac{\partial U^1/\partial C_1^1}{\partial U^1/\partial C_2^1} = \frac{\partial U^2/\partial C_1^2}{\partial U^2/\partial C_2^2} = p_1/p_2 = p$$

it follows that:

$$\frac{dU^1}{\partial U^1/\partial C_2^1} = pdC_1^1 + dC_2^1 = dY^1$$

$$\frac{dU^2}{\partial U^2/\partial C_2^2} = pdC_1^2 + dC_2^2 = dY^2 \tag{A3.1.6}$$

The left-hand side of equations (A3.1.6) can be interpreted as an index number of the change in real income, measured in terms of commodity 2; the $U$s cancel in the numerator and denominator leaving commodity 2 units. The final step in the argument is to trace the source of the income change.

For each country, the aggregate budget constraint must be satisfied. This is written as:

$$pC_1^1 + C_2^1 = pX_1^1 + X_2^1$$

$$pC_1^2 + C_2^2 = pX_1^2 + X_2^2 \qquad (A3.1.7)$$

Totally differentiating (A3.1.7) and using (A3.1.6), it follows that:

$$dY^1 = dp(X_1^1 - C_1^1) + (pdX_1^1 + dX_2^1)$$

$$dY^2 = -dp(C_1^2 - X_1^2) + (pdX_1^2 + dX_2^2) \qquad (A3.1.8)$$

The last term in each equation (A3.1.8) is equal to zero, since a change in output on the transformation frontier leaves real income unchanged. That is, the slope of the transformation frontier is given by $p = -dX_2^1/dX_1^1 = -dX_2^2/dX_1^2$ except at corner points (the Ricardian case with complete specialisation, where $dX_1^1 = dX_2^1 = dX_1^2 = dX_2^2 = 0$). Finally, note that $(C_1^2 - X_1^2) = M_1^2$ and, with balanced trade, $(X_1^1 - C_1^1) = M_2^1 \cdot 1/p$. Hence:

$$dY^1 = \hat{p}M_2^1$$

$$dY^2 = -\hat{p}M_1^2 p \qquad (A3.1.9)$$

Substituting (A3.1.9) into (A3.1.3) yields the desired expressions for the elasticities of demand for imports:

$$\varepsilon_m^1 = \hat{M}_2^1/\hat{p} = \eta^1 + \sigma^1 + \varepsilon_s^1$$

$$\varepsilon_m^2 = -\hat{M}_1^2/\hat{p} = \eta^2 + \sigma^2 + \varepsilon_s^2 \qquad (A3.1.10)$$

where

$$\eta^1 = -\frac{\partial C_2^1}{\partial(1/p)} \cdot \frac{(1/p)}{M_2^1}$$

$$\eta^2 = -\frac{\partial C_1^2}{\partial p} \cdot \frac{p}{M_1^2}$$

are the absolute values of the pure price elasticities of demand for imports:

$$\sigma^1 = \frac{\partial C_2^1}{\partial Y^1}$$

$$\sigma^2 = \frac{\partial C_1^2}{\partial Y^2} \cdot p$$

are the marginal propensities to consume imports measured in terms of commodity 2 and:

$$\varepsilon_s^1 = \frac{\partial X_2^1}{\partial (1/p)} \cdot \frac{(1/p)}{M_2^1}$$

$$\varepsilon_s^2 = \frac{\partial X_1^2}{\partial p} \cdot \frac{p}{M_1^2}$$

are the elasticities of supply of import competing production.

Thus, the Marshall–Lerner condition for balance of payments equilibrium is given by substituting (A3.1.10) into (A3.1.1) to yield:

$$(\eta^1 + \sigma^1 + \varepsilon_s^1) + (\eta^2 + \sigma^2 + \varepsilon_s^2) - 1 > 0 \quad \text{(A3.1.11)}$$

Condition (A3.1.11) simply says that the sum of the price and income elasticity of demand for imports plus the elasticity of supply of import-competing production in both countries must be greater than 1.

The purpose of the comparative static exercises is to analyse the effects of some shift in the reciprocal demand function or offer curves. The equations (A3.1.9) can also be modified by including the last terms in equations (A3.1.8) as shifts in the transformation functions, yielding:

$$dY^1 = \hat{p}M_2^1 + pdX_1^1 + dX_2^1$$

$$dY^2 = -\hat{p}M_1^2 p + pdX_1^2 + dX_2^2 \quad \text{(A3.1.12)}$$

When the pattern of trade is reversed:

$$dY^1 = -\hat{p}M_1^1 p + pdX_1^1 + dX_2^1$$

$$dY^2 = \hat{p}M_2^2 + pdX_1^2 + dX_2^2 \quad \text{(A3.1.12a)}$$

Equations (A3.1.12) and (A3.1.12a) are the expressions for the income change for the two possible patterns of trade made up of two components – the terms of trade effect and the income effects.

It is now possible to examine the consequences of a comparative static displacement of the model. This is achieved totally differentiating the balance of payments condition. Thus, the balance of payments condition:

$$M_2^1 - M_1^2 \cdot p = 0$$

when totally differentiated yields:

$$\hat{M}_2^1 - \hat{M}_1^2 - \hat{p} = 0 \qquad (A3.1.13)$$

Adding a shift factor to allow for any desired change in the import demand functions or offer curves at constant terms of trade, (A3.1.10) can be rewritten as:

$$\hat{M}_2^1 = \varepsilon_m^1 \hat{p} + \hat{M}_2^1|\bar{p}$$

$$\hat{M}_1^2 = -\varepsilon_m^2 \hat{p} + \hat{M}_1^2|\bar{p} \qquad (A3.1.14)$$

where the second terms on the right-hand side in equations (A3.1.14) are the shift factors. Substituting (A3.1.14) into (A3.1.13) yields:

$$\hat{p} = \frac{- \hat{M}_2^1|\bar{p} + \hat{M}_1^2|\bar{p}}{\Delta} \qquad (A3.1.15)$$

where: $\qquad \Delta = \varepsilon_m^1 + \varepsilon_m^2 - 1$

When the patterns of trade reverses, equation (A3.1.15) can easily be re-written as:

$$\hat{p} = \frac{\hat{M}_1^1|\bar{p} - \hat{M}_2^2|\bar{p}}{\Delta} \qquad (A3.1.15a)$$

Now, when there is specialisation in production in both countries, as in the Ricardian case, with country 1 importing commodity 2 and country 2 importing commodity 1 and a productivity change or increase in labour supply takes place in both countries:

$$\hat{M}_2^1|\bar{p} = \sigma^1 p dX_1^1/M_2^1$$

and $\qquad \hat{M}_1^2|\bar{p} = \sigma^2 dX_2^2/M_1^2$

and $\qquad \hat{p} = \frac{- \sigma^1 dX_1^1 + \sigma^2 dX_2^2}{\Delta} \cdot \frac{p}{M_2^1} \qquad (A3.1.16)$

Substituting (A3.1.16) into (A3.1.12) yields the effects on incomes as follows:

$$dY^1 = \frac{(\Delta - \sigma^1)dX_1^1 + \sigma^2 dX_2^2}{\Delta} \cdot p$$

$$dY^2 = \frac{\sigma^1 dX_1^1 + (\Delta - p\sigma^2)dX_2^2}{\Delta} \qquad \text{(A3.1.17)}$$

Part of the above analysis can be extended to deal with the $2 \times 3$ Lewis model discussed in Section 3.3. Since all three commodities are traded, here with country 1 producing and exporting commodities $X_1^1$ and $X_2^1$ and country 2 producing $X_2^2$ and $X_3^2$ and exporting commodity $X_3^2$, the terms of trade are determined by the underlying supply conditions. Given the linear transformation frontiers for both countries, the supply of food is perfectly elastic. The Marshall–Lerner condition for the stability of the balance of payments equilibrium will always hold since one of the two countries will be producing and importing food so that either $\varepsilon_s^1$ or $\varepsilon_s^2$ will be infinitely large.

The price relations in the $2 \times 3$ Lewis model are given by:

$$\ell_1^1 w^1 = p_1$$

$$\ell_2^1 w^1 = 1$$

$$\ell_2^2 w^2 = 1$$

$$\ell_3^2 w^3 = p_3 \qquad \text{(A3.1.18)}$$

where $p_1$ and $p_3$ are the prices of commodities 1 and 3 in terms of commodity 2. Totally differentiating (A3.1.18) yields:

$$\hat{\ell}_1^1 + \hat{w}^1 = \hat{p}_1$$

$$\hat{\ell}_2^1 + \hat{w}^1 = 0$$

$$\hat{\ell}_2^2 + \hat{w}^2 = 0$$

$$\hat{\ell}_3^2 + \hat{w}^2 = \hat{p}_3 \qquad \text{(A3.1.19)}$$

Thus it is clear that $\hat{w}^1 = -\hat{\ell}_2^1$ and $\hat{w}^2 = -\hat{\ell}_2^2$. Substituting for $\hat{w}^1$ and $\hat{w}^2$ in the first and last of the equations (A3.1.19) yields:

$$\hat{\ell}_1^1 - \hat{\ell}_2^1 = \hat{p}_1$$

$$\hat{\ell}_3^2 - \hat{\ell}_2^2 = \hat{p}_3 \qquad \text{(A3.1.20)}$$

Since $(p_1/p_3) = \hat{p}_1 - \hat{p}_3$, the manufactured goods to commercials terms of trade is governed by:

$$(\ell_1^1 - \ell_2^1) - (\ell_3^2 - \ell_2^2) = (\hat{p}_1 - \hat{p}_3) \qquad (A3.1.21)$$

The factoral terms of trade will be determined by the labour embodied in food production. As long as $\ell_2^1 > \ell_2^2$, the factoral terms of trade will be improving for country 1, since relatively less and less labour will be embodied in the comparable commodity 2, food, which is exchanged.

Following the utility approach, a measure of real income change can be defined along the same lines as before. The utility or social welfare functions can be written as:

$$U^1 = U^1(C_1^1, C_2^1, C_3^1)$$

$$U^2 = U^2(C_1^2, C_2^2, C_3^2) \qquad (A3.1.22)$$

Totally differentiating the social welfare function yields:

$$dU^1 = \frac{\partial U^1}{\partial C_1^1} \cdot dC_1^1 + \frac{\partial U^1}{\partial C_2^1} \cdot dC_2^1 + \frac{\partial U^1}{\partial C_3^1} \cdot dC_3^1$$

$$dU^2 = \frac{\partial U^2}{\partial C_1^2} \cdot dC_1^2 + \frac{\partial U^2}{\partial C_2^2} dC_2^2 + \frac{\partial U^2}{\partial C_3^2} \cdot dC_3^2 \qquad (A3.1.23)$$

Dividing through by $\partial U^1/\partial C_2^1$ and $\partial U^2/\partial C_2^2$, respectively, and noting the optimising conditions in consumption:

$$\frac{\partial U^1/\partial C_1^1}{\partial U^1/\partial C_2^1} = \frac{\partial U^2/\partial C_1^2}{\partial U^2/\partial C_2^2} = p_1$$

and:

$$\frac{\partial U^1/\partial C_3^1}{\partial U^1/\partial C_2^1} = \frac{\partial U^2/\partial C_3^2}{\partial U^2/\partial C_2^2} = p_3$$

it follows that the index of real income change is given by:

$$dY^1 = \frac{dU^1}{\partial U^1/\partial C_2^1} = p_1 dC_1^1 + dC_2^1 + p_3 dC_3^1$$

$$dY^2 = \frac{dU^2}{\partial U^2/\partial C_2^2} = p_1 dC_1^2 + dC_2^2 + p_3 dC_3^1 \qquad (A3.1.24)$$

As before, the budget constraint must be satisfied, that is:

$$p_1 C_1^1 + C_2^1 + p_3 C_3^1 = p_1 X_1^1 + X_2^1$$

$$p_1 C_1^2 + C_2^2 + p_3 C_3^2 = X_2^2 + p_3 X_3^2 \qquad (A3.1.25)$$

Totally differentiating (A3.1.25) and using (A3.1.24) yields:

$$dY^1 = (X_1^1 - C_1^1)dp_1 - C_3^1dp_3 + (p_1dX_1^1 + dX_2^1)$$

$$dY^2 = -C_1^2dp_1 + (X_3^2 - C_3^2)dp_3 + (dX_2^2 + p_3dX_3^2) \quad (A3.1.26)$$

As before, the last terms in both equations of (A3.1.26) are equal to zero for changes on the production possibilities frontier but pick up the changes of the frontier in the comparative state exercises. Using the definitions of $M_1^2$ and so on, (A3.1.26) simplifies to:

$$dY^1 = M_1^2dp_1 - M_3^1dp_3 + (p_1dX_1^1 + dX_2^1)$$

$$dY^2 = - M_1^2dp_1 + M_3^1dp_3 + (dX_2^2 + p_3dX_3^2)$$

or
$$\hat{Y}^1 = \chi_{e_1}^1\hat{p}_1 - \chi_{m_3}^1\hat{p}_3 + \chi_{x_1}^1\hat{X}_1^1 + \chi_{x_2}^1\hat{X}_2^1$$

$$\hat{Y}^2 = - \chi_{m_1}^2\hat{p}_1 + \chi_{e_3}^2\hat{p}_3 + \chi_{x_2}^2\hat{X}_2^2 + \chi_{x_3}^2\hat{X}_3^2 \quad (A3.1.27)$$

where $\chi_{e_i}^k$, $\chi_{m_i}^k$, $\chi_{x_i}^k$ are the shares of exports, imports or production of commodity $i$ in total income in country $k$.

The final step in the argument is to find an expression for the last two terms in each equation of (A3.1.27) in terms of changing labour productivities and workforce.

The labour demand and employment conditions (2.2), when expressed as an equality, extended to the 2 × 3 Lewis case and noting that the wages fund $K = wL$ when measured in terms of food, after multiplying through by real wages yield:

$$w^1\ell_1^1X_1^1 + w^1\ell_2^1X_2^1 = w^1L^1$$

$$w^2\ell_2^2X_2^2 + w^2\ell_3^2X_3^2 = w^2L^2 \quad (A3.1.28)$$

Totally differentiating and simplifying:

$$\chi_{x_1}^1\hat{X}_1^1 + \chi_{x_2}^1\hat{X}_2^1 = \hat{L}^1 - \chi_{x_1}^1\hat{\ell}_1^1 - \chi_{x_2}^1\hat{\ell}_2^1$$

$$\chi_{x_2}^2\hat{X}_2^2 + \chi_{x_3}^2\hat{X}_3^2 = \hat{L}^2 - \chi_{x_2}^2\hat{\ell}_2^2 - \chi_{x_3}^2\hat{\ell}_3^2 \quad (A3.1.29)$$

where $\chi_{xi}^k$ is as previously defined.

Substituting from equations (A3.1.20) and (A3.1.29) into equation (A3.1.27) yields:

$$\hat{Y}^1 = \chi_{e_1}^1(\hat{\ell}_1^1 - \hat{\ell}_2^1) - \chi_{m_3}^1(\hat{\ell}_3^2 - \hat{\ell}_2^2) - \chi_{x_1}^1\hat{\ell}_1^1 - \chi_{x_2}^1\hat{\ell}_2^1 + \hat{L}^1$$

$$\hat{Y}^2 = - \chi_{m_1}^2(\hat{\ell}_1^1 - \hat{\ell}_2^1) + \chi_{e_3}^2(\hat{\ell}_3^2 - \hat{\ell}_2^2) - \chi_{x_2}^2\hat{\ell}_2^2 - \chi_{x_3}^2\hat{\ell}_3^2 + \hat{L}^2$$
$$(A3.1.30)$$

It is now possible to combine the analysis of the terms of trade with the effects on income along the lines suggested in Section 3.4 of the text.

## NOTES

1. See, for example, K. Smith (1977).
2. Contrary to the results obtained by Burgstaller (1986) there is no possibility of an employment decline in the food exporting country with the opening of trade. The Burgstaller result depends on a specific form of the capitalist savings function which allows for temporary disinvestment when the rate of profit declines with the opening of trade. For results along Burgstaller lines, see Section 6.7. However, it is possible that the stationary state equilibrium with trade in the food exporting country has a lower level of employment than the autarky stationary state equilibrium. The opposite is possible in the manufactures exporting country. This possibility arises if the higher rate of investment in the manufactures exporting country, compared with autarky, leads to a higher rate of growth of population. In the food exporting country, the lower level of investment in the with-trade situation, compared with autarky, may lead to a lower rate of population growth. However, under the assumptions made, the total population under autarky and under free trade must be the same when the exogenously given long-run wage remains in the accumulation process.
3. The same point is made with respect to his dynamic theory of growth by Findlay (1974, 1984).
4. The presentation in the first part of this appendix draws on Caves and Jones (1981, pages 489–99), modified to fit the notation and examples used here.

# 4 · NEO-CLASSICAL THEORY: THE BASIC ELEMENTS

## 4.1 THE NEO-CLASSICAL VISION

Much of the driving force behind the critique of Ricardo and the development of neo-classical thought was an attempt to head off the radical interpretations of Ricardian theory by socialists, particularly Marx and the Marxian tradition (Bliss, 1975, Ch. 5). The net result of these wider developments in political economy was to move away from the classical vision to a more narrowly-based view of economic science based on subjective individualism.

Within the dynamic Ricardian framework developed in Chapters 2 and 3, capital is both a fund of money advanced to pay for wages during the period of production, and a homogeneous produced commodity, food. Time entered the analysis in a crucial way, both in the sense that social reproduction took time, and in the sense that production required the prior availability of a stock of wage goods and produced means of production. The static H–O–S model is timeless and the classical distinction between capital as produced means of production and capital as a fund of money is dropped. Capital is treated as a non-produced input, just like land in the Ricardian system. This theoretical procedure fits well with the neo-classical vision of capitalism as a pure exchange economy and the central neo-classical thesis that development best takes place through the extention and improvement of the market mechanism, aided by rational policy intervention by government.[1] In that context, a major focus in the neo-classical literature is on general efficiency arguments which can, to a considerable extent, be developed in a static context.

The textbook exposition of the H–O–S theory starts with the

static two-country, two-commodity and two-factor, or 2 × 2 × 2, model of trade. This serves two useful functions. It lays bare the theoretical foundations of the neo-classical approach whilst contributing to the development of the analytical building blocks required for the understanding of the neo-classical efficiency arguments and the models of growth and development.

The static H–O–S model is based on the extension of Ricardo's principle of limited marginal substitutability between land and labour to any other factor of production. The second non-produced input is sometimes called land and sometimes capital. This schizophrenia over the nature of capital reflects a real problem. Capital is both a factor of production, an ultimate or original input into the production process such as machines or ploughs as factors of production[2], and the monetary value of capital employed. Clearly, capital is important in both senses. In the exposition of the H–O–S theory and the more general treatment of non-produced factors of production provided in this chapter, confusion arising from the dual definition of capital is avoided by referring to any fixed factor as a 'resource'.

## 4.2   THE STATIC H–O–S MODEL: TWO COUNTRIES, TWO COMMODITIES AND TWO FACTORS

### 4.2.1   The model

The central differences between the autarky equilibrium conditions in production for the dynamic Ricardian model described in equations (3.11) to (3.15) and the static 2 × 2 × 2 H–O–S model are as follows: the returns to capital advanced over the period of production and the growth of the capital stock are eliminated; land or the resource enters into the production of both manufactures and food, commodities 1 and 2; and that wages are now determined endogenously. Thus, retaining all of the other simplifying assumptions set out in Sections 2.2.1 and 2.2.2, and adding the new one that each country has the same technology but that there is no factor intensity reversal, the equilibrium price and quantity relations for the 2 × 2 × 2 H–O–S model with generalised substitution between labour and the resource in production and incomplete specialisation are as follows:

*Nominal price (cost) relations, closed economy*

$$\text{wages and rents} \quad \text{revenue}$$
$$wL_1 + \pi R_1 \quad = \quad pX_1$$
$$wL_2 + \pi R_2 \quad = \quad pX_2 \qquad (4.1)$$

*Quantity relations (factor usage), closed economy*

$$\text{factor usage} \quad \text{factor supply}$$
$$L_1 + L_2 \quad = \quad \bar{L}$$
$$R_1 + R_2 \quad = \quad \bar{R} \qquad (4.2)$$

*Production functions*

$$X_1 = X_1(L_1, R_1)$$
$$X_2 = X_2(L_2, R_2) \qquad (4.3)$$

*Optimising conditions in production*

$$\text{marginal revenue products} \quad \text{factor price}$$
$$p_1 X_{1\ell} = p_2 X_{2\ell} \quad = \quad w$$
$$p_1 X_{1r} = p_2 X_{2r} \quad = \quad \pi \qquad (4.4)$$

where $L_1, L_2$ are the amounts of labour allocated to industries 1 and 2

$R_1, R_2$ are the amounts of resource allocated to industries 1 and 2

$\pi$ is the resource rental

$X_{1\ell}, X_{2\ell}$ are the marginal products of labour in industries 1 and 2, respectively

$X_{1r}, X_{2r}$ are the marginal products of resource in industries 1 and 2

$\bar{R}$ is the total amount of resource available

$p_1$, $p_2$, $w$, $X_1$, $X_2$ and $\bar{L}$ are prices, wages, outputs and labour supply as previously defined.

In words, equations (4.1) require that total costs be made up of wages and rents on wages. On account of the assumption of constant returns to scale (CRS), equations (4.1) can be divided through by outputs to yield the unit cost relationship:

$$w\ell_1 + \pi r_1 = p_1$$
$$w\ell_2 + \pi r_2 = p_2 \qquad (4.1a)$$

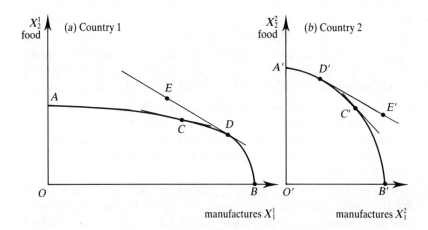

**Fig. 4.1**    Autarky and trading equilibrium for the $2 \times 2 \times 2$ H–O–S model.

where $\ell_i$ and $r_i$ are the labour and resource input requirements per unit of output as previously defined. Equations (4.2) require that factor usage equals factor supplies of labour and the resource, respectively. Generalised substitution in production in each industry is specified in equations (4.3) by neo-classical production functions with CRS. Finally, the set of equations (4.4) require that the marginal revenue products of each factor are equal to the commodity prices.[3] These equations can be used to derive the relationship between the marginal products of each factor and the factor price ratio, and the inverse relationship between the marginal products in each industry and the commodity price ratio. In other words the factor price ratio is equal to the marginal rate of substitution or MRS between the factors in both industries, and the commodity price ratio is equal to the marginal rate of transformation, or MRT, in production for both productive stocks.

The production system behind the H–O–S model can be illustrated using the standard production possibilities frontier, as shown for country 1 in Fig. 4.1(a). All points on the production possibilities frontier conditions reflect the inverse ratio of the marginal productivities, or the marginal rates of transformation. On account of a diminishing marginal rate of substitution for both factors, the production possibilities frontier is concave to the origin. Optimisation in production yields the equilibrium supply price ratio equal to the tangent to the production possibilities frontier such as the tangent to the production possibilities frontier at point $C$ in Fig. 4.1(a). If at point $C$ the optimising conditions in consumption are also satisfied, then the price ratio must also be equal to the marginal rates of substitution in consumption and $C$ will be the autarky production and consumption point in country 1.[4]

The opportunity to reap gains from trade at given world prices for the single small country follows on exactly the same lines as in the Ricardian case discussed in Section 3.5. Suppose, for country 1, the autarky and world relative prices of manufactures and food are such that, under autarky, manufactures are relatively cheaper, or $(p_1/p_2)_a^1 < (p_1/p_2)^*$. The autarky price ratio is represented by the slope of the tangent at point $C$ in Fig. 4.1(a), while the world price ratio is given by the gradient of line $DE$. By opening trade, country 1 can move its production from $C$ to $D$. It can now export manufactures in exchange for food along the consumption possibilities frontier $DE$ till the marginal rates of transformation in consumption are equal to the world price ratio, say, at point $E$.

To complete the H–O–S 2 × 2 × 2 model, it is necessary to consider a second country. In the static H–O–S model, differing factor endowments provide the paradigmatic explanation of pre-trade price differences and therefore comparative advantage. The technological blueprints underlying the production possibilities frontiers do not vary between countries and consumers have the same homothetic preference functions. Thus, suppose that manufactures are the labour-intensive commodity and that country 1 has a larger labour/resource endowment ratio compared with country 2.

It is intuitively obvious that country 1 will produce relatively more of the labour-intensive manufactures in comparison with country 2 under autarky. Following this intuition, the price ratios at points at the autarky equilibrium production and consumption points $C$ and $C'$ in Fig. 4.1(a) and (b), respectively, will be such that the price of manufactures relative to food will be lower in

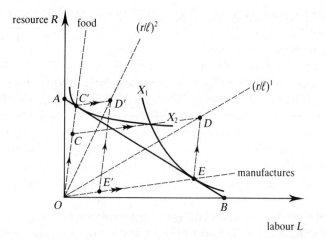

**Fig. 4.2**   Resource endowments and factor prices in the $2 \times 2 \times 2$ H–O–S model

country 1, or $(p_1/p_2)_a^1 < (p_1/p_2)_a^2$. The opening of profitable trade will therefore involve country 1(2) exporting its relatively cheaper manufactures (food) and importing commodity food (manufactures). If the equilibrium world price ratio is given by $DE$ and $D'E'$ in Figs 4.1(a) and (b), respectively, each country will shift its production point to $D$ and $D'$, respectively, trading along their consumption possibilities frontiers to the final consumption equilibrium points $E$ and $E'$, respectively. Country 1(2) exports commodity manufactures (food), which uses its relatively abundant factor, labour (resource), more intensively.

The above intuitive explanation of the basic H–O–S model can be made more precise. In Fig. 4.2, the isoquants for manufactures and food output at levels $X_1$ and $X_2$ are shown. On account of the CRS assumption, the isoquants are typical and all other isoquants will be some scalar multiples of those drawn. The isocost budget line $AC'EB$ is tangent to the isoquants $X_1$ and $X_2$ at $C'$ and $E$, respectively. For the given factor costs, the maximum obtainable outputs of each commodity are given by $X_1$ and $X_2$, respectively. The slope of each isoquant is given by the marginal rates of substitution in production which will be equal to the factor price ratio $w/\pi$ at $C'$ and $E$ and the optimising conditions in production given by equation (4.4) will be satisfied. Note that the isoquants only intersect once, reflecting the assumption that manufactures are labour intensive compared with food for all factor price ratios, so that there is no factor intensity reversal.

The isocost curve $AC'EB$ will be associated with a commodity price ratio for the outputs of manufactures and food. If this commodity price ratio is equal to the world price ratio $(p_1/p_2)^*$, then it is possible to show the output levels for each commodity in both countries for the with-trade equilibrium. Thus the rays $OD$ and $OD'$ through the origin in Fig. 4.2 show the resource to labour endowment ratios for country 1 and country 2, respectively. This reflects the assumption that country 1 has the lower resource/labour endowment ratio compared with country 2, or $\bar{R}^1/\bar{L}^1 < \bar{R}^2/\bar{L}^2$. On account of the CRS assumption, the resource endowment ratios can be written in terms of the average resource/labour ratios for each country or $(r/\ell)^1 < (r/\ell)^2$. If the with-trade level of output of manufactured goods in country 1 is given by point $E$, then the level of output of food can be found by completing the parallelogram to the point $D$ on the endowment ratio ray $OD$. The with-trade manufactures/food output ratio in country 1 will be given by $OE/ED$. Similarly, point $D'$ on the endowment ratio ray $OD'$ for country 2 can be found for a with-trade level of output of $OC'$ of food and the with-trade output ratio of manufactures relative to food in country 2 is given by $C'D'/OC'$. By construction, $OE/ED > C'D'/OC'$ and country 1 produces relatively more manufactures compared with food. The with-trade production points $D$ and $D'$ for each country, respectively, shown in factor space in Fig. 4.2, correspond to the with-trade production point $D$ and $D'$ in output space shown for each country in Figs 4.1(a) and (b), respectively. It therefore follows that country 1, because it has a lower resource/labour endowment ratio compared with country 2, exports the labour-intensive manufactures in exchange for the resource-intensive food. Similarly, country 2, on account of its higher resource/endowment ratio compared with country 1, exports the resource-intensive food in exchange for the labour-intensive manufactures.

### 4.2.2   Some properties of the model

In the previous section, the autarky and trading equilibrium positions in the basic H–O–S model were explained, and the

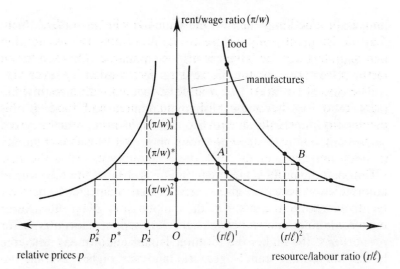

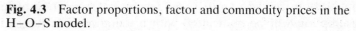

**Fig. 4.3**   Factor proportions, factor and commodity prices in the H–O–S model.

association of the pattern of trade with differences in the factor endowment ratios was established. Figure 4.2 can be used to construct a further diagram so that the most important properties of the model can be summarised.

The right hand side (RHS) of Fig. 4.3 shows the relationship between factor proportions and factor prices, and the left hand side (LHS) shows the relationship between commodity prices and factor prices. On the RHS, the curves for manufactures and food are derived from the isoquants for each commodity shown in Fig. 4.2. Thus, for a given level of output of manufactures and food, the ratio of resource/labour inputs increases as the rent/wage ratio declines. At any given factor price ratio, food always has the higher resource/labour input ratio compared with manufactures, reflecting the assumption that there is no factor-intensity reversal.

The relationship between factor prices and commodity prices can also be established from Fig. 4.2. Consider the iso-cost line $AC'EB$ and the associated factor price ratio $(\pi/w)^*$ and $(p_1/p_2)^*$. These are also the with-trade equilibrium prices shown in Fig. 4.3. As the iso-cost line $AC'EB$ is rotated clockwise around the $X_1$ isoquant, keeping the price of manufactures constant, the point of tangency with the $X_2$ isoquant must move outwards and the price of food must fall. At the same time as the manufactures/ food price ratio rises, the slope of the iso-cost curve is increasing and the wage/rent ratio must also be rising or $(\pi/w)$ must be falling. Thus the monotonic inverse relationship between the commodity price ratio $(p_1/p_2)$ and the factor price ratio $(\pi/w)$ in the LHS of Fig. 4.3 is established. It remains to be shown how the relationship between factor endowment ratios, factor prices and commodity prices can be shown in Fig. 4.3 for two countries entering into trade.

The paradigm[5] H–O–S assumption is that the two countries entering into trade are the same in every respect except their factor endowment ratios. On the supply side, given the inverse monotonic relationship between the factor price ratio and factor proportions, the higher the resource/labour endowment ratio, the lower will be the rent/wage ratio and the higher will be the commodity price ratio $(p_1/p_2)$. An increasing proportion of food consumption will be associated with a rising manufactures/food price ratio. The exact proportions of manufactures and food produced for any given factor price ratio will depend upon the interaction of the supply and demand conditions. Thus, when country 1 has a lower resource/labour ratio than country 2 and $(r/\ell)^1 < (r/\ell)^2$, the associated autarky equilibrium factor price and commodity price ratios can be read off from Fig. 4.3. Country 1 with the lower resource/labour ratio will have a higher rent/wage ratio and a lower relative price of commodity 1 so that $(\pi/w)_a^1 > (\pi/w)_a^2$. The opening of trade will therefore lead to country 1 exporting the labour-intensive manufactures whilst country 2 exports the resource-intensive food. At the common with-trade commodity price ratio $(p_1/p_2)^*$, the endowment ratios of both countries lie within the factor proportions required for manufactures and food production at the with-trade factor price ratio $(\pi/w)^*$, shown by points $A$ and $B$ in Fig. 4.3, and both countries are incompletely specialised with trade.

The essential properties of the H–O–S model are captured in four theorems which can now be explained with the aid of Fig. 4.2 and 4.3.

*The Heckscher–Ohlin theorem*
This theorem seeks to establish the relationship between factor scarcity and either the factor intensity of commodities traded or

factor embodiment in commodities traded. In its quantity form, the theorem states that a country will export (import) the commodity which intensively utilises or embodies the abundant (scarce) factor. When the quantity form of the theorem is based on the descriptive characteristics of commodities which enter trade according to their utilisation of factors, it is sometimes referred to as the commodity form of the theorem. The price form of the Heckscher–Ohlin or H–O theorem states that the country with the relatively cheap factor under autarky exports commodities which use or embody that factor relatively intensively.

It is clear from the discussion of the autarky and with-trade equilibrium positions in Fig. 4.3 that the price form of the H–O theorem with hold since relative factor scarcity is reflected in relative factor prices and in the pattern of trade. The labour- (resource-)intensive commodity 1(2) is relatively cheaper in country 1(2) in the pre-trade situation since country 1 is relatively well endowed with labour in comparison with country 2. Thus, when there are only two commodities and country 1(2) exports the labour- (resource-)intensive commodity, the exports of commodity 1(2) both utilise and embody more of the country's abundant factor labour (resource) compared with imports of commodity 2(1) in each country, respectively.

*The Stolper–Samuelson theorem*
The Stolper–Samuelson theorem is about the relationship between commodity and factor prices, first established by Stolper and Samuelson (1941). The theorem states that an increase (decrease) in the relative price of a commodity will raise (lower) the returns to the factor used intensively in producing that commodity in terms of all prices.

The monotonic inverse relationship between commodity prices and factor prices establishes the first part of this theorem. Thus, starting from the with-trade price ratio $(p_1/p_2)^*$, an increase in the relative price of manufactures which could arise if the resource-abundant country 2 protected its import-competing production of labour-intensive manufactures, would cause the rent/wage ratio to fall or $(w/\pi)$ to rise as required by the theorem. The second part of the theorem is established by noting that, at the lower rent/wage ratio, both industries in country 1 will be operating with a higher resource/labour ratio. This will raise the marginal product of labour in both industries and will raise wages in terms of both commodities.

### Factor price equalisation theorem

This theorem was first established by Samuelson (1948, 1949). It states that, when the paradigm H–O–S assumptions hold and there is incomplete specialisation with trade, the equalisation of commodity prices through trade will also equalise factor prices. This result follows for the $2 \times 2 \times 2$ case from both Figs 4.2 and 4.3. In Fig. 4.2, the iso-cost curve $AC'EB$ is associated with a common commodity price ratio and a common factor price ratio. Provided the two countries which enter trade have factor endowment ratios between the rays through $OE$ and $OC'$, both countries will remain incompletely specialised with trade and a common commodity price ratio will be sufficient to ensure a common factor price ratio. The equality of factor prices then follows from the fact that the quality of factors and the production function are the same in both countries. The same result follows from Fig. 4.3, provided the factor endowment ratio for each country lies between points $A$ and $B$ in the RHS of the diagram. The factor proportions for manufactures production associated with the ray passing through $OE$ is the same as indicated by point $A$ in Fig. 4.3. Similarly, the ray through $OC'$ in Fig. 4.2 and point $B$ in Fig. 4.3 are associated with the same factor proportions for food production. The range of factor endowment ratios for which factor price equalisation is possible bounded by the rays through $OE$ and $OC'$ in Fig. 4.2, and by points $A$ and $B$ in Fig. 4.3, is sometimes referred to as the cone of diversification.

### The Rybczynski theorem

In the comparative static analysis of the relationship between trade and growth, it is often useful to analyse the effect of changes in a country's factor endowments and the associated output responses. Rybczynski (1955) establishes the basic result, which states that an increase in the endowment of one factor at constant prices will increase the output of the commodity that uses that factor intensively and reduces absolutely the output of the other commodity. This theorem can be established with the aid of Fig. 4.2.

Consider the endowment ratio given by the ray passing through

$OD'$. If the endowment of resources remains constant but the supply of labour expands, then the endowment ratio ray will rotate to the right, say to that given by the ray passing through $OD$. Since by assumption the commodity price and factor price ratios remain unchanged, the value of output in the initial situation and in the final situation will be given by the iso-cost lines parallel to $AC'EB$ passing through $D'$ and $D$, respectively (not drawn). Since in the second position, the resource endowment has remained constant and the labour supply has increased, the iso-cost curve passing through $D$ must lie outside the iso-cost curve passing through $D'$.

Now suppose that the output of food is held constant at the level given by the length of the ray $OC'$, and the additional labour is available for employment in manufactures. However, at constant factor prices, the employment of resource and labour in food production will not change and the additional supply of labour will be unemployed. It therefore follows that the only way that the additional supply of labour can be employed is for the output of food to contract from $OC'$, releasing some of the resource for employment in manufactures. Therefore at the final production point $D$, the output of food must have contracted absolutely as the level of output of manufactures expanded.

## 4.3  SOME COMPLICATIONS

Consideration of many countries, commodities and factors, intermediate inputs and effective protection, and non-traded goods and transport costs, is complicated but does not fundamentally alter the spirit of the H–O–S model. Specific factors are also consistent with the H–O–S model provided they are not arbitrarily invoked to 'explain' any unexplained long-run comparative advantage. When taken together, the four sets of complications considered in this section tend to allow greater scope for incomplete specialisation in the world economy whilst retaining the spirit of the H–O–S model. The same cannot be said for economies of scale, an important set of excluded considerations from the discussion of the H–O–S model in this chapter. Generally speaking, the presence of scale economies increases the likelihood of complete specialisation in the with-trade situation and greatly complicates the analysis of the trading equilibrium. To the extent that the new literature on scale economies has most to say about intra-developed country trade, and little to say about developed/developing country trade (see the discussion in Section 1.4), exclusion of scale economies from the detailed set of complications considered in this section is justified.

### 4.3.1   Many countries (m), commodities (n) and factors (q)

In the discussion of the $m$-country and $n$-commodity Ricardian model in Section 2.3.1, it was argued on empirical grounds that the number of countries was less than 200 whilst the number of commodities was about 12,000, of which about 7,000 are traded. Therefore $m < n$ by a large order of magnitude. It is much more difficult to place a limit on the number of primary factors or non-produced inputs in the long run, as discussed in Section 2.3.2 in relation to specific factors. Within the Ricardian context, where exogenously-given technological differences underlie the explanation of trade, it was argued that it was useful to consider only a limited number of primary factors such as the irreducible qualities of nature and non-reproducible works of art. Within the H–O–S framework, however, the choice of the number of primary factors is more problematic. The explanation of the basis of trade is given in terms of differences in factor endowments between countries. The ad hoc expansion of the number of factors, particularly specific factors, therefore makes this explanation trivial. Here, the neo-classical tradition is quite schizophrenic. Ohlin (1933, Ch. V) has in mind the classical three-factor division, labour, land and capital. For most purposes, he suggested that a disaggregation of labour into three sub-categories, (a) unskilled, (b) skilled and (c) technical, would be sufficient, provided each group is non-competing with the other. Land or natural resources relevant for industrial activity could be disaggregated into five categories: (a) agriculture and forest growing, (b) fishing and hunting, (c) the production of minerals, (d) the production of water power and (e) transport activities. Capital should be expressed as a sum of money representing the net cost of reproduction after the deduction of obsolescence and depreciation, the price of capital being the rate of interest. This suggests that the number of factors considered for most purposes should be between three and nine or, $3 \leqq q \leqq 9$. In contrast, the major developments and formalisation of the H–O–S framework discussed in the previous section used the two-factor labour-resource model. More recently, the popular specific factors model (Jones, 1971 and Samuelson, 1971) has one mobile factor labour and a specific factor for each commodity in each country. In this case, the total number of factors in the world economy given by the product of the number of commodities and the number of countries plus one, or $q = mn + 1$, reducing the factor proportions explanation of the basis of trade to a tautology.

This suggests that the appropriate H–O–S model for the analysis of long-run comparative advantage will have many more commodities than countries, but many less factors than countries, or $n > m > q$.

It is quite straightforward to extend the analysis to deal with $m$ countries and $n$ commodities when there are only two factors for the case with and without factor price equalisation. The salient features of the analysis can be represented in two-dimensional factor space by considering an $m$ country and $n$ commodity version of Fig. 4.2, as shown in Fig. 4.4.

In Figs 4.4(a) and (b), the commodities are ranked in order of increasing resource/labour intensity for a given set of commodity prices. Only the extreme ends of the range of resource/labour endowments and intensities are considered, plus one or two in between commodities. Consider the case with factor price equalisation, shown in Fig. 4.4(a). Factor prices, given by the slope of the iso-cost line $AB$, will be equalised if all countries produce at least two commodities in common. This will certainly be the case if all countries produce both commodities 1 and $n$, but other combinations of common commodities produced are possible. Given that each country has the same homothetic preferences, it follows that at the common commodity prices the resource/labour ratio in consumption must lie between the extreme factor endowment ratios $(r/\ell)^m$ and $(r/\ell)^1$ rays shown. Further, it must be the case that, whatever combination of the $n$ commodities produced in each country, the average resource/labour ratio in production in each country must be the same as the country's endowment ratio.

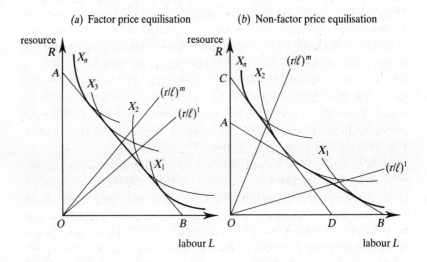

**Fig. 4.4**   Chains of comparative advantage in the $2 \times 2 \times 2$, H–O–S case.

An implication of the $n$ commodity extension of the two-factor model is that there is a fundamental indeterminacy in the production and trading patterns in the $2 \times n \times m$ H–O–S model. Further restriction of the model is required to resolve the indeterminacy in the pattern of trade. For example, the number of commodities produced in a country will increase if some of the commodities are effectively non-traded. However, as long as there are more tradable commodities than factors and transport costs are not high, the indeterminacy in the $2 \times n \times m$ H–O–S model will remain.

The case with factor price non-equalisation considered in Fig. 4.4(b) is for the countries at the extreme ends of the range of endowment ratios. As before, the equilibrium international prices are taken as given, but now countries 1 and $m$ only produce commodity 2 in common. The iso-cost lines for country 1 and country $m$ are given by $AB$ and $CD$, respectively. For a given range of resource/labour ratios in production, factor price equalisation is less likely the greater is the range of the endowment ratios of countries which enter trade. Without factor price equalisation, each country will tend to produce a range of commodities in the chain of comparative advantage.

In the two factor many-commodity case, the Heckscher–Ohlin, Stolper–Samuelson and Rybcyznski theorems require some reinterpretation. Consider first the Heckscher–Ohlin theorem. Because of the indeterminancy in the pattern of trade, it is no longer possible to predict which commodities will be traded from factor utilisation alone and the ranking of commodities traded. For example, it can be seen from Fig. 4.4(a) that the resource-abundant country $m$ could end up exporting commodity 3 and importing commodities 1, 2 and $n$, whilst the labour-abundant country 1 imports commodity 3 and exports commodities 1, 2 and $n$. In this case, the most resource intensive commodity $n$ would be exported by the labour-abundant country 1. However, as can be seen from the example shown in Fig. 4.4(a) with factor price equalisation, a country always exports a combination of commodities which embody relatively more of its abundant endowment than those which are imported and the Heckscher–Ohlin theorem holds in the factor embodiment form.

This problem does not arise when there is no factor price equalisation between countries, as can be seen in Fig. 4.4(b). In the case shown, commodity 2 is the common commodity produced, and it must be the case that the resource-abundant country $m$ produces this commodity with a higher resource/labour ratio than the labour-abundant country 1 on account of the factor price differences. Thus, any other commodities produced by country $m$ will have a higher resource/labour ratio than commodity 2 production at country $m$'s factor prices, and any other commodities produced by country 1 will have lower resource/labour ratios than commodity 2 production at country 1's factor prices. In this case, the Heckscher–Ohlin theorem holds in the commodity form and there will be a chain of commodities which can be ranked by their factor intensities. With many countries, the point at which any country enters the chain of comparative advantage will be dependent on its resource/labour endowment ratios. Further, it can be seen that a unit-value of any commodity exported by the resource-abundant country embodies more resource and less labour than any commodity exported by the labour-abundant country 1. As Brecher and Choudri (1982) have shown, this implies that, with balanced trade and no trade impediments, total exports from country $m$ have a higher resource embodiment than exports from country 1 and the Heckscher–Ohlin theorem holds in the factor content form in the absence of factor price equalisation.

In the presence of more than two commodities, the Rybczynski theorem can also be appropriately modified. By grouping commodities into those with factor intensities above or below the country average, the Rybcyznski theorem will continue to hold for those groups of commodities. Similarly, the additional commodities create little difficulty for the Stolper–Samuelson theorem. If the resource-abundant country $m$ exports commodities 3 and $n$, a uniform tariff on imports increases the relative price of the labour-intensive import-competing commodities 1 and 2 so that the Stolper–Samuelson result follows with a rise in the wage/rental ratio. In terms of Fig. 4.4(a), the factor price plane will rotate to the right as the relative prices of commodities 1 and 2 rise.

The most serious difficulties in generalising the H–O–S model arise when more than two factors are considered, or $q > 2$. For example, the factor-intensity characteristics of commodities does not generalise in an obvious manner. Consider the problem of ranking two commodities produced with three factors, say labour $L$ and two types of resource $R_1$ and $R_2$. Taking the first resource as the reference-input for ordering by factor intensity, the two commodities can be compared either by their $L/R_1$ or by their $R_2/R_1$ rankings. Alternatively, they can be compared by using the second resource as the reference-input so that the commodities are compared either by their $L/R_2$ or by their $R_1/R_2$ rankings. Clearly, such orderings will be different. One way in which the H–O–S model can be generalised to allow for more than two factors is for each commodity to be uniquely associated in an ordered manner with one factor. Restrictions must also be placed on the relationship between commodity and factor prices to give the many-dimensional equivalent of the assumption of no factor-intensity reversal. Then the factor-intensity characteristics of commodities can be re-interpreted in a statistical sense (Deardorff, 1982, 1984), and the commodity form of the Heckscher–Ohlin theorem holds as an average relationship. This result is useful for the empirical testing of the H–O–S model. Another resolution of the difficulties of generalisation is to focus on the underlying factor embodiments.

The factor embodiment form of the Heckscher–Ohlin theorem has the useful property that it bypasses the problem of the ranking of commodities by factor intensity when there are more than two factors, or $q > 2$. This result can be stated as follows. Suppose there are just two countries – the 'home' country 1 and 'the rest of the world' country 2, each capable of producing all commodities, and that the standard simplifying assumptions are maintained. Both countries produce a common subset of at least as many commodities as factors, so that factor price equalisation takes place. It follows that there will be a unique ranking of the relative endowments of the two countries and the factor content of trade. Thus, the number of general primary factors can be increased to $q$, so that $\bar{V}_i^k$ is the endowment of primary factors for $i = 1, q$ and $k = 1, 2$. If the factor endowments are such that:

$$\bar{V}_1^1/\bar{V}_1^2 > \bar{V}_2^1/\bar{V}_2^2 > \dots \bar{V}_q^1/\bar{V}_q^2 \qquad (4.5)$$

then it can be shown that:

1. The home economy country 1 will be a net exporter of the services of $V_1, V_2 \dots V_j$ and a net importer of the services of factors $V_{j+1}, V_{j+2} \dots V_q$.
2. When the common factor prices are known, $j$ will be determined and the net flow of each factor service can be exactly calculated.
3. The ranking of the net trade in factor services can also be made when relative factor endowments are measured in terms of factor shares rather than physical endowments.

These results are elaborated on in Appendix A4.1.

Many of the strong assumptions required to obtain this result can be relaxed, as already seen in the discussion of the two-factor many-commodity case shown in Fig. 4.4(b) above. Recall that in this case, the H–O theorem in its factor embodiment form is not dependent on there being factor price equalisation. Further, focus on the underlying exchange of factor services through trade means that the assumptions of the same technology, the same pattern of consumption and no factor-intensity reversal can all be dropped. As Deardorff (1982) has shown, the factor content form of the H–O theorem indeed generalises in the absence of factor price equalisation, with different technologies in each country, with no restriction on factor intensity reversal, and with differences in consumer preferences between countries. This result, combined with the treatment of the commodity form of the H–O theorem as a statistical relationship, help inform the empirical testing of the H–O theorem discussed in Section 9.2.

### 4.3.2 The Jones–Samuelson specific factors model

Since the early 1970s, there has been a revived interest in the specific factors model discussed in the Ricardian context in Section 2.3.2 (see Jones, 1971 and Samuelson, 1971). The specific factors model in its $n$-commodity and $n+1$-factors version appears incompatible with the observation that attention should be confined to cases where the number of commodities exceeds the number of factors, or $n > q$. However, the specific factors model has been used for shorter- and medium-run analysis where there is imperfect mobility of fixed capital between sectors. It is the short- to medium-run version of the specific factors model which is discussed here. Further discussion of the longer-run specific factors model is taken up in Sections 7.2 and 7.7.

Formally speaking, the single country $2 \times 3$ specific factors model requires modification of equations (4.1) and (4.4) as follows:

*Nominal price (cost) relations, closed economy*

$$\text{wages and rents} \quad \text{revenue}$$
$$wL_1 + \pi_1 R_1 \ = \ p_1 X_1$$
$$wL_2 + \pi_2 R_2 \ = \ p_2 X_2 \tag{4.6}$$

*Quantity relations (factor usage), closed economy*

$$\text{factor usage} \quad \text{factor supply}$$
$$L_1 + L_2 \ = \ \bar{L}$$
$$R_1 \ = \ \bar{R}_1$$
$$R_2 \ = \ \bar{R}_2 \tag{4.7}$$

*Production functions*

$$X_1 = X_1(L_1, R_1)$$

$$X_2 = X_2(L_2, R_2) \tag{4.8}$$

*Optimising conditions*

marginal revenue products    factor price

$$p_1 X_{1\ell} = p_2 X_{2\ell} \quad = \quad w$$

$$p_1 X_1 r_1 \quad = \quad \pi_1$$

$$p_2 X_2 r_2 \quad = \quad \pi_2 \tag{4.9}$$

where all the symbols are as previously defined, except $\bar{R}_1$, $\bar{R}_2$, $\pi_1$ and $\pi_2$ now refer to the specific resource rentals, respectively, associated with each sector.

It is apparent that factor price equalisation cannot take place through commodity trade, since there are more factors than commodities. Thus, with CRS, equation (4.6) can be rewritten in a coefficient form on the same lines as equation (4.1a):

$$w\ell_1 + \pi_1 r_1 = p_1$$

$$w\ell_2 + \pi_2 r_2 = p_2 \tag{4.6a}$$

Equation (4.6a) involves a relationship between three-factor prices and two-commodity prices. Thus, when commodity prices are equalised between countries through trade, there is insufficient information to determine factor prices.

The short-run specific factors model has strikingly different properties compared with the long-run H–O–S model discussed in the previous sections. Consider the case of a small country which exports commodity 1, oil, in return for commodity 2, manufactures. Suppose there is an increase in the price of commodity 1 whilst the price of commodity 2 remains fixed, as happened in the 1970s with oil price changes. There will be an incentive to increase the output of commodity 1 and to increase employment of labour in commodity 1 production. For the increase in employment to take place, given a fixed supply of the specific factor, there must be a decline in the wage in terms of commodity 1 on account of the diminishing marginal productivity of the additional labour. Correspondingly, with more units of labour per unit of the specific resource in industry 1, the real returns to that resource must increase and $\pi_1/p_1$ rises. Since by assumption the price of commodity 2 is fixed, the returns to the specific factor in industry 1 must also increase in terms of commodity 2 and $\pi_1/p_2$ also rises. In industry 2, there will be a lower employment of labour to allow for the transfer of labour to industry 1. As a result of this rise in the number of units of specific resource per unit of labour in industry 2, wages must rise and the specific factor rent must fall in terms of the price of both commodity 1 and commodity 2. Thus, there is an unambiguous increase in industry 1 specific factor rent in terms of both prices and an unambiguous fall in $\pi_2$ in terms of both prices. However, the effects on real wages are ambiguous. Real wages fall in terms of commodity 1 and rise in terms of commodity 2. The final effects on real wages will depend on the relative importance of commodity 1 and commodity 2 in worker consumption.

Changes in resource endowments also have some predictable effects. An increase in the amount of labour will lower the number of units of both resources per worker; real wages fall and real rents will rise in terms of both commodities. There will also be an increase in the output of both commodities, the amount depending on the relative responsiveness of the output in each industry to the increase in employment. A rise in the amount of either specific factor will increase the number of units of resource per unit of labour and the real wage will rise in terms of both commodities. Whichever industry experiences the rise in the availability of the specific factor will experience an increase in output, whilst the other will decline.

The attractiveness of the specific factors model stems from several considerations. First, the model easily generalises to the $n$-commodity $n+1$-factor case, as shown in Section 5.2.1 and in Appendix 5.1.2. Second, it provides a bridge between partial and general equilibrium analyses. While partial equilibrium analysis holds all economy-wide variables constant, the specific factors model holds the industry-specific variables constant and allows for some limited general equilibrium interactions. Third, it has been used to provide a bridge between short- and long-run analyses and temporal adjustment (for further discussion, see Jones and Neary, 1984 and Caves and Jones, 1981, pages 137–41). However, there is no capital as such in the Jones–Samuelson specific factors model, and it is much less useful when applied to long-run analyses without the introduction of capital as produced means of production. This issue is addressed more fully in Section 7.2.

### 4.3.3  Intermediate inputs and the concept of effective protection

For a long time, the neo-classical tradition was surprisingly resistant to incorporating intermediate inputs into the standard H–O–S trade model. As noted in Section 2.3.3, the Ricardian trade model was generalised to include intermediate inputs in the 1950s, but the central lesson drawn was that the potential gains from trade would be greater than with just final commodities entering trade. It was the recognition of the importance of intermediate inputs for the theory of protection which finally attracted a great deal of attention from the mainstream neo-classical trade literature.

The importance of intermediate inputs for the assessment of the protective effects of a system of tariffs and subsidies was often surprisingly well understood by government authorities charged with administering commercial policy. The conflicts of interest which arose between, for example, a general policy of protecting manufacturing industry, and the effects that protection of intermediate manufactured goods have as a tax on the users of such inputs in the production of final goods, were often all too evident to the experts on tariff commissions.[6] However, strong neo-classical interest in the problem of intermediate inputs only developed in the mid-1960s.[7] This section outlines the effects of the introduction of intermediate inputs into the H–O–S model, together with the concepts of effective protection.

Consider first the introduction of intermediate inputs into the single country 2 × 2 H–O–S case. Omitting the country superscript, the production functions and optimising conditions (4.3) and (4.4) will be modified to:

$$X_1 = X_1(L_1, R_1, X_{11}, X_{21})$$
$$X_2 = X_2(L_2, R_2, X_{12}, X_{22}) \qquad (4.10)$$

$$\begin{array}{ccc} \text{marginal revenue products} & & \text{input price} \\ p_1 X_{1\times 1} = p_2 X_{2\times 1} & = & p_1 \\ p_1 X_{1\times 2} = p_2 X_{2\times 2} & = & p_2 \end{array} \qquad (4.11)$$

where $X_1$ and $X_2$ now refer to gross outputs and the $X_{ixj}$s are the marginal products of commodity $j$ in the production of commodity $i$.

Equations (4.11) require that the marginal revenue products of the intermediate inputs are equal to the price of the product. In the case of the own product inputs, this amounts to the requirement that these inputs must, at the margin, produce just sufficient gross product to replace the inputs used.

In this timeless static model, the intermediate inputs attract no interest charge and the slope of the net production possibilities frontier is given by the ratio of the marginal productivities as before. As in the Ricardian model with intermediate inputs, discussed in Section 2.3.3, there are expanded possibilities of the gains from trade. The presence of intermediate inputs introduce no new difficulties into the factor price equalisation theorem, but some consequences follow for the Heckscher–Ohlin, Stolper–Samuelson and Rybczynski theorems.

With the introduction of intermediate inputs into the H–O–S model, it is the net, rather than gross, outputs which are relevant for the analysis of trade. The production functions defined in terms of gross outputs can be transformed to reflect the distinction between net and gross outputs. As shown in Appendix 4.2, equations (4.10) can be rewritten as:

$$C_1 = C_1^{\dagger}(L_1, R_1)$$
$$C_2 = C_2^{\dagger}(L_2, R_2) \qquad (4.10a)$$

where $\dagger$ indicates the net output production function. The resultant labour and resource requirements per unit of net output are sometimes referred to as the direct plus indirect input coefficients. In the $2 \times 2 \times 2$ case, the distinction between net and gross outputs does not affect the rankings of industries by factor intensity. However, as shown in Appendix 4.2, in the many-commodity case where $n > q = 2$, the direct plus indirect coefficients are required to rank industries by factor intensity. The commodity form of the Heckscher–Ohlin theorem breaks down in the many-commodity and many-factor case with intermediate inputs for the same reasons as discussed in Section 4.3.1. However, the presence of intermediate inputs presents no new difficulties for the factor content form of the Heckscher–Ohlin theorem. The Rybczynski and Stolper–Samuelson theorems, also restated in terms of direct and indirect input coefficients and net outputs, carry no new complications provided a suitable price index for net outputs or value added is defined.

The concept of effective protection revolves around the effects of tariffs and other forms of protection on the value added price index and the resource re-allocative effects which follow. Thus, in the presence of intermediate inputs, the price of value added for industry $i$ can be written as:

$$p_i^v = p_i - \Sigma_j a_{ij} p_j \qquad (4.12)$$

where $p_i^v$ is the value added price index, $p_i$ is the price of gross output, and the $a_{ij}$s are intermediate inputs. If the price of gross outputs is given by world prices, and the *ad valorem* tariffs on gross outputs are given by $t$, then the value added price index with protection is given by:

$$p_i^{vt} = p_i(1 + t_i) - \Sigma_j a_{ij} p_j (1 + t_j) \qquad (4.13)$$

The effective rate of protection for industry $i$ or $ERP_i$ is defined by the change in the value added price index induced by the structure of protection or:

$$ERP_i = (p_i^{vt} - p_i^v)/p_i^v \qquad (4.14)$$

In general, it is not possible to predict the direction of resource re-allocation from a knowledge of the ERPs alone. This point and the implications for the use of the ERPs to measure the resource re-allocative effects of a tariff structure are further discussed in Section 5.3.

### 4.3.4  Non-traded commodities and transport costs

Apart from their empirical importance, an additional reason for interest in transport costs within the H–O–S model is their role in breaking the fundamental indeterminacy in the H–O–S model, particularly when transport costs are infinitely high as in the case of non-traded commodities. This section examines some aspects of the role of non-traded commodities in the context of the long-run H–O–S model.[8] The analysis of radical technical change and terms of trade shifts developed for the Ricardian case in Section 2.3.4 is repeated for the three-commodity, two-factor, or 3 × 2 H–O–S, case when one of the commodities is non-traded. The final part of the section briefly examines Main-waring's concept of effective impedence, commenting on the consequences of the addition of more commodities and factors.

The three-dimensional production possibilities frontier required to illustrate the 3 × 2 H–O–S case can be collapsed to a two-dimensional frontier showing the trade-off between tradable and non-tradable production when one of the commodities is non-traded. Thus, the factor-intensity rankings of the first three commodities, as shown in Fig. 4.4(a), are altered so that commodity 1 is the most resource-intensive commodity and commodity 2 is labour-intensive and commodity 3 is in between. If the country $m$ is resource-abundant as shown and if commodity 3 is non-traded, commodity 1 will be exported in exchange for commodity 2. The production possibilities frontier showing the trade-off between tradables and non-tradables for country $m$ for given world prices of tradables $\bar{p}_1$ and $\bar{p}_2$ can now be drawn.

The linear segment $AC$ of the production possibilities frontier in Fig. 4.5(a) for given world prices $\bar{p}_1$ and $\bar{p}_2$ corresponds to the case shown in Fig. 4.4(a) when both tradable commodities 1 and 2 are produced. In this case, the allocation of resources between tradables and non-tradables can be altered along the segment without changing factor prices or the tradable/non-tradable price ratio. The segment $CB$ in Fig. 4.5(a) corresponds to a situation in which the importable is not produced and changing the allocation of resources between tradables and non-tradables requires that factor prices and the tradable/non-tradable price ratio change. The initial equilibrium production and consumption point chosen in Fig. 4.5(a) is assumed to be at $D$ on the income expansion path $ODEF$. In this case, both tradables will be produced with commodity 1 exported and commodity 2 imported.

Alternatively, when the non-tradable commodity 3 is the most labour-intensive commodity and the importable commodity 2 is in between, the production possibilities frontier between tradables and non-tradables will be as shown in Fig. 4.5(b) with an initial equilibrium at $J$. As before, the linear segment $HI$ of the production possibilities frontier corresponds to the situation

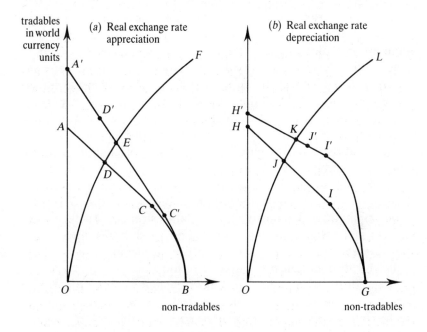

**Fig. 4.5**   Tradables and non-tradables in the 3 × 2, H–O–S model.

where both tradables are produced, and the concave portion *IG* corresponds to the case when the importable is no longer produced. In the initial position, there are no perceptible effects from the change in factor-intensity assumption but the response to the productivity change will be very different.

Now consider some form of radical technical change in the first case where the importable commodity 2 is the most labour-intensive commodity. For the purposes of illustration, suppose that there is Hicks-neutral technical improvement in the production of the exportable commodity 1. At constant international terms of trade, the maximal production of the two tradables alone will shift upwards from *A* to *A'* as shown in Fig. 4.5(a). There will be no change in the maximal production of the non-tradable, which remains fixed at point *B*. The new production possibilities frontier after the factor augmenting technical change will be given by *A'C'B*. The final consumption and production points will now be at $D'$. The price of the non-tradables will rise in terms of world currency units, which is equivalent to an appreciation of the real exchange rate. Because of this, the new equilibrium point will be to the left of the expansion path $ODEF$. The radical technical change in the export industry at constant international terms of trade is equivalent to an increase in the resource endowment, so the output of the export industry 1 will expand whilst the import-competing industry 2 will contract, but a net increase in the amount of tradable production will take place. Had the radical technical change taken place in the import-competing industry 2, the export industry would have contracted and the output of the importable would have increased. The effects on production of the non-tradable commodity 3 will be indeterminate, depending upon the relative strength of substitution effects in consumption which will tend to shift resources from non-tradables to tradables, compared with income effects which will tend to maintain non-tradable production.

The effects of a radical technical change on long-run factor prices and the price of the non-tradable $X_3$ will depend on the factor intensities of the three industries and the industry which experiences the technical change. Consider the case when technical change occurs in the exportable commodity 1. Since the technical change can also be treated as an effective price increase, application of the Stolper–Samuelson theorem indicates that effective resource rents will rise and wages will fall in terms of all commodity prices when the exportable industry 1 is resource intensive and when both tradables are produced. There will be a real appreciation, as shown in Fig. 4.5(a), since the importable commodity 2 is the most labour-intensive industry. With a wage fall and a resource rent rise, the relative price of the non-tradable commodity 3 must rise, since it has a higher resource intensity than the importable industry 2.

By a similar analysis, when the non-tradable is the most labour-intensive industry the results reverse when both tradables are produced. Commodity 3 is now labour intensive in comparison with the importable commodity 2 and will experience a fall in price as real wages fall, and there will be a real exchange rate depreciation. This is shown in Fig. 4.5(b) by the decrease in the slope of the linear segment of the production possibilities frontier (the slope of $H'I'$ is less than $HI$) as a result of the Hicks-neutral technical change in the resource-intensive export industry. For greater detail and an analysis of the equivalence between treating the technical change as either effective factor or effective price augmenting, the reader is referred to Appendix 5.1. The reader can also re-work the above analysis for the case of Hicks-neutral technical change in the import competing industry, reversing all of the above results.

The above effects of technical change in the resource-exporting sector are broadly the same as those observed when the world price of the exportable rises. On the demand side, a rise in the price of the resource-based export will lead to a switch in demand from the exportable to importables and non-tradables, provided that the commodities are substitutes in consumption. If the domestic consumption of the exportable is not large, this can be ignored. On the output side, it is no longer possible to depict the output of tradables as a composite commodity since by assumption the relative price of one of the commodities changes. However, if the amount of labour used in the booming export sector is relatively small, the additional export revenue can be treated as a capital inflow. In this case, the vertical axis in Fig. 4.5 will now represent importables only and the substitution effects in demand between the exportable and the other commodities can be ignored. In an exportable resource-based commodity price boom, the output of the importable industry 2 will contract as before, but the output of the non-tradable industry 3 will always expand when the labour requirements in export production are sufficiently small. The effects on factor prices and the price of the non-tradable commodity will then follow from the relative factor intensity of the importable and non-tradable commodities following the same pattern as above.

There are many other possible combinations of relative factor intensity assumptions and the location of the boom – in the exportable, importable or non-traded industries. The results are also sensitive to assumptions made about factor mobility between the sectors. These results are in contrast to the effects of radical technical change in the simpler Ricardian model discussed in Section 2.3.4, where radical technical change in the export sector always led to a rise in wages and/or the rate of profit, and the real exchange rate always appreciated. However, a final assessment of long-run Dutch disease effects must wait until a more satisfactory treatment of capital is incorporated into the models in Section 7.4.

Ideally, transport costs should be included systematically, rather than as zero for tradables and infinitely large for non-tradables. Mainwaring (1984b) argues that the standard trade theory literature treats transport costs rather like tariffs and other artificial impediments to trade which affect the volume but not the direction of trade. However, Mainwaring notes that the introduction of transport costs in the presence of intermediate inputs can have unpredictable effects on output and therefore the pattern of trade. These effects arise for reasons similar to those which give rise to perverse output responses in the effective protection literature discussed in Section 5.1. Mainwaring therefore introduces the concept of 'effective impedence' in his analysis of transport costs and the pattern of trade.

Given Mainwaring's caution, it is clearly important to take into account transport costs in any step towards increasing the realism of the simple model considered in this section. In so far as Dutch disease effects can take place through radical technical change in transport systems, as was the case with the introduction of refrigeration into shipping in the nineteenth century, Mainwaring's message that the analysis of the effects of transport costs will generally have more complicated and possibly perverse effects compared to those analysed above is well taken.

## APPENDIX 4.1   THE FACTOR CONTENT FORM OF THE HECKSCHER–OHLIN THEOREM

The commodity form of the Heckscher–Ohlin or H–O theorem discussed in Section 4.2.2 can be restated for the $2 \times 2 \times 2$ case using symbols as previously defined as follows;

if $$\bar{R}^1/\bar{L}^1 > \bar{R}^2/\bar{L}^2$$

and if $$r_1/\ell_1 > r_2/\ell_2 \qquad (A4.1.1)$$

then country 1 exports commodity 1 and country 2 exports commodity 2. In the $2 \times 3 \times 2$ case, the H–O theorem in its commodity form breaks down. Thus:

if $$\bar{R}^1/\bar{L}^1 > \bar{R}^2/\bar{L}^2$$

and if $\qquad r_1/\ell_1 > r_2/\ell_2 > r_3/\ell_3$

then all that can be said is that country 1 exports some combination of up to two of the three commodities that embody relatively more resource than labour compared with country 2, which exports some combination of up to two commodities embodying relatively more labour than the exports of country 1. The strict commodity form of the H–O theorem is violated, but it will still hold in its factor content form.

The factor content form of the H–O theorem can be stated for the 2 country, $n$ commodity and $q$ factor form following the discussion by Vanek (1968) as follows:

if $\qquad \bar{V}_1^1/\bar{V}_1^2 \geqq \bar{V}_2^1/\bar{V}_2^2 \ldots \geqq \bar{V}_q^1/\bar{V}_q^2$ $\qquad$ (A4.1.2)

is the ranking of factor endowment ratios for $q$ types of factors, then country 1 will be a net exporter of the services of $\bar{V}_1, \bar{V}_2 \ldots$ $\bar{V}_j$ and a net importer of the services of $\bar{V}_{j+1} \ldots \bar{V}_q$. Further, once factor prices are determined, the $j$th industry will be determined. It is convenient to divide the discussion of the H–O theorem in its factor content form into two cases, (a) where the number of commodities $n = q$, the number of factors, and (b) where $n > q$.

*Definitions*

$X^1(X^2)$ $\qquad$ is a $(n \times 1)$ column vector of country 1 (country 2) outputs.

$C^1(C^2)$ $\qquad$ is a $(n \times 1)$ column vector of country 1 (country 2) consumption or expenditure.

$\bar{V}^1(\bar{V}^2)$ $\qquad$ is a $(q \times 1)$ column vector of country 1 (country 2) factor endowment.

$v(\hat{v})$ $\qquad$ is a $(1 \times q)$ row vector $(q \times q$ diagnonal matrix) of world factor prices.

$V^x(V^c)$ $\qquad$ is a $(q \times 1)$ column vector of the primary non-produced input content of world output (expenditure).

$V^{x_1}(V^{c_1})$ $\qquad$ is a $(q \times 1)$ column vector of primary non-produced input content of country 1 output (expenditure).

$V^{x_2}(V^{c_2})$ $\qquad$ is a $(q \times 1)$ column vector on primary non-produced input content of country 2 output (expenditure).

$V^{t_1}(V^{t_2})$ $\qquad$ is a $(q \times 1)$ column vector of the primary non-produced input content of country 1 (country 2) trade.

$\Lambda^1(\Lambda^2)$     is a $(q \times n)$ matrix of primary non-produced input coefficients $\lambda_{ij}$ factor $i$ into commodity $J$,

$n = q$

Now, the primary non-produced input content of world output valued at equalised factor prices $v$ will be given by:

$$V^x = \hat{v}(\bar{V}^1 + \bar{V}^2)$$
$$= \hat{v}(\Lambda^1 X^1 + \Lambda^2 X^2)$$
$$= \hat{v}\Lambda(X^1 + X^2)$$

where     $\Lambda^1 = \Lambda^2 = \Lambda$     (A4.1.3)

The primary non-produced input content of world output can be decomposed:

$$V^x = V^{x_1} + V^{x_2} \qquad (A4.1.4)$$

With identical homothetic preferences in each country, the factor content of domestic expenditure in country 1 will be:

$$V^{c_1} = mV^x \qquad (A4.1.5)$$

where $m$ is a constant to be determined.

The net factor content of trade $V^t$ will be given by the difference between the factor content of output and the factor content of consumption for each country; for country 1:

$$V^{t_1} = V^{x_1} - V^{c_1} \qquad (A4.1.6)$$

The coefficient $m$ is determined by the requirement that there is balance of payments equilibrium. In terms of the factor content of trade, the balance of payments condition can be written as:

$$V^{t_1\prime}I = 0 \qquad (A4.1.7)$$

where $I$ is a column vector of 1s and $\prime$ indicates transpose.

The vector of the net factor content of trade for country 1 can be decomposed as follows:

$$V^{t_1} = \hat{v}\Lambda X^1 - m\hat{v}\Lambda(X^1 + X^2)$$
$$= \hat{v}(\bar{V}^1(1 - m) - m\bar{V}^2) \qquad (A4.1.8)$$

using equations (A4.1.3), (A4.1.4) and (A4.1.6).

The $j$th element of $V^{t_1}$, $V_j^{t_1}$ will be:

$$V_j^{t_1} = v_j(\bar{V}_j^1(1 - m) - m\bar{V}_j^2) \qquad \text{(A4.1.9)}$$

Once $v_j$ and factor endowments are given, equation (A4.1.9) is a linear function in $m$ and $V_j^{t_1}$ and can be graphed as in Fig. A4.1.1.

When $m = 0$, $V_i^{t_1} = v_i\bar{V}_i^1$ and $V_j^{t_1} = v_j\bar{V}_j^1$ the two points $V_i^{t_1}$ and $V_j^{t_1}$ on the vertical axis in Fig. A4.1.1 are defined. Similarly, when $V_i^{t_1} = V_j^{t_1} = 0$ equation (A4.1.8) can be solved for $m$, yielding:

$$m_i = 1/(1 + \bar{V}_i^2/\bar{V}_i^1)$$

$$m_j = 1/(1 + \bar{V}_j^2/\bar{V}_j^1) \qquad \text{(A4.1.10)}$$

Now from inequality (A4.1.2):

$$\bar{V}_j^2/\bar{V}_j^1 \geqq \bar{V}_i^2/\bar{V}_i^1 \text{ for } j > i$$

by assumption and therefore $m_j \leqq m_i$.

Thus, in Fig. A4.1.1, the two lines joining $V^{t_1}$ and $m_i$, $V_j^{t_2}$ and $m_j$ are drawn for the case where $V_j^{t_1} > V_i^{t_1}$ for $m = 0$, a condition which need not necessarily hold. For the two-factor case, $m_2 \leqq m \leqq m_1$, so that $m$ is chosen such that $V_1^{t_1} = -V_2^{t_2}$ and country 1 exports the services of factor 1 and imports the services of factor 2. For $q > 2$, Fig. A4.1.1 can be generalised and $m$ will be chosen such that the net exports of factor services is zero as required by equation (A4.1.7). Further, inequality (A4.1.2) can be rewritten in terms of factor shares (the $v_j\bar{V}_j$s) and the same results follow.

$n > q$

When $n > q$, the same results will hold provided there is incomplete specialisation in $q$ products and specialisation is in more than $(n - q)$ products.

For further discussion, see Vanek (1968).

## APPENDIX 4.2   INTERMEDIATE INPUTS IN THE H–O–S MODEL

As noted in Section 4.3.3, all observations about factor intensity and factor content in the H–O–S model must be reworked in terms of the direct and indirect input requirements when intermediate inputs are introduced.

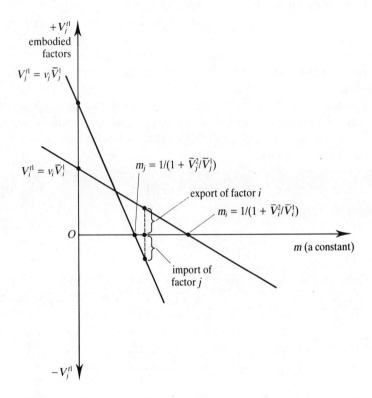

**Fig. A4.1.1**   Net trade in factor services in the H–O–S model.

The gross output production functions shown in equation (4.10) of the text can be rewritten as net output functions:

$$C_1 = C_1(L_1, R_1)$$

$$C_2 = C_2(L_2, R_2) \qquad (A4.2.1)$$

where $C_1$ and $C_2$ are net outputs. Equation (A4.2.1) can be extended for any number of commodities and factors; here, the $n$ commodity, two-factor case is considered.

Defining the direct and indirect factor input coefficients as $\ell_i^\dagger = L_i/C_i$ and $r_i^\dagger = R_i/C_i$, and writing $a_{ij} = X_{ij}/X_j$ for the intermediate input coefficients, the following relationships between net and gross outputs, direct and direct plus indirect input coefficients, will hold for any given set of commodity and factor prices:

$$[C] = [X] - [A][X]$$
$$= [I - A][X]$$

and
$$[X] = [I - A]^{-1}[C] \qquad \text{(A4.2.2)}$$

where $I$ is the identity matrix and $A$ is the matrix of coefficients $a_{ij}$. Now by definition:

$$\begin{bmatrix} L \\ R \end{bmatrix} = \begin{bmatrix} \ell \\ r \end{bmatrix} [\hat{X}] \qquad \text{(A4.2.3)}$$

where $\begin{bmatrix} L \\ R \end{bmatrix}$ and $\begin{bmatrix} \ell \\ r \end{bmatrix}$ are both $(2 \times n)$ matrices of total factor inputs and direct factor input coefficients, respectively, and $[\hat{X}]$ is a diagonal matrix of gross outputs. Substituting from (A4.2.2) into (A4.2.3) and writing $[C]$ as a diagonal matrix:

$$\begin{bmatrix} L \\ R \end{bmatrix} = \begin{bmatrix} \ell \\ r \end{bmatrix} [I - A]^{-1}[\hat{C}] = \begin{bmatrix} \ell^{\dagger} \\ r^{\dagger} \end{bmatrix} [C] \qquad \text{(A4.2.4)}$$

Thus it is clear from equation (A4.2.4) that the relevant definition of the direct and indirect factor input coefficients is:

$$\begin{bmatrix} \ell^{\dagger} \\ r^{\dagger} \end{bmatrix} = \begin{bmatrix} \ell \\ r \end{bmatrix} [I - A]^{-1} \qquad \text{(A4.2.5)}$$

In the $2 \times 2$ H–O–S, the ranking of industries by factor intensity will be the same whether in terms of the direct or the direct and indirect factor coefficients, but this result does not generalise. Thus the relevant factor intensities for the empirical testing of the H–O theorems about the pattern of trade should use the direct plus indirect factor intensities. The factor embodiment form of the H–O theorem discussed in Appendix 4.1 can be readily modified to take into account intermediate inputs. When technology is the same in all countries and there are no transport costs, the matrix $\Lambda$ of direct factor input requirements used in equation (A4.1.3) must be replaced by the matrix $\Lambda^{\dagger}$ of direct and indirect factor requirements and the vector $X$ of gross outputs must be replaced with the vector $C$ of net outputs and the analysis proceeds as before. For further discussion of the generalised H–O theorem and relaxation of the assumption, see Deardorff (1982).

## NOTES

1.  See, for example, Rowthorn (1974) and Steedman (1979a, Ch. 1) for a general discussion of these issues. For a general exposition and critique of the more extreme neo-liberal application of these arguments to development issues, see Toye (1987).
2.  Kaldor (1955, page 89, fn. 3) notes that Ricardo thought of machines and ploughs as factors of production, but not the monetary value of capital employed.
3.  For an introductory treatment of the optimising conditions in production, see Baumol (1977, Ch. 13). For a more advanced treatment, see Henderson and Quandt (1980, Ch. 4).
4.  For an introductory discussion of the optimising conditions in consumption, see Baumol (1977, Ch. 9). For a more advanced treatment, see Henderson and Quandt (1980, Ch. 2). See also Section 2.2.4 and the references cited in footnote 11.
5.  By 'paradigm' cases in trade theory, I mean differences in technology in static Ricardian theory and differences in resource endowments in the H–O–S theory as the basis for trade.
6.  See, for example, Brigden *et al.* (1929).
7.  Jones and Neary (1984) trace the neo-classical concern with the consequences of intermediate inputs back to Corden (1966). In turn, the early neo-classical interest in intermediate inputs was greatly stimulated by Barber (1955). However, these effects were not unknown to earlier writers such as Heckscher (1934) and Viner (1934).
8.  The presence of non-traded intermediate commodities provides a fertile ground for the possible breakdown of the basic theorems, particularly the Stolper-Samuelson and factor price equalisation theorems. For example, different factor prices can be associated with the same relative prices for the traded commodities when the price of the non-traded input varies. These issues are discussed in Woodland (1982).

# 5 · NEO-CLASSICAL THEORY: SOME PERSPECTIVES ON TRADE AND GROWTH

## 5.1 INTRODUCTION

Although the static H–O–S model presented in the previous chapter was timeless, the idea that economic processes take time was imposed exogenously. In the case of the standard $2 \times 2 \times 2$ H–O–S model, it was assumed that both labour and the resource were mobile within each country and that the time period was long enough for wages and rents to be equalised. In contrast, the short-run $2 \times 2 \times 3$ specific factors model assumed that the resource was immobile between sectors over the time period considered. When the specific factor is a natural resource such as oil deposits, resource immobility would also prevent the equalisation of returns to specific factor rents in the medium and long run. However, when the sector-specific factor is fixed capital, mobility may ensure the equalisation of the rental on capital in the medium and long run.

The first part of this chapter continues the development of the static H–O–S framework to consider some aspects of growth in a comparative static framework. Section 5.2.1 formalises the comparative statics of the single-country, two-commodity and two-factor H–O–S and the two-commodity and three-factor, specific factors model in terms of the magnification effects of exogenous changes in factor supply or prices. The remainder of Section 5.2 presents some standard single-country and two-country analyses of trade and growth, and Section 5.3 extends the comparative static analysis of the effects of protection in the presence of intermediate inputs. The final section aims to convey the essence of the neo-classical approach to long-run growth.

There are a number of different strategies which could be adopted to achieve this aim, each of which implies radically different levels of attention to detail and technical difficulty. In ignoring the finer details of the more general analysis, a virtue is made of the fact that much of the recent literature on trade and growth has been concerned to show that the essential propositions derived from static H–O–S theory carry over to the long-run dynamic context.

Marglin (1984a, b) suggests that the heart of the neo-classical approach to long-run growth is to treat the household with its sovereign consumers as the mainspring of capitalism.[1] Thus, for any exogenously-given growth of the workforce and technical change, profit and wage rates must adjust through market clearance mechanisms so that households as consumers, maximising utility as the discounted flow benefits arising from the flow of consumption over time, consent to save as much as is required to invest in order to grow at some exogenously specified rate. Similarly, household members as producers must adopt the techniques of production in response to relative price changes which contribute towards the same outcome. In this story, investment and consumption, aided by perfect foresight,[2] adjust to the exogenously-given growth rate, with the level of income depending critically upon the price efficiency of the economy.

These textures of neo-classical growth theory can be captured with a one-sector model. In order to introduce trade and growth considerations, however, the two-sector neo-classical growth model for the small open economy is also developed in this section. For the small open economy, the analysis can proceed along the same lines as for the one-sector model without greatly increasing the level of technical difficulty. The main focus of the analysis will be on the long-run steady state paths. The final section examines the consequences of dropping the abstinence or time preference theory of capital and interest by outlining some of the consequences for long-run growth of introducing wealth holding as an additional motive for saving.

## 5.2 SOME COMPARATIVE STATIC RESULTS

### 5.2.1 Magnification effects

The relationship between commodity prices, factor prices and resource re-allocation for both comparative static and comparative dynamic analyses in a single country can be made more rigorous with the aid of some algebra. Equations (4.1) and (4.2) can be totally differentiated to yield, after some manipulations, the following relationships:

$$\theta_{\ell_1}\hat{w} + \theta_{r_1}\hat{\pi} = \hat{p}_1$$

$$\theta_{\ell_2}\hat{w} + \theta_{r_2}\hat{\pi} = \hat{p}_2 \qquad (5.1)$$

where $\theta_{ij}$ for $i = \ell, r$ and $j = 1, 2$ is the share of the $i$th factor in unit costs in the $j$th industry and $\hat{}$ indicates the relative change in the variable or parameter, and:

$$\psi_{\ell_1}\hat{X}_1 + \psi_{\ell_2}\hat{X}_2 = \hat{L} + \delta_\ell(\hat{w} - \hat{\pi})$$

$$\psi_{r_1}\hat{X}_1 + \psi_{r_2}\hat{X}_2 = \hat{R} - \delta_r(\hat{w} - \hat{\pi}) \qquad (5.2)$$

In equation (5.2), the $^-$ symbol for exogenously-given factor supplies has been dropped for convenience. The $\psi_{ij}$ for $i = \ell, r$ and $j = 1, 2$ are the shares of factor $i$ allocated to industry $j$, $\delta_\ell$ and $\delta_r$ are positive coefficients involving the $\theta$s, the $\psi$s and the elasticities of substitution in production between labour and the resource, and $^\wedge$ is the relative change as before (equations (A5.1.4) and (A5.1.8) in Appendix 5.1). Equations (5.1) and (5.2) have some useful properties.

First, when commodity 1 is labour intensive, it follows that:

$$\hat{w} > \hat{p}_1 > \hat{p}_2 > \hat{\pi}$$

when                         $\hat{p}_1 > \hat{p}_2$

and                          $\hat{\pi} > \hat{p}_2 > \hat{p}_1 > \hat{w}$

when                         $\hat{p}_2 > \hat{p}_1 \qquad (5.1a)$

Jones (1965) refers to this as the magnification effect. Since the commodity price changes are weighted averages of the factor price changes, the factor price changes provide the upper and lower bounds to commodity price changes and the ranking of industries by factor intensity defines the ranking of the relative factor price changes.

Similarly, when commodity 1 is labour intensive and factor prices are unchanged ($\hat{w} = \hat{\pi} = 0$), there will be magnification effects in the output and factor allocations as follows:

$$\hat{X}_1 > \hat{L} > \hat{R} > \hat{X}_2$$

when

$$\hat{L} > \hat{R}$$

and

$$\hat{X}_2 > \hat{R} > \hat{L} > \hat{X}_1$$

when

$$\hat{R} > \hat{L} \qquad (5.2a)$$

Thus, changes in total factor usage are a weighted average of output changes and the ranking of the relative output and factor changes will be governed by the ranking of commodities by factor intensity.

In the case of the short- to medium-run, two–commodity, three–factor specific factors model, the magnification effects on factor process are more ambiguous so that either:

$$\hat{\pi}_1 > \hat{p}_1 > \hat{w} > \hat{p}_2 > \hat{\pi}_2$$

or

$$\hat{\pi}_2 > \hat{p}_2 > \hat{w} > \hat{p}_1 > \hat{\pi}_1 \qquad (5.3)$$

where the rents now have an industry subscript to indicate that the resources are industry specific. In both cases identified, the effects of the price change on real wages will be ambiguous, since real wages increase in terms of one of the commodities, but decrease in terms of the other. In the case of the expansion of either the labour supply or the supply of one or other of the specific factors, no clear-cut magnification effects take place.

Extension of the long-run H–O–S model to the three–commodity and two–factor case by the inclusion of a non-traded commodity can utilise the magnification effects already described. As before, commodities 1 and 2 are tradable, commodity 3 is non-tradable, and the two primary factors are labour and a resource. The magnification effects of radical technical change in the exportable industry 1, modelled by Hicks neutral technical change at constant world prices when both tradable commodities are produced, affects factor prices according to the factor–intensity ranking of the tradable commodities. Thus, if the Hicks neutral technical change in industry 1 is of an amount $-\hat{\tau}_1 > 0$, then when the export industry is labour intensive:

$$\hat{w} > -\hat{\tau}_1 > 0 > \hat{\pi}$$

and when the export industry is resource intensive:

$$\hat{\pi} > -\hat{\tau}_1 > 0 > \hat{w} \qquad (5.4)$$

The effects on the price of the non-tradable commodity will

depend on the factor intensity of the non-tradable compared with the importable. Thus, when the exportable is labour-intensive compared with the importable, the radical technical change raises wages according to the first inequality in (5.4). If the non-tradable commodity 3 is labour-intensive compared with the importable commodity 2, then the price of the non-tradable must rise, or $\hat{p}_3 > 0$, and the real exchange rate appreciates. Alternatively, when the non-tradable is resource intensive compared with the importable, the price of the non-tradable must fall, or $\hat{p}_3 < 0$, and the real exchange rate depreciates. The reverse pattern of results emerges when the export sector is resource-intensive.

### 5.2.2  Immiserising growth

When two countries are involved, the analysis of some of the comparative static changes of the H–O–S model to exogenously-specified growth of factors or technical change proceeds along similar lines to the analysis in Section 3.4 on the demand side. However, because incomplete specialisation can be readily specified in the H–O–S model, the final outcome is very much more varied. For example, it is possible within the H–O–S framework for the terms of trade in the faster growing country to improve provided the import-competing domestic production expands fast enough in the growth process. In all of the results reported here, attention will be confined to various combinations of factor supply growth. Similar types of results can be obtained when technical change with different types of bias takes place in one or other industry, or in the economy as a whole, but it is beyond the scope of this book to examine these cases in detail. In all of the results reported, it is assumed that country 1 has the abundant resource endowment and does not expand at all whilst country 2 has the abundant labour endowment and grows at some arbitrary rate. This simplifies the analysis whilst preserving the assumption that country 2 grows faster than country 1. In all cases, it is assumed that country 2 exports the labour-intensive commodity 1 in exchange for the resource-intensive commodity 2 exported by country 1, and that there is incomplete specialisation in both countries.

In all the cases considered, the income effects for the country which does not grow will be given by the terms of trade effects on imports, whereas for the growing economy the output growth will be added to the terms of trade effects. Thus:

$$dY^1 = -\hat{p}M_1^1 p$$

and $\qquad dY^2 = \hat{p}M_2^2 + pdX_1^2 + dX_2^2 \qquad\qquad (5.5)$

which is from equation (A3.1.12a) with $pdX_1^1 + dX_2^1 = 0$ or no output growth in country 1. The terms of trade effect will be given by:

$$\hat{p} = \frac{-\hat{M}_2^2|\bar{p}}{\Delta} \qquad\qquad (5.6)$$

from equation (A3.1.15a). The shift factor for the import demand function at constant prices, given by totally differentiating (A3.1.2) at constant prices for the reverse pattern of trade, will be:

$$dM_2^2|\bar{p} = dC_2^2 - dX_2^2$$

or $\qquad \hat{M}_2^2|\bar{p} = \phi_{c_2}^2 \hat{C}_2^2 - \phi_{x_2}^2 \hat{X}_2^2 \qquad\qquad (5.7)$

where the coefficients $\phi_{c_2}^2$ and $\phi_{x_2}^2$ express domestic consumption and production of commodity 2 as a share of imports. The essence of the analysis is to specify an exogenous shift of the transformation frontier and to specify the effects of this on the offer curve shift functions shown in (5.7).

The general possibility of immiserising growth can be illustrated with a single-country diagram (see Fig. 5.1). In Fig. 5.1, the initial production possibilities frontier for country 2 is given by $ABC$. Trade takes place along the consumption possibilities frontier $BD$ and the final consumption point chosen is at $D$. After growth in country 2 (with no growth in country 1), the new production possibilities frontier is given by $EFG$. If there is no change in the terms of trade there is an unambiguous gain from growth with trade, as the shift of the consumption possibilities frontier to $D'B'$ shows. When the terms of trade changes are also taken into account, however, the overall effect of growth is unambiguous. The new consumption possibilities frontier may be drawn as $FH$. Whether growth is immiserising or not depends upon whether the final equilibrium point to the left or right of $J$. The location of the equilibrium point in turn depends upon the structure of the demand conditions and social indifference func-

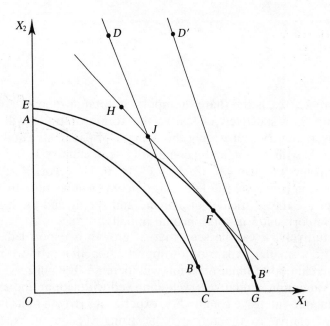

**Fig. 5.1**    Immiserising growth.

tions (not shown here). If the new consumption point is at $H$, social welfare will have fallen as a result of growth. Some of the conditions which give rise to the possibility of such immiserising growth can now be examined in turn.

### 5.2.3    Balanced growth

Suppose the transformation frontier in country 2 shifts out uniformly at the rate $\alpha$. In this case, $pdX_1^2 + dX_2^2 = \alpha Y^2$ and $\hat{M}_2^2|\bar{p} = \alpha$. Thus substituting into equations (5.5) and (5.6) yields:

$$\hat{p} = \frac{-\alpha}{\Delta} < 0$$

and

$$dY^1 = \frac{\alpha}{\Delta} M_1^1 p$$

$$dY^2 = \frac{\alpha}{\Delta} M_2^2 + \alpha Y^2$$

or
$$\hat{Y}^1 = \frac{\alpha}{\Delta}\chi^1_m$$

$$\hat{Y}^2 = \frac{\alpha}{\Delta}(\Delta - \chi^2_m) \qquad (5.8)$$

where $\chi^1_m$, $\chi^2_m$ is the share of imports in total income in countries 1 and 2, respectively. Clearly, the terms of trade will move against country 2 providing the balance of payments equilibrium is stable with $\Delta > 0$, and income will rise in country 1. In country 2, income will also rise if $(\Delta - \chi^2_m) > 0$. However, if $\chi^2_m > \Delta$, income in country 2 will fall. This outcome will be more likely the lower are the elasticities of demand and supply and the higher is the import share in total income initially.

Intuitively, it can be seen that, if growth is export-led, there will be a smaller expansion of import-competing production and the likelihood of immiserisation will increase. If country 2, which by assumption is relatively well-endowed with labour and exports the labour–intensive commodity, experiences growth of its labour-force relative to the resource, a strong version of export-led growth will emerge.

### 5.2.4  Export-led growth

From the magnification effects discussed in Section 5.2.1, when $\hat{L}^2 > 0$ and $\hat{R}^2 = 0$, it follows from inequality (5.2a) that $\hat{X}^2_1 > 0$. At constant commodity and factor prices, the shift in the transformation frontier and domestic consumption of the importable commodity will be given by:

$$pdX^2_1 + dX^2_2 = \alpha wL^2 = \alpha\chi^2_\ell Y^2$$

and
$$dC^2_2 = \alpha\chi^2_{c_2}\chi^2_\ell Y^2 \qquad (5.9)$$

where $w$ is the wage and $\chi^2_{c_2}$, $\chi^2_\ell$ are the shares of the importable commodity 2 and labour income in total income, respectively.

Expressions for the change in outputs are a little more complicated, but can be readily obtained by solving equations (5.2) for constant factor prices when $\hat{L}^2 = \alpha$ and $\hat{R} = 0$. Thus:

$$\hat{X}^2_1 = \frac{\psi^2_{r_2}}{|\psi^2|}\alpha$$

or
$$dX_1^2 = \frac{\psi_{r_2}^2}{|\psi^2|}\, \alpha X_1^2$$

and
$$\hat{X}_2^2 = -\frac{\psi_{r_1}^2}{|\psi^2|}\, \alpha$$

or
$$dX_2^2 = -\frac{\psi_{r_1}^2}{|\psi^2|}\, \alpha X_2^2 \qquad (5.10)$$

where the $\psi$s are the shares of labour and resource in each industry and $|\psi^2| = \psi_{\ell_1}^2 \psi_{r_2}^2 - \psi_{\ell_2}^2 \psi_{r_1}^2 > 0$ when commodity 1 is labour-intensive.

The terms of trade effects of labour expansion in country 2 can now be found. Substituting into equations (5.6) and (5.7) from equations (5.9) and (5.10):

$$\hat{p} = -\frac{(dC_2^2 - dX_2^2)}{M_2^2 \Delta}$$

$$= -\frac{\alpha}{\chi_m^2 \Delta}\left\{\chi_{c_2}^2 \chi_\ell^2 + \frac{\psi_{r_1}^2 \chi_{x_2}^2}{|\psi^2|}\right\}$$

$$< 0 \qquad (5.11)$$

when $\Delta > 0$. Clearly, the terms of trade effect will be unambiguously negative. Substituting (5.11) and (5.9) into (5.5) gives the income effects:

$$\hat{Y}^1 = \frac{\alpha}{\Delta}\left\{\chi_{c_2}^2 \chi_\ell^2 + \frac{\psi_{r_1}^2 \chi_{x_2}^2}{|\psi^2|}\, \frac{\chi_m^1}{\chi_m^2}\, p\right\}$$

$$\hat{Y}^2 = \frac{\alpha}{\Delta}\left\{\chi_\ell^2(\Delta - \chi_{c_2}^2) - \frac{\psi_{r_1}^2 \chi_{x_2}^2}{|\psi^2|}\right\} \qquad (5.12)$$

The income effect in country 1 will always be positive when $\Delta > 0$, but may be negative in country 2 if:

$$\Delta < \left\{\chi_{c_2}^2 + \frac{\psi_{r_1}^2 \chi_{x_2}^2}{|\psi^2| \chi_\ell^2}\right\} \qquad (5.13)$$

Thus, country 2 will suffer immiserising growth the lower are the elasticities $\Delta$, the higher is domestic consumption of the importable, the higher the share of the resource in export production, the higher the income shares of the importable, the closer the factor proportions ratios in the two industries, and the lower the overall share of labour in total income.

### 5.2.5 Import-substituting growth

A polar opposite case of import substituting growth can be obtained for the case where country 2 experiences the growth of the resource whilst its labour force does not grow at all. Thus, if $\hat{R}^2 = \alpha$ and $\hat{L}^2 = 0$, it follows from the magnification condition (5.2a) that when $\hat{R}^2 > 0$ and $\hat{L}^2 = 0$, then $\hat{X}_2^2 > 0$ and $\hat{X}_1^2 < 0$. Following the same methodology as for the export-led growth case, the shifts in the transformation function and offer curves will be:

$$pdX_1^2 + dX_2^2 = \alpha\pi R^2 = \alpha\chi_r^2 Y^2$$

$$dC_2^2 = \alpha\chi_{c_2}^2\chi_r^2 Y^2 \tag{5.14}$$

where $\pi$ is the resource rent and $\chi_r^2$ is the rental share in total income and all other symbols are as before. Similarly, expressions for changes in outputs can be found from equations (5.2):

$$\hat{X}_1^2 = -\frac{\psi_{\ell_2}^2}{|\psi^2|}\,\alpha$$

or

$$dX_1^2 = -\frac{\psi_{\ell_2}^2}{|\psi^2|}\,\alpha X_1^2$$

and

$$\hat{X}_2^2 = \frac{\psi_{\ell_1}^2}{|\psi^2|}\,\alpha$$

or

$$dX_2^2 = \frac{\psi_{\ell_1}^2}{|\psi^2|}\,\alpha X_2^2 \tag{5.15}$$

The terms of trade and income effects follow by substituting (5.14) and (5.15) into equations (5.5), (5.6) and (5.7) as before:

$$\hat{p} = \frac{\alpha}{\chi_{m}^2\Delta}\left\{\frac{\psi_{\ell_1}^2}{|\psi^2|}\,\chi_{x_2}^2 - \chi_{c_2}^2\chi_r^2\right\}$$

$$\hat{Y}^1 = \chi_m^2 \frac{\alpha}{\Delta} \left\{ \frac{\psi_{\ell_1}}{|\psi^2|} \chi_{x_2}^2 - \chi_{c_2}^2 \chi_r^2 \right\}$$

$$\hat{Y}^2 = \frac{\alpha}{\Delta} \left\{ \chi_r^2 (\Delta - \chi_{c_2}^2) + \frac{\psi_{\ell_1}^2}{|\psi^2|} \chi_{x_2}^2 \right\} \tag{5.16}$$

In this case, the terms of trade can go either way according to the condition:

$$\hat{p} \gtreqless 0 \text{ if } \frac{\psi_{\ell_1}^2}{|\psi^2|} \chi_{x_2}^2 \gtreqless \chi_{c_2}^2 \chi_r^2 \tag{5.17}$$

The terms of trade can improve for the growing country the larger the initial allocation of labour to the export industry, the larger the share of the import competing industry in total product, the closer the factor proportions are in the two industries, the lower the consumption share of the import competing industry and the lower the share of resource rent in total income.

The income effects in country 1 will follow the terms of trade effect as before whilst the immiserisation condition for country 2 will be given by the sign of the term inside the braces in the second equation in (5.16). Immiserisation will occur if:

$$\Delta < \chi_{c_2}^2 - \frac{\psi_{\ell_2}^2 \chi_{x_1}^2}{|\psi^2| \chi_r^2} \tag{5.18}$$

Clearly, the immiserisation condition for import-substituting growth is weaker than for the case of export-led growth, which can be seen from the comparison of (5.18) with (5.13). However, this will only be the case if the import substitution takes place without interference with the free-trade assumption which has been maintained so far in this section. When the import substitution is induced by tariff protection, it is more likely to be immiserising. The tariff-induced import substituting growth can be readily analysed using the above framework.

## 5.2.6 Tariff-induced import substitution

The analysis of possible immiserisation from tariff-induced import substitution is due to Johnson (1967). In this case, the terms of trade effects on growth are eliminated by adopting the

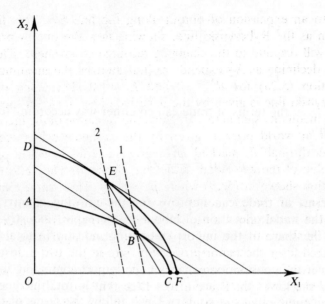

**Fig. 5.2**  Immiserising growth from protected import substitution.

small-country assumption. There is no growth in country 1 as before, now 'the rest of the world', and $\hat{Y}^1 = 0$. The possibility that $\hat{Y}^2$ might be negative can be seen from equation (5.5). Setting $\hat{p} = 0$ and substituting directly for $dX_1^2$ and $dX_2^2$ from (5.15) into (5.5) yields:

$$dY^2 < 0 \text{ if } p > \frac{\psi_{\ell_1}^2}{\psi_{\ell_2}^2} \frac{X_2^2}{X_1^2} = \frac{\ell_1^2}{\ell_2^2} \qquad (5.19)$$

The immiserising condition (5.19) can be illustrated diagrammatically, as in Fig. 5.2.

In Fig. 5.2, the initial position for country 2 is given by the production possibilities frontier $ABC$. Domestic prices are given by the price line tangent to the production possibilities frontier at $B$. World prices are given by the dashed line marked 1 through $B$. The price differential is maintained by a tariff which expands domestic production of $X_2^2$ compared with what it would be under free trade. If the tariff and world prices are held constant, then an expansion of the resource $R^2$ with $L^2$ held constant will lead to an expansion of output along the line $BE$. This line is known as the Rybczynski line, showing how the output proportions will respond to the changing resource endowment. Clearly, $X_1^2$ is declining as $X_2^2$ expands as indicated by the magnification condition (5.2a) for $\hat{R}^2 > 0$ and $\hat{L}^2 = 0$. The slope of the Rybczynski line is given by the negative of the term on the right of the inequality sign in (5.19). Now, the valuation of the increased output at world price is given by the dashed world price line passing through $E$, marked 2. Clearly, in terms of world prices, the value of the expanded output has declined. This reflects the condition shown in (5.19) where $p > \ell_1^2/\ell_2^2$. Thus, the expansion of output in the protected import substituting industry when valued at world prices is negative, so that growth is immiserising. It can be shown that, if the expanded resource used intensively in protected import substituting growth is foreign owned, then the national welfare is necessarily lowered regardless of the condition shown in (5.19) (see Brecher and Diaz Alejandro, 1977).

The literature on immiserising growth is a powerful reminder of how rich and varied results can be obtained from the $2 \times 2 \times 2$ H–O–S framework. However, as will be shown in Section 8.4, all the cases of immiserisation examined arise because of a failure of first best trade policy intervention. Thus, either the deterioration in the terms of trade is not offset by an optimal tariff policy designed to capture national monopoly power on world markets, or because distortions have been introduced through the protection of import-substituting industries. The estimation of the effects of a protective structure on resource allocation is discussed in the next section.

## 5.3   EFFECTIVE PROTECTION AND RESOURCE REALLOCATION

In the two-commodity, two-factor H–O–S model without intermediate inputs, a tariff on the import-competing industry will both raise the returns to the factor used intensively in import-competing production through the Stolper–Samuelson effect and induce a resource reallocation into import-competing production. However, the resource reallocative effects may be perverse once intermediate inputs enter into the picture. The fine tuning of the resource-reallocative effects of a tariff structure cannot be predicted without a knowledge of both resource endowments and the elasticities of substitution in production, thereby requiring much more information than the rates of effective protection themselves. These points can be illustrated by a simple extension of the single-country, $2 \times 2$ model developed in Section 5.2.1 and Appendix 5.1.

Suppose that the single country $2 \times 2$ H–O–S model used in Section 5.2.1 is modified to include a non-competing intermediate input. Thus, equations (4.1) and (4.2), rewritten in the coefficient form, are modified to:

$$w\ell_1 + \pi r_1 = p_1 - a_1 p_a = p_1^v$$

$$w\ell_2 + \pi r_2 = p_2 - a_2 p_a = p_2^v \qquad (5.20)$$

and
$$\ell_1 X_1 + \ell_2 X_2 = \bar{L}$$

$$r_1 X_1 + r_2 X_2 = \bar{R}$$

$$a_1 X_1 + a_2 X_2 = X_a \qquad (5.21)$$

where $\ell_i$ and $r_i$ are the labour and resource coefficients as previously defined for $i = 1, 2$; $a_i$ is the input coefficient for non-competing intermediate inputs for $i = 1, 2$; $p_a$ is the price of non-competing intermediate imports; $p_i^v$ is the price of value added for $i = 1, 2$; $X_a$ is the total amount of non-competing intermediate inputs. Factor prices are given by $w$ and $\pi$ and $X_i$ is output for $i = 1, 2$ as previously defined. As shown in Appendix 5.2, equations (5.20) and (5.21) can be totally differentiated to yield the proportional change relations similar to (5.1) and (5.2) as follows:

$$\theta_{\ell_1}^v \hat{w} + \theta_{r_1}^v \hat{\pi} = \hat{p}_1^v$$

$$\theta_{\ell_2}^v \hat{w} + \theta_{r_2}^v \hat{\pi} = \hat{p}_2^v \qquad (5.22)$$

and
$$\psi_{\ell_1} \hat{X}_1 + \psi_{\ell_2} \hat{X}_2 = \hat{L}^e$$

$$\psi_{r_1} \hat{X}_1 + \psi_{r_2} \hat{X}_2 = \hat{R}^e$$

$$\psi_{a_1} \hat{X}_2 + \psi_{a_2} \hat{X}_2 = \hat{X}_a^e \qquad (5.23)$$

All the variables are as previously defined, except the $\theta$'s which are cost shares in value added, the $\psi_a$s which are the proportions in which the intermediate input is used in each industry; the $\hat{L}^e$

and $\hat{R}^e$ are summary terms defining the effective factor or intermediate input supply given by:

$$\hat{L}^e = \hat{L} + \delta_{\ell_1}(\hat{w} - \hat{\pi}) - \delta_{\ell_2}(\hat{p}_a - \hat{\pi}), \hat{R}^e = \hat{R} - \delta_{r_1}(\hat{w} - \hat{\pi}) - \delta_{r_2}(\hat{p}_a - \hat{\pi})$$

and $\qquad \hat{X}_a^e = \hat{X}_a - \delta_{a_1}(\hat{w} - \hat{\pi}) - \delta_{a_2}(\hat{p}_a - \hat{\pi})$

where the $\delta$s are weighted averages of the elasticities of substitution. (Equation (5.22) is from equation (A5.2.3) and equation (5.23) is from equation (A5.5.10).)

It can easily be seen that equations (5.22) and (5.23) reduce to equations (5.1) and (5.2) when intermediate inputs are dropped. Further, $\hat{p}_1^v$ and $\hat{p}_2^v$ play the same role in the modified model as $\hat{p}_1$ and $\hat{p}_2$ in the model without intermediate inputs. Thus, when commodity 1 is the labour-intensive commodity relative to commodity 2, and $\hat{p}_1^v > \hat{p}_2^v$, it follows that:

$$\hat{w} > \hat{p}_1^v > \hat{p}_2^v > \hat{\pi} \qquad (5.24)$$

Similarly, when $\hat{L}^e > \hat{R}^e$, it follows that:

$$\hat{X}_1 > \hat{L}^e > \hat{R}^e > \hat{X}_2 \qquad (5.25)$$

To illustrate the 'perverse' output response to a change in the $\hat{p}^v$s, suppose that world prices are fixed and given, but a subsidy is introduced on non-competing intermediate inputs. If the intermediate input has a higher share in the cost of commodity 1 than in commodity 2, then $\hat{p}_1^v > \hat{p}_2^v > 0$. From inequality (5.24), it follows that $(\hat{w} - \hat{\pi}) > 0$. However, since $\hat{p}_2^v > 0$, the sign of $\hat{\pi}$ is indeterminate. Thus, with $\hat{p}_a < 0$, it follows that the sign of $(\hat{p}_a - \hat{\pi})$ will also be indeterminate and will depend on the particular elasticities of substitution and the resource endowments. The direction of the resource reallocation effects of the subsidy on intermediate inputs is given by (5.25). When $\hat{L} = \hat{R} = 0$ and with no intermediate inputs, then $\hat{X}_1 > \hat{L}^e > \hat{R}^e > \hat{X}_2$ and a 'normal' output response follows with protection of the labour-intensive commodity 1 leading to an increase in its output. With intermediate inputs, $(\hat{p}_a - \hat{\pi}) \gtreqless 0$ and the direction of the resource reallocative effects of the subsidy on intermediate inputs will be governed by the relative size of $\hat{L}^e$ and $\hat{R}^e$ according to:

$$\hat{L}^e \gtreqless \hat{R}^e \text{ as}$$

$$(\delta_{\ell_1} + \delta_{r_1})(\hat{w} - \hat{\pi}) \gtreqless (\delta_{\ell_2} - \delta_{r_2})(\hat{p}_a - \hat{\pi}) \qquad (5.26)$$

(Inequality (5.26) is the same as inequality (A5.2.11).) With some plausible patterns of bias in substitution possibilities, such as imported pesticides substituting for agricultural land or imported petroleum products enhancing the output of a blast-furnace discussed in the numerical example given by Ramaswamy and Srinivasan (1971), it is possible that $\hat{X}_2 > \hat{R}^e > \hat{L}^e > \hat{X}_1$. The labour-intensive commodity 1 is protected as before, but cheapening the intermediate input can lead to an increase in the use of both the intermediate input and an effective increase in the endowment of the resource relative to labour and a decline in the output of $X_1$ relative to $X_2$. However, real wages still rise because of the increased productivity of the additional intermediate input.

The possible perverse effects of a protective structure on resource allocation have not prevented generation and use of estimates of effective protection for trade policy analysis in many countries. However, Woodland (1982, page 321) has shown that there remains an average statistical relationship calculated over many industries and the resource-reallocative effects of a tariff structure. The alternative to using the available information as an average relationship, which provides a rough guide to the resource-reallocative effects of a protective structure, is to argue the case for the reform on general efficiency grounds and to argue that it is both beyond the capacity and the scope of governments to be concerned with the fine tuning of the resource-reallocative effects of a protective structure. These issues are taken up in Chapter 8.

## 5.4 DYNAMIC MODELS OF TRADE AND GROWTH

### 5.4.1 The open two-sector dynamic H–O–S growth model

The simplest two-sector neo-classical growth model has a capital and a consumption commodity. For convenience, commodity 1 will be treated as the capital good and commodity 2 as the consumption good. The main change in the dynamic context is that the all-purpose fixed resource $R$, the second factor of production in the static $2 \times 2$ H–O–S model, is dropped in the dynamic model and a capital good which can be produced within the economy is introduced in its place. Time now enters into the model in an essential way in that, in any time period, a decision can be made to increase the flow of future consumption by saving and investing in the capital good in order to expand the capital stock. Thus, in the dynamic two-sector neo-classical model, second primary factor is a produced input, capital, and time preference enters into the consumption-investment decision.

For any given time period, CRS, it is possible to re-write the production functions (4.3) in per-worker terms. Omitting the time subscript, the production functions (4.3) can be rewritten as:

$$x_1 = x_1(k_1/\ell_1)$$

$$x_2 = x_2(k_2/\ell_2) \tag{5.27}$$

where the $x$s are output per worker and the $k$s and $\ell$s are the capital/output and labour/output ratios.

For any given endowments of labour and capital expressed here in terms of a given economy-wide capital/labour ratio $(k/\ell)$, the long-run equilibrium conditions for the economy when both commodities are produced will be exactly the same as in equations (4.4), and it will be useful to bear this in mind throughout the discussion which follows. However, these conditions appear in a slightly different form when the analysis is conducted in per-worker terms, as is shown in Appendix A5.3 and developed intuitively below.

In the case of the small open economy, the world prices of the two commodities $\bar{p}_1$ and $\bar{p}_2$ will be given. Thus, denoting $y$ as income per worker, $i$ as investment per worker and $c$ as consumption per worker, the income and expenditure balance condition can be written as:

$$y = x_1\bar{p}_1 + x_2\bar{p}_2$$

$$= i\bar{p}_1 + c\bar{p}_2 \tag{5.28}$$

It is assumed that the production function in each sector is well-behaved, so that the marginal products of labour and capital are positive and all the second derivatives are negative. The relationship between the capital/labour ratio in each sector and total income per worker valued at world prices can be shown for each sector and for the economy as a whole as in Fig. 5.3. Output per worker for a given time period valued at fixed world prices of

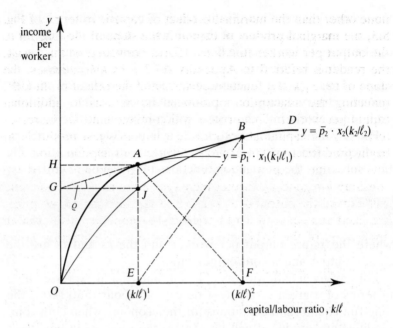

**Fig. 5.3**   Income per worker in the open H–O–S growth model.

consumption and capital commodities are drawn. Output per worker in both sectors increases with $k/\ell$ at a decreasing rate, reflecting the assumption of diminishing returns to additional amounts of capital per worker implied in the requirement that the production functions be well behaved. Notice that the consumption commodity is assumed to be capital intensive, and since the curves only intersect once, it is assumed that there is no factor-intensity reversal.[3] The common tangent $AB$ is drawn and extended to the vertical axis at $G$. The perpendiculars from $A$ and $B$ are also drawn together with the diagonals $AF$ and $BE$. The outer envelope curve or frontier $OABD$, representing the maximal income per worker which can be achieved with trade for different values of $k/\ell$, has some useful properties.

For an initial stock of capital per worker such as $(k/\ell)^0 < (k/\ell)^1$, the economy will specialise in the production of the labour-intensive investment good. If the stock of capital grows faster than the rate of growth of the workforce, capital per worker $k/\ell$ will rise. Intuitively, it can be seen that the increase in output per worker resulting from additional capital per worker is none other than the marginal product of capital. In terms of Fig. 5.3, the marginal product of capital is the slope of the tangent to the output per worker functions. (For a derivation of this result, the reader is referred to Appendix A5.3.) As $k/\ell$ increases, the slope of the $x_1(k_1/\ell_1)$ function declines and the rate of profit falls, reflecting the assumption of diminishing returns to additional capital per worker. This process will continue until $k/\ell$ increases to $(k/\ell)^1$, the capital/labour ratio at which it is just profitable to begin production of the capital-intensive consumption good.

Notice that once it is profitable to begin production of the consumption good $x_2$, further increases in the capital/labour ratio will expand the output of $x_2$ relative to $x_1$; since the output prices are fixed and equal to world prices by assumption, this is just an application of the Rybczynski theorem. Since commodity prices are fixed, factor prices remain unchanged as long as both commodities are produced. With incomplete specialisation, the rate of profit $\varrho$ is given by the slope of the linear segment $GAB$. Income per worker for the economy as a whole, as a function of $k/\ell$, is given by the common tangent $AB$. As total income per worker increases from $EA$ to $FB$, the income per worker of the investment good will decline along the diagonal $AF$ and the income per worker of the consumption good will increase along $EB$. Once $k/\ell$ reaches $(k/\ell)^2$, the economy becomes completely specialised in the production of the consumption good and further increases in $k/\ell$ lead to a monotonically-declining return to capital along $BD$.

The argument so far may now be summarised. In the two-sector, open, neo-classical growth model, the income per worker function $OABD$ has three distinct sections. For $0 < k/\ell < (k/\ell)^1$, the segment OA is relevant and the economy specialises in the production of the labour-intensive investment good. At the point $A$ with $k/\ell = (k/\ell)^1$, it is just profitable to begin production of the consumption good. Over the range $(k/\ell)^1 < k/\ell < (k/\ell)^2$, the linear segment $AB$ is relevant and the economy is incompletely specialised. At the point $B$, production of the investment good is just profitable but output is reduced to zero. For $k/\ell > (k/\ell)^2$, the range $BD$ on the income per worker function is relevant and the economy specialises in the capital-intensive consumption good.

The factor proportions $(k/\ell)^1$ and $(k/\ell)^2$ define the cone of diversification discussed in relation to the factor price equalisation theorem. Over the region of incomplete specialisation, the rate of profit is constant and equal to $\varrho$ in Fig. 5.3. Since the tangent of the angle $AGJ$ is equal to the rate of profit and $GJ$ is the amount of capital per worker when production is at $A$, $AJ$ ($= HG$) must be equal to the amount of profit per worker. Since $AE$ is total income per worker, $EJ$ ($= OG$) must be the wage rate.

It has been assumed so far that it is possible to increase the capital/labour ratio without limit. What determines the limit, or the equilibrium capital/labour ratio? By assumption, the equilibrium or steady state growth requires that the capital/labour ratio is unchanging, and that the amount of investment required to increase the capital stock in line with the growing workforce is equal to the desired savings of households. Suppose that the workforce is growing at some exogenously-specified rate $n$ whilst the capital stock wears out or depreciates each year at a constant rate $d$. There is Harrod-neutral technical change at the rate $\alpha$ per year. Writing the time derivatives of variables as $dK/dt = \dot{K}$ and so on:

$$\dot{K} = I - dK$$
$$\dot{L} = (n + \alpha)L \qquad (5.29)$$

Thus, when $\dot{K} - \dot{L} > 0$, $k/\ell$ will be increasing; when $\dot{K} < \dot{L}$, $k/\ell$ will be decreasing; and $k/\ell$ will remain unchanged when $\dot{K} = \dot{L}$. This latter condition defines the steady state or unchanging capital/labour ratio. As shown in Appendix A5.3.2, this may be rewritten in terms of $k/\ell$ as:

$$(k/\ell) = d(k/\ell)/dt$$
$$= i - (d + \alpha + n) \qquad (5.30)$$

The first term of equation (5.30) is investment per worker. The second term is made up of three separate components. The first is depreciation of the capital stock per worker, the second the rate of growth of capital per worker required to keep pace with the growth of the effective workforce through technical change, and the third the investment per worker required to keep pace with the growth of the workforce itself. The economy will be on a steady state growth path when $(k/\ell) = 0$ or $i = (d + \alpha + n)k/\ell$.

Investment per worker $i$ will be in equilibrium when the desired savings are just equal to the investment requirements for steady state growth. When $d = \alpha = 0$ for convenience, the steady state levels of investment per worker is given by $i = nk/\ell$.

Whatever the initial capital/labour endowment ratio, the economy will gravitate to the steady state growth path when the consumption good is the capital-intensive commodity.[4] Investigation of the stability conditions of the model would be important if the focus of the analysis was on the transition from short- to long-run equilibrium. However, pursuit of this route would add to the technical complexity of the argument without doing much to resolve the problem that the stability conditions of the model depend upon technology and the pattern of trade.

There are a number of different ways in which desired savings are determined. Here, the focus is on rational savings by the representative consumer. This form of the savings function is derived from the assumption that consumers make rational decisions about present and future consumption. The representative consumer maximises the utility derived from the discounted flow of consumption over time. The outcome of the optimising process for the representative consumer is to equate the rate of pure time preference to the rate of profit which, in this context, is the same as the rate of interest.[5] In other words, the familiar equilibrium conditions must prevail whereby the marginal rate of substitution in consumption is equated to the marginal rate of transformation in production, or:

$$\delta = \varrho \qquad (5.31)$$

where $\delta$ is the rate of pure time preference and $\varrho$ is the marginal product of capital or the rate of profit. (A more formal statement of this proposition can be found in Appendix 5.3.)

The equilibrium savings/investment ratio is found by equating the rate of profit to some exogenously-given rate of pure time preference, or:

$$\varrho = \bar{\delta} \qquad (5.32)$$

Figure 5.4 repeats the outer envelope $OABD$ from Fig. 5.3 which shows the income per worker as a function of capital per worker, or $y = y(k/\ell)$. The condition for steady-state savings – investment balance, $i = nk/\ell$, a straight line passing through the origin, is also graphed.

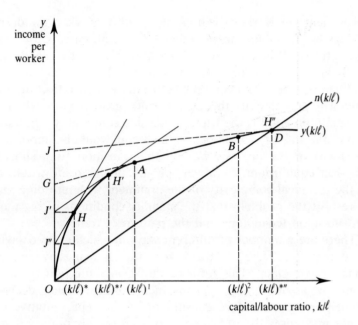

**Fig. 5.4** Equilibrium conditions in the two-sector, open H–O–S growth model.

For $\varrho = \bar{\delta} > n$, such an equilibrium income per worker would be given by the point $H$ where (5.32) holds and the equilibrium capital/labour ratio is $(k/\ell)^*$. When $\varrho = \bar{\delta} = n$, the equilibrium income per worker will be at $H'$ and the steady state capital/ labour ratio $(k/\ell)^{*'}$. Setting $\bar{\delta} = n$ is sometimes known as the biological rate of interest, or more commonly, it corresponds with the Golden Rule of Accumulation.

The Golden Rule of Accumulation requires that each generation bequeaths sufficient capital per worker to sustain the same level of consumption per worker as was possible to produce with inherited capital per worker. (For an introductory discussion of the Golden Rule of Accumulation and its biblical connotation, see H. Jones (1975, pages 208–14).) The Golden Rule of Accumulation can also be illustrated with the aid of Fig. 5.4. For any given capital/labour ratio, the steady state consumption per worker is the difference between total income per worker and steady state investment per worker, or:

$$c = y(k/\ell) - nk/\ell \qquad (5.33)$$

when $d = \alpha = 0$ for simplicity. In terms of Fig. 5.4, $c$ is the vertical distance between the $y(k/\ell)$ and the $nk/\ell$ functions. The Golden Rule of Accumulation requires the selection of $k/\ell$ such that $c$ is maximised, which is achieved for the capital/labour ratio $(k/\ell)^{*\prime}$ where the tangent to the income per worker function $H'$ is parallel to the steady state investment function $nk$. Thus, the tangent $J'H'$ to the income per worker function has a slope $\varrho = n$, the case where the rate of interest is equal to the rate of growth of the workforce.

It will be immediately apparent that the two-sector, open, dynamic neo-classical model will tend to be completely specialised in the steady state equilibrium. The rate of profit with incomplete specialisation, given by the slope of the linear segment $AB$, will only be equal to $n$ or $\bar{\delta}$ by chance. Since by convention $\bar{\delta} > n$ (the pure rate of time preference is assumed to be greater than the biological rate of interest $n$), the equilibrium income per worker will be on or to the left of the point $H'$. When the slope of $AB$ is less than $n$, this implies complete specialisation in the investment good. Alternatively, if the slope of $AB$ was greater than $n$, specialisation would be in the consumption good. Only in the case of some arbitrary aggregate savings ratio will it be likely for the growing economy to be incompletely specialised, an outcome which is dependent on the savings/investment equilibrium producing a steady state equilibrium capital/labour ratio in the range $(k/\ell)^1 < k/\ell < (k/\ell)^2$.

It is not possible to describe the small open economy illustrated in Fig. 5.4 as capital or labour abundant, since there is not a second economy for its capital intensity to be compared with. However, as already noted above, the economy behaves in some important ways like the static H–O–S model; the factor proportions $(k/\ell)^1$ and $(k/\ell)^2$ define the cone of diversification and the output response over the range of capital/output ratios $(k/\ell)^1 < k/\ell < (k/\ell)^2$ is as described by the Rybcyznski theorem. Comparative advantage, however, is now governed by the determinants of the equilibrium capital/labour ratio and not by the initial endowments. In the neo-classical case of rational savings by the representative consumer, a high rate of pure time preference $\delta$ implies a low rate of savings and a low steady state capital/labour ratio whilst a low rate of pure time preference implies a high rate of savings and a high steady state capital/labour ratio. The steady state income per worker is therefore dependent on the rate of time preference; a higher rate of pure time preference will increase the likelihood that the economy will specialise in the labour intensive investment good. In the case of the Golden Rule of Accumulation, comparative advantage will be dependent on the natural rate of growth of the workforce; the higher is $n$, the lower will be the steady state level of income per worker.

It is not convenient to introduce a second economy using the diagrammatic analysis used above, but some of the important qualitative results can be described (for a detailed analysis, see Stiglitz, 1970). If the second economy has identical production functions and identical rates of growth of the workforce but different rates of pure time preference, there will be a steady state equilibrium in which at least one of the two economies will be specialised; this must be the case since by assumption the rates of time preference and therefore the rates of profit and wages are different. The economy with lower steady state capital/labour ratio will have a lower wage than the economy with the higher steady state capital/labour ratio on account of the difference in the rate of profit. This outcome is independent of the initial stocks of capital per worker. If the country with the lower rate of time preference has the lower starting stock of capital per worker, there will be an initial period when this country will export the labour-intensive commodity. However, as the accumulation process proceeds, the pattern of trade will reverse and the country with the lower rate of time preference will end up with the higher steady state level of capital per worker, exporting the capital-intensive commodity regardless of the initial starting conditions. The application of the Golden Rule of Accumulation would imply an equalisation of the rate of profit and factor price equalisation, since by assumption the rate of growth of the workforce in both economies is the same. In this case, the amount of trade in steady state equilibrium will depend on whether or not the capital stock per worker is equalised. In this case, the economy with the higher steady state stock of capital per worker will be the one with the higher initial starting capital stocks. However, there will also be equalisation of the capital stock per worker under autarky in the long-run steady state equilibrium and the two economies will be indifferent between trade and no trade.

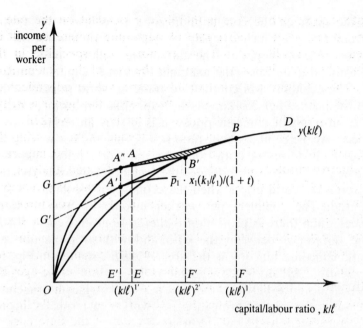

**Fig. 5.5** Protection in the open two-sector H–O–S growth model.

## 5.4.2 Protection in the dynamic context

There will be no static consumption costs of protection in the model described above since there is only one consumption commodity. However, it is a straightforward matter to show how production costs of protection affect the income per worker function and therefore consumption per worker over time.

Suppose there is a tariff (or export subsidy) on commodity 2, the consumption good. This introduces a differential between domestic and world prices; the effect is to lower the domestic price of the investment good from $\bar{p}_1$ to $\bar{p}_1/(1 + t)$ where $t$ is the tariff as a fraction of the world price. Thus, Fig. 5.3 is modified to Fig. 5.5.

In Fig. 5.5, the income per worker function in terms of domestic prices shifts downwards by the amount of the tariff (or export subsidy) as shown. In terms of domestic prices, the per worker income function shifts to $OA'B'BD$. The cone of diversification is now changed to $(k/\ell)^{1'}$ and $(k/\ell)^{2'}$ as shown in Fig. 5.5. The effect of the tariff on the consumption good is to lower the capital/ labour ratio at which complete specialisation in the investment commodity takes place. The fall in the relative price of the investment good raises the marginal product of capital from $\varrho$ to $\varrho'$. The economy will continue to trade at world prices, so that whilst income per worker at the capital/labour ratio $(k/\ell)^{1'}$ is $A'E'$ in terms of domestic prices, it is at $A''E'$ in terms of world prices. At the capital/labour ratio $(k/\ell)^{2'}$, income per worker will be $B'F'$ in terms of both domestic and world prices. The line segment $A''B'$ therefore defines the income per worker function in terms of world prices when the economy is incompletely specialised. The complete per worker income function at world prices when there is protection is therefore given by $OA''B'BD$. The difference between the with and without protection per worker income function is the area $A''ABB'$, shaded in Fig. 5.5 for clarity. At any $k/\ell$ such that $(k/\ell)^{1'} < k/\ell < (k/\ell)^{2'}$, the vertical distance between the two per worker income functions measures the cost of protection per worker in terms of income foregone, measured at world prices.

It is now a straightforward matter to note the cost of protection in the steady state equilibrium. If the economy is completely specialised in either $x^1$ or $x^2$ production before and after the tariff is introduced, there will be no costs of protection. The equilibrium income per worker at world prices will be either to the left of $A''$ or to the right of $B$. There will only be a cost of protection if the economy is incompletely specialised after protection, and the costs per worker for any equilibrium $k/\ell$ such that $(k/\ell)^{1'} < k/\ell < (k/\ell)^{2'}$ can be read off in the manner described above. With rational savings behaviour and an exogenously-given rate of pure time preference $\bar{\delta}$, both economies will normally be completely specialised in the steady state equilibrium in the two-commodity case, and there will be no cost (and no effects) of protection. However, any transitional path from a given stock of capital per worker to the final steady state equilibrium which involves capital/ labour ratios in the interval $(k/\ell)^{1'} < k/\ell < (k/\ell)^{2'}$ will incur a protective cost. A variety of other results from the analysis of protection can be obtained from the model when a second country is added, though in the case of the rational savings assumption the results are uninteresting in the steady state, since both economies will normally specialise. With non-steady state growth in the case of a single country with many consumption and investment commodities for the small and large economy cases (M. A. M. Smith, 1984), the results exactly parallel those already analysed for the static $2 \times 2 \times 2$ case. The effects of protection on the savings rate itself can also be analysed, but there is no presumption that protection will change the pure rate of time preference in one direction or another, if at all. Since there is little added to the essentials of the static and comparative static analysis of protection by the formal dynamic models, the empirical discussion of the effects of protection on trade and growth in Section 9.5 can proceed without further reference to the fully dynamic framework.

### 5.4.3  Wealth holding as a motive for saving

A central part of the modern neo-classical vision of the main-spring of capitalist growth stems from the abstinence or time preference theory of interest. Thus, in the open dynamic H–O–S model discussed above, the long-run steady state equilibrium position is established when the rate of profit is equal to an exogenously-given rate of pure time preference. This is shown by the equilibrium position $H$ in Fig. 5.4, when the rate of pure time preference is equal to the rate of profit.

A very different picture of long-run equilibrium emerges when the stock of capital or wealth enters directly into the individual welfare function along with the flow of consumption over time.

Steedman (1981) argues that even the strongest supporters of the abstinence theory of interest, including Irving Fisher, the most influential proponent of this view (see Fisher, 1931), recognise that the welfare of individual capitalists will be strongly affected by holding wealth, as well as by the future stream of income which may thereby be generated. Steedman (1981, page 226) summarises the motives for wealth holding considered by a range of economists, whose views cross the ideological and political spectrum, as follows.

1.  The desire for self-aggrandisement, social prestige and esteem, and the chance of rising social status.
2.  The desire to achieve political or other power and influence on the basis of wealth.

3. The desire for a manifest measure of one's success in life.
4. The satisfaction from mere possession, or from the process of acquiring wealth.
5. The intrinsic interest in owning a business and extending the field for the exercise of one's abilities.
6. The desire for independence and the power to act freely.

It is intuitively obvious that when wealth is included in the individual utility function, the rate of profit will be lower than would otherwise be the case when there are diminishing returns for additional investment. In fact, when capital is held for the intrinsic benefits derived, including conspicuous display, it may not be as effectively used for the production of future income and consumption. Thus, the additional motive for the accumulation of wealth at the expense of current consumption may increase investment and the rate of growth in the transition to the long-run steady state equilibrium. In terms of Fig. 5.4, the steady state equilibrium may be to the right of $H$, and the whole production function may be lower. During such a transition with consumption growing, and in steady state equilibrium, it may even be possible for the rate of profit to be lower than the rate of pure time preference. These observations are developed more formally in Appendix 5.3.

The above discussion assumes that causality runs from the pure rate of time preference of individuals to the economy-wide rate of profit. The rate of time preference is given exogenously and the rate of profit adjusts to it in the steady state. Such a view is consistent with the neo-classical preoccupation with subjective individualism. An alternative perspective is offered in the next two chapters. Thus, if the rate of profit is determined by mechanisms other than the rate of pure time preference and the nature of individual utility function, then the implied rate of pure time preference in capitalist societies may be higher than the rate of profit. This has important implications for the choice of model for examining comparative advantage and growth in open capitalist economies, for evaluating the intertemporal gains from trade, and more generally in the qualitative judgements made when evaluating alternative patterns of trade and growth.

# APPENDIX 5.1   MAGNIFICATION EFFECTS

## A5.1.1   The standard H–O–S model

The relationship between commodity prices, factor prices and resource re-allocation in the $2 \times 2$ single country H–O–S model set out in this appendix uses the framework set out by Jones (1965). Equations (4.1) in the text, when divided through by $X_1$ and $X_2$, respectively, yield:

$$w\ell_1 + \pi r_1 = p_1$$
$$w\ell_2 + \pi r_2 = p_2 \qquad (A5.1.1)$$

where $\ell_i$ and $r_i$ are defined by $L_i/X_i$ and $R_i/X_i$ for $i = 1, 2$, respectively. Totally differentiating (A5.1.1) and setting $\theta_{\ell_i} = w\ell_i/p_i$, $\theta r_i = \pi r_i/p_i$ and defining $\hat{\ }$ as the relative change or $\hat{w} = dw/w$ and so on, yields:

$$\theta_{\ell_1}\hat{w} + \theta_{\ell_1}\hat{\ell}_1 + \theta_{r_1}\hat{\pi} + \theta_{r_1}\hat{r}_1 = \hat{p}_1$$
$$\theta_{\ell_1}\hat{w} + \theta_{\ell_2}\hat{\ell}_2 + \theta_{r_2}\hat{\pi} + \theta_{r_2}\hat{r}_2 = \hat{p}_2 \qquad (A5.1.2)$$

Now, from the point of view of the individual firm, $\hat{w} = \hat{r} = \hat{p}_1 = \hat{p}_2 = 0$ as factor proportions change, since the firm is a price taker on commodity and factor markets. Substituting into (A5.1.2) yields:

$$\theta_{\ell_1}\hat{\ell}_1 + \theta_{r_1}\hat{r}_1 = 0$$
$$\theta_{\ell_2}\hat{\ell}_2 + \theta_{r_2}\hat{r}_2 = 0 \qquad (A5.1.3)$$

Equation (A5.1.3) says that the cost-minimising firm will always change its input proportions in such a way that the cost-weighted changes sum to zero. Imposing condition (A5.1.3) on (A5.1.2) yields, for the economy as a whole:

$$\theta_{\ell_1}\hat{w} + \theta_{r_1}\hat{\pi} = \hat{p}_1$$
$$\theta_{\ell_2}\hat{w} + \theta_{r_2}\hat{\pi} = \hat{p}_2 \qquad (A5.1.4)$$

Similarly, equality (4.2) in the text can be rewritten in coefficient form as:

$$X_1\ell_1 + X_2\ell_2 = \bar{L}$$
$$X_1 r_1 + X_2 r_2 = \bar{R} \qquad (A5.1.5)$$

Defining factor share coefficients $\psi_{\ell_i} = X_i \ell_i / \bar{L}$ and $\psi_{r_i} = X_i r_i / \bar{R}$ and $\hat{\ }$ as the relative change of a variable for $i = 1, 2$, respectively and dropping the $\bar{\ }$ symbol for convenience, total differentiation of (A5.1.5) and simplification yields:

$$\psi_{\ell_1}\hat{X}_1 + \psi_{\ell_1}\hat{\ell}_1 + \psi_{\ell_2}\hat{X}_2 + \psi_{\ell_2}\hat{\ell}_2 = \hat{L}$$

$$\psi_{r_1}\hat{X}_1 + \psi_{r_1}\hat{r}_1 + \psi_{r_2}\hat{X}_2 + \psi_{r_2}\hat{r}_2 = \hat{R} \qquad \text{(A5.1.6)}$$

Equation (A5.1.6) can be modified to eliminate $\hat{\ell}_i$ and $\hat{r}_i$ for $i = 1, 2$, by finding expressions for the change in input coefficients in terms of changes in factor prices and the elasticity of substitution of the production functions. The elasticities of substitution in production for each industry is defined as:

$$\alpha_1 = (\hat{r}_1 - \hat{\ell}_1)/(\hat{w} - \hat{\pi})$$

and $$\alpha_2 = (\hat{r}_2 - \hat{\ell}_2)/(\hat{w} - \hat{p}) \qquad \text{(A5.1.7)}$$

Combining the first and second equations of (A5.1.3) and (A5.1.7), respectively, equation (A5.1.6) may be written as:

$$\psi_{\ell_1}\hat{X}_1 + \psi_{\ell_2}\hat{X}_2 = \hat{L} + \delta_\ell(\hat{w} - \hat{\pi})$$

$$\psi_{r_1}\hat{X}_1 + \psi_{r_2}\hat{X}_2 = \hat{R} - \delta_r(\hat{w} - \hat{\pi}) \qquad \text{(A5.1.8)}$$

where $$\delta_\ell = \psi_{\ell_1}\theta_{r_1}\alpha_1 + \psi_{\ell_2}\theta_{r_2}\alpha_2$$

and $$\delta_r = \psi_{r_1}\theta_{\ell_1}\alpha_1 + \psi_{r_2}\theta_{\ell_2}\alpha_2$$

Some useful results follow easily once the relative factor intensities are given. Now, when commodity 1 is labour intensive:

$$\ell_1/r_1 > \ell_2/r_2$$

or $$\ell_1 r_2 > \ell_2 r_1 \qquad \text{(A5.1.9)}$$

Multiplying above by $w\pi$ and dividing by $p_1 p_2$, respectively, and using the definition of the $\theta$s yields:

$$(\theta_{\ell_1} - \theta_{\ell_2}) > 0 \qquad \text{(A5.1.10)}$$

When $\hat{p}_1 > \hat{p}_2$, rearranging equation (A5.1.4) yields:

$$(\theta_{\ell_1} - \theta_{\ell_2})\hat{w} > (\theta_{r_2} - \theta_{r_1})\hat{\pi}$$

or $$(\theta_{\ell_1} - \theta_{\ell_2})\hat{w} > (\theta_{\ell_1} - \theta_{\ell_2})\hat{\pi} \qquad \text{(A5.1.11)}$$

or $\qquad\qquad\qquad \hat{w} > \hat{\pi}$ using (A5.1.10)

Thus, when commodity 1 is labour intensive and inequality (A5.1.10) holds, $\hat{p}_1 > \hat{p}_2$ implies $\hat{w} > \hat{\pi}$. But from equation (A5.1.4), when the $\theta$s are positive and $\hat{w} > \hat{\pi}$:

$$\hat{w} > \hat{p}_1 > \hat{\pi}$$

and $\qquad\qquad\qquad \hat{w} > \hat{p}_2 > \hat{\pi} \qquad\qquad\qquad$ (A5.1.12)

Putting both inequalities in (A5.1.12) together yields:

$$\hat{w} > \hat{p}_1 > \hat{p}_2 > \hat{\pi} \qquad\qquad \text{(A5.1.13)}$$

When $\hat{p}_2 > \hat{p}_1$ but commodity 1 remains labour intensive:

$$\hat{\pi} > \hat{p}_2 > \hat{p}_1 > \hat{w} \qquad\qquad \text{(A5.1.14)}$$

When commodity 2 is labour intensive, the opposite results hold.

Changes in factor endowments at given commodity and therefore factor prices yield similar magnification effects. Thus, when commodity 1 is labour intensive, it can be shown by multiplying (A5.1.9) above and below by $X_1X_2$ and $LR$, respectively, and using the definitions of the $\psi$s, that:

$$(\psi_{\ell_1} - \psi_{r_1}) > 0 \qquad\qquad \text{(A5.1.15)}$$

When $(\hat{w} - \hat{\pi}) = 0$ and when $\hat{L} > \hat{R}$, it follows from equation (A5.1.8) that:

$$\hat{X}_1 > \hat{L} > \hat{R} > \hat{X}_2$$

and when $\hat{R} > \hat{L}$:

$$\hat{X}_2 > \hat{R} > \hat{L} > \hat{X}_1 \qquad\qquad \text{(A5.1.16)}$$

The reverse argument holds when commodity 2 is labour intensive.

### A5.1.2   The specific factors model

Magnification effects in the specific factors model can be analysed after a simple modification to the analysis in the previous sector. Adding a superscript to the resource rent variable in equation (A5.1.4) and identifying the specific resources separately in equation (A5.1.8), yields:

$$\theta_{\ell_1}\hat{w} + \theta_{r_1}\hat{\pi}_1 = \hat{p}_1$$

$$\theta_{\ell_2}\hat{w} + \theta_{r_2}\hat{\pi}_2 = \hat{p}_2 \qquad (A5.1.17)$$

and

$$\psi_{\ell_1}\hat{X}_1 + \psi_{\ell_2}\hat{X}_2 = \hat{L} + \psi_{\ell_1}\theta_{r_1}a_1(\hat{w} - \hat{\pi}_1) + \psi_{\ell_2}\theta_{r_2}a_2(\hat{w} - \hat{\pi}_2)$$

$$\hat{X}_1 = \hat{R}_1 - \theta_{\ell_1}a_1(\hat{w} - \hat{\pi}_1)$$

$$\hat{X}_2 = \hat{R}_2 - \theta_{\ell_2}a_2(\hat{w} - \hat{\pi}_2) \qquad (A5.1.18)$$

It is now possible to analyse the responses of the specific factors model to price and resource endowment changes along the lines of the Stolper–Samuelson and Rybczynski theorems, as follows:

1.   Consider $\hat{p}_1 > 0$, $\hat{p}_2 = 0$.

The rise in price for commodity 1 will induce an expansion of commodity 1 output or $\hat{X}_1 > 0$. For this to happen, there must be an increase in the labour-resource ratio in industry 1 and $(\hat{w} - \hat{\pi}_1) < 0$. From the first equation of (A5.1.17) it follows that $\hat{\pi}_1 > \hat{p}_1 > \hat{w}$.

In industry 2, there will be a fall in the labour-resource ratio and a decline in output so that $(\hat{w} - \hat{\pi}_2) > 0$ and $\hat{X}_2 < 0$ from equation (A5.1.18). Thus, from the second equation of (A5.1.17), the magnification effects give an unambiguous result for the specific factor rents; $\hat{\pi}_1 > \hat{p}_1 > w > \hat{p}_2 > \hat{\pi}_2$ and the specific factor rent for industry 1 rises unambiguously in terms of both prices and the specific factor rent for industry 2 falls unambiguously in terms of both prices. However, what happens to real wages depends on consumption proportions, since real wages fall in terms of commodity 1 prices but rise in terms of commodity 2 prices (for further details, see Ruffin and Jones, 1977).

The above argument generalises for the $n$ commodity case in the sense that, for any pair of commodities $i$ and $j$ for which there is an increase or a decrease in the allocation of labour following a price change, it will be true that:

$$\hat{\pi}_i > \hat{p}_i > \hat{w} > \hat{p}_j > \hat{\pi}_j \qquad (A5.1.17a)$$

However, for any pair of commodities for which there is either an increase or a decrease in the allocation of labour, the change in real wages will be ambiguous.

2.   Labour force growth or $\hat{L} > 0$ with $\hat{p}_1 = \hat{p}_2 = 0$.
When the labour force grows, the specific factor to labour ratio must fall in both industries and $(\hat{w} - \hat{\pi}_1) < 0$, $(\hat{w} - \hat{\pi}_2) < 0$. From equation (A5.1.17), it must also be true that real wages fall and real specific factor rents rise in terms of both commodities, and $\hat{X}_1 > 0$ and $\hat{X}_2 > 0$ from equation (A5.1.18).

3.   Growth of both specific factors or $\hat{R}_1 > 0$ and $\hat{R}_2 > 0$.
In this case, the resources to labour ratios must rise in both industries and $(\hat{w} - \hat{\pi}_1) > 0$ and $(\hat{w} - \hat{\pi}_2) > 0$. From equation (A5.1.17) real wages must rise in terms of either price, and real resource rents must fall in terms of both prices. From equation (A5.1.18), $\hat{X}_1 > 0$ and $\hat{X}_2 > 0$.

4.   If either $\hat{R}_1 > 0$ or $\hat{R}_2 > 0$, then ambiguous results follows.

### A5.1.3   The $3 \times 2$ H–O–S model with Hicks-neutral technical change

Suppose that $X_2$ is the importable commodity and that there is Hicks-neutral technical change in the exportable industry $X_1$, so that:

$$\ell_1 = \hat{r}_1 = \hat{\tau}_1$$

In this case:

$$\theta_{\ell_1}\ell_1 + \theta_{r_1}\hat{r}_1 = \hat{\tau}_1$$

since          $\theta_{\ell_1} + \theta_{r_1} = 1$ by definition.

Thus, equations (A5.1.4), when rewritten to include a non-tradable industry $X_3$ and Hicks-neutral technical change in $X_1$, will be:

$$\theta_{\ell_1}\hat{w} + \theta_{r_1}\hat{\pi} = \hat{p}_1 - \hat{\tau}_1$$
$$\theta_{\ell_2}\hat{w} + \theta_{r_2}\hat{\pi} = \hat{p}_2$$
$$\theta_{\ell_3}\hat{w} + \theta_{r_3}\hat{\pi} = \hat{p}_3 \qquad\qquad \text{(A5.1.19)}$$

Now consider the two tradable commodities only. With world terms of trade fixed and Hicks-neutral technical change in the exportable industry, $\hat{p}_1 = \hat{p}_2 = 0$ and $\hat{\tau}_1 < 0$. It then follows from equation (A5.1.11) that:

$$(\theta_{\ell_1} - \theta_{\ell_2})\hat{w} > (\theta_{\ell_1} - \theta_{\ell_2})\hat{\pi} \qquad\qquad \text{(A5.1.20)}$$

When $X_1$ is labour intensive, $(\theta_{\ell_1} - \theta_{\ell_2}) > 0$ and

$$\hat{w} > -\hat{r}_1 > 0 > \hat{\pi} \qquad \text{(A5.1.21)}$$

Similarly, when $X_1$ is resource intensive:

$$\hat{\pi} > -\hat{r}_1 > 0 > \hat{w} \qquad \text{(A5.1.22)}$$

Thus, the Hicks-neutral technical change will raise real wages when the exportable industry is labour intensive and will raise resource rents when it is resource intensive.

The effects of the assumed technical change in the price of the non-tradable $X_3$ can be found by considering the second two equations in (A5.1.19). There are several possibilities:

1. Suppose that $\hat{p}_3 < 0$ and, as before, $\hat{p}_2 = 0$. By altering the numbering in equation (A5.1.11), it follows that:

$$(\theta_{\ell_2} - \theta_{\ell_3})\hat{w} > (\theta_{\ell_2} - \theta_{\ell_3})\hat{\pi} \qquad \text{(A5.1.23)}$$

Now, recall that when $X_1$ is labour intensive, $(\hat{w} - \hat{\pi}) > 0$. Thus, for (A5.1.23) to be true, it must be the case that $\theta_{\ell_2} > \theta_{\ell_3}$. In other words, the import-competing industry $X_2$ has a labour intensity in between the exportable and non-tradable industries.

2. When $X_1$ is resource intensive, $(\hat{w} - \hat{\pi}) < 0$. For (A5.1.23) to hold with $\hat{p}_3 < 0$ and $\hat{p}_2 = 0$ as before it must be the case that $\theta_{\ell_1} < \theta_{\ell_2} < \theta_{\ell_3}$. The non-tradable $X_3$ is now labour intensive and the importable $X_2$ is in between, as before.

3. Now suppppose that $\hat{p}_3 > 0$ with $\hat{p}_2 = 0$, so that inequality (A5.1.23) is modified to:

$$(\theta_{\ell_2} - \theta_{\ell_3})\hat{\pi} > (\theta_{\ell_2} - \theta_{\ell_3})\hat{w} \qquad \text{(A5.1.24)}$$

When $X_1$ is labour intensive, $(\hat{w} - \hat{\pi}) > 0$ in which case, for (A5.1.24) to be true it must be the case that $(\theta_{\ell_3} - \theta_{\ell_2}) > 0$. In other words, when the importable $X_2$ is the most resource-intensive industry in relation to both $X_1$ and $X_3$, the Hicks-neutral technical change will raise wages and the relative price of the non-tradable $X_3$.

4. When $X_1$ is resource intensive, $(\hat{w} - \hat{\pi}) < 0$. With $\hat{p}_3 > 0$ and $\hat{p}_2 = 0$ as in case 3, inequality (A5.1.24) will only be the case when $(\theta_{\ell_2} - \theta_{\ell_3}) > 0$. In this case, the importable industry $X_2$ will be labour intensive in relation to both the exportable and non-tradable industries.

**Table A5.1.1**   Magnification effects of Hicks-neutral technical change in the $3 \times 2$ H–O–S model summarised.

| Factor intensity of industry. Exportable industry $X_1$ | Factor price changes | Non-tradable $X_3$ price changes |
|---|---|---|
| $X_1$ resource intensive compared with $X_2$ and $X_3$ | $\hat{\pi} > 0 > \hat{w}$ | $\hat{p}_3 < 0$ (real depreciation) when $X_3$ most labour intensive $\hat{p}_3 > 0$ (real appreciation) when $X_2$ labour intensive compared with $X_1$ and $X_3$ |
| $X_1$ labour intensive compared with $X_2$ and $X_3$ | $\hat{w} > 0 > \hat{\pi}$ | $\hat{p}_3 < 0$ (real depreciation) when $X_3$ the most resource-intensive industry $\hat{p}_3 > 0$ (real appreciation) when $X_2$ the most resource-intensive industry |

It should be noted that the factor price changes noted will be unchanged when measured in terms of either $p_1$, $p_2$ or $p_3$. This result follows in a quite straightforward way from the magnification effects in which the factor price changes are always greater in absolute value than the absolute value of the induced price change in the non-tradable industry $X_3$.

The results can now be summarised in Table A5.1.1. It can be seen from Table A5.1.1 that there will be a real depreciation when the factor intensity of the non-tradable industry $X_3$ has an extreme factor intensity compared with the exportable industry $X_1$, whilst real appreciation occurs when the importable was an extreme factor intensity compared with the exportable industry $X_1$. For further reading, see Corden and Neary (1982).

## APPENDIX 5.2   EFFECTIVE PROTECTION AND RESOURCE ALLOCATION

The simplest way to model the resource-reallocative effects of protection of intermediate inputs is to include a non-competing intermediate input into the $2 \times 2$ single-country H–O–S model. Thus, equality (4.1) rewritten in coefficient form is modified to:

$$w\ell_1 + \pi r_1 + a_1 p_a = p_1$$
$$w\ell_2 + \pi r_2 + a_2 p_a = p_2 \qquad (A5.2.1)$$

where $a_i$ is the non-competing imported intermediate input coefficient and $p_a$ is the price of the non-competing imported input. If the definition of factor shares $\theta_{\ell_i}$ and $\theta_{r_i}$ is extended to include $\theta_{a_i}$ for the non-competing imported intermediate input, then following the same methodology as in the previous sections, total differentiation of equation (A5.2.1) and noting that $wd\ell_i + \pi dr_i + p_a da_i = 0$ yields:

$$\theta_{\ell_1}\hat{w} + \theta_{r_1}\hat{\pi} = \hat{p}_1 - \theta_{a_1}\hat{p}_a$$
$$\theta_{\ell_2}\hat{w} + \theta_{r_2}\hat{\pi} = \hat{p}_2 - \theta_{a_2}\hat{p}_a \qquad (A5.2.2)$$

If $p_i^v$ is defined as the price of value added for $i = 1, 2$, and if $dp_i^v \equiv (dp_i - a_i dp_a)$, then equation (A5.2.2) can be rewritten as:

$$\theta_{\ell_1}\hat{w} + \theta_{r_1}\hat{\pi} = \hat{p}^{v_1}$$
$$\theta_{\ell_2}\hat{w} + \theta_{r_2}\hat{\pi} = \hat{p}^{v_2} \qquad (A5.2.3)$$

Notice that this definition of $p_i^v$ is not unambiguous, since if:

$$p_i^v = p_i - a_i p_a$$

then $\qquad dp_i^v = dp_i - a_i dp_a - p_a da_i \qquad (A5.2.4)$

Thus, the definition of $dp_i^v$ used in equation (A5.2.3) can be thought of as a linear approximation of the correct definition of $dp_i^v$. For present purposes, the linear approximation will suffice; for further discussion, see Woodland (1982, pages 316–24).

Similarly, the factor and intermediate input supply and demand balance relationships will follow from equality (4.2) re-written in coefficient form:

$$\ell_1 X_1 + \ell_2 X_2 = \bar{L}$$
$$r_1 X_1 + r_2 X_2 = \bar{R}$$
$$a_1 X_1 + a_2 X_2 = X_a \qquad (A5.2.5)$$

Using the definition of $\Psi_{\ell_i}$ and $\Psi_{r_i}$ and extending in an obvious way to $\Psi_{a_j}$, and dropping the $^-$ symbol for convenience, (A5.2.5) when totally differentiated simplified yields:

$$\Psi_{\ell_1}\hat{X}_1 + \Psi_{\ell_1}\hat{\ell}_1 + \Psi_{\ell_2}\hat{X}_2 + \Psi_{\ell_2}\hat{\ell}_2 = \hat{L}$$

$$\Psi_{r_1}\hat{X}_1 + \Psi_{r_1}\hat{r}_1 + \Psi_{r_2}\hat{X}_2 + \Psi_{r_2}\hat{r}_2 = \hat{R}$$

$$\Psi_{a_1}\hat{X}_1 + \Psi_{a_1}\hat{a}_1 + \Psi_{a_2}\hat{X}_2 + \Psi_{a_2}\hat{a}_2 = \hat{X}_a \qquad (A5.2.6)$$

The magnification effects on the price side analysed in Appendix 5.1.1 hold for net or value added prices. Thus, when commodity 1 is labour intensive and $\theta^v_{\ell_1} - \theta^v_{\ell_2} > 0$, then either:

$$\hat{w} > \hat{p}^v_1 > \hat{p}^v_2 > \hat{\pi} \qquad \text{or} \qquad \hat{\pi} > \hat{p}^v_2 > \hat{p}^v_1 > w \qquad (A5.2.7)$$

Similarly, for unchanged factor and commodity prices, $\hat{\ell}_i = \hat{r}_i = 0$ for $i = 1, 2$ and the Rybczynski results follow on the same lines as in Appendix 5.1.1. When commodity 1 is labour intensive, and $(\psi_{\ell_1} - \psi_{r_1}) > 0$, either:

$$\hat{X}_1 > \hat{L} > \hat{R} > \hat{X}_2$$

or: $$\hat{X}_2 > \hat{R} > \hat{L} > \hat{X}_1 \qquad (A5.2.8)$$

However, when commodity and factor prices change, the output response is a little more complicated and does not necessarily follow the direction of the net price or value added price change.

Rewriting the definition of the elasticity of substitution in production from (A5.1.7) and extending to include intermediate inputs in an obvious way yields:

$$\alpha_{r\ell_i} = (\hat{r}_i - \hat{\ell}_i)/(\hat{w} - \hat{\pi})$$

$$\alpha_{ra_i} = (\hat{r}_i - \hat{a}_i)/(\hat{p}_a - \hat{\pi})$$

$$\alpha_{\ell a_i} = (\hat{\ell}_i - \hat{a}_i)/(\hat{p}_a - \hat{w})$$

$$\text{for } i = 1, 2 \qquad (A5.2.9)$$

Following the same steps as carried out in Appendix A5.1.1, equation (A5.2.6) can be rewritten as:

$$\Psi_{\ell_1}\hat{X}_1 + \Psi_{\ell_2}\hat{X}_2 = \hat{L}^e$$

$$\Psi_{r_1}\hat{X}_1 + \Psi_{r_2}\hat{X}_2 = \hat{R}^e$$

$$\Psi_{a_1}\hat{X}_1 \; \Psi_{a_2}X_2 = \hat{X}^e_a$$

where the augumented or effective factor supplies are defined by:

$$\hat{L}^e = \hat{L} + \Psi_{\ell_1}[\alpha_{r\ell_1}(1 - \theta_{\ell_1})(\hat{w} - \hat{\pi}) - \alpha_{ra_1}\theta_{a_1}(p_a - \hat{\pi})]$$
$$+ \Psi_{\ell_2}[\alpha_{r\ell_2}(1 - \theta_{\ell_2})(\hat{w} - \hat{\pi}) - \alpha_{ra_2}\theta_{a_2}(p_a - \pi)]$$
$$= \hat{L} + \delta_{\ell_1}(\hat{w} - \hat{\pi}) - \delta_{\ell_2}(\hat{p}_a - \hat{\pi})]$$

$$\hat{R}^e = \hat{R} - \Psi_{r_1}[\alpha_{r\ell_1}\theta_{\ell_1}(\hat{w} - \hat{\pi}) + \alpha_{ra_1}\theta_{a_1}(\hat{p}_a - \hat{\pi})]$$
$$- \Psi_{r_2}[\alpha_{r\ell_2}\theta_{\ell_2}(\hat{w} - \hat{\pi}) + \alpha_{ra_2}\theta_{a_2}(\hat{p}_a - \hat{\pi})]$$
$$= \hat{R} - \delta_{r_1}(\hat{w} - \hat{\pi}) - \delta_{r_2}(\hat{p}_a - \hat{\pi})$$

and

$$\hat{X}_a^e = \hat{X}_a - \psi_{a_1}[\alpha_{r\ell_1}\theta_{\ell_1}(\hat{w} - \hat{\pi}) - \alpha_{ra_1}(1 - \theta_{a_1})(\hat{p}_a - \hat{\pi})]$$
$$- \Psi_{a_2}[\alpha_{r\ell_2}\theta_{\ell_2}(\hat{w} - \hat{\pi}) - \alpha_{ra_2}(1 - \theta_{a_2})(\hat{p}_a - \hat{\pi})]$$
$$= \hat{X}_a - \delta_{a_2}(\hat{w} - \hat{\pi}) + \delta_{a_2}(\hat{p}_a - \hat{\pi}) \qquad (A5.2.10)$$

where the $\delta$ are defined in an obvious way. Notice that $\hat{L}^e = L$, $\hat{R}^e = R$ and $\hat{X}_a^e = \hat{X}_a$ when there are no price changes.

Now consider the introduction of a subsidy on non-competing imported intermediate inputs. Thus, if $\theta_{a_1} > \theta_{a_2}$ and $\hat{p}_a > 0$, provided commodity 1 is labour intensive, $(\hat{w} - \hat{\pi}) > 0$ from the first of the inequalities (A5.2.7). However, $(\hat{p}_a - \hat{\pi}) \lessgtr 0$, depending on the size and sign of $\hat{\pi}$. It will be possible that $\hat{\pi} > 0$, since with $\hat{p}_a < 0$, there will be more intermediate input per unit of both labour and resource; the marginal productivity of both labour and the resource will rise and $(\hat{p}_a - \hat{\pi}) < 0$.

With $\hat{L} = \hat{R} = 0$, from (A5.2.10), the relationship between $\hat{L}^e$ and $\hat{R}^e$ is given by $\hat{L}^e \gtrless \hat{R}^e$ as:

$$(\delta_{\ell_1} + \delta_{r_1})(\hat{w} - \hat{\pi}) \gtrless (\delta_{\ell_2} - \delta_{r_2})(\hat{p}_a - \hat{\pi}) \quad (A5.2.11)$$

Since the $\delta$s are weighted averages of the substitution elasticities, they will be positive. Thus, when there are no intermediate inputs, and with $(\hat{w} - \hat{\pi}) > 0$, it immediately follows that $\hat{L}^e > \hat{R}^e$. Substituting $\hat{L}^e$ and $\hat{R}^e$ into (A5.2.8) yields the normal Stolper–Samuelson result of $\hat{X}_1 > \hat{X}_2$ when $(\Psi_{\ell_1} - \Psi_{r_1}) > 0$. However, with intermediate imputs, it is readily apparent from (A5.2.11) that with some forms of biased substitution possibilities, and with an uncertain sign for $(\hat{p}_a - \hat{\pi})$, it could easily be that $\hat{R}^e > \hat{L}^e$ even with $(\hat{w} - \hat{\pi}) > 0$. Substitution into (A5.2.8) yields $X_2 > X_1$ when $(\Psi_{\ell_1} - \Psi_{r_1}) > 0$, which is a 'perverse' response to the subsidy on the imported input. This outcome is not just a theoretical possibility. As noted by Ramaswamy and Srinivasan (1971, page 297), there are many cases where such bias in the substitution possibilities is readily conceivable, such as between fertiliser and land in agriculture, or between imported petroleum products and blast-furnace capacity in steel. For further discussion of this result, see Ramaswamy and Srinivasan (1971) and Woodland (1982, pages 316–24).

## APPENDIX 5.3   OPTIMISING CONDITIONS OVER TIME

### A5.3.1   The marginal productivity conditions in per worker terms

For any sector, the CRS production function with labour and a single capital commodity can be written as:

$$X_i = X_i(L_i, K_i) \qquad (A5.3.1)$$

Since (A5.3.1) is homogenous to the first degree as a consequence of the CRS assumption, (A5.3.1) can be rewritten for the aggregate single commodity case by ignoring the subscript $i$:

$$X = L \cdot x(k/\ell) \qquad (A5.3.2)$$

where $k$ and $\ell$ are as previously defined and $x(k/\ell)$ is the production function in per worker terms.

Partially differentiating (A5.3.2) with respect to $K$ and $L$:

$$\varrho = \partial X/\partial K = L \cdot \frac{\partial x(k/\ell)}{\partial(k/\ell)} \cdot \frac{\partial(k/\ell)}{\partial K}$$

$$= x'(k/\ell)$$

$$w = \partial X/\partial L = x(k/\ell) + L \cdot \frac{\partial x(k/\ell)}{\partial(k/\ell)} \cdot \frac{\partial(k/\ell)}{\partial L}$$

$$= x(k/\ell) - x'(k/\ell) \cdot (k/\ell) \qquad (A5.3.3)$$

It is clear from the second equation of (A5.3.3) that the partial derivative of the production function expressed in per worker terms is equal to the rate of profit. The wage is simply the difference between total product per worker and profit per worker. These relationships are expressed graphically in Fig. A5.3.1.

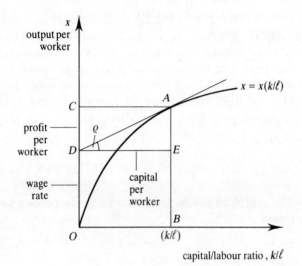

**Fig. A5.3.1**   Output per worker, wage and profit rates.

Output per worker is graphed in Fig. A5.3.1. For a given amount of capital per worker $(k/\ell)$, output per worker is given by the point $A$ and is equal to the distance $AB = CO$. The tangent to the output per worker function is given by $DA$, and the slope of this tangent $AE/DE$ is the rate of profit $\varrho = x'(k/\ell)$. Since the distance $DE$ is the amount of capital per worker, it must be true that $AE$ (equal to $CD$) is the amount of profit per worker, or the term $x'(k/\ell)$ in the first equation of (A5.3.3). Since the first term of this equation is the total product per worker or $AB = CO$ in Fig. A5.3.1, it follows that the wage rate is given by $DO$.

### A5.3.2   The equilibrium growth conditions

The time derivation of the capital/labour ratio $(k/\ell)$ is given by:

$$\frac{d(k/\ell)}{dt} = \frac{1}{L} \cdot \frac{dK}{dt} + \frac{K\partial(1/L)}{\partial L} \cdot \frac{dL}{dt}$$

$$= \frac{1}{L} (\dot{K} - (k/\ell)\dot{L}) \qquad (A5.3.4)$$

Substituting for $\dot{K}$ and $\dot{L}$ from equations (5.29) in the text yields:

$$(k/\ell) = i - (k/\ell)(d + n + \alpha) \qquad (A5.3.5)$$

The Golden Rule of Accumulation can be derived from equation (A5.3.5) by setting $d = \alpha = 0$ for simplicity and noting that $i = (x(k/\ell) - c)$ where $c$ is consumption per worker, yielding:

$$c = x(k/\ell) - (k/\ell) - nk/\ell \qquad (A5.3.6)$$

Since the Golden Rule path is, by assumption, a steady state path, it must be true that $(k/\ell) = 0$. Thus, the problem reduces to finding that $(k/\ell)$ which maximises $c$, or:

$$\frac{\partial c}{\partial (k/\ell)} = x'(k/\ell) - n = 0$$

or: $\qquad\qquad\qquad\qquad\qquad \varrho = n \qquad (A5.3.7)$

### A5.3.3  Optimising conditions in consumption

In this section, it is useful to make the utility function explicit. Consider an individual's intertemporal utility function, assumed to be additive in discrete time of the form:

$$U = U(C_1) + \frac{U(C_2)}{(1 + \delta)} + \cdots \frac{U(C_t)}{(1 + \delta)^t} + \frac{U(C_{t+1})}{(1 + \delta)^{t+1}} \cdots +$$

$$\frac{U(C_T)}{(1 + \delta)^T} \qquad (A5.3.8)$$

where the subscripts refer to the same commodity consumed in different time periods and $\delta$ is the rate of subjective time preference. Consider this function in two time periods $t$ and $t + 1$ where $1 < t < t + 1 < T$. Totally differentiating (A5.3.8) yields for constant utility $dU = 0$ and $dC_i = 0$ for $i = 1, \ldots t - 1, t + 2, \ldots, T$:

$$\frac{\partial U/\partial C_t}{\partial U/\partial C_{t+1}} = \frac{\partial U(C_t)/\partial C_t}{\partial U(C_{t+1})/\partial C_{t+1}} (1 + \delta)$$

$$= \frac{U_{c_t}}{U_{c_{t+1}}} (1 + \delta) \qquad (A5.3.9)$$

Thus, the slope of the intertemporal utility function in two time periods is given by the ratio of the marginal utilities adjusted for the rate of subjective time preference.

Suppose for simplicity that the individual has a constant income stream $\bar{Y}$ and, at any time $t$, a stock of wealth $W_t$ which earns an income at the constant and given rate of profit $\varrho$. Then, in any two time periods, the optimal consumption choice given all other levels of consumption and wealth implies a decision to save, dissave or to consume at a constant level between the two periods, leaving the stock of wealth in periods $t$ and $t + 1$ unchanged. These possibilities can be illustrated in a simple diagram (see Fig. A5.3.2).

In Fig. A5.3.2, the levels of consumption and income in the two time periods $t$ and $t + 1$ are shown on the horizontal and vertical axes. The reader can check that, with a constant income stream $\bar{Y}$ and an initial stock of wealth $\bar{W}_t$, combined with the possibility of borrowing or lending at the given rate of profit or interest $\varrho$, the consumption possibilities frontier for the two time periods will be given by the straight lines $AD'DBC$, $ABC$ or $ABDC$ in Figs A5.3.2(a), (b) and (c), respectively, with a slope equal to $(1 + \varrho)$. Thus, the two-period optimal choice of consumption requires that:

$$\frac{\partial U/\partial C_t}{\partial U/\partial C_{t+1}} = (1 + \varrho)$$

or:

$$\frac{U_{c_t}}{U_{c_{t+1}}} = \frac{(1 + \varrho)}{(1 + \delta)} \tag{A5.3.10}$$

using (A5.3.9). Notice that the first equality in (A5.3.10) has exactly the same form as the optimising conditions in consumption in the static case except that the intertemporal price ratio is given by $(1 + \varrho)$, the ratio of the opportunity cost of consuming now rather than in the next period, because of the possibility of investing at the rate of profit $\varrho$.

Now, when the optional consumption choice is at a point such as $D$ on indifference curve 1 in Fig. A5.3.2(a), $C_{t+1} > C_t$ and there is saving in period $t$ equal to $\Delta W_t$ which is consumed in period $t + 1$. Similarly, consumption choice at the points $B$ or indifference curve 2 and $D$ or indifference curve 3 in Figs A5.3.2(b) and (c), respectively, are for $C_{t+1} = C_t$ and $C_{t+1} < C_t$, respectively. Under normal assumptions concerning marginal utilities which imply a diminishing marginal utility of consumption as consumption grows:

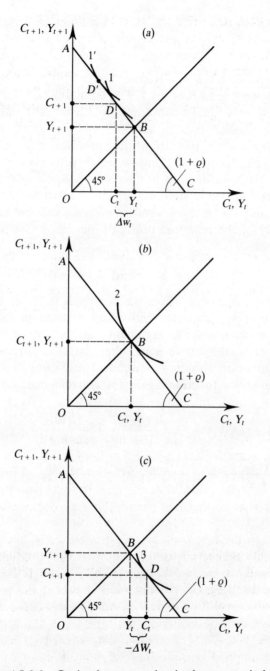

**Fig. A5.3.2**  Optimal consumption in the two-period case.

$$U_{c_t}/U_{c_{t+1}} \gtreqless 1 \quad \text{as} \quad C_{t+1}/C_t \gtreqless 1$$

and $\qquad \delta - \varrho \gtreqless 0 \quad \text{as} \quad C_{t+1}/C_t \gtreqless 1 \qquad$ (A5.3.11)

This is known as the Keynes–Ramsey rule and is the discrete time result corresponding to Ramsey (1928, equation 9). It simply says that, when an individual's consumption is rising, the rate of time preference is smaller than the rate of profit (interest), and when consumption is falling, the rate of time preference is greater than the rate of profit (interest). Only when there is no consumption growth will the rate of time preference be equal to the rate of interest. Thus, in steady state growth, the rate of subjective time preference and the rate of profit (interest) will be the same. Alternatively, if the marginal utility of income is assumed to be constant, then:

$$U_{c_t}/U_{c_{t+1}} = 1 \quad \text{and} \quad \varrho = \delta$$

An interesting argument arises when wealth is included in the utility function specified for individual consumers. Steedman (1981) has summarised the argument that capitalists may wish to accumulate wealth for reasons other than the purpose of the future consumption stream generated. Thus, using the additive form of the utility function again for convenience, (A5.3.8) is rewritten as:

$$U = U(C_1) + U(W_1) + \ldots \frac{U(C_t)}{(1 + \delta)^t} + \frac{U(W_t)}{(1 + \delta)^t}$$

$$+ \frac{U(C_{t+1})}{(1 + \delta)^{t+1}} + \frac{U(W_{t+1})}{(1 + \delta)^{t+1}} + \ldots \frac{U(C_T)}{(1 + \delta)^T}$$

$$+ \frac{U(W_T)}{(1 + \delta)^T} \qquad (A5.3.12)$$

in which utility is derived from the flow of consumption in each period as well as the stock of wealth. Totally differentiating (A5.3.12) and setting $dU = 0$ and $dC_i = 0$ for $i = 1, t - 1, t + 2, \ldots, T$ and $dW_i = 0$ for $i = 1, \ldots, t - 1, t + 1, \ldots, T$ yields:

$$\frac{dC_{t+1}}{dC_t} = U_{c_t} \bigg/ \left( \frac{U_{c_{t+1}}}{1 + \delta} + \frac{U_{w_t}}{\varrho} \right)$$

$$= (1 + \varrho)$$

and
$$\frac{U_{c_t}}{U_{c_{t+1}}} = \frac{1 + \varrho}{1 + \delta} + \frac{1 + \varrho}{\varrho} \cdot \frac{U_{w_t}}{U_{c_{t+1}}} \qquad (A5.3.13)$$

Notice that (A5.3.13) reduces to (A5.3.10) when $U_{w_t} = 0$.

The presence of the wealth term alters the analysis significantly, depending on the relative weight of $C$ and $W$ in the utility function. In terms of Fig. A5.3.2, the utility functions 1, 2 and 3 will rotate and shift in either direction depending on the power and direction of the wealth effect. The normal result in Fig. A5.3.2(a) will be to shift the utility function in a $NW$ direction yielding a new equilibrium at a point such as $D'$ on the new utility function $1'$, indicating that there is capital accumulation for non-consumption reasons. Thus, when there is already accumulation of wealth for the purpose of reallocating consumption through time, it is likely that there will initially be increased accumulation of wealth when the wealth effects are taken into account. More generally, it can be seen from equation (A5.3.13) that, for any given ratio of the marginal utility of income and any given rate of profit, the rate of subjective time preference will be higher than would be the case without taking the wealth effect into account and it is no longer possible to relate the rate of time preference to the rate of profit in the simple way described in (A5.3.11). This means that, other things being equal, taking wealth into account is likely to lead to a heavier discounting of the benefits of future consumption than would otherwise be the case. In particular, it is possible that the LHS of equation (A5.3.13) is greater than one, indicating that consumption is growing, and for the rate of profit to be less than the rate of pure time preference. The consequences of this for the intertemporal gains from trade are discussed in Section 6.2.5.

## NOTES

1. This is not to say that neo-classical economists do not consider other institutional elements which profoundly modify this perspective. For example, Meade (1961) introduces a central monetary authority to co-ordinate investment and savings decisions. Johansen (1960) introduces the state as the co-ordinator of savings and investment decisions using taxes and subsidies as policy instruments.

2. It is not necessary to assume perfect foresight in order to get steady state growth, but the dynamics of any transition path to the steady state path will be dependent upon the assumptions made to deal with the inherently unknowable nature of the future. For a useful discussion of some of these issues see Shackle (1972). Shaw (1984) has a useful elementary discussion of rational expectations and other approaches to the introduction to expectations into economic models.

3. The reason for assuming that the consumption goods industry is capital intensive arises from the stability conditions of the model. These conditions are discussed further below.

4. In the two-commodity, two-country case, stability of the equilibrium also requires that the consumption commodity is capital intensive relative to the investment commodity. This restriction is also required for the single closed economy version of the two-sector dynamic H–O–S growth model. For a useful introductory discussion and heurisitic explanation of this result, see H. Jones (1975, pages 110–13).

5. In this formulation, no allowance is made for the fact that population is also growing through time. Stigliz (1970, page 460) chooses the difference between the pure rate of time preference and the rate of growth of the population as the net rate at which future utility is discounted. This is equivalent to weighting the utility of per capita consumption by the size of the population.

# 6 · NEO-RICARDIAN THEORY

## 6.1 WHICH WAY FROM RICARDO?

### 6.1.1 The neo-Ricardian and neo-classical routes

Findlay (1984, page 190) argues that the open Ricardian trade model discussed in Section 3.5 naturally leads to both the standard H–O–S and the Jones–Samuelson specific factors models discussed in the previous two chapters. There are, however, important qualifications which must be made to this observation since the specific factors model is a short- to medium-run model whereas the open Ricardian growth model and the standard H–O–S model are long-run models.

Ohlin (1933, page 76) is quite clear about what is meant by capital in the long run. He suggests that:

> For the purposes of comparison between countries the capital available in each of them is expressed as a sum of money which represents the cost of reproducing the capital goods in existence, after deduction of depreciation and obsolescence. The price of the use of this capital during a time period is the rate of interest.

The simplest class of models with heterogeneous capital goods, consistent with the concept of capital used by Ohlin, has been developed within the neo-Ricardian trade theory (see Steedman (ed.), 1979, Steedman, 1979a and Pasinetti, 1981). This can be done in a quite straightforward way in a long-run model with just labour and circulating or commodity capital, in which the problems of fixed capital and joint production are ignored. In effect, a single-period snapshot is taken of an economy experiencing proportional growth. When additional primary factors are included, it is not possible to model the economy in steady state growth except under the extreme assumption that all primary factors grow at the same rate, usually set at a zero rate of growth. The neo-Ricardian literature uses the latter class of models as a critical device against the core idea of factor proportions theory, that factor prices are governed by relative factor scarcities.

The chosen modelling compromise within the neo-Ricardian literature is the two-country labour and circulating capital model in which the returns to one of the factors are exogenuously determined. When produced means of production form a large share of world trade, it is argued that a deeper understanding of the relationship between class, income distribution and comparative advantage is obtained through the analysis of the equilibrium characteristics of steady state models than through the neo-classical alternatives. The latter use models of non-steady state growth with some other form of simplification, either through descriptive or through behavioural assumptions, to make the models tractable. For example, the dynamic H–O–S model described in the previous section works with a single capital good and excludes wealth holding from the intertemporal welfare function. The purpose of this chapter is to assess the merits of the neo-Ricardian theory and to lay the foundations for the discussion of trade and growth from a neo-Marxian perspective in Chapter 7.

### 6.1.2  On the definition of equilibrium and on causality in the theory of comparative advantage

The choice of equilibrium concept is closely related to the emphasis which has been given to the determination of income distribution independently from market clearance mechanisms. Thus, Steedman (1979a, page 8) defines the relevant long-period equilibrium for the neo-Ricardian approach as one which:

> ... displays the methods of production, the inputs, the outputs and the prices consistent with the existence of a uniform rate of profit.

This definition of long-period equilibrium only requires consistency with a uniform rate of profit.[1] The more generally-accepted definition treats equilibrium as the outcome of the behavioural characteristics of a model rather than of the outcome of the initial assumptions. For most applications, it is an assumed characteristic of equilibrium in neo-Ricardian theory that the rate of profit will be equalised between branches, and that either the rate of profit or the wage rate are set exogenously without reference to maximising behaviour or market clearance mechanisms. Relative prices and the rate of profit are assumed to be independent of the composition and allocation of outputs. They are constrained to be on the balanced growth path, and the level of activity is not determined. (For a useful discussion, see Walsh and Gram, 1980, Chs 11 and 12.) Garegnani (1983) argues that this definition of equilibrium follows the methodology of classical political economy, so that the long-run equilibrium prices are the classical natural prices which act as 'centres of gravity' around which actual market prices fluctuate. A closely related issue is the choice of the concept of comparative advantage.

The theory of comparative advantage as developed by Torrens and Ricardo requires a comparison of independently-determined autarky prices between potential trading partners. Strict adherence to the orginal concept of comparative advantage implies that the heterogenous stock of capital goods be valued at autarky prices when making statements about the role of the capital stock as a determinant of comparative advantage (see Metcalfe and Steedman, 1981). This leads to a breakdown of the Heckscher–Ohlin theorem in the circulating capital model with a single primary non-produced input, labour. For this and other reasons, the neo-Ricardian trade theory focuses on exogenously determined income distribution and technological differences as the fundamental determinants of comparative advantage.

Ethier (1979, 1981) argues that when the autarky capital stocks are valued at common prices, the Heckscher–Ohlin results reappear. Metcalfe and Steedman conclude from this observation that the Heckscher–Ohlin theorems lose their causal power and can only describe the trading equilibrium. Against this, it can be argued that the transformed theorems do predict the characteristics of the trading equilibrium when the equilibrium is defined as the outcome of the behavioural assumptions of the model. If the redefined equilibrium concept is accepted, the only point of dispute is the legitimacy of redefining the concept of comparative advantage to allow autarky comparisons of the stocks of commodity capital at common prices prior to the opening of trade.

Neither the original nor the altered concept of comparative advantage is an accurate description of the opening of trade between capitalist economies whose profit-maximising agents are suddenly given the opportunity to trade. However, the role of the autarky construct in the theory of comparative advantage is an aid to thought rather than a description of an observable process. Moreover, for the most part, only with-trade situations are observable and empirical tests of any theory of comparative advantage must rely on observation of the characteristics of the trading equilibrium (see Deardorff, 1984, for discussion). In this case, it is not clear why the altered concept of comparative advantage is unacceptable.

### 6.1.3 An analytical Marxian perspective

The approach to modelling capitalist economies exemplified by the neo-Ricardian trade theory has also been criticised by Roemer (1981, Section 1.2). In his typical model of a capitalist economy, Roemer constrains the level of output for any particular capitalist by their initial endowment of capital goods. When added up for the economy as a whole, and when there is no fixed capital, this is just the Ricardian wages fund augumented by the stock of intermediate inputs required during the period of production. The initial endowment of capital goods held by workers is by assumption equal to zero. Maximisation of income over a finite time period generates an equilibrium with a positive rate of profit when wages are exogenously given. The supply of capital is insufficient to drive the rate of profit to zero over the period of production. The level of activity is governed by the constraint on the initial endowment of capital goods for the economy as a whole.

It turns out that, for an equalised rate of profit to be achieved, the initial endowment of capital goods must be suitably close to the proportions required for balanced growth. The valuation of the capital goods can then be made at the equilibrium prices. This equilibrium concept is essentially the same as that used by Ethier (1979) and other neo-classical economists when working with a circulating capital model described in the previous section. The relative merits of circulating capital models for the understanding of trade and growth issues must therefore be decided on grounds other than their use within neo-Ricardian theory as a critical device against H–O–S theory.

The choice of model depends on a judgement about the best way to capture some strategic elements of the problem under analysis, whilst retaining analytical tractability. As a rough empirical approximation, the period over which long-run equilibrium is established might be thought of as 15–20 years (see Marglin, 1984a, b). There are obvious problems with using a steady state model to take a 'snapshot' of a long-run non-steady state equilibrium of a growing economy. First the steady state equilibrium requires that the exogenously-specified rates of growth of primary factors be equal, an uninteresting trivial case. The steady state model only gives a rough approximation to long-run, non-steady state equilibrium when the exogenously specified growth rates will not be equal. Second, the comparative dynamic analysis across steady states does not take into account transitional gains or losses and therefore should be used with care when making welfare judgements.

The merit of using the labour, resource and circulating capital model described in Section 6.4 as the starting point for the analysis of trade and growth is that it captures a role for both produced means of production and resource-based trade, whilst leaving open a possible role for the institutional determination of one of the factor prices. It can also be used as the starting point for comparative dynamic analyses, further developed in Chapter 7. The equilibrium characteristics of the model make it analytically tractable, yet it is sufficiently complex to take into account some strategic characteristics of economies which enter trade such as those described. This aspect of the labour, resource and circulating capital model is further developed in the next chapter, where examples of nineteenth century colonial trade and imperialism, and of twentieth-century North–South trade are discussed.

## 6.2 ALTERNATIVE THEORIES OF INCOME DISTRIBUTION

Typically, a formal economic model can only capture the requirements of physical reproduction over time. The deeper Marxian notion of reproduction through time as embodying institutional and ideological reproduction must be added to any more complete view of the reproduction of an economy in real historical time. It is not surprising then to find a greater interest in theories of income distribution in the non-neo-classical literature, which relies on institutional mechanisms which are inherently difficult to model. Some of those are described in this section.

The separation of the theories of income distribution from the rest of the trade model, or the distribution closure after Sen (1963), rests on the idea that a common set of determinants of relative prices and outputs might be associated with very different theories of distribution. In the case of steady state CRS models discussed over the next two chapters, the separation is complete when relative prices and relative outputs are independent of the level of activity (see, for example, the non-substitution theorem of Metcalfe and Steedman, 1973). These ideas can now be formalised. We have already discussed the macroeconomic equilibrium condition that savings and investment must be equal both *ex post* and *ex ante* for the Ricardian and H–O–S cases in Sections 2.2. and 5.4 respectively. For simplicity,the classical savings function which underlies equation (2.6) is retained. Thus, macroeconomic equilibrium requires that:

$$I = S$$

or
$$g = s_c \varrho \qquad (6.1)$$

The equilibrium condition (6.1) establishes the relationship between the equalised rate of profit and the balanced growth rate. Since the capitalists propensity to save lies between zero and one or $0 \leqq s_c \leqq 1$, the classical savings function is always steeper than the 45° line through the origin shown in Fig. 6.1(a).

The Ricardo–Marx distribution closure sets:

$$w = \bar{w}^a \qquad (6.2)$$

where $\bar{w}^a$ is the autarky wage given in part by convention – the

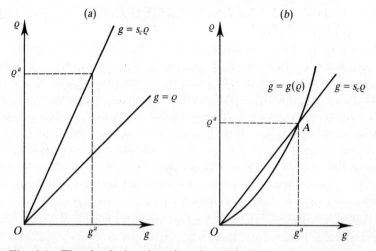

**Fig. 6.1**   The classical savings function with the classical and neo-Keynesian distribution closures.

subsistence wage in classical political economy, or the wage determined by the cost of reproduction of labour power in Marxian political economy. In both the Ricardian and Marxian cases, the real wage is not a biologically-determined subsistence wage, but a conventional wage influenced by historial, cultural and moral components.[2] In the Lewis case discussed in Section 3.3, the real wage is governed by the average product of labour in the subsistence sector. For some purposes, it is enough to treat the average product of labour in the subsistence sector as constant, capturing the essential classical spirit of the Lewis surplus labour model. Equation (6.2) can therefore be referred to as the Ricardo–Marx–Lewis closure rule. In the Ricardian case discussed in Section 2.2, the closed economy or autarky rate of profit $\varrho^a$ is determined once the real wage is given so that the equilibrium growth rate $g^a$ can then be read off from the savings function, as shown in Fig. 6.1(a). The line of causality is clear in that the long-run rate of growth is determined once the rate of profit is known.

An alternative closure to the distribution system from the profit side, sometimes called the Cambridge or neo-Keynesian closure, is based on the hypothesis that the level of investment is an increasing function of the expected rate of profit, or:

$$I = I(\varrho^e) \qquad (6.3)$$

where $\varrho^e$ is the expected rate of profit. The 'animal spirits' of capitalists is often invoked as a determinant of the shape and position of the investment function – the psychology of the investment community.[3] Following Marglin (1984b, pages 122–3), a long-run neo-Keynesian view of the formation of expectations can be specified by setting the expected rate of profit equal to the actual rate of profit, or $\varrho^e = \varrho$. Substituting into (6.3), the long-run neo-Keynesian equilibrium will be as shown in Fig. 6.1(b), providing the investment function intersects the savings function from below at a point such as $A$. The equilibrium rates of profit and growth $\varrho^a$ and $g^a$, respectively, can be read off from the diagram.

The relationship between the equilibrium or warranted rate of growth $g^a$, the rate of growth of the workforce, $n$, and the level of activity, will differ in each case. In the Ricardian model without land, the initial stock of capital will determine the level of activity. The rate of growth of the population, $n$, and therefore of the workforce, will be equal to the warranted rate of growth, $g$, in the long run through the Malthusian population principle. In the Marxian case, with a 'reserve army' of labour and relative surplus population, the initial capital stock will also determine the level of activity. The rate of growth of the workforce and the rate of growth of the population, and the warranted rate of growth and the rate of growth of the workforce, are not connected. This means that $g^a \gtreqless n$ over a long-run period of 15–20 years, an outcome which is possible because the model refers to the rate of growth of the capitalist sector.

When the equilibrium rate of growth of the capitalist sector is greater than the rate of growth of population, or $g^a > n$, labour is being drawn into production from the reserve army – from unemployed workers, from the non-capitalist sectors, from immigration, or from the entry of women into the paid labour force. When the rate of growth of the capitalist sector is less than the rate of growth of population, or $g^a < n$, the reserve army is being replenished. Only by accident will the rate of growth of the capitalist sector be the same as population growth and $g^a = n$. In the neo-Keynesian case, both the initial capital stock and labour supply determine the level of activity, but labour market equilibrium, $g^a = n$, will be achieved only by chance.

Marglin (1984b, page 123) argues that the neo-Keynesian argument that the equilibrium growth rate may be above the rate of growth population, or $g^a > n$, is less convincing than the neo-Marxian rationale, suggesting that a rate of growth up to the rate of growth of population, or $g^a \leqq n$, is a more appropriate representation of the neo-Keynesian case. In the neo-Marxian case, excess supply of wage labour at the going wage rate implies that there is an alternative to wage labour through some form of non-capitalist activities – subsistence agriculture as in the Lewis model, reliance on the informal sector or some kind of petty commodity production, the family, or the welfare state. In the neo-Keynesian case, the rate of profit is determined, somewhat unrealistically, through the investment function without direct reference to the conditions of labour.[4]

Causality runs in very different directions in the Ricardian, neo-Marxian, neo-Keynesian cases, which also differ from the neo-classical analysis. Growth is prior to exchange in the neo-classical view and is determined by biology and exogenously-determined technical change, and the rate of profit is determined by subjective time preference. In the neo-Marxian view, a combination of the wage rate and technology determine the rate of profit which, given the rate of capitalist savings, determines the rate of growth. The rate of growth and the rate of profit are determined through the interaction of production and exchange and the rate of growth can be greater than or less than both the rate of growth of the workforce and the rate of growth of the population for long periods of time. Furthermore, in the neo-Marxian case, all the parameters of the model have a strong element of social determination. Causality is reversed in the neo-Keynesian story, where a combination of the 'animal spirits' and the rate of savings of capitalists determines the rate of profit and the rate of growth, with technological conditions determining the wage rate.

The interaction between the alternative distribution closures, trade and growth is taken up in the next section, where the neo-Ricardian trade model with labour and circulating capital is developed.

## 6.3   LABOUR AND CIRCULATING CAPITAL IN THE TWO-COUNTRY, TWO-COMMODITY CASE

Surprisingly little modification is required to transform the Ricardian model set out in Section 2.2 into a neo-Ricardian model. The essential change is to include a set of fixed intermediate input–output coefficients, $a_{ij}$, along the lines of Section 2.3.3. There is an interest charge on the intermediate inputs or circulating capital advanced and used up during the period of production. To simplify the algebra, it is assumed that wages are not advanced at all, but circulating capital is advanced for the period of production. Both labour and capital used are explicitly deferred so that activity levels can be determined when the distribution closure is chosen. Thus, retaining basic simplifying assumptions of CRS, no externalities, no joint production and no capital intensity reversal, the closed economy model will have the following equilibrium price and quantity relationships.

*Nominal price relations, closed economy*

$$\underset{\text{wages}}{w\ell_1} + \underset{\substack{\text{circulating capital} \\ \text{and profit}}}{(1 + \varrho)(a_{11}p_1 + a_{21}p_1)} \geqq \underset{\text{price}}{p_1}$$

$$w\ell_2 + (1 + \varrho)(a_{12}p_1 + a_{22}p_2) \geqq p_2 \qquad (6.4)$$

*Quantity relations, closed economy*

$$\underset{\text{consumption}}{C_1} + \underset{\text{circulating capital}}{(1 + g)(a_{11}X_1 + a_{12}X_2)} \leqq \underset{\text{output}}{X_1}$$

$$C_2 + (1 + g)(a_{21}X_1 + a_{22}x_2) \leqq X_2 \qquad (6.5)$$

$$\underset{\text{labour demand}}{\ell_1 X_1} + \underset{\text{labour use}}{\ell_2 X_2} = L \qquad (6.6)$$

$$\underset{\text{capital demand}}{k_1 X_1} + \underset{\text{capital use}}{k_2 X_2} = K \qquad (6.7)$$

*Non-negativity constraints*

$w \geqq 0$, $\varrho \geqq 0$, $p_1 \geqq 0$, $p_2 \geqq 0$, $C_1 \geqq 0$, $C_2 \geqq 0$, $g \geqq 0$, $X_1 \geqq 0$, $X_2 \geqq 0$, $L \geqq 0$, $K \geqq 0$

where all the parameters and variables are as previously defined, except the industry capital/output ratios defined by $k_i = (pa_{i1} + a_{i2})$.

Inequality (6.4) is very similar to the equivalent inequality (2.1) for the Ricardian model, except that circulating capital is no longer a wages fund, but circulating capital made up of the intermediate inputs used up during the period of production. The output balance relation (6.5) is the same as for inequality (2.10), except for the allowance for increments in the stock of circulating capital through the introduction of the rate of growth of output, $g$.

With no given supply of labour or initial stock of circulating capital, no demand conditions and no macroeconomic balance conditions, the model is incompletely specified. However, since the output variables do not enter the pricing system it can be treated as an independent sub-system. Thus, rewriting (6.4) as equalities consistent with the full equilibrium and no corner solutions, it can be seen that there are two equations in four unknown distribution variables and relative prices $w$, $\varrho$, $p_1$ and $p_2$. Without loss of generality, the equations can be normalised in terms of one of the prices. There are now two equations in three unknown wages, profits and relative prices $w$, $\varrho$ and $p$, where $w$ is the real wage in terms of commodity 2 and $p = p_1/p_2$. A distribution closure must therefore be chosen to complete the determination of the price side of the model. Similarly, prices do not enter into the determination of the quantity relations (6.5) so that, with CRS, the output disposition inequalities can be rewritten in per worker units. Thus, the relationships between wages, profits and prices on the one hand, and consumption, growth and output proportions on the other, which are consistent with the equilibrium of the economy, can also be illustrated diagrammatically.

First, notice that (6.4) written with equalities can be used to find an expression for relative prices, $p$, in terms of the rate of profit, $\varrho$, and the production parameters:

$$p = \frac{(1 - a_{22}P)\ell_1 + a_{21}\ell_2 P}{(1 - a_{11}P)\ell_2 + a_{12}\ell_1 P} \qquad (6.8)$$

where $$P = (1 + \varrho)$$

Notice that, when there are no intermediate inputs, or $a_{ij} = 0$, (6.8) reduces to:

$$p = p_1/p_2 = \ell_1/\ell_2 \qquad (6.8a)$$

which is none other than the Ricardian case where prices are proportional to the direct labour input coefficients. Alternatively, (6.4) can be used to find an expression for real wages, $w$, in terms of profits or the wage–profit frontier. Thus, the factor price frontier will be:

$$w = \frac{(1 - a_{11}P)(1 - a_{22}P) - a_{12}a_{21}P^2}{(1 - a_{11}P)\ell_2 + a_{12}P\ell_1} \qquad (6.9)$$

From the output relations (6.5) expressed in per worker terms using lower-case symbols, setting $c_1 = 0$ so that commodity 2 is the consumption commodity and $c_2 = c$ is consumption per worker, and using (6.6), output per worker $x_1$ and $x_2$ can be solved out leaving the consumption–growth or $(c - g)$ frontier:

$$c = \frac{(1 - a_{11}G)(1 - a_{22}G) - a_{12}a_{21}G^2}{(1 - a_{11}G)\ell_2 + a_{12}G\ell_1} \qquad (6.10)$$

where $G = (1 + g)$. Notice that wages and *per capita* consumption ($w$ and $c$), and profits and growth ($P$ and $G$) can be interchanged in equations (6.9) and (6.10); in the CRS world, the wages–profit ($w-\varrho$) and consumption–growth ($c-g$) frontiers coincide.

The properties of the wage–profit and consumption–growth frontiers, and the price–profit locus, are analysed in detail in Appendix 6.1. For the closed economy, the frontiers may be graphed as in Fig. 6.2. It is intuitively obvious that relative price, $p$, will be a decreasing function of the rate of profit when commodity 1 is labour intensive, and an increasing function when commodity 1 is capital intensive, as shown in the lower quadrants Figs 6.2(a) and (b), showing an inverse relationship between wages and profits, and consumption and growth, respectively. The wage–profit and consumption–growth frontiers will always be downward sloping, as shown in the upper quadrants of Figs 6.2(a) and (b). However, it is less obvious that the convexity or concavity of the wage–profit and consumption–growth frontiers will also be governed by the relative size of the capital/labour ratios in each sector. Thus, recalling that the industry capital/output ratios are given by:

$$k_i = (a_{1i}p + a_{2i}) \qquad (6.7a)$$

the wage–profit ( $w$–$\varrho$) and consumption–growth ($c$–$g$) frontiers will be:

| | | |
|---|---|---|
| concave to the origin | $k_1/k_2 > \ell_1/\ell_2$ | industry 1 capital intensive |
| convex to the origin | when $k_1/k_2 < \ell_1/\ell_2$ | industry 1 labour intensive |
| a straight line | $k_1/k_2 = \ell_1/\ell_2$ | equal factor intensities (6.11) |

The reason for the variation in the shape of the frontier follows intuition. In each sector, changing the wage rate or the rate of profit has a direct effect which is modified by the indirect effects of the price change for circulating capital purchased relative to the price of the wage good. When sector 1 has the lower capital/labour ratio, a rise in the rate of profit lowers the relative price of the labour-intensive commodity 1 and the price of circulating capital falls relative to the wage good, commodity 2. As the rate of profit increases, the wage decline on account of the direct effect of the increase in the rate of profit is modified by the indirect effect of the falling price of circulating capital relative to wage goods, and the wage rate falls at a decreasing rate, as shown in Fig. 6.1(a). On the other hand, when industry 1 is capital intensive, as the rate of profit increases the direct effects on the wage are increased by the rising relative price of circulating capital compared with the wage good and the wage falls at an increasing rate, as shown in Fig. 6.1(b). The same argument can be repeated, replacing the wage rate with per capita consumption, and the rate of profit with the rate of growth. (The mathematical argument is set out in Appendix 6.1.1.)

The determination of the distribution relations and relative prices for the closed economy, together with the steady state warranted growth rates, can be illustrated with the aid of Figs 6.1 and 6.2. In the case of the classical Ricardo–Marx–Lewis closure, a given autarky wage $\bar{w}^a$ implies an equilibrium autarky rate of profit $\varrho^a$ which can be read off directly from Fig. 6.2(a). This rate of profit implies an equilibrium steady state growth rate $g^a$ which can be read off from Fig. 6.1(a), and an equilibrium level of per worker consumption $c^a$ which can be read off from Fig. 6.2(a). The difference between $c^a$ and $\bar{w}^a$ is capitalist consumption. Finally, given the autarky rate of profit $\varrho^a$, the autarky price ratio

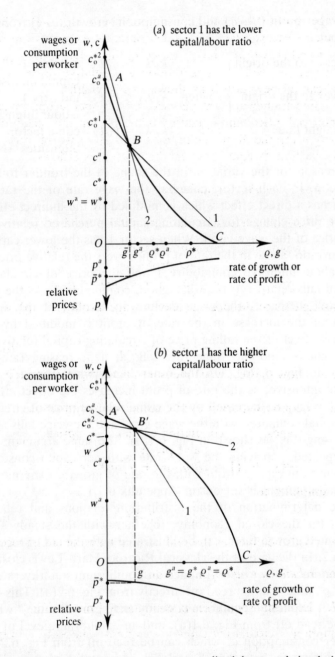

**Fig. 6.2**  The two-country, two-commodity labour and circulating capital model with a single technique.

$p^a$ can be read off from the lower quadrant of Fig. 6.2(a). Similarly, the neo-Keynesian closure determines the equilibrium rates of profit and growth $\varrho^a$ and $g^a$ shown in Fig. 6.1(b). The equilibrium wage, per worker consumption and relative prices $w^a$, $c^a$ and $p^a$ can all be read off as shown in Fig. 6.2(b).

The same framework can be used for the open economy case. The nominal price and quantity relations for the small open economy using the above definitions with given world prices, $\bar{p}_1$ and $\bar{p}_2$, written as equalities, can be set out as follows:

*Nominal price relations, small open economy*

*Case 1.*   Economy specialises in commodity 1 production

| wages | circulating capital and profit | price |
|-------|-------------------------------|-------|

$$w\ell_1 \; + \; (1 + \varrho)(a_{11}\bar{p}_1 + a_{21}\bar{p}_2) \; = \bar{p}_1$$

which simplifies to the open economy wage–profit $(w - \varrho)_1$ frontier:

$$w = (\bar{p} - Pk_1)/\ell_1 \qquad (6.12)$$

where $w$ is now the real wage measured in terms of commodity 2.

*Case 2.*   Economy specialises in commodity 2 production

| wages | circulating capital and profit | price |
|-------|-------------------------------|-------|

$$w\ell_2 \; + \; (1 + \varrho)(a_{12}\bar{p}_1 + a_{22}\bar{p}_2) \; = \bar{p}_2$$

which simplifies to:

$$w = (1 - Pk_2)/\ell_2 \qquad (6.13)$$

where $w$ is also defined as the real wage in terms of commodity 2.

*Quantity relations, small open economy*

*Case 1.*   Economy specialises in commodity 1 production

| consumption | circulating capital | exports | imports | output |
|-------------|--------------------|---------|---------|--------|
| $c_1$ | $+ \;\;(1 + g)a_{11}x_1$ | $+ \;\; e_1$ | | $= \;\; x_1$ |
| $c_2$ | $+ \;\;(1 + g)a_{21}x_1$ | | $- \;\; m_2$ | $= \;\; 0$ |

balance of payments

$$\bar{p}_1 e_1 - \bar{p}_2 m_2 = 0$$

labour demand

$$\ell_1 x_1 = 1$$

(6.14)

where all variables as expressed in per worker terms.

*Case 2.* Economy specialises in commodity 2 production

| consumption | circulating capital | imports | exports | output |
|---|---|---|---|---|
| $c_1$ | + $(1 + g)a_{12}x_2$ | − $m_1$ | | = 0 |
| $c_2$ | + $(1 + g)a_{22}x_2$ | | + $e_2$ | = $x_2$ |

balance of payments

$$\bar{p}_1 m_1 - \bar{p}_2 e_2 = 0$$

labour demand

$$\ell_2 x_2 = 1$$

(6.15)

where all variables are expressed in per worker terms.

Corresponding to the linear open economy wage–profit or $(w-\varrho)$ frontiers (6.12) and (6.13), the open economy consumption–growth or $(c-g)$ frontiers can be found by setting $c_1 = 0$ in equations (6.16) and (6.17) so that commodity 2 is the consumption commodity and solving for *per capita* consumption $c$ in terms of growth $g$, yielding:

*Case 1.* Economy exports commodity 1

$$c = (\bar{p} - Gk_1)/\ell_1$$ (6.16)

*Case 2.* Economy exports commodity 2

$$c = (\bar{p} - Gk_{12})/\ell_2$$ (6.17)

Using a subscript to denote the commodity of specialisation, notice that the open economy wage–profit and consumption–growth frontiers for each pattern of specialisation $(w-\varrho)_1$ and $(c-g)_1$, $(w-\varrho)_2$ and $(c-g)_2$ frontiers, respectively, are identical as in the closed economy case. The open and closed economies may now be combined for the analysis of trade.

The open economy frontiers for specialisation in commodity 1 and commodity 2 are marked 1 and 2 respectively, in Figs 6.2(a) and 6.2(b). These frontiers are defined for given world prices $\bar{p}^*$, intersecting the closed economy frontiers at point $B$ in Fig. 6.2(a) and at point $B'$ in Fig. 6.2(b). At the wage and profit combinations associated with the points $B$ and $B'$, the two economies will be indifferent to trade; this will not be the case for other wage–profit combinations.

Now consider Fig. 6.2(a). The wage–profit frontier is convex to the origin when commodity 1 is labour intensive for all commodity prices, or $\ell_1/\ell_2 > k_1/k_2$. Suppose there is excess supply of labour at a fixed wage which determines both the autarky and the with-trade wage, so that $\bar{w}^a = \bar{w}^*$. The autarky rate of profit $\varrho^a$ and the autarky price ratio $p^a$ can then be read off from the diagram. If the opportunity for trade opens up at given world prices such that $\bar{p}^* > p^a$, it will be profitable to export the labour-intensive commodity 1 in exchange for the capital-intensive commodity 2. At unchanged wages, the free trade rate of profit will increase to $\varrho^*$ as shown in Fig. 6.2(a). What happens to the steady state level of consumption per worker will depend on capitalist savings.

When all capitalist income is invested so that the rate of growth and the rate of profit are equal, per worker consumption will also be given by the real wage. If under autarky all capitalist income is also invested, then autarky growth and profit rates are also equal, the effect of opening trade will be to increase the rate of growth. More generally, with some capitalist consumption so that $0 \leqq s_c \leqq 1$, the opening of trade will affect both the steady state rate of growth and the level of consumption per worker as shown in Fig. 6.2(a). In this case, a result emerges which at first sight may seem surprising.

Consider the case of simple reproduction with zero growth, or $g^a = g^* = 0$. The steady state levels of consumption per worker under autarky and with specialisation in commodity 1 will then be at the points $c_0^a$ and $c_0^{*1}$, respectively, in Fig. 6.2(a). Since the open economy frontier for specialisation in commodity 1 intersects the closed economy frontier $ABC$ from below, the autarky steady state consumption per worker is higher than for free trade or $c_0^a > c_0^{*1}$. More generally, with the capitalists propensity to save between zero and one or $0 \leqq s_c \leqq 1$, the open economy frontier 1 lies below the frontier autarky to be left of the point $B$ and the associated growth rate $\bar{g}$. The difference in the autarky and free trade steady state levels of consumption per worker $(c^a - c^*)$ when commodity 1 is exported is given by the vertical distance between the two frontiers. The consumption–growth frontier 1 lies above the closed economy frontier to the right of $B$ and the free trade steady state level of consumption rises. The possibility that the steady state level of consumption per worker under free trade might be lower than under autarky has been much discussed in the literature and will be taken up in Section 6.7.

Consider now Fig. 6.2(b). The analysis of the opening of trade and the consequences for steady state levels of consumption follow very similar lines to the discussion of Fig. 6.2(a) above. In Fig. 6.2(b), the wage–profit and consumption–growth frontiers are now concave to the origin, so that commodity 1 is now capital intensive relative to commodity 2, and $k_1/k_1 > \ell_1/\ell_2$. In this case, the open economy frontiers, which pass though the closed economy frontier at $B$ for world prices equal to $\bar{p}^*$, have reversed their order. The labour-intensive commodity has the lower slope as before, but this is now commodity 2. Given the neo-Keynesian distribution closure assumed for Fig. 6.2(b), the autarky and free trade rates of profit will be the same so that $\varrho^a = \varrho^*$. Thus, if the autarky price and world price ratio differ, given by $p^a > \bar{p}^*$, the labour-intensive commodity 2 will be exported. As a result of the opening up of trade, the steady state wage will rise from $w^a$ to $w^*$. However, the steady state gains from trade will depend on the rate of growth. Since under the neo-Keynesian closure the rate of profit remains unchanged with the opening of trade and with constant capitalist savings, the rate of growth will also remain unchanged. Steady state consumption per worker will rise or fall with the opening of trade, according to whether or not the with-trade rate of growth is greater than or less than that associated with the point $B'$ in Fig. 6.2(b) or $g^* \gtreqless \bar{g}$ as before.

The above analysis of the pattern of trade and gains from trade per worker was quite independent of the level of activity. However, in the Ricardian and neo-Marxian case, the level of activity is determined by the availability of stocks of commodity capital. Thus, when equation (6.7) is totally differentiated and the real value of the capital stock is held constant, the required condition is that:

$$(a_{11}X_1 + a_{22}X_2)dp = dK \qquad (6.7a)$$

Equation (6.7a) makes it clear that the composition of the capital stock may change whilst the only change in the nominal value of the total capital stock permitted is the compensating change which adjusts for the price change. In other words, equation (6.7a) holds the total real value of the capital stock constant.

The above analysis can be easily extended to deal with trade between two countries by reinterpreting Figs 6.2(a) and (b). First, consider the situation depicted in Fig. 6.2(a), where industry 1 is labour intensive or $\ell_1/\ell_2 > k_1/k_2$. For two countries 1 and 2 with identical techniques of production, profitable trade will only arise if the autarky income distribution is different in the two economies, say with $w^{a_1} > w^{a_2}$ (not drawn). The two different wage rates can be shown on the same diagram and the autarky price ratios can then be read off from the lower quadrant of the diagram. Thus, with commodity 1 relatively cheaper in country 1 or $p_a^1 < p_a^2$, the opportunity to trade will lead to country 1 exporting commodity 1 and country 2 exporting commodity 2. If the free–trade price ratio is given as previously by $\bar{p}^*$, then the open economy wage–profit and consumption–growth frontiers can be defined, shown as the straight lines 1 and 2 passing through the point $B$ as before. With free trade at world prices $\bar{p}^*$, there will be the possibility of either higher wages, or higher profits, or some of both, in each country, respectively. The analysis of the steady state gains (or losses) from trade follows easily from the previous discussion.

Steady state equilibrium requires that both countries grow at the same rate. For free trade growth rate less than $\bar{g}$ shown in Fig. 6.2(a), country 1 exporting commodity 1 will have a lower per worker consumption under free trade compared with autarky. The difference, as before, is given by the vertical distance between the autarky consumption–growth frontier and the open economy consumption–growth frontier. The opposite will be true for country 2, whose steady state per worker consumption is higher under free trade compared with autarky. When the steady state growth rate is greater than $\bar{g}$, country 2 experiences the decline in per worker consumption and country 1 experiences the rise in per worker consumption when free trade and autarky are compared. In the special case where the free trade steady state growth rate is equal to $\bar{g}$, the two economies will be indifferent between trade and no trade. The analysis of the effects of the opening of trade on the level of activity in each country when there is a Ricardian and neo-Marxian wages closure is taken up in Section 6.7, where the intertemporal gains from trade are discussed.

When industry 1 is capital intensive, or $k_1/k_2 > \ell_1/\ell_1$, as in Fig. 6.2(b), the analysis of the opening of trade between two countries with the same techniques of production can proceed on similar lines. When the two countries have different techniques, it is necessary to combine separate diagrams for each country, defining the with-trade wage–profit and consumption–growth frontiers at a common world price ratio. The choice of technique can also be introduced into the analysis, taken up in Section 6.5.

## 6.4  LABOUR, RESOURCE AND CIRCULATING CAPITAL IN THE TWO-COMMODITY CASE

In the model described in this section, a second primary factor land or resource is required in the production of both commodities. All of the same set of simplifying assumptions used in the labour and circulating capital are retained, plus three additional assumptions. First in line with the descriptive assumption made in the Ricardian models discussed in Chapters 2 and 3, commodity 1 is manufactures and commodity 2 is food. Thus manufactures always have a lower resource/labour ratio and a lower resource/capital ratio than food. Second, it is assumed that in the equilibrium solutions considered, that either the rate of profit or the real wage is determined exogenously. In this case, the two remaining distribution variables will be endogenously determined and it is assumed that both associated factors will be fully employed. Finally, the equilibrium growth solutions considered explicitly only relate to simple reproduction, or zero growth.

The addition of a general homogenous resource to the circulating capital model, set out in the previous section, for the special case when the rate of growth is zero leads to a straightforward modification of the price and quality relations (6.4) to (6.7). Rewritten as equalities consistent with the full equilibrium and no corner solutions for the closed economy, the relations are as follows:

wages rent          circulating capital          price
                    and profit

$w\ell_1 + \pi r_1 + (1 + \varrho)(a_{11}p_1 + a_{21}p_2) = p_1$

$w\ell_2 + \pi r_2 + (1 + \varrho)(a_{12}p_1 + a_{22}p_2) = p_2$      (6.18)

consumption    circulating capital        output

$\qquad C_1 + (a_{11}X_1 + a_{12}X_2) = X_1$

$\qquad C_2 + (a_{21}X_1 + a_{22}X_2) = X_2$      (6.19)

labour demand     labour use

$\qquad \ell_1X_1 + \ell_2X_2 = L$      (6.20)

resource demand    resource use

$\qquad r_1X_1 + r_2X_2 = R$      (6.21)

capital demand    capital use

$\qquad k_1X_1 + k_2X_2 = K$      (6.22)

Setting $p = p_1/p_2$ and $P = (1 + \varrho)$ as before, and defining $z = \pi/w$, (6.18) can be solved for relative prices $p$ in terms of the distribution variables $P$ and $z$:

$$p = \frac{(1 - a_{22}P)(\ell_1 + zr_1) + a_{21}P(\ell_2 + zr_2)}{(1 - a_{11}P)(\ell_2 + zr_2) + a_{12}P(\ell_1 + zr_1)} \qquad (6.23)$$

Notice that (6.23) reduces to (6.8) when $z = 0$.

The relationship between the rate of profit, rent and wages can be established through the closed economy wage–profit–rent frontier. This frontier can be defined by solving (6.18) for wages $w$ in terms of profits $P$ and rent $\pi$ when both wages and rent are measured in terms of commodity 2, yielding:

$$w = \frac{(1-a_{11}P)(1-a_{22}P)-a_{12}a_{21}P^2}{(1-a_{11}P)\ell_2+a_{12}P\ell_1} - \pi\frac{(1-a_{11}P)r_2+a_{12}Pr_1}{(1-a_{11}P)\ell_2+a_{12}P\ell_1}$$

$$(6.24)$$

It is quite straightforward to establish the properties of the three-dimensional factor–price frontier described by equation (6.24) and graphed in Fig. 6.3. (For details of the mathematical argument, see Appendix 6.1.)

Equation (6.23) reduces to a linear relationship between wages $w$ and rent $\pi$ when profits are zero or $P = 1$. It is also a linear

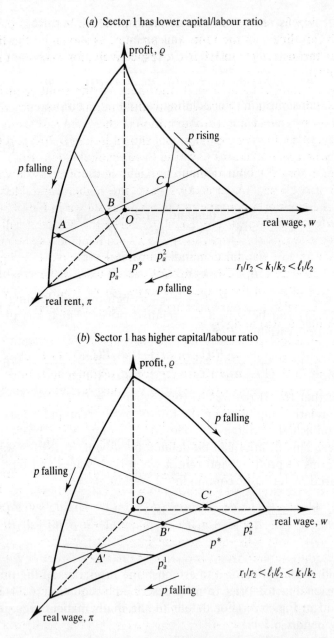

(*a*) Sector 1 has lower capital/labour ratio

(*b*) Sector 1 has higher capital/labour ratio

Sector 1 always has the lower resource/labour and resource/capital ratio

**Fig. 6.3**   Factor price frontier of the labour, resource and circulating capital model with a single technique of production. Sector 1 always has the lower resource/labour and resource/capital ratio.

relationship for any given rate of profit $\varrho$. Thus, both Figs 6.3(a) and (b) are linear in the rent–wages plane, as shown by the lines passing through $ABC$ and $A'B'C'$, respectively, for a constant rate of profit.

When rent is zero or $\pi = 0$, the shape of the frontier in Figs 6.3(a) and (b) will vary according to the ranking of manufactures and food by their capital/labour ratios in the same way as in the labour and circulating capital model shown in Figs 6.2(a) and (b). Thus, when manufactures have the lower capital/labour ratio, the frontier is convex to the origin in the wage–profit plane as shown in Fig. 6.3(a). When manufactures have the higher capital/labour ratio, the frontier is concave to the origin as shown in Fig. 6.3(b). Similarly, when wages are equal to zero, the frontier will be concave towards the origin in the rent–profit plane as shown in Figs 6.3(a) and (b) since manufactures always have the higher capital/resource ratio. This result follows on exactly the same line as the derivation of the shape of the wage-profit frontier shown in Fig. 6.2(b), where labour and wages play the same role as land and rent in Figs 6.3(a) and (b).

The relationship between factor prices and relative commodity prices can be readily established in the same way. Thus, when the rate of profit is zero, the relative price of manufactures must fall as the rent/wage ratio rises, or $p$ falls, since manufactures have the lower resource/labour ratio. Similarly, when the wage rate is zero, the relative price of manufactures must fall as the rent/profit ratio rises since manufactures also have the lower resource/capital ratio. Finally, when rent is zero, the relative price of manufactures will rise as the profit/wage ratio falls when manufactures have the lower capital/labour ratio as shown in Fig. 6.3(a). Similarly, when manufactures have the higher capital/labour ratio, the relative price of manufactures will fall as the profit/wage ratio falls, as shown in Fig. 6.3(b).

An additional important property of the three-dimensional factor-price frontier shown in Fig. 6.3 is that it is made up of a series of linear iso-price lines. This can be seen from the equilibrium price conditions when both commodities are produced so that (6.18) holds as equalities. For any given relative price ratio $\bar{p}$, (6.18) defines a linear relationship between the three factor prices or a plane in $w$, $\pi$ and $\varrho$ space. Thus the surface of the factor price frontier is made up of a series of linear iso-price contours as shown in Figs 6.3(a) and (b).[5] In Fig. 6.3(b), all of the iso-price contours slope in a northwest direction as shown for the three lines marked $p_a^1$, $p^*$ and $p_a^2$ and passing through $A'$, $B'$ and $C'$ respectively. This is a straightforward consequence of the factor-intensity assumptions. When manufactures have the higher capital/labour and capital/resource intensity, a fall in the rate of profit will always lower the relative price of manufactures for any given rent/wage ratio. To hold relative prices constant, the fall in the rate of profit must be associated with a fall in the rent/wage ratio. However, when manufactures have the lower capital/labour ratio as in the case shown in Fig. 6.3(a), a fall in the rate of profit will raise the relative price of manufactures for lower values of the rent/wage ratio. Thus, to hold relative prices constant, a fall in the rate of profit must be associated with a rise in the rent/wage ratio and the iso-price line will slope to the northeast, as shown for low values of the rent/wage ratio in Fig. 6.3(a). For some rent/wage ratio, the iso-price line will be vertical and for higher values of the rent/wage ratio it will slope to the northwest as before.

It is now apparent that the factor price combinations associated with autarky and trade between two countries with identical techniques and demand conditions can be established. Thus, if both countries have the same factor-price frontiers as shown in Fig. 6.3(a) or (b) and the same rates of profit, equilibrium autarky combinations of factor prices for country 1 and country 2 might be as shown for the points $A$ and $C$, respectively, in Fig. 6.3(a) and $A'$ and $C'$, respectively, as shown in Fig. 6.3(b). In both cases, the pre-trade price ratios will be such that manufactures have the lower relative price in country 1, or $p_a^2 < p_a^2$. Thus, the possibility of gainful trade will be open to both countries at some equilibrium price ratio such as $p^*$ and equilibrium factor prices as shown by the points $B$ and $B'$ in Figs 6.3(a) and (b), respectively. In both cases, the opening of trade will be associated with a fall in the rent/wage ratio in country 1 and a rise in the rent/wage ratio in country 2.

An obvious basis for trade in the cases outlined above lies in a combination of different institutional determination of one of the factor prices and different endowment ratios for the remaining factors in the two countries. This is analysed in the next section, where the properties of the labour and circulating capital model, and the labour, resource and circulating capital model, are further developed.

## 6.5   SOME PROPERTIES OF THE CIRCULATING CAPITAL MODELS

There has been an intense debate in the literature over the extent to which the neo-Ricardian trade models yield different results from the timeless static H–O–S model.[6] Some aspects of this debate can be discussed once choice of technique has been added to the models discussed in the previous section. In all of the cases examined, comparable assumptions are made wherever possible and the results are presented using summary diagrams of the same form as Fig. 4.3 used in the discussion of the 2 × 2 × 2 H–O–S model. For consistency of the discussion, commodity 1 will be referred to as manufactures and commodity 2 will be referred to as food for both models.

### 6.5.1   The basic theorems in the labour and circulating capital model

Consider first the case of the circulating capital model with a single primary factor and a choice of many discrete techniques. A technique of production is defined as a combination of CRS fixed proportions activities for the production of each commodity. Such techniques may be compared pair-wise when one of the activities is common to both techiques. When manufactures are the labour-intensive commodity over all possible ranges of wage and profit rates so that there is no factor intensity reversal, each technique must be associated with wage-profit frontiers which are convex to the origin as shown in the upper part of Fig. 6.2(a). The factor price frontier will therefore be made up of the outer envelope of the single technique frontiers. Similarly, for each technique, commodity prices and factor prices will be related in the same way as shown in the lower part of Fig. 6.2(a) and the relative price of manufactures will rise as the profit/wage ratio falls. The commodity price/factor price locus with many techniques will be made up from the lower envelope of the single technique loci, corresponding to the outer envelope of the factor price frontier.[7]

The same set of arguments may be applied to the construction of the factor price frontier and the commodity price/factor price loci when there are many discrete techniques available and manufactures are always capital intensive, as in Fig. 6.2(b). The many technique factor price frontier will be made up of the outer envelope of the single technique frontiers in the upper part of Fig. 6.2(b), and the upper envelope of the single technique commodity price/factor price loci.

Consider now the effect of changes in factor prices or factor intensity. By assumption, factor intensity reversal is ruled out. However, the reswitching of techniques is not. In this case, the capital/labour ratios in each sector may not vary monotonically with the factor price ratio. To see why this is the case, consider the case when manufactures are labour intensive. The maximum total consumption per worker and the total product per worker when the rate of growth is zero is given by the amount $c_0^a$ at the point $A$ on the factor price frontier shown in Fig. 6.2(a). For any given wage such as $\bar{w}^a$, the payment to capital per worker will be given by the difference between total product per worker and the wage, or $(c_0^a - \bar{w}^a)$. This is none other than the value of the capital stock per worker or the capital/labour ratio multiplied by the rate of profit. Thus, the capital/labour ratio is given by the (payments to capital per worker)/(rate of profit) or $(c_0^a - \bar{w}^a)/\varrho^a$, the slope of the line joining the point $A$ and the equilibrium factor price chosen on the factor price frontier. When two techniques are compared at common factor price and commodity price ratios or switch point, it is always the case that one of the activities producing one of the commodities is common to both techniques. It therefore follows that, when comparing the overall capital/labour ratios of two techniques at a switch point, the capital/labour ratio for one of the activities will be unchanged and the change in the overall capital/labour ratio is induced by the change in the capital/labour ratio for the activity producing the other commodity.

Now consider what happens when there is a choice of technique such that technique 1 is chosen at high and low profit/wage ratios and technique 2 is chosen at some in between profit/wage ratio. By assumption, technique 1 always has a higher capital/

labour ratio in manufactures compared with technique 2 and manufactures are always the labour-intensive industry. For the purposes of the argument, it is supposed that the activity producing food is common to both techniques so that all changes in capital/labour ratios refer to the activities producing manufactures only. At an initial low profit/wage ratio, technique 1 is optimal and has a higher capital/labour ratio. As the profit/wage ratio is increased, a switch point is reached where factor and commodity prices are common to both techniques. Technique 2 is associated with a lower capital/labour ratio in manufactures so that as the profit/wage ratio rises and techniques change from 1 to 2, the capital/labour ratio will fall in manufactures and in the whole economy in the same way as in the neo-classical resource and labour model shown in Fig. 4.3.

As the profit/wage ratio is further increased, another switch point is reached, beyond which technique 1 is profitable. Technique 1 is still associated with the higher capital/labour ratio in manufactures compared with technique 2. Thus, as the profit/ wage ratio increases beyond the switch point value and technique 1 is chosen again, there will be a rise in the capital/labour ratio in manufactures as the profit/wage ratio increases. This is counter to the neo-classical case shown in Fig. 4.3. Thus, in general in the two-commodity labour and circulating capital model, there will not be a monotonic relationship between factor intensity and factor price ratios. Furthermore, for a given fixed proportions activity, the capital/labour ratio might rise as the profit/wage ratio rises on account of Wicksell effects.[8] This will happen, for example, when manufactures are labour intensive as in the above example, but food has a higher weight than manufactures in the circulating capital requirements. Thus, as the profit/wage ratio rises and the relative price of food rises, the capital/labour ratio for manufactures valued at equilibrium prices will also rise.

The commodity price/factor price and factor price/factor intensity relationships for the labour and circulating capital model, with choice of many techniques, when manufactures are always labour intensive are summarised in Fig. 6.4. The monotonic relationship between commodity prices and factor prices is shown in the LHS of Fig. 6.4. This has the same shape as the single technique case shown in the lower part of Fig. 6.2(a). The factor price/factor intensity ratios described above are shown in the

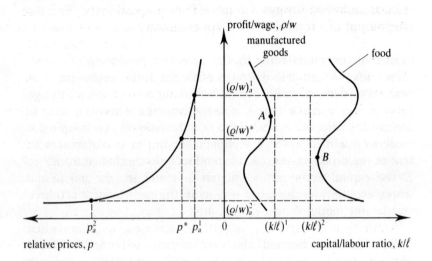

**Fig. 6.4**   Factor proportions, factor and commodity prices re labour and circulating capital model with a choice of techniques.

RHS of Fig. 6.4 with the continuous lines. On account of both reswitching of techniques and Wicksell effects, there are ranges of factor price ratios for which the capital/labour ratios rise in both sectors as the profit/wage ratio rises.

It is now possible to consider the four basic theorems for the labour and circulating capital model.

*The Rybczynski theorem*
At constant commodity and factor prices, the endowment of capital $K$ in equation (6.7) can be treated as a constant, although as the long-run equilibrium output proportions vary, the composition of the capital stock will change. Thus as long as there is no factor-intensity reversal, so that manufactures are always labour intensive, the expansion of the capital stock measured at constant prices with a constant stock of labour will always increase the output of the capital-intensive food and decrease absolutely the output of the labour-intensive manufactures, as shown in Section 4.2.2 for the two-commodity, two-factor labour and resource H–O–S model and in Appendix 6.1 for the circulating

capital case. In proportionate terms, an increase in the capital/ labour endowment ratio will more than proportionately increase the output of the capital-intensive commodity.

*The Heckscher–Ohlin theorem*
Consider two countries with the same production techniques and the same demand conditions which enter into trade. Country 2 always has a higher capital/labour ratio than country 1 at all common factor price ratios. When either the rate of profit or the real wage is exogenously given, profitable trade will arise when the exogenously given factor prices are different. Because re-switching of techniques is possible, it will not be possible to associate the pre-trade factor price differences with the relative factor intensity of the commodities traded, and comparative advantage is governed by differences in income distribution. When factor prices are determined endogenously and each country has given endowments of labour and real capital, a different picture emerges. When the factor endowment ratios are measured at the equilibrium commodity price ratios such as those given by $(k/\ell)^1$ and $(k/\ell)^2$ in Fig. 6.4, the H–O theorem will hold in the quantity form. This follows because, according to the proportionate form of the Rybcynski theorem, at common factor and commodity price ratios, country 1 will always have a greater relative supply of the labour-intensive manufactures compared with country 2 when the demand conditions are the same. In this case there will be an equilibrium with-trade price ratio, such as $p^*$ in Fig. 6.4 at which the relatively labour-abundant country 1 exports the labour-intensive manufactures in exchange for the capital-intensive food exported by the relatively capital-abundant country 2. The cone of diversification measured at autarky prices is given by the vertical lines at the points $A$ and $B$ in the RHS of Fig. 6.4. The endowment ratios such as $(\bar{k}/\ell)^1$ for country 1 and $(\bar{k}/\ell)^2$ for country 2 measured at the equilibrium prices lie within the cone of diversification defined in this way and there will be incomplete specialisation in the trading equilibrium. The H–O theorem will also hold in its price form. The demonstration of this theorem requires taking into account the constraint (6.7a) which defines the sense in which the real stock of capital is held constant and is relegated to Appendix 6.1.

The requirement that the relevant comparisons of autarky

prices and factor intensities be made at common commodity prices modifies the classical concept of comparative advantage, whereby countries open trade without any knowledge of the other country except their autarky price ratios. If the classical concept of comparative advantage is adhered to, as suggested by Metcalfe and Steedman (1981), the H−O theorem may break down in its quantity form. Thus, suppose in Fig. 6.4 that the factor-intensity ratios were closer together without violating the requirement of no factor-intensity reversal at common factor prices. In this case, comparison of the factor intensities at autarky prices could easily reverse. This undermines the H−O theorem in the quantity form when the classical concept of comparative advantage is applied.

*Factor price equalisation theorem*
It is clear from the LHS of Fig. 6.4 that trade at common commodity prices will lead to factor price equalisation, when both countries are incompletely specialised.

*The Stolper-Samuelson theorem*
As in the case of the factor price equalisation theorem, the Stolper-Samuelson theorem is dependent on the monotonic relationship between commodity and factor prices, as shown in the LHS of Fig. 6.4. Thus, if at given world prices, country 2 which imports the labour-intensive manufactures increases the domestic price of manufactures, for example through tariff protection, then the equilibrium profit/wage ratio will fall.

### 6.5.2  The basic theorems in the labour, resource and circulating capital model

The introduction of choice of techniques in the labour, resource and circulating capital model follows on exactly the same lines as in the labour and circulating capital case discussed above. The commodity price/factor price and factor price/factor intensity relationships, when either the rate of profit, or the real wage, is exogenously given can be constructed along the same lines as Fig. 6.4.

In Fig. 6.5(a) the wage rate is exogenously given and in Fig. 6.5(b), the rate of profit is exogenously given. In both cases, the

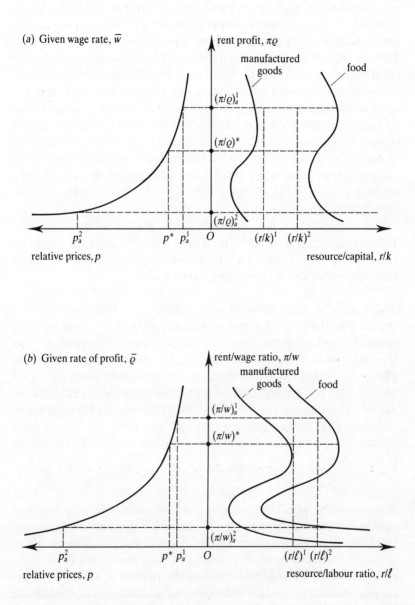

(a) Given wage rate, $\overline{w}$

rent profit, $\pi \varrho$

manufactured goods

food

$(\pi/\varrho)_a^1$

$(\pi/\varrho)^*$

$(\pi/\varrho)_a^2$

$p_a^2$     $p^*$   $p_a^1$   $O$     $(r/k)^1$   $(r/k)^2$

relative prices, $p$            resource/capital, $r/k$

(b) Given rate of profit, $\overline{\varrho}$

rent/wage ratio, $\pi/w$

manufactured goods   food

$(\pi/w)_a^1$

$(\pi/w)^*$

$(\pi/w)_a^2$

$p_a^2$      $p^*$   $p_a^1$   $O$     $(r/\ell)^1$   $(r/\ell)^2$

relative prices, $p$           resource/labour ratio, $r/\ell$

**Fig. 6.5** Factor proportions, factor and commodity prices in the labour, resource and circulating capital model with a choice of technique.

food industry always has the higher resource/labour ratio and resource/capital ratio, but sector 2 may have a higher or lower capital/labour ratio when compared with manufactures. When the wage rate is exogenously given, the monotonic inverse relationship between commodity prices and the rent/profit ratio is as shown in the LHS of Fig. 6.5(a). With both the reswitching of techniques and Wicksell effects, the rent/profit ratios and resource/capital intensities can vary, as shown in the RHS of Fig. 6.5(a). Similarly, the monotonic inverse relationships between commodity prices and the rent/wage ratio is as shown in the LHS of Fig. 6.5(b). With both the reswitching of techniques and Wicksell effects, the rent/wage and resource/labour intensities can vary as shown in the RHS of Fig. 6.5(b). For a fuller exposition refer to Appendix 6.2.

Consider now the four basic theorems for the labour, resource and circulating capital model.

*The Rybczynski theorem*
When the wage rate is fixed, labour use defined by equation (6.20) will be endogenously determined, but the resource and capital use defined by equations (6.21) and (6.22) will be constrained by the respective factor supplies when the capital stock is measured at constant commodity prices. As before, the sense in which the real stock of capital is held constant is given by equation (6.7a). In this case the model reduces to the same form as the labour and circulating capital model discussed in the previous section, with the resource replacing labour as a constraining factor and again the Ryczynski theorem holds, as shown in Appendix 6.1.

When the rate of profit is exogenously fixed, size and composition of the capital stock defined in equation (6.22) will vary endogenously whilst the labour and resource use will be constrained by the respective factor supplies defined in equations (6.20) and (6.21). As long as there is no factor intensity reversal, so that manufactures always have the lower resource/labour ratio, an increase in the amount of the resource with a constant labour supply will always increase the output of the resource-intensive food industry and decrease absolutely the output of the labour-intensive manufactures. This is the same as in the labour and resource H–O–S model discussed in Section 4.2.2 and shown for the circulating capital case in Appendix 6.1.

In both of the above cases, a proportionate change in the endowment ratios for those factors associated with the endogenously-determined factor prices will more than proportionately increase the output of the commodity with the correspondingly higher factor intensity.

*The Heckscher–Ohlin theorem*
Consider two countries with the same production techniques and the same conditions of demand. In order to focus on the role of resource endowments in the determination of the pattern of trade, the exogenously-determined factor price is assumed to be the same in both countries. When the rate of profit is exogenously determined, the H–O theorem will also hold in the quantity form. This can be readily seen from the RHS of Fig. 6.5(b). The relative price of commodities does not influence the resource/labour ratio so that the possibility of gainful trade can be considered with circulating capital valued at the autarky price ratios. In the case shown in Fig. 6.5(b), country 1 has the lower resource/labour endowment ratio and the higher rent/wage ratio compared with country 2. Country 1 exports manufactures with the lower resource/labour intensity in return for food with the higher resource/labour intensity.

However, the H–O theorem does not hold in the price form in either case. This can be seen by noting that for any given pattern of pre-trade relative commodity price differences between countries could be associated with a lower or higher factor price ratios. This is not immediately obvious from Fig. 6.5(a) but the reader can readily check that this is possible in Fig. 6.5(b). However, once trade is opened, a trading equilibrium will be established with country 1 always having an excess supply of the labour-intensive commodity 1 compared with country 2 at common trading prices in both cases.

*Factor price equalisation*
In the LHS of Figs 6.5(a) and (b), there is a monotonic relationship between commodity prices and the endogenously-determined factor prices. Thus, when the exogenously-determined factor prices are the same in both countries, and when there is incomplete specialisation, trade at common commodity prices will lead to factor price equalisation.

*The Stolper–Samuelson theorem*
The monotonic relationship between commodity prices and endogenously-determined factor prices guarantees that the Stolper–Samuelson theorem will also hold. A rise in the relative price of commodity 1 will raise the returns to the factor which is used intensively in commodity 1 production.

The two-country, two-commodity labour, resource and circulating capital model illustrates how the stock of the primary factor with an exogenously-determined price has no role in determining the pattern of trade when the exogenously-determined factor price is common to both countries. However, the fact that there are now multiple equilibria, leading to a breakdown of the Heckscher–Ohlin theorem in its price form, would not seem to justify the conclusions drawn by the neo-Ricardian writers, namely that factor endowments theory does not provide a useful theory of comparative advantage. Rather, what has been illustrated is that in both the labour and circulating capital and the labour, resource and circulating capital models, the relationship between factor prices and factor intensity may not be independent of the final equilibrium. This observation simply underlines the care with which one must interpret any model of trade which attempts to capture some of the essential determinants of comparative advantage and the pattern of trade.

### 6.5.3   History and the distribution of income

Whilst the exact specification of the distribution closures varies widely in the literature, at least part of the reason for the reluctance of non-neo-classical authors to include market clearance conditions in all factor markets stems from a desire to allow for unspecified or unspecifiable but powerful social forces such as class struggle or monopoly power to have an independent role in determining the distribution of income in any particular long-run period. In the labour, resource and circulating capital model, the failure of factor prices to reflect factor scarcities was cited as a major reason for abandoning the H–O–S framework. This aspect of the neo-Ricardian approach has long been criticised by neo-classical authors, and some Marxists, for example Rowthorn (1974), who expressed some puzzlement that the neo-Ricardian tradition remained wedded to the idea that supply and demand had no role in the determination of the distribution of income.

One possible reconciliation of the polar positions represented here by the neo-classical and neo-Ricardian positions relies on a combination of historical determinants and supply and demand mechanisms. Roemer (1984) argues that there are roughly three positions, as follows:

1. The economic determinist position which argues that the distribution of income is entirely determined by supply and demand. This is, of course, the standard neo-classical proposition.

2. The historicist position which suggests that the description of the relative power and organisation of contending ·classes determine the distribution of income, depending on the particular historical circumstances, overriding market determination.

3. An intermediate position which suggests that market forces may be sufficient to explain the basic trends in the distribution of income, but that the relevant equilibrium may depend on history in the sense of being influenced by particular historical events.

Roemer develops his argument for the intermediate position in relation to the discussion of the distribution of income between wages and rent before and after the Black Death in medieval Europe. He speculates that, in a landlord-peasant economy with two classes of land, each having associated with it a technique of production, there may be three equilibrium positions, only two of which will be stable. One of these will be a low wage equilibrium in which some peasants sell their labour power to the landlords who own the good land, whilst the rest are marginalised in a subsistence peasant economy on the poor land. The second stable equilibrium is characterised by a high wage at which even some of the good land is not utilised. Roemer speculates that the low wage equilibrium characterised the distribution of income prior to the Black Death, whilst after the catastrophe of the Black Death, a hysteresis effect followed. The radical drop in population size led to a shift from the low wage to the high wage equilibrium in Western but not Eastern Europe, due to the differential impact of the Black Death. Subsequent population growth and the course of the distribution of income were dependent on the parameters governing the different equilibrium positions. Roemer makes no particular claim for his model other than the observation that it is consistent with the stylised historical facts and that everything is explained as equilibrium behaviour, after taking into account the historical catastrophe which led to a switch in the equilibrium position for some parts of Europe.[9] History may affect the choice of the equilibrium, and the parameters determining such an equilibrium will take over thereafter.

It was found in the previous section that the relative scarcity of factors whose prices are endogenously determined may not be reflected by relative factor prices in the labour, resource and circulating capital model. Thus, history may affect the choice of equilibrium in the context of the opening of trade or a change in the trading equilibrium. Perhaps more powerfully, the labour, resource and circulating capital model also allows for historical and social forces to have a direct impact on the institutional wage or an exogenously-determined rate of profit. For example, the nineteenth-century emigration of Europeans to the lands of recent settlement set a much higher floor under the real wages in the lands of recent settlement compared with that in the tropical colonies, where the availability of Indian and Chinese coolie labour or African slave labour provided an elastic supply of labour at a much lower wage. These issues are taken up in the next chapter.

## 6.6   COMPLICATIONS REVISITED

Some of the complications to the labour and resource H–O–S model which arise from extensions to include different techniques of production, different patterns of demand, many commodities, factors and countries, and non-traded goods and transport costs, have already been spelt out in Chapter 4. With two important caveats, these extensions can be carried over into the circulating capital models discussed in this chapter.

The first caveat concerns the institutional determination of one or more factor prices. In so far as this is the case, then the number of separate factors which will play a role in determining comparative advantage will be reduced. Thus attention need only focus on the endowments for which factor prices are endogenously determined when examining the basis of trade. For those factors whose prices are exogenously determined, direct attention needs to be given to the determinants of the returns to such factors.

The second caveat concerns the role of specific factors. As the discussion of the Jones-Samuelson specific factors model in Section 4.3.2 made clear, there is some schizophrenia in the literature between treating specific factors as resources (including capital) which are immobile between sectors in the short run, and long-run sector-specific natural or other resources. In the short run, the treatment of all immobile factors as sector specific facilitates the application of the Jones–Samuelson specific-factors model to the analysis of such important problems as the Dutch disease, or more recently the Dutch disease in reverse. However, this is obviously unsatisfactory in the long run, where capital mobility is possible between sectors but where some resources remain sector specific. The danger is that the concept of a specific factor can be overworked, so that it explains everything and nothing. The terms of trade model discussed in the next chapter provides an example of a case where it is useful to introduce specific factors in a long-run model of trade and growth.

Finally, it cannot be emphasised too often that models and theorems which elucidate the properties of models are of interest in so far as they are aids to the understanding of real-world phenomena. In this regard, it is noteworthy that not all of the elaborate theoretical reasons for the breakdown of the standard theorems have empirical relevance. This is perhaps most obvious in the case of the factor price equalisation theorem. In this case, the obvious failure of the theorem is empirical, rather than theoretical, because the initial premises of the theorem are not fulfilled. Above all else, international inequality of incomes is due to the lack of access of poor countries to best practice techniques of production, and to lower levels of skills and training. Nevertheless, it is of considerable interest to know if particular patterns of trade, demand, factor accumulation, technical change and changes in exogenously-determined factor returns contribute to or diminish the equality of returns to factors. In this context, it may be of interest to understand the theoretical conditions under which factor price equalisation could be achieved. Some of these issues will be addressed in Chapter 7.

## 6.7   THE INTERTEMPORAL GAINS FROM TRADE

In the discussion of the two-commodity labour and circulating capital model in Section 6.3, attention was drawn to a possible decline in the steady state level of consumption per worker in the transition from autarky to free trade. Thus, in Fig. 6.2(a), manufactures are labour intensive and $p^a < \bar{p}^*$, so that with simple reproduction and no growth, the opening of trade and specialisation in manufactures production leads to fall in consumption per worker from $c_0^a$ to $c_0^{*2}$. Alternatively, for some other set of autarky prices $p_a^2 > \bar{p}^*$ (not shown on the diagram), the country could have specialised in food production with a steady state consumption per worker $c_0^{*2} > c_0^a$. Superficially, it might appear that the opening of trade resulted in a welfare loss in the first case and a welfare gain in the second case. However, this is not necessarily so when the welfare effects of the transition from autarky are accounted for.

Consider first what happens when trade opens and takes place at world prices equal to the autarky prices. Thus, suppose that the autarky price ratio was the same as the world price ratio $\bar{p}^*$ shown in Fig. 6.2(a), so that the autarky and free trade wage and profit rates are given by $\varrho^a = \varrho^* = \bar{g}$ and $w^a = w^* = \bar{c}$. In this case, the opening of trade does not affect either the wage or the profit rate. Since the wage is unchanged, employed workers will be indifferent between autarky and free trade regardless of the pattern of specialisation. However, when the country specialises in manufactures production at the same level of employment after the opening of trade there may be an initial capital consumption and a loss of future consumption for capitalists. Alternatively, there may be an initial capital outlay in return for an increased consumption stream when the country specialises in food production. On the other hand, if the level of activity is governed by the real endowment of capital as in the neo-Marxian case, there may be an expansion of the level of employment when the country specialises in the labour-intensive manufactures and a fall in the level of employment when there is specialisation in the capital-intensive food industry. It is therefore pertinent to consider the intertemporal gains or losses from the opening of trade for the capitalists in the two cases outlined.

Consider first the standard neo-classical specification of the international social welfare function which includes only the utility derived from the consumption of commodities. Holding a stock of capital derives utility from the future consumption stream obtained. Thus, when there is full employment with the same endogenously-determined factor prices, under both autarky and free trade, there may be a lowering of the economy-wide capital/labour ratio and the release of wealth. With simple reproduction, this could be consumed in the transition from autarky to free trade to specialisation in the labour-intensive manufactures. When the future loss of capitalist consumption per worker is discounted at the rate of profit, the present value of the future loss of consumption exactly offsets the consumption of wealth from the running down of the capital stock. Alternatively, when the opening of trade leads to specialisation in capital-intensive food production, there could be an initial rise in the stock of capital per worker, which is exactly offset by the present value of the increased consumption per worker when discounted at the rate of profit. Finally, there could be no change in the capital stock and the economy remains indifferent to trade. As far as capitalists are concerned, rational behaviour suggests that they will be indifferent between autarky and trade in either commodity, a result which fits with the sensible observation that trade at prices equal to autarky prices will leave both capitalists and workers just as well off as in the initial situation. When autarky prices are different from with-trade prices, there will be overall gains from trade and factor prices will change according to the pattern of specialisation.

The transition argument under simple reproduction is rather different in the neo-Marxian case, when the level of activity is governed by the initial stock of capital. When trade takes place at prices equal to autarky prices and with an unchanged real wage, there will be no change in the rate of profit and capitalists will be indifferent between autarky and free trade as before. If specialisation takes place in the labour-intensive manufactures, there may be an expansion of the level of employment and to that extent, workers will be better off. When specialisation is in the capital-intensive food industry, there is a fall in the level of employment and workers are worse off. Thus, free trade at the autarky prices leaves capitalists just as well off, but the consequences for workers depends on changes in the level of employment. If free trade prices are different from autarky prices, the rate of profit will increase when both commodities enter into the ' wage bundle and when real wages remain unchanged. Capitalists therefore will be better off in both cases. In so far as the rise in the rate of profit leads to an increase in the growth rate, the welfare of workers will be enhanced due to increased employment. In the first case, this is additional to the transitional employment benefits. In the second case, the higher rate of growth of employment will mean a higher level of future employment to be offset against the present transitional losses. These arguments can be illustrated with the aid of some simple diagrams (see Fig. 6.6).[10]

In the case where there is full employment before and after the opening of trade and when the rate of profit remains unchanged with the opening of trade, the argument can be conducted in per worker terms. In Fig. 6.6(a), per worker consumption is shown on the vertical axis and time is shown on the horizontal axis. The per worker consumption streams for autarky and for free trade with specialisation in the labour-intensive commodity manufactures shown by the dashed horizontal lines corresponding to the case set out in Fig. 6.2(a). Suppose that the transition to free trade takes place at the beginning of time period zero, so that consumption per worker drops immediately. Recall that the circulating capital only lasts for a single period of production, so that the increase in consumption available as the capital stock declines with the opening of trade is given by $c_0^{*1} - \Delta k_0^1$, where $\Delta k_0^1$ is change in capital stock per worker. The change in capital stock per worker will be equal to the change in profit per worker/ rate of profit or $(c_0^{*1} - c_0^a)/\varrho^*$. The net increase in consumption per worker in time period 0 is shown by the shaded area. From the beginning of period 1, there is no longer a boost to consumption per worker and the steady state level of consumption declines to $c_0^{*1}$ and the loss of consumption per worker is given by the shaded area from the beginning of time period 1 onwards.

The loss in per capita consumption per period into perpetutity under free trade is $\varrho^* \Delta k_0^1$, with a present value of $\varrho^* \Delta k_0^1/\varrho^* = \Delta k_0^1$ when discounted at the with-trade rate of profit $\varrho^*$. This is exactly equal to the gain of $\Delta k_0^1$ from capital consumption in time period zero, and the two effects exactly cancel out. Similarly, in Fig. 6.6(b), which corresponds to the case shown in Fig. 6.2(b),

(a) Constant employment and specialisation in labour-intensive commodity 1

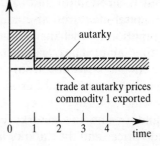

(b) Constant employment and specialisation in capital-intensive commodity 2

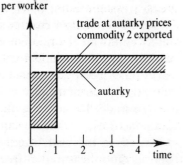

(c) Neo-Marxian case with specialisation in labour-intensive commodity 1

(d) Neo-Marxian case with specialisation in capital-intensive commodity 2

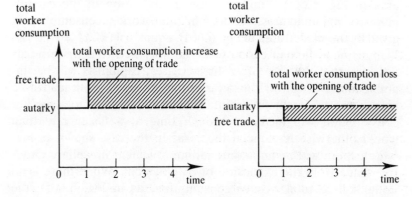

**Fig. 6.6** Intertemporal gains from trade in the two-commodity labour and circulating capital model.

the initial drop in consumption per worker of $\Delta k_0^2$ is equal to $(c_0^{*2} - c_0^a)/\varrho^*$ in time period 0. This is exactly equal to the present value of the gains into perpetutity of the increased consumption derived from the higher captial stock per worker $\varrho^* \Delta k_0^2 / \varrho^* = \Delta k_0^2$. In the first case, capitalists realise their capital gains now in return for future income losses, whilst the opposite intergenerational income transfers occur when the opening of trade raises the capital stock per worker. Since workers and capitalists will be indifferent between autarky and trade and may potentially gain from trade when the with-trade prices are different from the autarky prices, there is an intertemporal gain from the opening of trade from the point of view of both capitalists and workers.[11]

The neo-Marxian case is set out in Figs 6.6(c) and (d). For a given endowment of commodity capital measured at equilibrium with-trade prices, capitalist consumption is unchanged when autarky and free-trade prices are the same. Thus, capitalist consumption is constant through time in the transition from autarky to free trade. However, with specialisation in the labour-intensive manufactures, worker consumption increases by $\bar{w}(\ell_1^*/k_1^* - \ell^a/k^a)\bar{K}$ where $\bar{w}$ is the real wage, $k^a$ and $\ell^a$ and the autarky capital/output ratio measured at free trade prices and the autarky labour/output ratio, $k_1^*$ is the free trade capital/output ratio for manufactures measured at with-trade prices, $\bar{\ell}_1^*$ is the with-trade labour/output ratio for manufactures and $\bar{K}$ is the given capital stock. The increase in total worker consumption is given by the shaded area in Fig. 6.6(c). Similarly, for specialisation in the capital-intensive manufactures, the loss in total worker consumption is given by the shaded area in Fig. 6.6(d), equal to $\bar{w}(\ell_2^*/k_2^* - \ell^a/k^a)\bar{K}$. In both neo-Marxian cases, when autarky and free trade prices differ so that the rate of profit increases, capitalists will be unambiguously better off. In so far as the increased profit leads to a higher rate of growth both capitalist consumption and total worker consumption will increase through time at a faster rate than would otherwise have been the case. In the case shown in Fig. 6.6(c), there will be an additional improvement in welfare under free trade from the expansion of employment. When there is an initial fall in total worker consumption, as in Fig. 6.6(d), the decline in worker income will have to be offset by the benefits of future employment at a higher rate of growth. The total welfare effects for workers will therefore depend crucially on the rate of discount chosen.[12]

The neo-classical interpretation of the result with a constant level of employment is quite straightforward. Recall from Section 5.4 that the country with the lower rate of time preference will be the country which specialises in the capital-intensive commodity, and the country with the higher rate of time preference specialises in the labour-intensive commodity. Thus, the 'impatient's country dissaves and will take the gains from the opening of trade now at the expense of future consumption income, whilst the 'patient' country will save and incur a capital outlay now in return for a future enhanced consumption stream (M. A. M. Smith, 1984, page 306). However, this interpretation of the motives behind the intertemporal reallocation of consumption is very narrow.

The grounds for including wealth holding as a motive for saving in the welfare function, particularly for capitalists, were outlined in Section 5.4.4. The inclusion of wealth holding in the welfare function for capitalists will obviously affect the above arguments about the intertemporal gains from trade. The key to these effects hinges on the relationship between the rate of profit and the rate of subjective time preference in the presence of wealth holding for its own sake.

In the standard case, when there is full employment and the only motive for saving is to alter the time path of consumption, the Keynes–Ramsey rule holds and the rate of profit is equal to or greater than the rate of individual pure time preference as the rate of growth of consumption is equal to or greater than zero, or $\varrho \gtreqqless \delta$ as $\dot{C} = 0$, where $\dot{C}$ is the change in consumption over time as shown in equation (A5.3.11). Thus in the steady state case discussed above, where the rate of growth of consumption is zero, or $\dot{C} = 0$, it is entirely proper to equate the rate of profit with the rate of subjective time preference as is the normal neo-classical procedure.

Once wealth is included in the welfare function, this result is no longer generally true. It is perfectly possible that the rate of profit is equal to, greater than, or less than the rate of pure time preference, or $\varrho \gtreqqless \delta$, depending on the relative marginal utilities of wealth holding compared with consumption (see Appendix 5.3.3 and equation (A5.3.13)). Several possibilities now emerge.

Consider what happens when there are direct wealth effects and the rate of profit is less than the rate of pure time preference and $\varrho < \delta$. When the transition to trade would lower the stock of capital as in Fig. 6.6(a), the rational capitalist may prefer to stick to autarky with a higher level of wealth and forego an increase in present consumption and the future consumption loss is discounted at a rate which is greater than the rate of profit. Similarly, the rational capitalist may have second thoughts about a transition to trade when there is an increase in the capital stock as in Fig. 6.6(b). In this case, the direct wealth effect may be insufficient to offset the present consumption costs when the future consumption benefits are discounted at a rate which is higher than the rate of profit. In both cases, the outcome will be indeterminate, depending on the relative weights of the direct wealth effects compared with consumption in the utility function and the capitalist may forego the potential benefits from the inter-temporal gains from trade.

Second, from the point of view of society, it may be argued that a more appropriate social discount rate is such that the rate of time preference is less than the rate of profit, or $\varrho > \delta$. In this case, it will not be appropriate to take into account wealth effects. This situation could easily arise when the rate of profit is governed by the real wage, as in the neo-Marxian case, or by the investment function as in the neo-Keynsian case (for a discussion of the issues, see Mainwaring, 1984). When the transition is to a higher income stream at the cost of investment now, setting the rate of time preference less than the rate of profit will enhance any estimate of the gains from free trade, as in the example shown in Fig. 6.6(b). When the free trade consumption stream falls, as in the example shown in Fig. 6.6(a), at constant prices the transition to trade will yield present consumption gains and a future consumption loss. When discounted at a rate of time preference lower than the rate of profit there will be higher weight given to future losses and a net loss from the transition to trade when autarky and with-trade prices are the same. When there is a change in relative prices in the transition to trade, there will be an off-setting gain in future per capita consumption, so that the result is indeterminate. In the neo-Marxian case, when specialisation in the labour-intensive manufactures leads to an increase in employment, as in Fig. 6.6(c), the estimated gains from free trade will be enhanced by the choice of a social discount rate lower than the rate of profit. When the transition is to the capital-intensive commodity as in Fig. 6.6(d), the lower rate of time preference will increase the welfare benefits of future gains in employment from a higher rate of growth.

From the point of view of capitalists, the presence or absence of the wealth effect in the intertemporal utility function has dramatic effects on the analysis of the transition from autarky to trade when there is full employment. Welfare-maximising capitalists may choose autarky rather than trade when a more narrowly defined welfare function suggests that there will be intertemporal gains from trade. The effects are less dramatic in the neo-Marxian case. In both sub-cases discussed in Figs 6.6(c) and (d), there is never any disinvestment so that the sharp conflict between wealth holding and consumption never arises. However, insofar as the rate of profit increases with trade, the increased future consumption may increase the propensity to invest and therefore further increase the rate of growth.

The inclusion of direct wealth effects in the welfare function does not affect any of the arguments about the rationality of the agents or the principle of welfare maximisation over time. However, the example suggests that it is generally incorrect to equate the rate of time preference with the rate of profit in steady state equilibrium, and therefore incorrect to associate intertemporal optimality with free trade when the full employment assumption is made. When there is unemployment and the rate of profit is determined by the real wage, the presence of wealth effects adds little to the standard arguments for divorcing the rate of discount from the rate of profit.

## APPENDIX 6.1   FACTOR PROPORTIONS, FACTOR PRICES AND COMMODITY PRICES IN THE CIRCULATING CAPITAL MODELS

The properties of the circulating capital models described in Sections 6.3 and 6.4 for a single technique can be established by totally differentiating equations (6.18) and (6.20) to (6.22) of the text, substituting the rent terms for terms in the rent/wage variable $z$, noting that $P = (1 + \varrho)$ and that $k_i = (pa_{1i} + a_{2i})$:

$$\ell_1 dw + r_1(wdz + zdw) + k_1 dP = (1 - Pa_{11})dp$$

$$\ell_2 dw + r_2(wdz + zdw) + k_2 dP = -Pa_{12}dp \qquad \text{(A6.1.1)}$$

$$\ell_1 dX_1 + \ell_2 dX_2 = dL \qquad \text{(A6.1.2)}$$

$$r_1 dX_1 + r_2 dX_2 = dR \qquad \text{(A6.1.3)}$$

$$k_1 dX_1 + k_2 dX_2 + p(da_{11}X_1 + da_{12}X_2)$$
$$+ (a_{11}X_1 + a_{22}X_2)dp = dK \qquad \text{(A6.1.4)}$$

where all other variables are as previously defined.

Consider first the price equation. For $dz = 0$, one of the equations (A6.1.1) can be used to solve out the relative price terms $dp$ to yield the downward sloping factor price frontier:

$$\frac{dw}{dP} = -\frac{Pa_{12}k_1 + (1 - Pa_{11})k_2}{(l_1 + zr_1)Pa_{12} + (\ell_2 + zr_2)(1 - Pa_1)} \quad (A6.1.5)$$

Similarly, for $dz = 0$, the slope of the price/profit locus can be established by using one of equations (A6.1.1) to solve out the wage terms to yield:

$$\frac{dp}{dP} = -\frac{k_1(\ell_2 + zr_2) - k_2(\ell_1 + zr_1)}{(1 - Pa_{11})(\ell_2 + zr_2 + Pa_{12}(\ell_1 + zr_2)} \quad (A6.1.6)$$

The denominator of (A6.1.6) is always positive, so that the slope of the price/profit locus is governed by the factor intensity condition:

$$\frac{dp}{dP} \gtreqless 0 \quad \text{as} \quad \frac{k_1}{k_2} \gtreqless \frac{\ell_1 + zr_1}{\ell_2 + zr_2} \quad (A6.1.7)$$

Notice that when $z = 0$, (A6.1.6) reduces to a condition governing the capital/labour ratios. Similarly, when $z \to \infty$, $(\ell_1 + zr_1)/(\ell_2 + zr_2) \to (r_1/r_2)$, and (A6.1.6) reduces to a condition governing the capital/resource ratios.

When the rate of profit is constant or $dP = 0$, equations (A6.1.1) are linear and can be used to solve out the wage terms to yield the locus of relative price changes as the rent/wage ratio changes or:

$$\frac{dp}{dz} = \frac{r_1(\ell_2 + zr_2) - r_2(\ell_1 + zr_1)}{(1 - Pa_{11})(\ell_2 + zr_2) + Pa_{12}(\ell_1 + zr_1)} \quad (A6.1.8)$$

Again, the sign of $dp/dz$ is governed by the factor intensity condition:

$$\frac{dp}{dz} \gtreqless 0 \quad \text{as} \quad \frac{r_1}{r_2} \gtreqless \frac{(\ell_1 + zr_1)}{(\ell_2 + zr_2)} \quad (A6.1.9)$$

and $\quad \dfrac{dp}{dz} \lesseqgtr 0 \quad$ for $\quad 0 \lesseqgtr z \lesseqgtr \infty \quad$ when $\quad \dfrac{r_1}{r_2} < \dfrac{\ell_1}{\ell_2}$

Similarly, when the wage rate is constant or $dw = 0$, equations (A6.1.1) can be used to find:

$$\frac{dp}{dP} = \frac{k_1 r_2 - k_2 r_1}{(1 - P a_{11}) r_2 + P a_{12} r_1}$$

and $\quad \dfrac{dp}{dP} < 0 \quad$ when $\quad \dfrac{k_1}{k_2} > \dfrac{r_1}{r_2}$ $\qquad$ (A6.1.10)

The convexity or concavity of the factor price frontier can be established by taking the second derivative of equation (A6.1.5) and substituting for $dp/dP$ from (A6.1.6). Thus, calling the denominator of (A6.1.5) $D$:

$$\frac{d^2 w}{dP^2} = -\frac{dp}{dP} \frac{a_{12}}{D} \qquad (A6.1.11)$$

Thus, the sign of the second derivative of the factor price frontier is opposite to the slope of price/profit locus. The convexity or concavity of the factor price frontier for $dz = 0$ is therefore governed by the factor-intensity conditions in (A6.1.7). Since the consumption–growth frontiers in the labour and circulating capital model have exactly the same form as the factor price frontier when $z = 0$, the same conditions govern the convexity or concavity conditions of the consumption–growth frontiers. Thus, the factor price frontier will be:

concave to the origin $\quad$ when $\quad \dfrac{k_1}{k_2} > \dfrac{\ell_1 + z r_1}{\ell_2 + z r_2}$

convex to the origin $\quad$ when $\quad \dfrac{k_1}{k_2} < \dfrac{\ell_1 + z r_1}{\ell_2 + z r_2}$ $\quad$ (A6.1.12)

a straight line $\quad$ when $\quad \dfrac{k_1}{k_2} = \dfrac{\ell_1 + z r_1}{\ell_2 + z r_2}$

When $dw = 0$, $\pi$ replaces $w$ in (A6.1.11). The labour coefficients disappear and the $z$s cancel in (A6.1.12).

The slope of the iso-price curves can be established by setting $dp = 0$ and using one of equations (A6.1.1) to solve out terms in $dw$ to yield:

$$\frac{dP}{dz} = -\frac{w[r_1(\ell_2 + z r_2) - r_2(\ell_1 + z r_1)]}{k_1(\ell_2 + z r_2) - k_2(\ell_1 + z r_1)} \qquad (A6.1.13)$$

It can be readily seen that the numerator of (A6.1.13) will always be negative on account of the factor-intensity assumptions. Thus the sign of $dP/dz$ will vary with the sign of the denominator so that:

$$\frac{dP}{dz} \gtreqless 0 \quad \text{as} \quad \frac{k_1}{k_2} \gtreqless \frac{\ell_1 + zr_1}{\ell_2 + zr_2} \quad (A6.1.14)$$

Given the factor intensity assumptions that $r_1/r_2 < \ell_1/\ell_2$ and $r_1/r_2 < k_1/k_2$, the slopes of the various functions as graphed in Figs 6.2 and 6.3 for a single technique can be readily established, as $z$ varies between zero and infinity, including the cases when the rate of profit does not vary and the wage rate does not vary. The argument can be extended in a straightforward way to deal with the many technique cases shown on Figs 6.4 and 6.5.

In the many technique case, the cost-minimising set of production coefficients are chosen from the convex set of possible production techniques. For constant prices, these coefficients do not change so that the Rybczynski theorem can be shown to hold from equations (A6.1.2) to (A6.1.4). In the labour and circulating capital case, the displacement of the equilibrium outputs at constant commodity prices as factor supply changes will be given by solving equations (A6.1.2) and (A6.1.4) for the change in outputs:

$$dX_1 = \frac{1}{\ell_1 k_2 - \ell_2 k_1} (k_2 dL - \ell_2 dK)$$

$$dX_2 = -\frac{1}{\ell_1 k_2 - \ell_2 k_1} (k_1 dL - \ell_1 dK) \quad (A6.1.15)$$

thus when
$$\frac{\ell_1}{\ell_2} > \frac{k_1}{k_2},$$

$dK = 0$ and $dL > 0$, $dX_1 > 0$ and $dX_2 < 0$. When $dL = 0$ and $dK > 0$, $dX_1 < 0$ and $dX_2 > 0$ and the Rybczynski theorem holds.

In the labour, resource and circulating capital case, when the wage is given, labour use will not be constrained by the labour supply but the level of output will be constrained by the supply of the resource and capital. Thus, the Rybczynski theorem for changes in $dR$ and $dK$ also holds with the resource replacing the labour constraint in (A6.1.15). Similarly, when the rate of profit is constant, the binding constraints are for labour use and resource use. In this case, (A6.1.15) has the resource replacing capital and the Rybczynski result follows along the same lines as before.

## APPENDIX 6.2   CHOICE OF TECHNIQUE AND THE NET OUTPUT FRONTIER

It remains to investigate the conditions under which the H–O theorem in its price form will hold when there is choice of technique. To achieve this, it is necessary to find the relationship between net outputs and relative commodity prices, interpreting all input coefficients as the cost minimising set chosen from the set of available techniques. The net output constraint for the labour and circulating capital model is given by equations (6.5) and (6.6) in the text, and by (6.19)–(6.22) for the labour, resource and circulating capital case. When the rate of growth is zero, (6.5) and (6.19) will be the same in both cases. Thus, (6.19) can be used in conjunction with varying combinations of equations (6.20) to (6.22) and the real capital stock constraint (6.7a) to yield the desired net output frontier for the two models with different closure rules. Thus, totally differentiating (6.19) and multiplying by prices yields:

$$pdC_1 + dC_2 = [p(1 - a_{11}) - a_{21}]dX_1 + [-pa_{12} + (1 - a_{22})]dX_2$$
$$- (pda_{11} + da_{21})X_1 - (pda_{12} + da_{22})X_2$$

$$(A6.2.1)$$

From (6.18), the value of net output after dividing through by $p_2$ is given by

$$w\ell_1 + \pi r_1 + \varrho(pa_{11} + a_{21}) = p(1 - a_{11}) - a_{21}$$

$$w\ell_2 + \pi r_2 + \varrho(pa_{12} + a_{22}) = -pa_{12} + (1 - a_{22}) \quad (A6.2.2)$$

Substituting in (A6.2.1) yields:

$$pdC_1 + dC_2 = \varrho(pa_{11} + a_{21})dX_1 + \varrho(pa_{12} + a_{22})dX_2$$
$$+ (w\ell_1 + \pi r_1)dX_1 + (w\ell_2 + \pi r_2)dX_2$$
$$- (pda_{11} + da_{21})X_1 - (pda_{21} + da_{22})X_2$$

$$(A6.2.3)$$

Now, total differentiation of the labour and resource use conditions (6.20) to (6.22) and using the definition of $k_i = pa_{1i} + a_{2i}$ yields:

$$\ell_1 dX_1 + \ell_2 dX_2 = dL - d\ell_1 X_1 - d\ell_2 X_2$$

$$r_1 dX_1 + r_2 dX_2 = dR - dr_1 X_1 - dr_2 X_2$$

$$(pa_{11} + a_{21})dX_1 + (pa_{12} + a_{22})dX_2$$
$$+ (pda_{11} + da_{21})X_1 + (pda_{12} + da_{22})X_2$$
$$= dK - (a_{11}X_1 + a_{12}X_2)dp \qquad (A6.2.4)$$

Substituting (A6.2.3) into (A6.2.4) yields after some rearrangement:

$$
\begin{aligned}
pdC_1 + dC_2 = &- \varrho(a_{11}X_1 + a_{12}X_2)dp \\
&- [wd\ell_1 + \pi dr_1 + (1 + \varrho)(pda_{11} + da_{21})]X_1 \\
&- [wd\ell_2 + \pi dr_2 + (1 + \varrho)(pda_{12} + da_{22})]X_2 \\
&+ wdL + \pi dR + \varrho dK \qquad (A6.2.5)
\end{aligned}
$$

Now, cost minimisation for firms requires that the value of input coefficient changes sum to zero or:

$$[wd\ell_1 + \pi dr_1 + (1 + \varrho)(pda_{11} + da_{21})]X_1$$
$$+ [wd\ell_2 + \pi dr_2 + (1 + \varrho)(pda_{12} + da_{22})]X_2 = 0 \quad (A6.2.6)$$

Using (A6.2.6), (A6.2.5) simplifies to:

$$pdC_1 + dC_2 = wdL + \pi dR + \varrho[dK - (a_{11}X_1 + a_{12}X_2)dp]$$

$$(A6.2.7)$$

Equation (A6.2.7) expresses the value of changes in net outputs in terms of changes in the value of the stocks of labour, resource and capital used in production. It is now possible to examine the shape of the net output frontier and the relationship between the slope of the net output frontier and output prices.

Since the underlying set of production techniques is convex, the net output frontier will always be concave to the origin (see Ethier, 1979, and Metcalfe and Steedman, 1972). However, it will not generally be the case that the price line is tangent to the net output frontier when one of the factor prices is exogenously determined. To see why this is so, consider the case of the labour and circulating capital with fixed supplies of labour and a given real stock of capital; i.e., $dL = 0$, equation (6.7a) holds and all coefficients and prices referring to the resource are zero. Thus,

$pdC_1 + C_2 = 0$ and the price vector is normal to the production possibilities frontier and the price line is tangent to the production possibilities frontier. In this case, the net output ratio $C_1/C_2$ is positively related to relative prices $p$ since the net output frontier is concave. Alternatively, when the wage rate is exogenously fixed, $dK - (a_{11}X_1 + a_{12}X_2)dp = 0$ and the price line cuts the net output frontier.

By similar argumentation, in the labour, resource and circulating capital model, with either wages exogenously determined as in the neo-Marxian case, or the rate of profit exogenously determined as in the neo-Keynesian case, the price line will cut the net output frontier.

Whenever the price line cuts the net output frontier, it is possible for techniques to re-switch as discussed in Section 6.5.1. When re-switching of techniques occurs, the net output ratio $C_1/C_2$ will no longer be monotonically related to relative prices $p$. Thus, consider an initial relative price $p_0$ and the associated net outputs $(C_1/C_2)_0$. Suppose $p$ now increases to $p_1$ and the net outputs increase to $(C_1/C_2)_1$ as the combination of discrete technologies change. If $p$ increases further to $p_2$ but techniques re-switch to those associated with $p_0$, then net outputs will also fall to $(C_1/C_2)_0$ and the ratio of net outputs will not be monotonically related to relative prices.

It is now possible to summarise implications of the above for the H–O theorem in the price form.

(i)  Suppose that two economies entering trade are specified a labour and circulating capital model with endogenous factor prices and the stocks of labour and of real capital given, when both countries have identical homothetic demand conditions and the same techniques of production and no factor intensity reversal, and commodity 1 (manufactures) has the higher labour intensity. Then the country with the lower autarky price ratio will have a relatively lower net output of manufactures and a lower wage/profit ratio. Thus the country with the lower wage profit ratio will export the labour intensive manufactures as required by the price form of the H–O theorem.

(ii)  Suppose that two economies entering trade are specified by a labour, resource and circulating capital model with either wages or profits exogenously determined and equal in the two countries and with the stocks of factors associated with the endogenously determined factor prices given. When both countries have identical homothetic demand conditions and the same techniques of production and no factor intensity reversal, and commodity 1 (manufactures) has the lower resource/labour and resource/capital ratio, then the country with the lower autarky price ratio will not necessarily have a relatively lower rent/wage or rent/profit ratio and the H–O theorem in the price form fails.

## NOTES

1. Whilst Steedman has chosen this equilibrium concept as the one most relevant to neo-Ricardian theory, he has also developed an open von-Neuman model which deploys the more generally-accepted definition of equilibrium which is the outcome of the behavioural characteristics of the model rather than the initial assumption of the outcome. See Steedman (1979a).
2. See Chapter 2, note 7, for a discussion of Ricardo's view of the subsistence wage. For discussion of Marx's views on wages, see Rowthorn (1980) and Marglin (1984a, b).
3. The term 'animal spirits' is used in a rather loose way here. It was introduced by Keynes in the discussion of the position of the short-run marginal efficiency of capital (MEC) function. As noted by Marglin (1984b, page 122), some shifts in the short-run MEC function due to a change in 'animal spirits' may not mean a shift in the long-run investment function. For example, a shift in the prospective real wage which influences expected profits involves a shift in the short-run MEC function but a shift along the long-run investment function.
4. These remarks draw heavily on the excellent summary of some of these issues by Marglin (1984b). This reconciliation of the neo-Marxian and neo-Keynesian views inevitably involves shorter-run monetary considerations and dynamic adjustment processes which are beyond the scope of this book.
5. I am grateful to Ian Steedman for pointing this out to me.
6. There has been a considerable debate in the literature over the role of heterogenous capital *versus* non-traded goods in producing situations where some of the standard theorems breakdown (see Metcalfe and Steedman, 1973 and Bliss, 1973). Mainwaring (1976) has shown, for the labour and circulating capital model case, the breakdown of the factor price equalisation, the Stolper–Samuelson theorem and the Heckscher–Ohlin theorems is not dependent on

the introduction of additional non-traded commodities. The discussion in this section refers to the two-commodity case so that these criticisms are not relevant here.

7. The reason why it is the lower envelope of the commodity price/factor price frontier can be easily established. Consider a suboptimal choice of technique inside the outer envelope of the factor price frontier at a given real wage and commodity price ratio. By assumption, another technique compared at the same commodity price ratio has a higher rate of profit. Therefore the relevant commodity price/factor price envelope is the lower one in the lower part of Fig. 6.2.

8. For a useful discussion of price-Wicksell effects, see Bliss (1975, pages 111 and 118). The original statement of the distinction between the physical components of the capital stock and the exchange value of the capital stock is due to Wicksell (1934).

9. Roemer's model may be criticised on the grounds that it implies a backward bending supply curve for labour, and as such is a misspecification of the historical situation described. However, his basic methodological point has merit.

10. The intergenerational income transfers arising from the opening of trade shown in Figs 6.6(a) and (b) are special cases of the more general argument developed by Smith (1984, Figs 3.3 and 3.4) and are independent of any assumptions regarding the length of life or commodity composition of capital assets.

11. There is an extensive literature on optimal intertemporal trade policy with surplus labour. See, for example, Bardhan (1970, Ch. 9) and Brecher (1974).

12. When two countries entering into trade are considered, it is quite possible for the employment gains in the country exporting the labour intensive commodity to be offset by the employment losses in the country exporting the 'capital' intensive commodity. The results obtained from exercises which examine the employment gains and losses in non-steady state equilibrium depend upon the pattern of trade, any demand differences between the countries entering trade, the specific form of the investment function and the responsiveness of the long-run wage to increases or decreases in the rate of profit, and the responsiveness of the rate of growth of the work force to any changes in the long-run rate of profit. The results obtained by Burgstaller (1986) for a dynamic Ricardian model are sensitive to the form of the investment function chosen. Specifically, Burgstaller allows for disinvestment in the country which experiences a decline in the rate of profit with the opening of trade. In the results reported in the text, employment losses arise only on account of differences in the pattern of trade.

# 7 · AN ANALYTICAL MARXIAN PERSPECTIVE ON TRADE AND GROWTH

## 7.1 ON THE CHOICE OF A MODEL FOR THE ANALYSIS OF COMPARATIVE ADVANTAGE AND GROWTH

The theoretical models of trade and growth favoured by the Marxian and structuralist-institutionalist literature often fail to take into account the role of resource endowments as one of the determinants of comparative advantage and growth. This may be the result of a negative vision of dependent but resource-abundant nations remaining hewers of wood and drawers of water, or because the positive virtues of industrialisation are seen as an end in themselves. Such imagery is not in accord with empirical reality.

The standard of patterns of the manufacturing share of commodity GDP (GDP excluding services) shown in Table 7.1(a) for per capita GDP of US$400 (1970) and US$1000 (1970) are strongly affected by resource endowments. The full analysis of standard patterns of manufacturing shares of commodity GDP in World Bank (1987, page 55) shows clearly that small resource-abundant countries have been able to achieve high levels of GDP per capita with significantly smaller shares of manufactures than for larger countries. Moreover, a large amount of world trade is in commodities which require some form of natural resources for their production, as can be seen from Table 7.1(b). Thus, in 1980, about 44 per cent of total world trade and about 36 per cent of intra-developed market economy trade was resource based. Trade between developed market and developing countries is still

**Table 7.1(a)**   Shares of manufactured goods in commodity GDP (per cent).
(a)

|  | Per capita GDP (1970 $) | |
|---|---|---|
|  | 400 | 1000 |
| small countries with ample resources, primary orientation | 20 | 39 |
| small countries with ample resources, industrial orientation | 36 | 56 |
| large countries | 44 | 58 |

*Source:* World Bank (1987, page 55).

**Table 7.1(b)**   Shares of resource-based trade in 1980 (per cent).
(b)

| | |
|---|---|
| intra-developed market economies | 36 |
| imports of developed market economies from developing countries | 79 |
| exports of developed market economies to developing countries | 23 |
| total world trade | 44 |

*Source:* Appendix 9.1, Table A9.1.3.

dominated by the exchange of manufactures (77 per cent of developed market economy exports) for resource-based commodities (79 per cent of developed market economies imports from developing countries). This structural dominance of resource-based trade from developing country exports should not mask the rapidly rising share of manufactured exports in developing countries, which has been important since the mid-1960s.

The neo-Ricardian labour and circulating capital model discussed in Section 6.3, and the dynamic H–O–S model with labour and a single capital good discussed in Section 5.4, do not fit the above stylised facts, since there is no resource input. In contrast, the open economy version of Ricardo's dynamic model with labour, land and a single capital good discussed in Section 3.5 fits one aspect of the empirical reality to be understood by the inclusion of land. In many ways, the open dynamic Ricardian model is the natural starting point for the analysis of trade and growth. However, the long-run stationary state equilibrium arises from the particular assumptions made about wage determination and population growth which bring the rate of growth of capital and population into equilibrium with the rate of growth of the supply of land.

A more useful starting point is the two-commodity labour, resource and capital model discussed in Section 6.4. This model, which is a special case of the more general non-steady state circulating capital model developed by M. A. M. Smith (1984), captures a role for both produced means of production and resource-based trade in the analysis of comparative advantage and growth whilst leaving open the possible institutional determination of one of the factor prices. It can also be used as the starting point for comparative dynamic analysis, as seen in Section 7.3.

The choice of a model depends on a judgement about the best way to capture some strategic elements of the problem under analysis. Whereas mainstream trade models are almost all non-steady state models, whether static models (including the new models with differentiated products, monopolistic competition and scale economies), or the non-steady state dynamic models, the labour, resource and circulating capital model is a long-run equilibrium model. It is precisely this characteristic which gives the model its simplicity, its institutional richness and consistency with stylised facts. In fact, some of the most enduring lessons of economic theory have come from the study of equilibrium models. Typically, the simpler mainstream models have a narrower focus. The circulating capital model is particularly useful because it captures some of the essential institutional and economic characteristics of capitalist economies. Furthermore, as developed in this chapter, the model is consistent, with some important stylised facts which characterised nineteenth-century trade between England and the lands of recent settlement, such as North and parts of South America and Australasia. It can also be adapted to allow for a dual economy, so that the model captures some important stylised facts about twentieth-century North–South trade, thus enriching the comparative dynamic analysis of North–South and South–South trade.

## 7.2   NINETEENTH-CENTURY TRADE BETWEEN ENGLAND AND AMERICA

There are few examples of attempts to use simple analytical models to analyse the basis of trade and factor movements in the historical context of colonial trade and imperialism under competitive conditions. The Marxian literature on this subject has been concerned with the study of imperialism in terms of the expansion of capitalism as a social system.[1] Recently there has been recognition of the need to explain precisely particular features of this expansion of capitalism internationally, such as its timing and the mechanisms through which it comes about (see Murray, 1978, page 18). It would seem that the application of trade theory, by clarifying the economic motives and the economic analysis, might help to answer these questions in the historical study of the processes and forms of imperialism.[2]

From a neo-classical perspective, Jones (1971) sets out the typical stylised facts about the pattern of trade and factor movements between England and North America in the nineteenth century, namely England exporting manufactures, capital and labour, and North America exporting corn whilst importing capital and labour. The example can easily be extended to include many countries such as Argentina in South America exporting beef. For consistency in referring to North and South America as America, 'corn' in the Jones example is referred to here as 'food'. Jones argues that the stylised facts cannot be explained within the context of the simplest paradigm $2 \times 2 \times 2$ H–O–S model, because incompletely specialised trade leads to factor price equalisation even without factor movements. Instead, he explains the stylised facts using the specific factors model described in Section 4.3.2, where factor price equalisation does not take place. The labour, resource and circulating capital model described in Sections 6.4 and 6.5.2 does not imply factor price equalisation through trade when the institutionally-determined factor returns are not equal between countries and produces results consistent with Jones's stylised facts. Both countries may be assumed to have access to the same technology (on account of trade and factor movements which ensured that the lands of recent settlement had access to the same technology as in England), to have homogenous endowments of primary factors which differ only in their relative supply, to be incompletely specialised, with England exporting manufactures in exchange for food, and with America having both a higher wage and a higher rate of profit.[3]

For present purposes it is sufficient to consider the factor price frontier for a single technique of production defined by equation (6.18) and shown in Fig. 6.3, when wages and rent are measured in terms of commodity 2, where sector 2 always has the higher resource/labour ratio and a higher resource/capital ratio, but the ranking of the sectors in terms of their capital/labour ratios may vary. This is shown in Fig. 7.1.

Consider now the opening of trade between two economies identical in every respect except the exogenously-determined distribution variable and endowments. First, suppose that under autarky, America has more of the resource relative to capital when measured at a common price, higher exogenously-given real wage and a higher rate of profit compared to England. The capital stocks are those required for simple reproduction in both countries. The autarky positions for England and America, indicated by $E^a$ and $A^a$ in Figs 7.1(a) and (b), respectively, have autarky price ratios $p^{aE}$ and $p^{aA}$, respectively. Both wages and profits are high at $A^a$ compared with $E^a$, satisfying Jones's stylised facts in the autarky position. The autarky price ratios are such that England exports commodity 1 (manufactures) and imports commodity 2 (food). In the case shown in Fig. 7.1(a), a trading equilibrium when transport costs are zero at price $p^*$ yields a higher rate of profit at the higher real wage in America at $A^*$ compared with England at $E^*$, in line with the stylised facts. However, at the common trading price $p^*$ in Fig. 7.1(b) the rate of profit is lower at the higher real wage in America at $A^*$ compared with England at $E^*$, contrary to Jones's stylised facts. Only with transport costs included, which prevent the full equalisation of commodity prices through trade, could a trading equilibrium be consistent with the stylised facts in the latter case.

Second, suppose that profits are exogenously determined and are higher in America than in England. If in addition America has the smaller endowment of labour relative to the resource, then the above argument with respect to the pattern of trade and configurations of distribution variables can be repeated. The

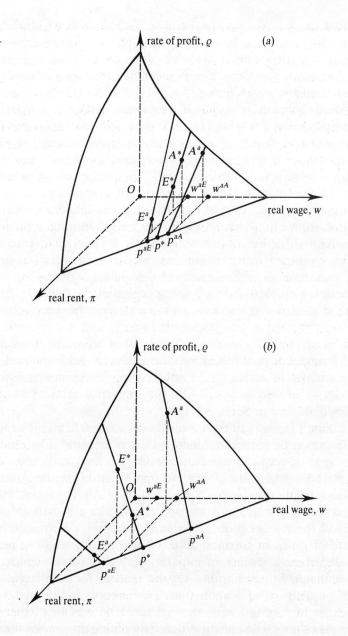

**Fig. 7.1**  Nineteenth-century trade between England and America.

argument can be extended to the many technique cases in which the iso-cost curves will be made up of piecewise linear segments on the factor price frontier made up of the outer envelope of the single technique frontiers. The number of countries can also be expanded on the usual lines.

It would therefore appear that the labour, resource and circulating capital model making H–O–S 'paradigm' case assumptions can be used to construct a story of nineteenth-century trade between England and America which satisfies Jones's stylised facts for a more general case than with the specific factors model. Whilst a finer cut with Occam's razor is not everything in model building, the above example suggests that the labour, resource and circulating capital model provides a useful starting point for the analysis of the basis of trade and potential factor movements between countries with the same or similar techniques but differing endowments and institutional determinants of one of the distribution variables. The circulating capital model has the additional virtue of taking into account the difference between reproducible capital and non-reproducible factors, a source of endless forced assumptions or even confusion when using the timeless H–O–S model or the timeless specific factors model in the analysis of comparative advantage.[4] Furthermore, the circulating capital model is also consistent with the empirical tests of trade theories discussed in Section 8.1.

No attempt is made to establish why the wage rate and the rate of profit might be higher in America than in England. One route might be to specify a wages closure for England and America along Ricardo–Marx lines, with the opportunities on the American land frontier inducing a higher wage. Alternatively, one might consider a wages closure for England along Ricardo-Marx lines, and the rate of profit in America might be determined by the rate of profit in England adjusted for a risk premium, plus some differential because of imperfect capital mobility which is not eliminated in equilibrium. Or the reasons for a differential rate of profit from an examination of differences in the financial institutions in England and America could be specified exogenously.[5] Another variant might proceed by noting that, when there is capital export in search of raw materials or land and climate suitable for plantation agriculture, some form of a dual economy model with specific factors may be more appropriate for the second trading economy. This possibility is discussed in the next section.

## 7.3   A MODEL OF TRADE BETWEEN ENGLAND AND THE TROPICS

Ideally, the choice of model for the analysis of trade and growth prospects for developing countries should allow for the endogenous specification of competing hypotheses. In practice, the choice of model reflects the prior position taken on the alternatives. This problem is no more evident than in empirical and policy debates over the long-run terms of trade and over the transmission of growth through trade.

In the Lewis model of trade between 'temperate' England and the Tropics discussed in Section 3.3, the terms of trade are governed by purely supply-side effects. This is in contrast with the supply and demand side considerations which underlie the models discussed in Sections 5.2.2 to 5.2.6. The Prebisch–Singer terms of trade thesis (Prebisch, 1950; Singer, 1950, 1975, 1984), the more recent terms of trade models in the Kaldorian tradition by Vines (1984) and Thirlwall (1986), and contributions by Findlay (1981 and 1984), all take into account supply and demand considerations. Within the Lewis model, there is no scope in the analysis for the changes in labour productivity to be decomposed into technical change and change in the supply of the productive inputs labour, resource and capital. Also, the static Ricardian framework does not permit the endogenous analysis of a second traded activity in the Tropics such as manufactures production, initially as an import substituting activity, and possibly as an emerging export activity. Given the very rapid rate of growth of manufactured exports from the so-called newly industrialising countries (NICs) in the 1970s, this is a serious limitation of the static Ricardian framework. These deficiencies can be overcome in the dual economy version of the labour, resource and circulating capital model. The model described here is similar to the timeless, dual-economy, specific factors model developed by Bardhan (1982), but does not have the limitations of the neo-classical specific factors model already discussed.

Suppose that the price and quantity relations of the model for

England (producing manufactures, commodity 1 and temperate food, commodity 2) is described by a slightly modified version of the relations (6.18) to (6.22) to allow for the traded Tropical commodity commercials (commodity 3) in the specification of circulating capital, and for distortion in the labour market through the degree of unionisation. This model can be further modified so that the Tropics, the second economy entering trade, is a dual economy in which there is a capitalist sector and a subsistence sector under some form of pre-capitalist relations of production. Extending the Lewis case discussed in Section 3.3, the tropical dual economy has a capitalist sector 3 producing crops for export, or commercials for short, and the subsistence farming sector 4 producing tropical food with individual holdings of land. The dual economy may be modelled with mobile labour between both sectors, but no capital or resource mobility.[6]

In contrast with the Lewis model described in Section 3.3, tropical food is treated as a non-traded commodity which must pass through some form of processing in the capitalist commercials sector before entering into trade.[7] Thus, using a superscript $E$ to describe England and the superscript $T$ to describe the Tropics, the equilibrium price and quantity relations for a single technique, excluding the demand conditions, the balance of payments conditions, and the distribution closure for England, are given by:

*England*

wages      rent         circulating capital              price
                          and profit

$$w^E \mu_1^E \ell_1^E + \pi^E r_1^E + (1 + \varrho^E)(a_{11}^E p_1 + a_{21}^E p_2 + a_{31}^E p_3) = p_1$$
$$w^E \ell_1^E \quad + \pi^E r_2^E + (1 + \varrho^E)(a_{12}^E p_1 + a_{22}^E p_2 + a_{32}^E p_3) = p_2 \qquad (7.1)$$

consumption      circulating         output
                      capital

$$C_1^E + (a_{11}^E X_1^E + a_{12}^E X_2^E) = X_1^E$$
$$C_2^E + (a_{21}^E X_1^E + a_{22}^E X_2^E) = X_2^E \qquad (7.2)$$

labour demand      labour use
$$\ell_1^E X_1^E + \ell_2^E X_2^E \quad = \quad \bar{L}^E \qquad (7.3)$$

resource demand      resource use
$$r_1^E X_1^E + r_2^E X_2^E \quad = \quad \bar{R}^E \qquad (7.4)$$

capital demand    capital use
$$k_1^E X_1^E + k_2^E X_2^E = K^E \qquad (7.5)$$

*Tropics*

wage    rent                    circulating capital
                                 and profit                           price
$$w^T \mu_3^T \ell_3^T + \pi_3^T r_3^T + (1 + \varrho^T)(a_{13}^T p_1 + a_{23}^T p_2 + a_{33}^T p_3 + a_{43}^T p_4) = p_3$$
$$w^T \ell_4^T \qquad\qquad + \qquad\qquad (a_{14}^T p_1 + a_{24}^T p_2 + a_{34}^T p_3) \qquad\quad = p_4$$
$$(7.6)$$

consumption        circulating        output
                      capital
$$C_3^T \qquad + (a_{33}^T X_3^T + a_{34}^T X_4^T) = X_3^T$$
$$C_4^T \qquad + \qquad a_{43}^T X_4^T \qquad = X_4^T \qquad (7.7)$$

labour demand    labour use
$$\ell_3^T X_3^T + \ell_4^T X_4^T = L^T \qquad (7.8)$$

sector specific resource demand    and use
$$r_3^T X_3^T \qquad\qquad = R_3^T$$
$$r_4 X_4^T \qquad\qquad = R_4^T \qquad (7.9)$$

sector specific capital demand    and use
$$k_3^T X_3^T \qquad\qquad = K_3^T$$
$$k_4^T X_4^T \qquad\qquad = K_4^T \qquad (7.10)$$

where $E$ stands for England, $T$ stands for the Tropics, $\mu_i^E$ is a parameter respresenting the degree of unionisation in manufactures in England (sector 1), which enters into the wage costs for $\mu_1^E \geqq 1$, $\mu_3^T$ is the effect of unionisation in the Tropics in bringing the wage in the capitalist sector above the wage given by the average product of labour in the subsistence sector, $C_i^k$ for $k = E$, $T$ and $i = 1, 2$ is consumption plus net exports and all other variables and parameters are as previously defined.

England's equilibrium conditions are characterised by either an institutional wage set exogenously or by full employment and a rate of profit which is fixed exogenously. As before, it is assumed that temperate agriculture always has the higher resource/labour and resource/capital ratio compared with manufactures.

The behaviour of the model for England follows the analysis of the effects of price and quantity changes in the two-commodity labour, resource and circulating capital model described in Section 6.5.2 with profits and rents (or wages and rent) being the endogenously-determined factor prices and wages (or the rate of profit) being exogenously determined. As a result of the basic factor intensity condition, any change on the cost side which favours temperate agriculture (commodity 2) will increase rent relative to profit (or wages) when the exogenously-determined factor price is the wage rate (or the rate of profit); the opposite will be the case if manufactures (commodity 1) are favoured relative to temperature agriculture. For the Tropics, the results follows from the typical magnification effects of a two-sector specific factors model discussed in Section 4.3.2. These observations are made a little more precise in the next section.

## 7.4   SOME COMPARATIVE DYNAMIC RESULTS

Suppose for England that the endowments of capital and the resource are given when wages are set exogenously, or the endowments of labour and the resource are given when the rate of profit is fixed exogenously. In the Tropics, the endowments of labour and sector-specific capital and resources are given. Then the standard Stolper–Samuelson relationship between commodity prices and the endogenously-determined factor prices discussed in Section 6.5.2 will hold. These are shown in Figs 7.2(a) and 7.2(b) for England and Fig. 7.2(c) for the Tropics.

The with-trade equilibrium commodity and factor prices are denoted by the superscript * for given demand condition in both England and the Tropics. The equilibrium combinations of the rent/profit ratio in England as the manufactures/temperate food price ratio varies (for given Tropical prices and no unionisation) are shown in Fig. 7.2(a) when the wage rate is given exogenously. In Fig. 7.2(b), the equilibrium combinations of the rent/wage ratio as the manufactures/temperate food price ratio varies (with given Tropical prices and no unionisation) are shown when the rate of profit is given exogenously. Similarly, from a straightforward application of the specific factors model, the equilibrium combinations of the rate of profit in commercials (assumed for simplicity to move in proportion to specific factor rent) and the

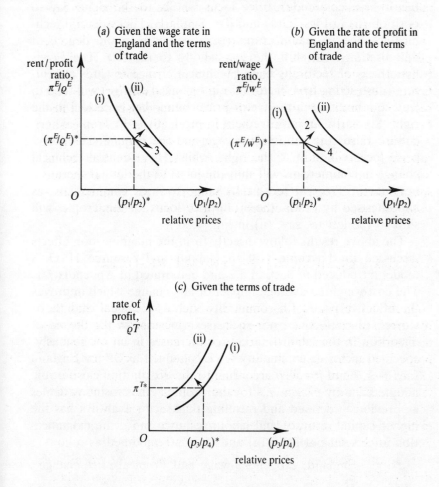

**Fig. 7.2**   Trade between England and the Tropics: factor prices and terms of trade.

internal Tropical terms of trade or the commercials/Tropical food price ratio for given equilibrium prices in England are shown in Fig. 7.2(c).

Now consider the effects of technical change or a change in the degree of unionisation in England. Hicks-neutral technical change in temperate agriculture in England will increase the rent/wage ratio for any given commodity price ratio, shifting the factor price/commodity price locus wholly to the right, say to position (ii) in Figs 7.2(a) and (b). Similarly, Hicks-neutral technical change in manufactures (or a decrease in the degree of unionisation) will shift the loci wholly to the left. The Lewis hypothesis of sectorally-biased technical change towards agriculture (abstracting from factor bias in technical change) will tend to lead to a net shift in the factor price/commodity price loci to the right. Similarly, an improvement in productivity in Tropical agriculture raises the subsistence wage and the commercials profit/price locus will shift to the right, whilst Hicks-neutral technical change in commercials will shift the locus to the left. If there is a net bias in Tropical technical change towards commercials, as hypothesised by Lewis, the profit/price locus for the Tropics will shift to the left to, say, (ii) in Fig. 7.2(c).

The above results follow directly from the magnification effects discussed in the context of the labour and resource H–O–S model introduced in Section 5.2 and elaborated in Appendix 7.1. The cost-weighted average impact of any change which improves the effective price of a commodity such as technical change, or worsens the effective price such as an increase in the degree of distortion in the labour market, or increases in an exogenously-specified factor or commodity price is defined by $\hat{p}_i^{ej}$ for England for $i = 1, 2$ and $j = w, \varrho$ according to the distribution closure rule adopted and by $\hat{p}_i^e$, $i = 3, 4$ for the Tropics. Thus, using variables as previously defined and recalling that sector 1 always has the higher capital/resource and labour/resource ratio, the magnification effects set out in (5.1a) and (5.3) are modified as follows:

England, exogenous wage and Tropical price change

either $\quad \hat{\varrho}^E > \hat{p}_1^{ew} > \hat{p}_2^{ew} > \hat{\pi}^E$

or $\quad \hat{\varrho}^E < \hat{p}_1^{ew} < \hat{p}_2^{ew} < \hat{\pi}^E$

England, exogenous profit and Tropical price change

either $\quad \hat{w}^E > \hat{p}_1^{e\varrho} > \hat{p}_2^{e\varrho} > \hat{\pi}^E$

or $\quad \hat{w}^E < \hat{p}_1^{e\varrho} < \hat{p}_2^{e\varrho} < \hat{\pi}^E$

Tropics

either $\quad \varrho^T > \hat{p}_3^e > \hat{w}^T > \hat{p}_4^e$

or $\quad \varrho^T < \hat{p}_3^e < \hat{w}^T < \hat{p}_4^e$ $\qquad$ (7.11)

Note that it is assumed that the change in the rate of profit in commercials in the Tropics is proportional to the change in the specific factor rent in commercials.

Thus, when wages are constant in England, when commodity prices are constant and when technical change is biased towards temperate agriculture, it can be seen from the second inequality in (7.11) that the rent/profit ratio must rise, as shown in Fig. 7.2(a). Similarly, when the rate of profit is constant, and technical change is biased towards temperate agriculture, the rent/wage ratio rises at constant commodity prices as shown in the fourth inequality in (7.11) and in Fig. 7.2(b). In the Tropics, when technical change is biased towards commercials production, it follows that profits must rise relative to both subsistence wages as shown in the second-last inequality in (7.11) and Fig. 7.2(c).

The technical change described above will have an impact on the supply of commodities. Whilst this will have an eventual effect on commodity prices and the terms of trade, it is useful to consider the supply-side effects at constant commodity prices. This follows from a straightforward analysis of the magnification effects on the supply side. Thus, using the superscript $^e$ to indicate the weighted average effects on factor supply of factor-augmenting technical change and induced factor substitution, the output magnification effects can be summarised by:

England, exogenous wage

either $\quad \hat{X}_1^E > \hat{K}^{eE} > \hat{R}^{eE} > \hat{X}_2^E$

or $\quad \hat{X}_1^E < \hat{K}^{eE} < \hat{R}^{eE} < \hat{X}_2^E$

England, exogenous rate of profit

either $\quad \hat{X}_1^E > \hat{L}^{eE} > \hat{R}^{eE} > \hat{X}_2^E$

or $\quad \hat{X}_1^E < \hat{L}^{eE} < \hat{R}^{eE} < \hat{X}_2^E$

Tropics

$$\hat{X}_3^T = \hat{R}_3^{eT}$$

$$\hat{X}_4^T = \hat{R}_4^{eT} \tag{7.12}$$

For the complete definition of the augmented or effective factor supplies, see Appendix 7.1.

Thus it can be seen from the second and fourth inequalities in (7.12) that technical change in England, when biased towards temperate agriculture and which is not offset by a negative-induced factor substitution effect, will increase the supply of temperate agriculture relative to manufactures. Similarly, it can be seen from the last two equalities in (7.12) that technical change in the Tropics when biased towards commercials will increase the supply of commercials relative to tropical food. The terms of trade and final distribution effects follow from an analysis of the patterns of excess demand and excess supply created by the technical change or other exogenous shifts.

Consider the Lewis case, in which it is hypothesised that technical change in England is sectorally biased toward temperate agriculture and towards commercials in the Tropics. For the moment, suppose that the absolute level of technical change is the same in both England and the Tropics so that attention can be focused on the sectorally-biased technical change hypothesis. Sectorally-biased technical change in England towards temperate food will tend to raise the supply of temperate agriculture relative to manufactures. It is possible that the supply of manufactures will fall absolutely, but this is less likely the higher the overall rate of technical change in England for any relative degree of sectoral bias in technical change. In the Tropics, biased technical change towards commericals will tend to raise the supply of commercials relative to tropical food. Thus, with a proportional change in income in England and the Tropics, there will tend to be excess supply of temperate food and commercials and excess demand for manufactures and Tropical food. Market clearance will require a deterioration in the temperate food/manufactures and the commercials/manufactures terms of trade with indefinite effects on the temperate food/commercials terms of trade. As in the original Lewis model this result is independent of any sectoral bias in the demand side. If the income and price elasticities of demand for temperate food, commercials and tropical food are less than one and for manufactures are greater than one, the temperate agriculture/manufactures and the commercials/manufactures terms of trade will tend to deteriorate rather more than for the case when all of the income elasticities are equal to one. Thus, the Lewis result, that the commercials/manufactures terms of trade will tend to worsen as a result of sectorally-biased technical change, will occur within the model described even without sectoral differences on the demand side. The Engel curve effects on the demand side will tend to reinforce this result.

The above patterns of biased technical change and shifts in the terms of trade will modify the previous analysis of the distribution of income, summarised by the direction of the arrows shown in Figs 7.2(a) to (c). For a given rate of profit and price of commercials in terms of tropical food, the improvement in the terms of trade for manufactures in terms of food in England will tend to offset the initial effects of technical change in shifting the distribution of income away from profit or wages and in favour of rent, as shown by arrows 1 and 2 in Figs 7.2(a) and (b), respectively. If the price substitution effects dominate the initial effects of the biased technical change, it is also possible for the distribution of income to move in favour of wages or profit in each case, shown by arrows 3 and 4, respectively.

The patterns of biased technical change which induce shifts in the terms of trade and the distribution of income will be further modified when substitution effects in production are taken into account. If the induced factor substitution effects dominate the initial effects of the sectorally-biased technical change, it is possible for the pattern of supply responses to be reversed. However, given that empirical estimates of the elasticities of substitution in production are almost always less than one, this possibility is unlikely.

Similarly, the analysis of the terms of trade and income distribution must take into account changes in factor supplies. To the extent that the supply of both capital and labour grow faster than the supply of the resource in England, the effects of any bias in technical change towards agriculture will be offset. This will lessen the likelihood that the temperate food/manufactures and the commercials/manufactures terms of trade will deteriorate. The analysis will also be modified when differences in the rate of technical change between England and the Tropics (or between the North and the South) are taken into account, as emphasised by Singer (1975, 1984). To the extent that the benefits of technical change in the North are captured as Schumpeterian rents, the model would have to be modified to take this into account.

The outcome of the model for international factor price differences is indeterminate. For example, with biased technical change in the Tropics towards commercials, the subsistence wage will always rise, albeit by less than the rise in Tropical profits and rent. If the wage is institutionally given in England, then in this case the international wage differential will decrease. When the rate of profit is exogenously fixed in England, biased technical change towards temperate agriculture may be associated with a rise in wages as can be seen from the third inequality in (7.11) and the implications for international wage inequality are indeterminate. To the extent that technical change in England is biased towards manufactures rather than temperate agriculture, international wage inequalities are more likely to be increased. Equally, to the extent that technical change in the Tropics is biased towards subsistence agriculture rather than commercials, international wage inequalities are likely to be lowered. In respect of both terms of trade and factor returns, the combined effects of biased technical change, factor supply change, induced factor substitution or changes in the degree of unionisation can only be determined empirically. This is taken up in Section 8.3.


## 7.5   NORTH–SOUTH TRADE IN THE PRESENCE OF SKILLED AND UNSKILLED LABOUR

One of the criticisms of the Lewis terms of trade model discussed in Section 3.4 is that it excludes the possibility that import-substituting manufacturing production could begin in the Tropics or the South. The simplest modification to the model of the Tropics described by relations (7.6) to (7.10) to allow for this is to make the specific factor in commercials production into a generally mobile resource. In this case, the introduction of import-competing manufactures transforms the model of the capitalistic part of the South economy into the same form as the labour, resource and circulating capital model as described for England or the North. The accumulation of capital at constant commodity prices and an unchanging subsistence wage will lead to a faster rate of growth of manufactures compared with commercials when manufactures production has the higher capital/resource ratio. This result follows from a straightforward application of the Rybczynski theorem. As growth and the accumulation of capital take place, there will be offsetting effects on the subsistence wage. The withdrawal of labour from the subsistence sector will tend to raise the average product of labour, as will any technical change which raises the average product of labour. Offsetting these changes will be the development of capitalist agriculture and the separation of labour from land within the agricultural sector itself, leading to the development of agricultural wage labour which no longer receives the average product of subsistence agriculture. However, from the point of view of the fully capitalistic sectors of the economy, the rate of growth will be strongly influenced both by the rate of profit which can be achieved given the subsistence wage and the availability of food as a wage-good in the capitalistic sector.[8] Roughly speaking, the analysis of capital accumulation and North–South trade can proceed on the basis of an institutionally determined wage or a Ricardo–Marx–Lewis closure of the model of the capitalistic sector in the South.

Both the development strategy and the pattern of trade will depend very much on the resource endowments available for the development of the capitalistic sector. To the extent that new resources are brought into capitalist production, either through the opening up of land frontiers or through mineral discoveries, the bias towards manufactures production as capital accumulation takes place arising from the underlying factor intensity conditions will be offset by the expansion of the supply of the resource. In this case, it is likely that manufacturing production will remain import competing, even when very high levels of per capita income have been reached, as in the case of Australia, Canada and New Zealand, even in the present period. To the extent that resources remain sector specific but are sufficiently important for a South economy's manufacturing sector to remain import competing, the analysis of the country's terms of trade will follow on the same lines as the analysis of the commercials/manufactures terms of trade for the Tropics in the previous section. The presence of the import-competing manufactures will offset the welfare costs of any decline in the commercials/manufactures terms of trade. Where the resource is abundant and not sector specific, such as with agricultural land, the country's terms of trade will follow more closely the analysis of the temperate food/manufactures terms of trade for England or the North.

For some Newly Industrialising Countries of the South (NICs), particularly the resource-scarce 'Four little tigers', South Korea,

Taiwan, Hong Kong and Singapore, the patterns of accumulation, growth and trade will be very different. To the extent that these countries were able to accumulate capital fast enough to become net exporters of manufactures, the terms of trade analysis of the commercials/manufactures terms of trade in the previous sector is turned on its head. There is, however, an important missing element in the application of the labour, resource and circulating capital models to the case of the East Asian NICs.

So far, no mention has been made of the importance of both primary education and basic literacy in the development of wage labour which can enter into employment in the capitalistic sector, or of the role of skills in the development of manufactures. If the development of primary education and literacy is an important prerequisite for the development of the unskilled wage labour, the development of a skilled labour force is an important complementary process as the accumulation of capital takes place. This has important consequences for the analysis of North–South trade.[9]

In order to focus on the role of skilled labour in the process of growth and development in North–South trade, consider the extreme case where the resource endowments in the South and the North are so small that only urban based commodities are produced without any resource at all and skilled labour replaces the resource in the model. Suppose now that two manufactured commodities are produced, a capital good and a wage good. Sector 1 produces machinery with a low capital/skilled labour ratio and sector 2 produces clothing with a higher capital/skilled labour ratio. When the unskilled wage is institutionally determined, the capital/unskilled and skilled/unskilled factor intensity relationships will not govern comparative advantage. In contrast to the wages closure for the determination of the unskilled wage in the North and the South, the rewards for skilled labour and capital are endogenously determined. In the initial situation, both the South and the North are incompletely specialised. The South has a low endowment of skilled labour relative to capital and exports clothing with the higher capital/skilled labour intensity ratio in return for machinery produced in the skill-abundant North. Now consider the case when the South grows faster than the North through the accumulation of capital. For simplicity, this can be

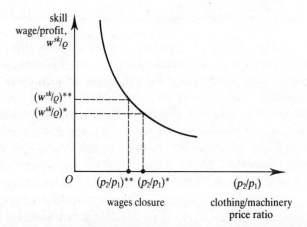

**Fig. 7.3** North–South terms of trade in a circulating capital model with unskilled and skilled labour.

modelled by assuming that there is no accumulation of capital or skills in the North, or of skills in the South. Thus, the accumulation of capital in the South will lead to an expansion of clothing production and an excess supply of clothing and an excess demand for machinery at the initial equilibrium prices. In terms of derived factor demand, there will be an excess demand for skilled labour and an excess supply of capital. Removal of the excess supply of clothing will require that the terms of trade will move against clothing. The fall in the clothing/machinery price ratio will increase the skilled labour/profit ratio in both the North and the South, as can be seen from Fig. 7.3.

Figure 7.3 is constructed on exactly the same lines as Fig. 7.2(a), except that skilled labour replaces the resource. Sector 2 has the higher capital/skilled labor ratio and sector 1 (machinery) has the lower capital/skilled labour ratio compared with sector 2. Thus, the fall in the clothing/machinery price ratio required to remove the excess supply of clothing resulting from a faster rate of accumulation of capital in the South will raise the skilled wage/ profit ratio. If the unskilled wage is fixed in terms of clothing and the skilled wage is also measured in terms of clothing, the skilled wage will also rise absolutely following the magnification conditions described in (7.11) and modified as required for the present example. Thus:

$$\hat{w}^{sk} > \hat{p}_1 > \hat{p}_2 > \hat{\varrho} \qquad (7.13)$$

where $\hat{w}^{sk}$ is the change in the skilled wage and the other variables are as previously described. This pattern of accumulation also has important implications for the pattern of employment.

In the simplified case where there is accumulation of capital in the South, no accumulation of capital in the North, and a constant supply of skilled labour in the South and the North, the output of clothing increases absolutely and the output of machinery declines at constant prices. More generally, adaptation of the magnification conditions described in (7.12) yields:

$$\hat{X}_2 > \hat{K} > \hat{L}^{sk} > \hat{X}_1 \qquad (7.14)$$

where $\hat{L}^{sk}$ is the change in supply of skilled labour and all other variables are as previously defined. If clothing has the lower capital/unskilled labour ratio or a higher unskilled labour/capital ratio, there will be increased employment of unskilled labour in the South and the available supply of skilled labour will be allocated to the less skill-intensive clothing sector. At the initial prices, there will be no change in the output of either machinery or clothing in the North, because these is no change in the supply of either capital or skilled labour.

However, once adjustment of prices takes place in order to eliminate the pattern of excess demand and excess supply created by the accumulation of capital in the South, the output of machinery must expand and the output of clothing must contract in the North. In this case, the available supply of skilled labour will be more heavily concentrated on machinery production and the employment of unskilled labour will fall.

The above analysis has important implications for income distribution and employment in both the North and the South. In the South, the initial effects will tend to improve the distribution of income. The rate of profit falls in relation to both skilled and unskilled wages, and there is an increase in the employment of unskilled labour. In so far as the increased employment of unskilled labour reduces the available sources of surplus labour, the accumulation of capital may put upward pressure on the subsistence or institutional wage paid to unskilled workers, further improving the unskilled wage relative to profit and offsetting the improvement in the relative position of skilled workers. The final effect on the distribution of income is an empirical matter which will depend on the factor intensities in each sector, particularly the relative skilled/unskilled labour intensity in each sector of substitution in production, the price and income elasticities of demand, the initial supplies of skilled labour and capital, and the initial level of employment of unskilled labour. Since clothing also has the higher unskilled labour/capital intensity ratio compared with machinery, the employment of unskilled labour may also expand faster than the capital stock. In this case, it is more likely that the total income share going to unskilled labour will also increase.

The virtuous circle of the benefits of the accumulation of capital in the South in improving the employment position of unskilled labour and raising the unskilled wage/profit ratio masks the distribution consequences of increasing the skilled/unskilled wage ratio when the supply of skilled labour is low. This is not the case in the North, where the combined effects of an increased skilled/ unskilled wage ratio, a decreased employment of unskilled labour and a larger initial supply of skilled labour relative to employed unskilled labour may dramatically worsen the position of unskilled labour. To the extent that the fall in employment of unskilled labour puts downward pressure on the institutional wage for the unskilled, the skilled/unskilled wage differential will be further increased. The social tensions and adjustment difficulties which arise in the North over the conflict between skilled and unskilled labour may overshadow the improved distribution of income between skilled labour and capital. The rapid rise of protectionism in the North to prevent the growth of North–South trade along these lines testifies to the importance of this issue.

The rapid accumulation of capital and the relative exhaustion of new sources of unskilled labour alters the above picture. The consequent increase in the degree of skill intensity of production more typical in a multi-commodity world needs to be taken into account. It is also necessary to take into account the consequences of increasing the supply of skilled labour. These issues are taken up in the next section.

## 7.6   SKILL-INTENSIVE SOUTH–SOUTH TRADE

In the discussion of the many-commodity and many-country version of the labour and resource H–O–S model in Section 4.3, it

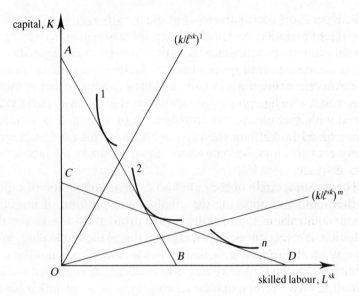

**Fig. 7.4**   Skilled labour in North–South and South–South trade.

was suggested that, outside of the context of factor price equalisation, North–South trade would reflect the standard presumption that South countries would export their most labour-intensive commodities. However, this model suggested that South–South trade would involve more resource-intensive commodities than those which entered into North–South trade. This argument can be extended to the case of the circulating capital model with unskilled and skilled labour and a Ricardo–Marx–Lewis distribution closure discussed in the previous section.

Figure 7.4 is similar to Fig. 4.4 but with capital and skilled labour replacing the resource and unskilled labour. With many countries, many commodities and no factor price equalisation between countries, a possible range of capital/skilled labour ratios and associated factor price ratios for producing three commodities are considered. The poorest South countries with the highest capital/skilled labour endowment ratio (or lowest skilled labour/capital ratios), such as $(k/\ell^{sk})^1$, will tend to have the highest skilled wage/profit ratios. For such countries, the production of commodities with iso-quants such as those marked 1 and 2 will be chosen in the equilibrium solution at the factor price ratio given by the iso-cost curve $AB$. Such countries would be net exporters of the least skilled labour-intensive commodity 1 and net importers of commodity 2 with a higher skilled labour/capital ratio. Alternatively, countries with low capital/skilled labour endowment ratios (or a higher skilled labour/capital ratio) and a lower skilled wage/profit ratio given by the iso-cost line $CD$ can profitably produce commodity 2 and commodity $n$. The countries with the high skill endowments will tend to be net exporters of the most skill/capital-intensive commodity $n$ and net importers of the less skill/capital-intensive commodity 2.

North–South trade will tend to be characterised by countries at the extreme end of the range of endowment ratios. The poorest South countries will tend to be net exporters of commodities with a low skill/capital intensity and North countries will tend to be exporters of high skill/capital-intensive commodities. However, Southern NICs which have began to expand their supply of skilled labour relative to their capital stock, for example countries whose sources of supply of unskilled labour have become exhausted in the short run and their opportunities for further accumulation of capital and export of the commodities with the lowest skill/capital intensity have become limited, may have an in-between capital/ skilled labour endowment ratio. Such NICs export less skill/ capital-intensive commodities. However, in their trade with other South countries the NICs will be net exporters of intermediate skill/capital-intensive commodities in exchange for the least skill-intensive commodities.

The movement of NICs up the broadly specified chain of comparative advantage has implications for the North as well. The discussion of North–South trade in the previous section focused on the effects on the North of increased imports of the least skill/capital-intensive commodities. In so far as the NICs are also rapid accumulators of skilled labour, the threat to North countries moves from the producers of the lower skill/capital-intensive commodities to the producers of the higher skill/capital-intensive commodities. If the NICs begin to accumulate skills faster than countries in the North, the expansion of more skill/ capital-intensive commodities will place skilled workers under the same threat as the less skilled workers in the argument of the previous section. In this case, the distribution of income in the

North will move in favour of profits and away from skilled labour
with the implication for unskilled labour depending on the respective unskilled/skilled labour ratios and the unskilled labour/
capital-intensity ratios.

This discussion of the dynamics of North–South and South–
South trade has deliberately abstracted from technical change
and associated changes in the character of skills. Some of these
issues, and the empirical evidence on the characteristics of
North–South and South–South trade, will be taken up in the final
chapter.

## 7.7    SPECIFIC FACTORS AND THE DUTCH DISEASE IN REVERSE

The typical reverse Dutch disease problems for primary exporters
are both macro and micro. The macro adjustment problem appears as a combination of required real exchange rate, real wage
rate and government expenditure changes. The micro adjustment
problem appears at the sectoral level through the impact of
changes in the pattern of comparative advantage produced by the
primary export slump. The particularly difficult set of policy
decisions which now face primary exporting countries revolve
around how these macro and micro adjustments are to be man-
aged in the short run whilst maintaining a coherent medium and
long-run development strategy.

The inherited framework within which the Dutch disease and
reverse Dutch disease problems have been analysed has been
heavily influenced by the neo-classical specific factors model discussed in Sections 4.3.2 and 5.2.1. In these models the key
relative prices which must change as a part of the adjustment
process are the real exchange rate (the price of tradables relative
to non-tradables) and the real wage rate. The major structural
changes required are shifts in the allocation of labour between
sectors and, in so far as the fluctuation in primary commodity
prices affect government revenue, there must be a flexible response of government expenditure. However, in the longer run,
attention must also be given to the intersectoral reallocation of
capital and the effects of institutional wages. The model of the

South described in Sections 7.3 and 7.4 can be modified for this purpose.

Suppose that there are three types of tradable commodities produced under capitalist relations of production, sector 1 producing manufactured, sector 2 producing non-traditional primary and sector 3 producing traditional primary commodities. In non-tradable production, 'services' are produced capitalistically (sector 4) whilst non-tradable agricultural commodities are produced in the non-capitalist sectors. In all capitalist sectors, production requires some kind of sector-specific resource – urban land with infrastructure suitable for manufactures, resources with attendant infrastructure for non-traditional primary commodities, resources for traditional primary commodities with attendent infrastructure, urban land suitable for services, and land used in non-traded agriculture. In addition, the capitalist sectors require both mobile capital and labour. For the most part, it is assumed that labour is homogenous without skill differentiation. As before, it is assumed that there are diminishing returns to additional amounts of both physical capital and labour when applied to a fixed amount of a specific factor. Little attention will be paid to labour mobility between the capitalist and non-capitalist sectors so that the institutional wage refers to the capitalistic sector. In so far as the non-capitalist sector produces non-traded agricultural commodities, this simplification will not be of too much consequence for present purposes.

Consider now the consequences of a longer-run change in the price of primary exports with constant world prices of tradable manufacturing and non-traditional primary commodities. This will have direct effects in the traditional primary export sector, as well as powerful indirect effects through the change in the real exchange rate on the rest of the economy.

If real wages are fixed in terms of some bundle of tradable and non-tradable commodities and if traditional primary commodities play no role as reproducible capital, the analytical characteristics of the model will mirror the specific factors model described in Section 5.2.1 and the multi-sector extension described in Appendix A5.1.2 with the change in the rate of profit replacing the wage rate change in inequalities (5.3) and (A5.1.17a). The full impact of the direct effects of a decline in traditional primary export prices will be a fall in traditional primary resource rents and the returns to capital: traditional primary resource rents will decline absolutely in terms of all prices, but the returns to capital will rise in terms of all other prices. On account of the rise in the rate of profit in terms of all other prices, there will be a fall in the specific factor rents outside the traditional primary commodity sector at a constant real exchange rate.

As a result of a fall in traditional primary commodity prices, the economy will obtain fewer tradables relative to non-tradables, so that there will be a rise in the price of tradables relative to non-tradables. This is equivalent to a depreciation of the real exchange rate which can be achieved without a fall in the absolute price of non-tradables through an adjustment of the exchange rate. This effect is the same as that shown in Fig. 4.5, except that in the specific factors case there is no linear segment on the transformation frontier between tradables and non-tradables. The fall in the relative price of non-tradables will lead to a further fall in the rent on specific resources used in non-tradables relative to all other prices, and a fall in the rate of profit in terms of non-tradables. In so far as an important component of the capital stock is made up of non-tradables, the depreciation of the real exchange rate will further increase the rate of profit in the tradable manufactures and non-traditional primary sectors.

At a fixed real wage rate, the main burden of the price adjustments falls on specific factor rents, particularly in the traditional primary and non-tradable sectors and on the returns to capital in terms of traditional primary commodities and non-tradables. Since the most important specific factor used in non-traded 'service' production is urban land, the main indirect beneficiaries of the original Dutch disease boom will have been the owners of urban land. Therefore from most perspectives, it would be readily agreed that it is appropriate that a major part of the reverse Dutch disease adjustment should be borne by such property owners. Equally, such property owners could form a sufficiently important interest group opposed to adjustment by taking action which prevents a decline in the real exchange rate.

The direction and extent of the overall change in the returns to capital is not clear from the above analysis. Since the returns to capital decline in terms of the price of both traditional primary and non-tradable service prices, but increases in terms of manufactures and non-traditional primary prices, the direction and extent of the change in the overall rate of profit will depend on the relative size of sectors and on the extent to which the indirect effect of a fall in the price of non-tradables leads to an increase in the returns to capital in the non-traditional tradables.

The above analysis assumed that the real exchange rate depreciation required by the reverse Dutch disease effects could be accommodated without a decline in real wages. However, for a large decline in the long-run traditional primary export prospects, this is unlikely to be sufficient. To the extent that non-traditional tradables have a lower labour to capital intensity compared to non-traded services, a lowering of the real wage will facilitate a further decline in the price of non-tradables relative to tradables and will increase the general rate of profit.

In so far as reverse Dutch disease affecting primary commodities has an impact on resource allocation through relative price changes, the results of the above analysis can be summarised as follows. On the production side, there will be an incentive for both mobile labour and capital to move from traditional primary and non-tradable sectors into non-traditional primary and manufacturing activities. On the expenditure side, there will be an incentive to switch into the consumption of non-tradables. From the point of view of longer-run adjustment policy, how much of the burden of adjustment will have to be borne by the owners of capital and specific resources and how much to lower wages, will depend crucially on the extent to which the adjustment can be made without a real wage change.

From the viewpoint of the formulation of trade strategy and policy in response to reverse Dutch disease, the above analysis leaves out two crucial dynamic aspects of adjustment. First, it assumes that the supply of both specific factors and capital is fixed. Second, it ignores the possibility that a longer-run development policy response to reverse Dutch disease will involve productivity-enhancing technical change. Since a real wage decline is difficult to achieve politically, and is undesirable from most perspectives, it is important to consider the extent to which these dynamic considerations can assist in the longer-run adjustment to the reverse Dutch disease. Such possibilities can only be explored in a specific policy context.

## APPENDIX 7.1  MAGNIFICATION EFFECTS IN THE MODEL OF TRADE BETWEEN ENGLAND AND THE TROPICS

To obtain the magnification effects described in conditions (7.11) and (7.12) of the text, an efficiency parameter $\tau$ was added to the input coefficients described in equations (7.1) to (7.10). An increment in technical efficiency is therefore indicated when the change in the efficiency parameter is less than zero, or $\hat{\tau} < 0$, when the size of the input coefficient decreases. The sum of all of the exogenous changes, as they effect the effective price of a commodity, is incorporated into an effective price change, $\hat{p}^e$, which is defined for each of the distribution closures in England and for the Tropics. Thus, log differentiating equations (7.1) and (7.6), using the factor-intensity condition that sector 1 in England always has the higher capital/resource and labour/resource ratio, and simplifying, yields the price magnification effects:

England, wage and Tropical price change exogenously given

either $\quad \hat{p}^E > \hat{p}_1^{ew} > \hat{p}_2^{ew} > \hat{\pi}^E$

or $\quad \hat{\varrho}^E < \hat{p}_1^{ew} < \hat{p}_2^{ew} < \hat{\pi}^E$

England, profit and Tropical price change exogenously given

either $\quad \hat{w}^E > \hat{p}_1^{e\varrho} > \hat{p}_2^{e\varrho} > \hat{\pi}^E$

or $\quad \hat{w}^E < \hat{p}_1^{e\varrho} < \hat{p}_2^{e\varrho} < \hat{\pi}^E$

Tropics, England price changes exogenously given

either $\quad \hat{\varrho}^T > \hat{p}_3^e > \hat{p}_4^e > \hat{w}^T$

or $\quad \hat{\varrho}^T < \hat{p}_3^e < \hat{p}_4^e < \hat{w}^T$ $\qquad$ (A7.1.1)

where

$$\hat{p}_i^{ew} = \hat{p}_i - \left( \hat{\tau}_{\ell_i}^E - \theta_{\ell_i}^E + \hat{\tau}_{r_i}^E \theta_{r_i}^E + \sum_j \hat{\tau}_{k_{ji}}^E \theta_{k_{ji}}^E \right)$$
$$- \hat{w}^E \theta_{\ell_i}^E - \hat{p}_3^T \theta_{k_{i3}}^E - \hat{\mu}_i^E \theta_{\ell_i}^E$$

$$\hat{p}_i^{e\varrho} = \hat{p}_i - \left( \hat{\tau}_{\ell_i}^E \theta_{\ell_i}^E + \hat{\tau}_{r_i}^E \theta_{r_i}^E + \sum_j \hat{\tau}_{k_{ji}}^E \theta_{k_{ji}}^E \right)$$

$$- \varrho^E \sum_j \theta^E_{k_{ji}} - \hat{p}^T_3 \theta^E_{k_{i3}} - \hat{\mu}^E_i \theta^E_{\ell_i}$$

for $i = 1, 2$ and $j = 1, 2, 3$, and

$$\hat{p}^e_i = - \left( \hat{t}^T_{\ell_i} \theta^T_{\ell_i} + \hat{t}^T_{r_i} \theta^T_{r_i} + \sum_j \hat{t}^T_{k_{ji}} \theta^T_{k_{ji}} \right)$$
$$- \hat{p}^E_1 \theta^E_{kji} - \hat{p}^E_2 \theta^T_{kji} - \hat{\mu}^T_i \theta^T_i$$

for $i = 3, 4$.

The $\hat{t}$s are changes in the technical efficiency parameters and the $\theta$s are cost shares with super and subscripts defined in an obvious way. All other variables are as previously defined and $\hat{\mu}^E_2 = \hat{\mu}^T_4 = 0$ for notional convenience, since the unionisation parameter does not enter sector 2 in England or sector 4 in the Tropics.

It can be readily seen from condition (A7.1.1) that an increase in productivity leads to an improvement in effective price, as does a fall in the price of commercials inputs, whereas an increase in the degree of unionisation or an increase in the exogenously-fixed factor price lowers the effective price. The shifts in the commodity price/factor price loci shown in Fig. 7.2 and described in the text follow from these observations.

The quantity magnification effects follow when equations (7.3) to (7.5) and (7.8) to (7.10) are log differentiated at constant commodity and exogenous factor prices, and the same factor-intensity conditions are applied as before. For simplicity, it is assumed that the underlying production functions are such that the capital goods are treated as a composite commodity and are nested with substitution between capital and labour, and between combined bundles of capital and labour substituting with the resource. Thus, using the superscript '$e$' to indicate augumented or effective factor supply, the results of this exercise are:

England, wages given exogenously

either    $\hat{X}^E_1 > \hat{K}^{eE} > \hat{R}^{eE} > \hat{X}^E_2$

or    $\hat{X}^E_1 < \hat{K}^{eE} < \hat{R}^{eE} < \hat{X}^E_2$

England, profits given exogenously

either    $\hat{X}^E_1 > \hat{L}^{eE} > \hat{R}^{eE} > \hat{X}^E_2$

or $\quad \hat{X}_1^E < \hat{L}^{eE} < \hat{R}^{eE} < \hat{X}_2^E$

Tropics

$$\hat{X}_3^T = \hat{R}_3^{eT}$$

$$\hat{X}_4^T = \hat{R}_4^{eT} \qquad\qquad\qquad\qquad (A7.1.2)$$

where

$$\hat{K}^{eE} = \hat{K}^E - \sum_i \psi_{k_i}^E \{\hat{t}_{k_i}^E - \theta_i^E(\hat{w}^E - \hat{p}_{k_i}^E)\alpha_{k\ell_i}^E$$

$$- \theta_{r_i}^E(\hat{\pi}^E - \hat{p}_{k \text{ and } \ell_i}^E)\alpha_{k \text{ and } \ell, r_i}^E\}$$

$$\hat{R}^{eE} = \hat{R}^E - \sum_i \psi_{r_i}^E\{\hat{t}_{r_i}^E - [\theta_\ell^E\theta_{r_i}^E\theta_{k_i}^E(\hat{w}^E - \hat{p}_{k_i}^E)\alpha_{k\ell_i}^E$$

$$+ (1 - \theta_{r_i}^E)^2(\hat{\pi}^E - \hat{p}_{k \text{ and } \ell_i}^E)\alpha_{k \text{ and } \ell, r_i}^E]/(1 - \theta_{r_i}^E)\}$$

$$\hat{L}^{eE} = \hat{L}^E - \sum_i \psi_{\ell_i}^E\{\hat{t}_{\ell_i}^E + \theta_{r_i}^E(\hat{\pi}^E - \hat{p}_{k \text{ and } \ell_i}^E)\alpha_{k \text{ and } \ell, r_i}^E$$

$$- \theta_{k_i}^E(\hat{w}^E - \hat{p}_{k_i}^E)\alpha_{k\ell_i}^E/(1 - \theta_{k_i}^E)\}$$

$$\hat{R}_3^{eT} = \hat{R}_3^T - \hat{t}_{r_3}^T - [\theta_{\ell_3}^T\theta_{r_3}^T\theta_{k_3}^T(\hat{w}^T - \hat{p}_{k_3}^T)\alpha_{k\ell_i}^T$$

$$+ (1 - \theta_{r_i}^T)^2(\hat{\pi}_3^T - \hat{p}_{k \text{ and } \ell_3}^T)\alpha_{k \text{ and } \ell, r_3}^T/(1 - \theta_{k_i}^T)]$$

and

$$\hat{R}_4^{eT} = \hat{R}_4^T - \hat{t}_4^T$$

The $\hat{t}$s are the changes in the technical efficiency parameters, the $\psi$s are the factor shares in each sector, the $\theta$s are cost shares, the $\alpha$s are the partial elasticities of substitution, the $\hat{p}_k$s are the weighted average changes in the cost of capital, induced either by commodity price change or changes in the rate of profit, and the $\hat{p}_{k \text{ and } \ell}$s are the weighted average changes in the cost of capital and labour. No substitution terms have been included in the subsistence sector.

It can be readily seen, for example, that an increase in rent relative to the cost of capital and labour will lead to an increase in the size of the labour coefficients, which in turn act to lower the supply of labour as shown in the definition of $\hat{L}^{eE}$. Similarly, technical change which increases labour productivity, ($\hat{t}_{\ell_i}^E < 0$), will increase the effective supply of labour. The patterns of excess demand and excess supply arising from technical change and induced factor substitution described in the text follow from the above quantity magnification effects.

## NOTES

1. For an excellent survey of Marxian theories of imperialism, see Brewer (1980). See also Willoughby (1987).
2. Not all of the relevant issues are addressed by trade theory, as noted by Robinson (1974). For example, Robinson (1951) clarified the role of trade between capitalist and non-capitalist areas in improving the incentive to invest, the driving mechanism in Luxemburg's theory of imperialism. Barratt-Brown (1974) drew on what he called 'ultra Keynesian' theory to shed light on the nature of competition between imperialist nation states.
3. It may be objected that it is not correct to assume that America had the same institutions as England, namely a class which only owns land, as well as a class which owns circulating capital and a working class. Initially, this may not be the case, as in the example discussed by Marx (1867, Ch. 33) in relation to Wakefield's theory of colonisation. When there is abundant land which is freely available for immigrants to take immediate possession, there will be none of the institutional requirements for the operation of a labour market. The present argument requires that capital and labour markets are operating with intersectoral mobility of capital and labour, and that homogenous land can be used in both sectors. Agents who own both land and circulating capital receive the same rate of profit (interest) when the price of land is the capitalised value of rent.
4. For example, Krueger (1977) and Havrylshyn (1985) use the specific factors model for the analysis of comparative advantage in which it is necessary to assume that no capital is used in agriculture and mining. Similarly, UNIDO (1986) incorrectly expresses concern over the fact that capital endowments are valued at traded prices rather than autarky prices for the analysis of comparative advantage.
5. This is in fact the approach adopted by Binswanger and Rosenweig (1986) and Binswanger and McIntire (1984) in the discussion of financial institutions in land-scarce South-Asian agriculture and land-abundant Africa.
6. For the purposes of the argument, all that is required is that there is no equalisation of the rate of profit or resource rents. The lack of mobility of resource use between capitalist and subsistence sectors could flow from different infrastructural requirements, even when the physical characteristics of the land used in both sectors is the same.
7. Tropical food can also be treated as tradable and in long-run competition with temperate food produced in England, as in the Lewis case, but it seems both more realistic and is analytically simpler

to treat it as internationally non-tradable before processing in the commercials sector.

8. For further discussion, see the survey of dual economy models by Kanbur and McIntosh (1984). See also Taylor (1979) and Kalecki (1976).

9. The ideas behind this discussion are based on Wood (1986). Exploration of the consequencs of the endogenous production of skilled labour in the context of perfect information and perfect foresight has been carried out by Findlay and Kierzkowski (1983). In the approach followed here, the focus is on the consequences of North–South trade for given endowments of skilled and unskilled labour. Given the imperfections in the market for the production of skills, and the ample role for motivation in skill acquisition other than income maximisation, it makes sense to treat the acquisition of skills as exogenous. This allows the analysis to focus on the distributional consequences of capital or skill accumulation in the context of North–South trade.

# 8 · NORMATIVE TRADE THEORY AND THE INSTITUTIONS OF TRADE POLICY

## 8.1 INTRODUCTION

At several points the analysis has touched upon issues of normative trade theory, or the theory of commercial policy, particularly in the context of surplus labour and longer-run growth. It is therefore useful to draw these strands of analysis with normative trade policy implications together in the context of a discussion of the neo-classical theory of domestic market distortions.[1]

The central focus of the theory of domestic market distortions is market inefficiency, and the policies designed to eliminate such market inefficiencies are market-corrective mechanisms. Thus, trade intervention such as tariffs and quotas, fair trade laws, minimum wage legislation, interest rate ceilings, capital gains taxes or government subsidies and so on are identified as forms of government control to be subjected to scrutiny within the theory of domestic market distortions. In terms of the distinctions made in Chapter 1, the neo-classical ideal is to achieve efficient forms of parametric state intervention in the market mechanism. The pervasive forms of state intervention which form an important part of the armoury of the developmental state are seen as highly inefficient or are not seen at all. This reflects a systematic neglect within the neo-classical tradition of many forms of intervention in the development process at the micro and macro level.

It is not possible to discuss the application of trade policy instruments without an implicit or explicit view of the role of the state in the development process. For example, the more extreme applications of the theory of domestic market distortions by neo-liberal economists are often combined with the advocacy of a minimalist role of the state, often contradicted by the authoritarianism of strong central governments which implement policies of market liberalisation (see, for example, Toye, 1987). The final section of this chapter therefore outlines an alternative perspective on the role of the state in development and the scope for the application of the theory of domestic market distortions in the institutional contexts observed in developing countries.


## 8.2 THE OPTIMALITY OF FREE TRADE: A RÉSUME

Underlying the argument that free trade is best, the following assumptions have been centrally important. They are divided into three groups – those which are useful for simplifying the argument, those which are problematic but are retained by convention within the neo-classical tradition, and those which can be varied in the analysis of the theory of domestic market distortions, as follows:

1 a. Two commodities.
 b. Balanced trade.
2 a. Welfare is governed by the individual consumption of commodities, and the problem of income distribution is dealt with via the compensation principle, whether or not actual redistribution takes place.
 b. Abstraction of all social relations of production and exchange from the analysis.
3 a. Given factor endowments.
 b. Given production functions.
 c. Constant returns to scale, or CRS.
 d. The country is 'small'.
 e. Perfect competition and Pareto optimum conditions exist.
 f. Full employment.

The statement of the gains from trade argument or 'free trade is best' will not be repeated, but some brief exploration of the effects of relaxing the assumptions under points 2 and 3 will be considered. Attention is focused first on the common final arguments which arise when some of the assumptions under point 3 are relaxed before turning to the more controversial implications of the assumptions listed under point 2.

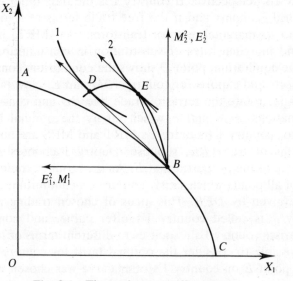

**Fig. 8.1** The optimum tariff argument.

### 8.2.1 Optimum tariffs

The idea that, for a single country, it may be desirable to drop the small country assumption (point 3d), was first articulated by Bickerdyke (1906). The optimum level of intervention through import or export taxes can be formalised as in Fig. 8.1. In Fig. 8.1, the neo-classical production function for two commodities and two factors $ABC$ is shown for country 2. With production at $B$ and world prices given by the price line $BD$, the 'normal' small country result would be for country 2 to trade along $BD$ to the point where the MRS between commodities 1 and 2 in consumption equals the MRT. Say $D$ is such a point. In this case country 2 will export commodity 1. However, when the 'small' country assumption is dropped, consumption at $D$ is not necessarily best from the point of view of country 2.

Suppose the production point $B$ and the price line $BD$ were chosen with some other considerations taken into account. Take country 2's production at $B$ as fixed for the moment, and draw in two new axes to show country 2 exports $E$ or country 1 imports $M$, and country 2 imports $M$ or country 1 exports $E$. Consider country 1's perspective. If country 1 is the only other country in the world economy and if the free trade terms of trade $BD$ are equal to its marginal rates of transformation (MRT) in production and marginal rates of substitution in consumption (MRS), then the equilibrium point $D$ shows the equilibrium combinations of imports and exports for country 1, $M$ and $E$. Now taking $B$ as the origin, rotate the terms of trade line $BD$ and consider other combinations of $M$ and $E$ which satisfy the optimal MRT and MRS for country 1 (country 1's MRT and MRS are not shown). At terms of trade $BE$, suppose country 1 chooses $M$ and $E$ according to the proportions at $E$. As the terms of trade vary, the locus of all points which satisfy country 1's equilibrium conditions will be given by $DEB$. This locus of chosen trading points for country 1 is called country 1's offer curve, and conveniently summarises country 1's responses to different terms of trade. It is now possible to consider the optimal tariff for country 2.

The point $E$ on country 1's offer curve was chosen with some very special properties. It is assumed to be the point on country 1's offer curve which enables country 2 to reach its highest social indifference curve (not shown) consistent with a free-trading equilibrium for country 1. This is achieved by country 2 requiring its consumers and producers to trade at the prices given by $BD$, whilst trading with country 1 at the prices given by $BE$. Thus, using the $*$ to indicate world prices, country 2's internal price ratio will be $p^*/(1 + t^m)$ where $t^m$ is the optimal import tariff imposed on country 2's imports as a fraction of world prices. Alternatively, the same result could be achieved with an export tax given by $(1 - t^e) = 1/ (1 + t^m)$ where $t^e$ is the export tax also expressed as a fraction of world prices.[2]

For present purposes, there are three observations which can usefully be made. First, even in the absence of an optimal tariff, free trade is better than autarky. This can be seen by noting that the country 1 offer curve shown in Fig. 8.1 could be redrawn for every point on the production possibilities frontier $ABC$, forming an envelope curve showing country 2's consumption possibilities frontier for every possible terms of trade (not drawn). This envelope curve will touch $ABC$ at one point where the tangent to $ABC$ is the same as the autarky MRS and MRT for country 1. This MRS and MRT will coincide with country 2's autarky price ratio, and there will be no basis for trade between the two countries. However, for any other production point for country 2, there will be the possibility of gainful free trade; the failure to exploit the optimum tariff does not destroy the gains-from-trade argument. Second, in the presence of powerful terms of trade effects with potential immiserising growth consequences, as discussed in Section 5.2.2, the argument above suggests that the best policy intervention to prevent immiserising growth is to impose an optimal export tax or import tariff. In the example of immiserising growth shown in Fig. 5.1, it can readily be shown that the envelope curve showing the consumption possibilities frontier after growth with an optimal tariff policy in operation will lie wholly outside the initial consumption possibilities frontier, and immiserising growth need not take place. Finally, the optimal tariff argument was conducted from the perspective of the individual country, not from an international world perspective. Since country 2's gain will be country 1's loss, to reach a world perspective requires some judgement about the desirability of the shift in world income distribution.

The most common guise under which the optimal export tax argument arises is in the context of fallacy of composition arguments against structural adjustment policies and more outward-oriented policies. Such situations arise where a group of developing countries have sufficient market power to make collective intervention to improve their terms of trade desirable. The extent to which such situations may arise, and the extent to which it is either feasible or desirable for a group of countries to attempt to improve their terms of trade, is taken up in the context of the empirical discussion of the terms of trade in Section 9.5.

### 8.2.2 Factor price distortions

There are a variety of factor market distortions discussed in the literature, some of which relate to sector-specific distortions and some of which affect factor markets economy-wide. The $2 \times 2$ H–O–S model is not very suitable for the analysis of many of these distortions because it assumes the economy-wide mobility of both factors, whereas in the static Ricardian representation of the same phenomenon, only labour mobility was assumed. Much of the neo-classical literature on domestic distortions uses the

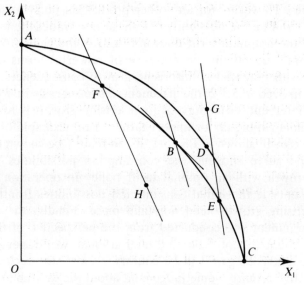

**Fig. 8.2** Factor pricing differentials.

specific factors model discussed in Section 4.3.2 to overcome this difficulty. However, in this section, the fiction of perfect mobility of the resource between sectors will be maintained. The exposition will focus on two types of underlying distortion mechanisms and subsistence agriculture will be treated as resource-intensive relative to manufacturing.

The analysis here focuses on three cases of institutional determination of the wage rate (which does not, of course, necessarily imply a fixed real wage). Section 3.3 introduced the Lewis surplus labour example, and this was contrasted with the Marxian reserve army of labour theory in Section 6.2. The case of urban–rural wage differentials is also examined below.

The surplus labour argument arises from payment of labour in agriculture according to its average rather than its marginal productivity. The consequences of such factor pricing differentials on the H–O–S model can be illustrated as in Fig. 8.2. In Fig. 8.2, the undistorted production possibilities frontier is given by $ADC$ and the with-distortions frontier is given by $AFBEC$. The reason why the with-distortion frontier lies inside the without-distortion frontier follows from the observation that, in the absence of the factor price distortions and in the presence of generalised substitution in productivity, it is possible to reallocate factors and obtain more output of one commodity without a decline in the output of the other.

The Lewis-type distortion raises the relative price of labour of the resource-intensive industry 2, subsistence agriculture, above its marginal productivity. Thus, at the autarky prices, production and consumption will be at some point such as $B$ rather than at $D$ with undistorted prices. At $B$, the social MRT given by the slope of the production possibilities frontier is less than the private cost ratio which is equated to the MRS, indicated by the price line through B which cuts the transformation frontier. The private cost of the labour-intensive commodity 1 is therefore higher than its relative social costs, because the resource-intensive subsistence agriculture raises the price of labour above its marginal product. With the introduction of trade, specialisation could go in either direction, depending on the relationship of world prices to the private cost ratio at $B$. Specialisation in $X_2$ production at $F$ is in the wrong direction since at the world price ratio $FH$, specialisation when autarky prices are given by the social MRT (given by the slope of the production possibilities frontier at $B$) would be in the opposite direction, $X_1$. Worse, free trade at the production point $F$ with consumption at $H$ yields a lower level of social welfare than autarky. This can be seen from Fig. 8.2 where the free trade social indifference curve tangent to $FH$ at $H$ (not drawn) will be lower than the social indifference curve for autarky. As discussed in Section 3.3, free trade specialisation in the 'wrong' direction lowers social welfare. Alternatively, specialisation could be in the right direction, such as point $E$ on the world price line $EG$. In this case, trade along the consumption possibilities frontier $EG$ to $G$ will improve welfare compared with the autarky point $B$. The without-distortion autarky point $D$ could be to the left or to the right of the consumption possibility frontier $EG$ and no ranking of distorted free trade and undistorted autarky position is possible.

Another type of factor price distortion discussed at length in the literature could be a wage or profit differential between the two sectors, again to be thought of in this context as agriculture and industry (Manoilesco, 1931; Hagen, 1958; Lewis, 1954). Obviously this example is compatible with surplus labour conditions. In this case, the distortion usually raises industrial wages above agricultural wages, or subsidises capital or 'rent' in the industrial sector. The lack of equalisation of wage rates will lead to a sub-optimal allocation of factors in production and production inside the without-distortion production possibilities frontier. Similarly, a rigid factor price, say a fixed real wage, will produce a distortion which lowers output and, in this case, leads to the unemployment of labour. The analysis of these and other factor market distortions proceeds along the same lines as discussed for the surplus labour model using Fig. 8.2. *In no case will the optimal policy intervention designed to eliminate the factor market distortion involve a restriction of trade.* Rather, it will require a subsidy to industrial wages in the case of both the surplus-labour and agriculture-industry price distortion cases, and the direct removal of any interest-rate or 'rental' subsidies to industry. When there is a fixed or rigid real wage as in the last case discussed, the optimum neo-classical policy recommendation would be either a general subsidy to all wage employment or, even better, the removal of the fixed real wage in the first place. As noted in Section 3.3, each of these first-best policy interventions requires a taxing capacity to meet the wage subsidy, a condition which may not always be feasible.

In principle, economic growth and development could eliminate surplus labour. This would allow the analysis to revert to the standard cases. However, there are two important qualifications. Firstly, the substantial elimination of unemployment does not exclude the possibility of institutional intervention directly and indirectly to influence the level and change of wages. Secondly, the condition of surplus labour or a reserve army of the unemployed – depending on one's theoretical viewpoint – persists throughout the Third World. Thus the end of this condition in one, probably small, country could be overturned by importing labour from other LDCs, or other policies discussed in Section 6.2 designed to match the long-run supply of labour to the demand for labour at an institutionally given wage.

### 8.2.3 The infant industry case

The standard theoretical case for protection is that of the infant industry. The neo-classical analysis is well set out in Corden

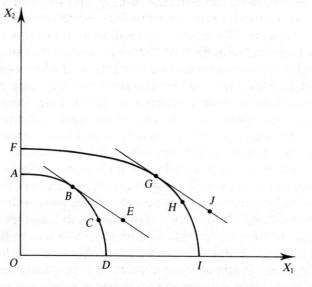

**Fig. 8.3**    The infant industry argument.


(1974, Ch 9). As he points out, the argument is essentially an argument for temporary protection. There are three necessary ingredients for the argument, as follows:

1. Time must enter the argument in an essential way.
2. Some form of imperfection and/or externality.
3. The dynamic or time element must enter the argument in a biased way, affecting some industries but not others.

Corden identifies two routes to establish the infant industry argument, through dynamic internal and dynamic external economies. Here, the argument is briefly illustrated with the aid of a single diagram (see Fig. 8.3).

In Fig. 8.3 the production possibilities frontier in the initial position is given by $ABCD$. With free trade, production would be at $B$ and consumption at $E$ on social indifference curve 2 (not drawn) on the consumption possibilities frontier $BE$. If industry 1 were protected, shifting the production and consumption point to $C$ and consumption to a point to the left of $E$ on social indifference curve 1 (not drawn), there would be a static welfare loss. Suppose the initial increase in domestic production of industry 1 leads to some powerful dynamic effect which only benefited industry 1, such as irreversible learning economies, or reciprocal external economies confined to the firms in industry 1. The production possibilities frontier might then shift to *FGHI* over time. In this case, the autarky consumption and production point at *H* on social indifference curve 3 (not drawn) will be superior to the initial free trade equilibrium consumption at *E*, but may be inferior to free trade on the with-growth production possibilities frontier, with production at *G* and consumption at *J* on social indifference curve 4 (not drawn). (In this case, any external economies have been assumed away by the second period.) In the first example, a sufficient imperfection to require infant industry protection would be a failure of the capital market to foresee the benefit of the dynamic learning possibilities which would offset the initial costs of establishing the industry. There are many variants of both types of effects which can be found in the literature, but for present purposes two points need to be stressed. First, in neither case will a tariff be the first-best policy for protecting the infant industry. Provided the budget revenue constraint is not overriding, it would be preferable to subsidise the industry and not incur a consumption distortion cost as well. Secondly, it is essential that there is a bias in the possibilities of dynamic effects in industry 1 rather than industry 2. If industry 1 and 2 are manufacturing and agriculture, then it must be established that there are dynamic effects which are confined to the manufacturing industry and which warrant protection. This is what List called the 'infant nation' argument, already encountered in Section 3.3, which overlaps to some extent the arguments for the development of industrial capitalism in the manufacturing industry whilst leaving subsistence agriculture untouched. Alternatively, if the infant industry argument is confined to some particular branches of manufacturing industry, for example capital goods rather than consumer goods, then the bias in the dynamic effects *within* the manufacturing sector must be established. This form of the infant industry argument is sometimes referred to as the Marshallian argument (see Corden, 1974, page 259). Another infant industry protection argument relies upon economics of scale, when the individual maximisation by producers does not take into account the effects of scale on their costs.

It is not possible here to do justice to the richness and variety of neo-classical analyses – theoretical or empirical – of protection. However, it is worth noting that although in general neo-classical analysis would recommend maximum protection of 10–20 per cent for five to eight years for infant industries, some historical evidence suggests that some successful NICs have pursued policies of selective infant industry promotion with very much higher levels of protection lasting for considerably longer time periods using conventional and unconventional forms of trade intervention (see Evans and Alizadeh, 1984; Bell *et al.*, 1984 and Pack and Westphal, 1986). These arguments are further developed in an empirical context in Section 9.6.


### 8.2.4 DUP and incentives

Neo-classical analysis tends to ignore the class and elite power groups role in development and their relationship to the state. The result is a pessimistic view of the effectiveness of interventionist policies. This is well illustrated by the theory of directly-unproductive profit-seeking activities (DUP). In the analysis of all distortions to the price mechanism so far, it was assumed that the different forms of government intervention had no resource cost. Bhagwati (1982) draws together and synthesises a great deal of work carried out in the 1970s which examined the legal and illegal responses of economic agents to a variety of government control mechanisms. Since the response of agents to such controls involves the expenditure of additional resources designed to overcome the control which would not otherwise take place, such DUP activity leads to production inside the production possibilities frontier. However, if the initial situation is distorted and the DUP activity partially eliminates the distortion, the final result may lead to a welfare improvement. In one early study of rent-seeking activity designed to overcome direct quantitative controls, Krueger (1974) found that the size of such control-induced rents in India and Turkey was at least 7 per cent and 15 per cent of GDP, respectively. For example, if import licenses for imported inputs are allocated according to installed productive capacity, it will pay to install additional productive capacity in order to secure a greater share of import quotas, even if such capacity remains underutilised. The economic principles behind the DUP literature can be illustrated with reference to the dis-

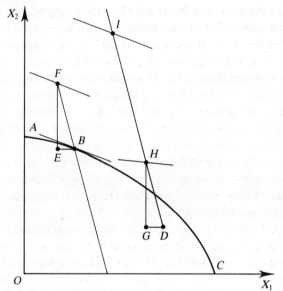

**Fig. 8.4** Import controls as an example of directly unproductive profit-seeking activity (DUP).

tinction between import quotas and tariffs for country 2 (see Fig. 8.4).

In Fig. 8.4, the initial production point is at *B*. With an import quota of *EF* and production remaining at *B* on the production possibilities frontier, *EB* of $X_1$ will be exported to pay for *EF* of $X_2$ imports and the final consumption point will be at *F* on social indifference curve 2 (not drawn). The same result could have been achieved with an import tariff which establishes the divergence between world prices given by the slope of *BF* and the slope of the domestic MRT and MRS given by the slopes of the production possibilities frontier at *B* and the social indifference curve 2 at *F* (not drawn). Now, if there is DUP activity designed to increase the allocation of import quotas to particular agents, the net benefits of protection will be less and some resources will shift into $X_1$ production. However, because real resources are expended in DUP activity, the final production point will be at some point such as *D*. As long as import controls remain in place, so that the maximum imports of commodity $X_1$ are constrained to *GH = EF*, there will still be a welfare loss since trade along *DHI* will be restricted to point *H*. At this point, social indifference curve 1 will be reached, which is lower than social indifference curve 2 passing through $F$ (indifference curves not drawn). However, if there was a tariff in the initial situation which triggered the DUP activity, there will be trade along $DHI$ to reach $I$ and social indifference curve 3 (not drawn) in the final situation. Thus, if the initial DUP activity was triggered by a quota, there will always be a welfare loss even though the DUP activity offsets the benefits of the quota in favour of the producers of commodity $X$. When the initial distortion is a tariff, the DUP activity will lead to a partially-offsetting welfare gain because the consumption costs of the tariff are not so tightly constraining.

There are many other forms of DUP activities designed to offset the effects on particular agents of tariffs, quotas or taxes, and the final outcome depends on the presence or absence of distortion in the initial and final situations. For a summary and further analysis, see Bhagwati (1982) and Bhagwati and Srinivasan (1982).

Two important critical comments on DUP theory can be entered here. Firstly, because neo-classical analysis ignores social class and power, it overlooks potential extensions of DUP analysis. For example, there is no counterpart within the neo-classical tradition to the literature on the labour process discussed in Evans (1989, section 4), which might be characterised by the acronym DPC or directly profit-seeking control. Such profit-seeking control within the hierarchically-controlled capitalist labour process might well be inefficient by straightforward welfare criteria, but the efficient alternative may be inconsistent with accepted social norms, or even outside the possible solutions with capitalistic or any other presently-known relations of production. Such control will often increase productivity through increases in the intensity of work and other such measures, but not always as the periodic crises in the social relations of capitalism, and more recently, existing socialism testify.[3] Secondly, DUP analysis ignores the possibility that the state could provide incentives to promote compliance with its policies. A good example of this is making the granting of import licences conditional on achieving a certain level of exports. More generally, credit, protection, government orders, etc., can be made subject to clearly defined performance criteria, and thus such incentives used as part of the strategic development plan. Clearly this depends both on the capacity of the state as an information centre, and the efficiency of its political and administrative capacity in resisting diversionary pressures, such as conception. These issues are further developed in the next section.

## 8.3   THE INSTITUTIONS OF TRADE POLICY

The interventionist arguments outlined in the previous section are in the mainstream neo-classical tradition. They may be extended to encompass a view of the state as an agent with imperfect knowledge and foresight, in which case the appropriate response is for indicative planning rather than for a detailed hands-on industrial policy planned by central government. Admitting a lack of information on the part of government may also open the way for the standard neo-liberal response, that an imperfect market solution may be much better than imperfect government intervention. This view is reinforced by the literature on DUP(E) activities and interest group politics. However, there is much that is left out of the story about the state by both the mainstream neo-classical and neo-liberal views which has important implications for the discussion of trade policy.

A preliminary sketch of the role of the developmental state can be found in Bardhan (1984). Although Bardhan's primary concern is with the Indian state, nevertheless his formulation has wider applicability to other developing countries. He argues that the state elite, with a sufficiently unified sense of ideological purpose about the desirability of national economic development, is the main instigator of development policies. Whilst there is a divergence in views about the extent of the autonomy of the state from class forces, Bardhan argues that in many cases of state-directed industrialisation, the leadership genuinely considers itself as the holder of the nation's deeply held normative aspirations. In a world of international military and economic competition, these aspirations often take the form of striving for industrialisation and rapid economic growth.

The state in many developing countries, in addition to providing the basic infrastructure and institutional framework, has substantial power over control and ownership in circulation (banking, credit, transport, distribution and foreign trade) and over production (directly manufacturing much of the basic and capital commodities output). The state also regulates the patterns of private investment, direction of resource allocation, choice of technology and import control. However, while the state from its commanding heights formulates goals and policies, nevertheless it often cannot ignore the serious constraints on effective implementation of policies posed by the articulated interest of proprietied classes. When there is significant conflict of interests among those proprietary classes, there may be serious repercussions for the implementation of development policies.

A similar view of the state is presented by White and Wade (1988), who compare the nation-building strategies of the ruling elites of Taiwan and South Korea with those used in Latin America. They argue that in the former countries the state has pursued a strategy of minimising commitments to existing social groups, particularly as a result of land reform which took place in the early 1950s. Whilst some bureaucratic authoritarian regimes in Latin America may have wanted to do the same, many existing groups already had a considerable autonomy from the state and a capacity to influence against it. These groups could only be put down by the exercise of great violence. In contrast, both Taiwan and South Korea experienced about 50 years of hard, growth-oriented Japanese colonial rule which permitted the non-Japanese inhabitants almost no political activity or autonomous organisation of any kind. Later on, independent channels of interest aggregation and interest articulation were successfully prevented from joining together and acquiring independent power. As a result, the state managers in both countries have enjoyed considerable autonomy to define national goals, and unusual powers to get those goals accomplished. It has not been necessary to enter into the bargaining process and shifting alliances which have characterised the policy process even in the more authoritarian regimes of Latin America, or the democratic regimes of India described by Bardhan.

The strength of the state at the national level in the formulation of development policy and strategy contrasts with the weakness of international state power for resolving economic conflict and developing international policies more conducive to development (Brett, 1985). Rather, domination by states at the international level for the enforcement of property relations and the maintenance of political and military alliances through direct and threatened use of military power is all too evident. More subtly, military expenditure itself may have economic effects which makes the resolution of economic conflict in trade and macro adjustment problems more difficult (see, for example, Smith and Smith, 1983 and Kaldor and Walker, 1988).

It is difficult to bridge the gap between such general perspectives on the role of the state in development, the institutions and state bodies charged with the formulation of economic policies, the institutions and agents within the economy whose behaviour is to be influenced by the policy environment, and the normative trade theory as outlined.

From a wide variety of perspectives, the extensive literature on the internal organisation of the firm and the organisation of work agrees that there is a deep conflict between individual and collective rationality at the point of production in any social system.[4] Profit or growth maximisation is likely to conflict with welfare maximisation and may lead to authoritarian forms of organisation of production. Moreover, concern with narrowly-conceived market efficiency may require that the state has strongly centralised power to operate against price distorting and welfare lowering interest groups. Often, there is a contradiction between 'economic liberalisation', and the authoritarian forms of government which are required to implement pro-market reforms. These observations underline the need to identify and define desirable and feasible forms of politics to go hand in hand with interventionist trade and industrial policies.

The mainstream view often ignores the central importance of ideology in the developmental state.[5] A strong developmental ideology may do much to facilitate hands-on intervention without state employees engaging in significant rent-seeking behaviour, as seems to have been the case to some extent in South Korea, to cite one example. Often non-market forms of intervention are also important. For example, state capacity for strategic decisions and more intermediate levels of state intervention have made a major contribution to the development of successful industrialisation strategies. The economic rationale for much of the successful East Asian state intervention is the provision of a clearing house for information and technology in the face of market failure.[6]

The above considerations suggest that trade policy instruments cannot be ranked in terms of their impact on efficiency and growth applied independently of the institutional context within which they were applied. For example, quantitative controls have always been important in the South Korean case, and certainly more important than revealed by the measured change in the use of quantitative controls.[7] To some extent, the potential for rent-seeking behaviour has not materialised, partly because of the role of ideology already mentioned above. More potently, quantitative controls were often tied to crude incentives in the South Korean case, for example import licenses tied to the export performance of the firm. This gave the state instruments of direct control over firms necessary for their industrial policies, which neither tariffs nor subsidies could achieve. In such cases, the standard ranking of tariffs as a more efficient protective instrument than quotas cannot be sustained. Quantitative controls tied to incentives, however crude, may also be superior to tariffs, precisely because they provide the instruments for implementing an interventionist industrial strategy. In terms of Fig. 8.4, firms have an incentive to expand exports in order to obtain import licenses, in much the same way that tariff protection may be associated with greater trade from $D$ to $I$, compared with import controls alone which only allow for trade from $D$ to $H$ when production is at $D$. In addition, the successful interventionist trade strategy may lead to fewer rent-seeking costs than implied by the production point $D$, and an outward-shifting production possibilities frontier as shown for the infant industry case in Fig. 8.3.

In other contexts, the choice of policy instruments may more closely approximate the ranking suggested by the theory of trade policy. For example, in an economy dominated by very small firms, the appropriate forms of intervention at the sector level may stress policies which encourage networking between firms combined with joint-venture co-operative arrangements for key activities which enjoy externalities and scale economies, either between firms, between firms and local government, or between firms and central government.[8] In effect, the industrial strategy may seek to combine interventionist policies, normally associated with a central government, with a small firm strategy designed to give the sector the type of benefits derived by the head office of very much larger firms. Within this context, the institutional arrangements may be sufficiently strong to permit the targetting of any subsidies which may be required to overcome market imperfections without incurring severe central or local government revenue constraints.

Class relations often have an important, if not crucial, bearing on the way in which comparative advantage is developed. This view is often emphasised in the structuralist-institutionalist, dependency and Marxian traditions.[9] This observation cuts two ways. If class relations have had an important historical influence on the development of long-run comparative advantage, then future changes in a country's comparative advantage might well be blocked by the classes who benefit from the present arrangements. In this case, the desired trade and development strategy can only proceed if the class forces that have shaped the historical development are changed or transformed.[10] Note that it is the class forces which must be overthrown in this case, not the principle of comparative advantage, as so often happens in the dependency and Marxian traditions.

The extent to which the principle of comparative advantage and the theory of trade policy built upon it can inform our understanding of development policy issues can only be assessed in the light of an examination of the empirical and policy record of developing countries, taken up in the next chapter.

## NOTES

1. The theory of trade policy discussed in this chapter draws heavily on the elegant exposition of Michaely (1977). See also Corden (1974, 1984), Bhagwati (1982), Bhagwati and Srinivasan (1982) and Bliss (1989).
2. At point $E$, the optimal import tariff is equal to the elasticity of country 1's offer curve less one:

   or $\qquad \eta - 1$ where $\eta = \dfrac{dE}{dM} \cdot \dfrac{M}{E}$

   For a discussion of the relationship between the optimal export tax and the elasticity of demand for exports, see Corden (1974, pages 160–8). For a fuller discussion of the optimal tax argument, see also Michaely (1977, pages 24–38).
3. See, for example, Williamson (1975, 1985), Lazear (1981), Bowles (1985) and Pagano (1985) and the summary in Evans (1989, Section 4.1).
4. See footnote 3.

5.  A notable exception is North (1981).
6.  This rationale is a summarised view in the 1987 World Development Report (World Bank, 1987, Box 4, page 71).
7.  See, for example, Wade (1989).
8.  For example, see the application of some of these ideas to an industrial strategy for Cyprus described in Murray *et al.* (1987).
9.  On this, see, for example, Sideri (1970), de Janvry (1981, 1984) and Sheehan (1987, 1988).
10.  For suggestions along these lines in the Nicaraguan case, see Fitzgerald (1986).

# 9 · EMPIRICAL TESTS AND TRADE STRATEGIES

## 9.1 INTRODUCTION

The usefulness of the trade theories discussed in the previous chapter for understanding and influencing the relationship between trade and development is ultimately an empirical one. In Chapter 1, it was suggested that five basic questions have been explored in the field of trade and development. This chapter examines some of these questions from an empirical perspective.

Inevitably, the coverage of the empirical literature is highly selective, and the discussion is intended to be illustrative rather than extensive. Most of the empirical material discussed relates to the post-war period.

To some extent, the answer to all of the questions asked depends on the prior answer given to question four. Are the classical and neo-classical theories of international trade suitable for application to the situation of developing countries? One way in which the empirical literature throws light on this question is through the empirical tests of the capacity of trade theories to predict the pattern of trade discussed in Section 9.2.

The role of trade in the process of economic development is pursued empirically through a discussion of the competing hypotheses that trade is the engine versus trade as handmaiden of growth in Section 9.3. The patterns of international exchange which best serve the objectives of developing countries are difficult to establish empirically. One of the problems frequently cited in the literature which limit the usefulness of the historical patterns of trade, whereby developing countries export primary commodities in exchange for manufactures produced in developed countries, is pursued in Section 9.4 through a discussion of the terms of trade. This line of enquiry is further developed in Section 9.5, where the fallacy of composition argument against outward-oriented trade strategies is discussed.

It was argued that the consequences of various instruments used by developed and developing countries aimed at achieving the desired pattern of trade cannot be viewed outside the institutional context in which the various instruments are used. This question is explored empirically in Section 9.6 through a discussion of inwards versus outward-oriented trade policies. The final section of this chapter draws together some of the implications of the theoretical and empirical findings of this book for the formulation of trade strategies.

## 9.2 PREDICTING THE PATTERN OF TRADE

### 9.2.1 Testing trade theories

The most important difficulty to be faced in testing predictions about the pattern of trade, using the classical concept of comparative advantage, is that unobservable knowledge of autarky price differences is required. In a multi-commodity framework with heterogeneous capital goods, pre-trade price differences based on a common price for valuing capital goods are required. It would therefore seem that it is necessary to derive indirect tests of trade theories based on the observation of with-trade equilibrium positions.

In the case of the simple Ricardian theory, the obvious indirect test is the ranking of industries between countries by their bilateral ranking of relative labour productivities, as set out in inequalities (2.8), compared with the pattern of bilateral trade. However, the pattern of trade in England from Ricardo's time until the end of the nineteenth century showed that natural resources and resource-based commodities were important (see Table A9.1.1). The exclusion of other factors such as natural resources from the simple Ricardian model may therefore undermine its predictive power.

The tests of the labour-time Ricardian theory have been surprisingly successful in establishing the predicted relationship between rankings of industries by relative labour productivities and the pattern of trade.[1] However, the tests do not discriminate between the simple Ricardian and H–O–S theories, since without the equalisation of wages or profits, differences in labour productivities may be the result of systematic differences in the endowments of other factors. It is difficult to establish the extent to which wages and profits differ internationally (see section 1 of Table A9.1.2 which sets out the differences in per capita GDP for 1960 and 1982 for several groups of countries). Apart from measurement difficulties, some of which are summarised in World Bank reports (1984, pages 274–5), it is not possible to separate the international differences in per capita GDP arising from differences in the underlying endowments of productive stocks or assets from other causes of productivity differentials.[2] Estimates of wage differentials between developing and developed countries for several different industries show that the difference between the average wage measured in terms of a common currency varies by a factor of between 3.5 and 6.1, depending on the industry and the time period (see Table A9.1.2, section 2). However, these data in themselves tell one nothing about labour productivity differentials since no allowance was made for differences in the endowments of other productive factors, differences in techniques of production, differences in intensities of labour and other factors which may influence productivity.

There is some evidence on the international differences in corporate profitability which suggest that there was some movement towards equalisation of rates of return over the period from 1962–4 to 1970–3, although the differences began to reassert themselves by 1974–6 (see Table A9.1.2 sections 3(a) and (b)). However, the lowest differential rate of profit between the six countries was 2.6 times. A similar picture emerges from section 3(b) when American private overseas investment is considered. There is a differential of over 2.7 times between the rates of return between countries or groups of countries in the latter part of the 1960s. There was no clear tendency towards overall equalisation of the returns to productive stocks between countries.

In order to test the H–O theorem in its quantity form, it is necessary to establish a relationship between three things: factor endowments, factor intensity of production and consumption, and trade patterns. The direction of causality is from the interaction between factor endowments and factor intensities to the pattern of trade, requiring a knowledge of a country's factors endowments and the world factor endowment. It is a salutary reminder of how difficult it is to test the H–O–S theory that, with the important exception of Leamer (1984), none of the tests of the H–O theorem use direct estimates of factor endowments, relying instead on casual empiricism. However, on the positive side, it is also worth recalling that the factor embodiment form of the H–O theorem can be modified to take into account some of the complications discussed in Sections 4.3, 6.5 and 6.6 concerning differences in consumption patterns and non-balanced trade. Differences in technology, factor prices and the possibility of factor intensity reversal can also be allowed for, and heterogeneous capital goods can be taken into account provided the tests are based on the with-trade equilibrium in which capital goods are measured at the same commodity prices. On the negative side, the presence of economies of scale may undermine the predictions of the factor proportions model, since relative prices are a function of the levels of output as well as the endowment of productive inputs. Transport costs and barriers to trade will blunt the extent to which the average trading patterns will reflect the underlying factor endowments. In addition not all of the endowments of productive inputs will be determinants of any pattern of trade.

In the dynamic H–O–S model and in the circulating capital models considered in Chapter 6, the role of the stock of capital, and of the endowment of labour, as a determinant of comparative advantage was undermined by the arguments in favour of including the exogenous specification of the long-run rate of profit or wages, which can be strongly influenced by social and institutional factors.[3] More generally, if the price of any stock is exogenously determined in the long run, it is the price of the services derived from using the stock and not the size of the stock itself which is the determinant of comparative advantage. The causal interpretation described above can only be established once the endogenous and exogenous components of price formation are fully specified.

For all of the above reasons, the empirical research on the testing of the H–O theorem, for the most part, only establishes the extent to which observed trading patterns are consistent with some of the variables indirectly associated with stocks embodied in trade. The sceptic who protests that the violation of so many of the assumptions of the model renders any empirical testing invalid should await the discussion of some of the results of empirical tests before reaching any conclusions.

### 9.2.2 Resource shares in world trade

In the absence of empirical estimation of the world endowment of productive stocks and the distribution of these endowments between countries, it is necessary to rely on a combination of casual empiricism on the relative endowments of productive stocks and indirect as well as direct indicators of stock intensities of production and trade. Further, without detailed case studies to determine which stocks have a role in determining comparative advantage and which stocks have exogenously-determined prices, it is not possible to make any strong statements about the causal determinants of comparative advantage. It is interesting to enquire how much of the observed patterns of trade is consistent with a factors-endowments theory of comparative advantage on the basis of casual empiricism. To this end, an aggregate world trade matrix for six commodity groups between seven regions for 1980 was constructed (see Table A9.1.3).

The estimate of the shares of resource-based trade are based on the shares of food, minerals and other fuels, and other primary commodities, for different groupings of countries. It is generally true that the production of minerals and fuels are critically dependent on endowment-specific natural resources. Also, food and other primary commodities require resources which will generally not be required for the production of other commodities. Such endowments of specific resources must also be combined with a set of relations of production which allow those resources to be employed productively. The three resource-based activities considered in Table A9.1.3 embrace Ohlin's breakdown of resource activities into agriculture and forestry, fishing and hunting, and minerals, the difference being that the classification in Table A9.1.3 is by end use rather than by resource type. The share of resource-based trade in world trade derived from the world trade matrix set and in Table A9.1.3 has already been summarised in Table 7.1.

It is therefore striking that no less than 44 per cent of all world trade, 36 per cent of intra-developed market economy trade and 23 per cent of developed market economy exports to developing countries or the 'South' are accounted for by the first three resource-based industries. Such resource-based trade also makes up 79 per cent of 'South' exports to the developed market economies or the 'North'. It is also apparent from Table A9.1.3 that resource-based trade is very important in intra-centrally planned economies trade, and in overall intra-developing country or South–South trade where it accounts for 66 per cent, 75 per cent and 43 per cent of 'South–South' exports for developing Africa, developing America and for developing Asia, respectively. The very high shares of resource commodities in trade even between the developed market economies provides *prima facie* evidence of the importance of the endowments of resources as a key element in describing comparative advantage and the pattern of trade. On this count alone, it would seem that the neo-Ricardian rejection of factor endowment theories of comparative advantage leaves out of account well over 40 per cent of world trade.[4]

The other commodity groups identified, namely textiles and clothing, machinery and transport, and other manufacturing (see Table A9.1.3) do not typically require the immediate presence of natural resources, although the proximity of water and power resources, and of transport resources, can have powerful indirect effects on the location of manufacturing activities. However, labour and capital generally make up the bulk of the costs of manufactured commodities and it is therefore pertinent to ask how successful the H–O–S theory is for at least describing the observed patterns of manufacturing trade.

The vast bulk of all manufactured trade takes place between the developed market economies themselves and between the centrally-planned economies, as can be quickly verified with reference to Table A9.1.3. Of a total world manufactured exports of US$(1980) 1150 billion, 77.7 per cent was from the developed market economies. The principal market for manufactured exports was the developed market economies themselves (46.9 per cent), the remaining markets being the centrally planned economies (5.9 per cent) and the developing or 'South' economies (33.7 per cent). On the imports side, 82.0 per cent of developed market economies imports of manufactures was from the developed market economies themselves with 4.3 per cent from the centrally planned economies and the remaining 13.7 per cent from the 'South' economies. In the overall exchange between 'South' and 'North', there is a strong division of labour. The overwhelming dominance of resource-based exports from 'South' has already been noted. In manufactured trade, 'North' exported US$130 billion worth of machinery and transport equipment in exchange for only US$14.5 billion imports in 1980 in the same category from 'South'. Similarly, 'North' exports of other manufactures of US$165.4 billion over-shadows 'South' exports of US$67.1 billion in the same category in 1980. This balance in 1980 is reversed only for textiles and clothing, where 'North' exports were US$7.2 billion in exchange for US$13.5 billion imports from 'South'.

Manufactured exports from 'South' economies, as is widely recognised, have been growing very rapidly for over 20 years, even though these exports remain a small percentage of manufactured imports into the developed market economies. Thus, for the period 1965–80, manufactured exports from all developing countries grew at about 8 per cent per annum faster than the rate of growth of all merchandise exports from developing countries (see World Bank, 1984, Table 3.3). However, these exports are not evenly distributed between 'South' economies. The largest absolute and relative shares of manufactures in exports is concentrated in the 'developing other Asia' group, with intra-group trade in manufactures being second only to the exchange of manufactures between 'developing other Asia' and the 'developed market economies' (see Table A9.1.3). Given the overall importance of manufactured trade and the overwhelming dominance of the intra-developed market economies trade in manufactures, it is pertinent to ask how much of this trade is consistent with the H–O–S factor endowments theory.

Unlike the specific resources which underlie trade in food, minerals and other fuels, and other primary commodities, the endowments of commodity capital and of skilled and technical labour which are more important in manufactured trade are not specific to any particular activity in the long run. It is therefore not possible to make any judgements about the accuracy of the factor endowments theory for describing manufactured trading patterns on the basis of Table A9.1.3.

### 9.2.3    Further evidence on the role of factor endowments in trade

A full scale test of the factor embodiment form of the H–O theorem is based on the relationship between factor embodiment in trade and a country's excess supply of factors where the factors included are those for which the country's supply is exogenously given. Thus, when the number of factors equals the number of commodities and all of the incredible assumptions required for the theorem to hold are satisfied, the factor content of country $k$'s trade will be given by:

$$\underset{\text{in net trade}}{\text{factors embodied}} \qquad \text{net factor supply}$$
$$V^{tk} \qquad = \qquad V^{xk} - \hat{\chi}^k V^w \qquad (9.1)$$

where $V^{tk}$ is a vector of the factor content of country $k$'s trade, $V^{xk}$ is the vector of factor endowments or factor supply used in producing country $k$'s output or GNP and factor demand $\hat{\chi}^k V^w$ is the product of a diagonal matrix $\hat{\chi}^k$ of country $k$'s share of world expenditure adjusted for differences in consumption patterns and non-balanced trade and $V^w$, the vector of endowments of the rest of the world.

Equation (9.1) may be rewritten by decomposing the vector of factor endowments in trade into the net trade in each commodity group multiplied by the matrix of direct and indirect factor input coefficients required in production, or:

$$\Lambda^k T^k = V^{xk} - V^w \qquad (9.2)$$

where $\Lambda^k$ is a matrix of direct and indirect factor inputs in production in country $k$, $T^k = E^k - M^k$ is the vector of net trade in country $k$ and all other variables are as previously defined. Equation (9.2) may also be rewritten as the trade intensity of the net supply of factors

$$T^k = [\Lambda^k]^{-1} [V^{xk} - \hat{\chi}^k V^w] \qquad (9.3)$$

Thus, a full test of the H–O theorem in its factor embodiment form based on equations (9.2) or (9.3) requires a knowledge of the direct and indirect factor input coefficients $\Lambda^k$, net trade in commodities $T$, the country's factor endowment or supply of factors $V^{xk}$ and the country's demand for factors $\hat{\chi}^k V^w$.

Most tests of the H–O theorem in its factor embodiment form

rely on only four of the nine types of information described above for the full test. Thus the early tests pioneered by Leontief (1953) for the United States use data on exports, imports and factor intensities to calculate the capital/labour ratios of exports and imports. However, in this ratio form, the results of these tests cannot be used to impute the excess supply of factors in all cases. As Leamer (1980, 1984) has shown, a direct estimate of the factor content of trade, the left-hand side of equation (9.2), can be used to estimate the excess supply of factors on the right-hand side of the equation. When this is done, it can be shown that the Leontief ratio form of the test of the H–O theorem is only correct when the embodied flows of capital and labour have the opposite sign, a situation which need not arise in a multi-factor world.

The most serious test of the H–O theorem is by Leamer (1984) who uses a reduced form version of equation (9.3) in cross-country regressions which relate net trade flows to factor endowments, estimating the reduced form coefficients of the universe matrix of factor intensities econometrically.

Leamer bases his tests on a very large database compiled for sixty-one countries for 1958 and 1975 using ten aggregate commodities and eleven types of factors. He fits equations of the form:

$$T = b_1 V^x + U_1 \qquad GNP = b_2 V^x + U_2 \qquad (9.4)$$

from the sample of sixty-one countries, where the net export and factor endowment vectors $T$ and $V^x$ are as previously defined, the matrix $b_1$ is an empirical estimate of the reduced form matrix of factor intensities, $b_2$ is the vector of factor returns, GNP is factor income and $U_1$ and $U_2$ are stochastic error terms (for details of the tests, see Leamer, 1984, Sections 2.2 and 6.2). He finds, after exhaustive econometric tests, that the essence of his findings are captured by fitting the simple linear model set out in equation (9.2).

The most important aspects of the Leamer findings are first, that with some important exceptions, the inter-country differences in the pattern of trade in the ten aggregate commodity groups are well captured by the eleven aggregate resource endowment variables for most of the commodities requiring endowments of natural resources. Second, the important exceptions occur in the role of the different categories of labour and capital in the equations for manufactured trade. Thus, capital played an insignificant role in predicting the pattern of manufactured trade in 1958, skilled labour had a negative impact on comparative advantage in manufactures in 1975, and one of the least satisfactory equations was for the export of labour-intensive manufactures (see Table A9.1.4).

Part of the reason for the failure of Leamer's results in explaining the pattern of trade in manufactures lies in the incomplete and inadequate measures of the underlying factor endowments, in spite of the very considerable efforts to overcome the conceptual and empirical difficulties. For example, the measured capital stock from fifteen-year investment flows correlates very highly with GDP; the cross-country differences between savings rates and growth rates are not sufficient to provide estimates of the capital stock which are significantly different from GNP. Further, the stocks of skilled labour are measured by the number of workers classified as professional or technical in each country without adjustment for inter-country differences in the degree of skill and the length of time required in education or other forms of training to be included in these classifications.

Leamer's results should not be interpreted as an evidence of failure of the H–O theorem in its quantity form, since the avenues for improving the database, particularly in relation to key variables such as skill endowments, may considerably improve the results. Further, information on the role of institutional variables in determining the underlying comparative advantage through the exogenous specification of one or more factor returns could be used to further refine the analysis.

In spite of the limitations to the Leontief form of the test of the H–O theorem and the difficulties posed by the institutional determination of some factor prices, particularly labour, there is considerable literature which estimates the capital/labour ratios for imports and exports over a large number of countries. That is, the ratio form of the test of the H–O theorem calculates the capital/labour ratio for imports and divides this by the capital/labour ratio for exports. If this ratio is less than one and if the underlying flows of capital and labour are of opposite signs, then it can be imputed that the country in question is a net importer of embodied labour and a net exporter of embodied capital.

There is no easy way to summarise the results of these tests but the studies of Baldwin (1971, 1979) and Havrylyshyn (1983) which estimate the embodiment of commodity capital and labour imports and exports for forty countries are representative. The Baldwin study uses the input-output coefficients for the USA, the EEC and Japan to provide alternative estimates of the relative capital to labour ratios in imports and exports, whilst Havrylyshyn uses Indian coefficients. In addition, Havrylyshyn estimates the 'human capital' to total labour requirements in exports and imports (some of these results are reported in Table A9.1.5).

Using casual empiricism to judge the relative endowments of capital and 'human capital' compared with total labour, the results for each country can be checked for approximate consistency with the H–O theorem on the assumption that the underlying flows of capital and labour have opposite signs. If the ratio of capital (or 'human capital') to labour ratio is higher in imports than for exports, then the ratios will be greater than one. Thus, for example, if it is assumed that all of the developed market economies are capital abundant relative to labour, then one would expect to find that all of the coefficients shown in the table for these countries are less than one. Similarly, if it is assumed that the developing market economies are capital scarce, all of the coefficients in the table should be greater than one.

On this criterion, the results are very pessimistic for the factor endowments theory in respect of capital to labour ratios (see the summary of the results in Table A9.1.5). However, this judgement is premature, first because the flows of capital and labour may not have opposite signs, and second because it may not be correct to describe some countries such as Greece, Portugal and Spain in the early 1960s as capital abundant relative to labour on the basis of calculations with the American and EEC factor-intensity coefficients. Thus, discounting the results for Greece obtained with American and EEC coefficients, the results are consistent with the proposition that both countries are net importers of embodied capital relative to labour in their trading patterns. Similar considerations may be used in classifying the results for all other countries in the studies as 'consistent' or 'inconsistent' with the factor endowment theory. In addition, where specific studies have been carried out which resolve the apparent 'paradox', these results were drawn on. An obvious case in point here is the illustration of the ratio form of the famous Leontief 'paradox' which suggests that the USA is a net importer of embodied capital through trade (see Table A9.1.5).

As discussed at length in the literature, the Leontief 'paradox' can be resolved in a variety of ways, principally though the disaggregation of labour into technical and other skill categories (see the results reported in Table A9.1.6). The 'paradox' can also be resolved by taking into account imbalances in the American pattern of trade, as discussed in Leamer (1980, 1984) and Deardorff (1984).[5]

On the rough criterion described above, using judgement and casual empiricism, the results summarised in Table A9.1.5 are not quite so inconsistent with the factor endowments theory as might appear at first sight. Thus, it would appear that thirty out of forty country estimates of the relative embodiment of capital to labour in trade might well be consistent with the H–O theorem and twelve out of twelve estimates of the relative embodiment of 'human capital' to total labour in Havrylyshyn (1983) are consistent with the theorem. If the countries are grouped into developed and developing countries, then the results are inconsistent for nine out of twenty-one developed market economies. The single inconsistent result for a developing country, Ghana, is probably dominated by the effects of extremely high protection combined with the use of developed country coefficients. The apparent failure of the factor endowments theory in relation to capital and labour is therefore confined mainly to the developed market economies, where there are a number of cases where the ratio form of the Leontief 'paradox' results are obtained. Further investigation of these cases along the lines of Leamer's resolution of the Leontief paradox might yield more consistent results. Given the overwhelming dominance of the developed market economies in the world manufactured trade, and given the similarity of their stock endowments as a group when compared with the 'South' economies, this result is not really surprising.

The vast bulk of other tests of the H–O theorem are much more loosely specified. They are based on regressions of the form:

$$T = b_3 \Lambda + U_3 \tag{9.5}$$

where $T$ is as previously defined, $b_3$ is a vector of parameters, $\Lambda$ is the matrix measuring the factor intensity in the production, and $U_3$ is a stochastic error term. When a Cobb-Douglas production function is specified, a simple measure of $\Lambda$ will be the cost-shares of the services of factors in each industry (see Deardorff, 1984, pages 485–6). Whilst these empirical studies do not constitute a test of the underlying H–O theorem in its quantity form, the results of some of these studies are suggestive of other determinants of comparative advantage in those areas not illuminated by the studies discussed so far. A useful way of summarising some of these results is to draw on the studies by Baldwin (1971, 1979) (see Table A9.1.6. for a summary).

The results summarised provide a great deal more detail about variables associated with the country patterns of trade. Roughly speaking, of the twenty-nine country results reported, seventeen are consistent with the H–O theorem. As was previously found, most failures were confined to the developed market economies. Thus, of the ten developed country failures indicated, three were due to the extremely poor fit of the regressions (Finland, Switzerland and Yugoslavia), three were due to the strong presence of Leontief 'paradox' results (West Germany, Italy and the UK) and four were due to the presence of strong scale economy effects (Australia, Belgium–Luxemburg, Greece and Japan). In the latter case, some factor endowment variables were also significant in the equations fitted, so that the exclusion of these countries somewhat overstates the failure of the factor embodiment description of the developed market economies. For the developing market economies, the failures were for Ghana and Libya.

The results show interesting new factor-related variables played a significant role in describing the country trading patterns. In the remarks which follow, attention is focused only on statistically significant variables. For example, the percentage of engineers and scientists in the industry workforce is positively associated with the net balance of trade by industry in the USA and is negatively associated with the trading pattern for Italy and Spain. This variable could be regarded as primarily reflecting the importance of differential stock of highly skilled labour in determining the pattern of trade at a point in time, or as a variable which reflects a more dynamic determinant of comparative advantage through the association of the employment of engineers and scientists with R&D expenditure. Other variables reflecting the possible importance of unskilled labour are important for three of the other developing Asian countries (Hong Kong, South Korea and Taiwan). Finally, a proxy for the importance of agricultural land in determining comparative advantage is significant, with a positive or negative coefficient in no less than fifteen countries. This result appears broadly to conform to casual empiricism on the relative endowments of agricultural land relative to labour.

In spite of all the limitations discussed, results of the empirical studies of the pattern of trade suggest a surprising degree of descriptive consistency of trading patterns with the predictions of the H–O theorem in its quantity form. However, it is much more difficult to establish causality. Take, for example, the Australian case. Australia could be regarded as a price taker on the international capital market as well as for most commodities traded. If the rate of profit is taken as exogenous and the wage rate endogenous, the relevant stocks which have a primary role in determining comparative advantage will be the resource to labour ratios. Alternatively, it could be argued that the strong institutional element in the determination of wages through the Australian arbitration system fixes the wage, with the rate of profit being exogenous. In this case, the relevant endowment ratios which determine comparative advantage will be the capital to resource ratios. If either hypothesis is correct, the positive and significant coefficient on the number of farmers and farm labourers found in the studies by Baldwin (1971, 1979) could be interpreted as a proxy for the stock of agricultural land per capita (see Table A9.1.6). This confirms the obvious point that Australia is a net exporter of natural resources, and the embodied flows of labour and capital would have to be interpreted in the light of adjustment for a current account deficit and the choice of the institutionally-determined factor return.

Another case which seems consistent with the H–O theorem is that of South Korea. It is widely recognised that South Korea had a surplus labour economy up until some point in the 1960s. In this case, the relevant factor endowments which determine comparative advantage in the surplus labour period are the capital to resource ratios. This is entirely consistent with the overwhelming importance of resource-based exports in South Korea's trade in

1960 (see World Bank, 1984, Table 10). Once the immediate sources of surplus labour in agriculture were exhausted, the role of exogenous determinants of the wages are more difficult to disentangle from other determinants (see the discussion of institutional wage determination in Sections 3.3 and 6.2). However, the confirmed rapid rise in manufactured exports throughout the 1970s and 1980s is consistent with a limited capacity to expand resource-based exports over and above the home consumption requirements. The empirical studies which suggest that South Korea is a net importer of capital in its trading pattern in the early 1970s are consistent with this interpretation (see, for example, the results shown in Table A9.1.5). However, a more complete study of the South Korean case would have to distinguish between skilled and unskilled labour, and the role of institutional determination of unskilled wages after the immediate sources of surplus labour were used up by the end of the 1960s along the lines suggested in Section 7.5.

## 9.3 TRADE AS ENGINE VERSUS TRADE AS HANDMAIDEN OF GROWTH

### 9.3.1 Trade and growth

The very broad association between periods of growth of exports and the rate of growth of GDP shown in Table 1.1 does not establish the direction of causality between trade and growth. The latter can only be established within the context of a theoretical model. The models of comparative advantage and growth discussed in this book have very different implications for the direction of causality.

A key determinant of the relationship between trade and growth lies in the choice of distribution closure discussed in Section 6.2. Models of long-run comparative advantage with a classical Ricardo–Marx–Lewis closure suggest that trade is likely to increase the rate of growth through the effect of trade on the rate of profit. For the small open economy, resource constraints will not be relevant, but these constraints may operate for the world economy as a whole. Alternatively, the neo-Keynesian closure discussed in Section 6.2 had no mechanism built in for increasing the rate of growth as a result of the opening of trade. However, such a mechanism could be readily included within the specification of the investment function, working either through scale economies and the size of market or through the realisation of effective demand through trade. Finally, the dynamic H–O–S model discussed in Sections 5.4 and 6.2 suggests that the primary effect of trade is on the level of economic activity and any stimulus to growth from trade is likely to work through the effects of scale economies and competition on the growth of factor productivity. It is within this broad context that empirical literature on the idea that trade is the engine of growth versus trade as the handmaiden of growth is discussed.

### 9.3.2 Trade as the engine of growth

In the context of Ricardo–Marx–Lewis closure of the theoretical model, the opening of trade will indeed increase the rate of growth, all else being given. Thus the idea that trade is the engine of growth has a very respectable pedigree. Lewis (1980) provides the most recent statement of the argument. He suggests that the rate of growth of output in the developing world for the past one hundred years has depended on the rate of growth of output in the developed world, and that the principal link through which the latter controls the former is through trade. Thus:

> The growth rate of world trade in primary products over the period 1873 to 1913 was 0.87 times the growth rate of industrial production in the developed countries; and just about the same relationship, about 0.87, also ruled in the two decades to 1973.... We need no elaborate statistical proof that trade depends on the prosperity of the industrial countries. (Lewis, 1980, page 556)

Thus, the demand for South exports can be written as:

$$E_s = E_s(X_n) \tag{9.6}$$

where $E_s$ is developing country or South exports and $X_n$ is industrial production in the North. Using total world trade of primary products as a proxy for South exports, Lewis fits a regression of the form:

$$\log E_s = \text{constant} + \alpha \log X_n + \text{stochastic error term} \tag{9.7}$$

to obtain the estimated value of $\alpha$ of 0.87 reported in the above quote.

However, there are a number of potentially important influences which may modify the relationship between primary commodity trade and the rate of growth of the industrial countries. The original list of six factors contributing to the failure of trade to act as the engine of growth for developing countries identified by Prebisch (1950), Singer (1950) and by Nurkse (1959), summarised by Cairncross (1960), were:

1. The change in industrial structure favouring of industries with a low import content of imported raw materials.
2. The rising share of services in total output of advanced countries.
3. The low income elasticity of consumer demand for many agricultural products.
4. Agricultural protectionism.
5. Economies in the use of raw materials, e.g., through the reprocessing of scrap.
6. The introduction of synthetic materials.

A more complete specification of the demand for South exports would try to separate at least some of the influences in the Nurkse–Cairncross list, to be modelled and included in equation (9.7). The fitted Lewis equation (9.7) only picks up effects 1, 5 and 6, relating to the use of materials in industry. Since industrial production is not a good proxy for income changes (among other things because of 2), the income elasticity effects, 3, are not captured in the Lewis equation. Price effects do not appear in either the Lewis equation or the Cairncross list, but it could be argued that these can be excluded on the demand side if the hypothesis that the price elasticity of demand for South exports is low is correct, and if the supply side of the surplus labour argument is correct.

Given the absence of historical data which would permit the estimation of a more complete model, a first step towards checking the robustness of the model can be made by testing for the stability of the coefficients over time, and for different groups of commodities, particularly commodities and manufactures. Whilst this has not been done directly in the literature, it can be done indirectly on the basis of the summary data on the rates of growth of world trade from Kravis (1970) (see Table A9.2.1 for a summary).

It is clear from the Kravis findings that there is a marked difference between the rates of growth of primary commodity exports from the underdeveloped compared with the developed countries in different time periods, undermining the Lewis assumption that the rate of growth of total primary product trade is a good proxy for the rate of growth of developing country trade. More significantly, there is a very marked difference between the rate of growth of manufactured exports from the developing countries and the developed countries (96 per cent and 36 per cent, respectively, over the first thirty-five year period from 1876–80 to 1913). In the second period, from 1913 to 1953, the relative position of the developing countries in primary commodities and manufactures reverses, with primary commodities from developing countries experiencing a relative boom over this period. In the final period, from 1953 to 1966, both primary commodity and manufactured exports from developing countries slumped compared with developed country trade in both groups. Thus, the Kravis data provides strong evidence that the aggregate engine of growth relationship fitted by Lewis for the earlier period would not stand up to disaggregation between primary commodities and manufactured exports within each time period, and the evidence suggests that any fitted relationships will not be stable over time.

A second body of empirical evidence which undermines the Lewis form of the trade as engine of growth hypothesis has been assembled by Riedel (1983). A test of the hypothesis was first made by regressing the log of world primary exports against the log of production of manufactures in developed countries for the period 1953–77. Riedel's aggregate estimate of the slope coefficient was close to Lewis's estimate for the period 1953–73, using slightly different data, but he found that the constant term and slope coefficients varied significantly over time. More interestingly, Riedel assembled consistent data for the period 1960–78 to test the trade as engine of growth hypothesis with aggregate and disaggregated developing country export data (see Table A9.2.2 for a summary).

In regression 1, the log of total developing country non-fuel exports is regressed on the log of GDP for the OECD-North countries with dummy terms to test for constant and slope differences between the 1960s and 1970s. The estimated slope coefficients for the 1960s are very close to the Lewis estimate, but the coefficient increases sharply in the 1970s. When the exercise is repeated with developing country non-fuel exports disaggregated to manfactured, raw material and food exports, a very different picture emerges. For manufactures, the value of the slope coefficient increases dramatically in the 1970s, whilst the coefficient for raw materials drops sharply. Only in the case of food exports is there no statistical difference in the slope coefficient for the two periods. Since the dramatic increase in manufactured exports took place in the 1970s against a background of declining growth rates in the North, secularly declining shares of manufactures in North GDP and rising protectionism, Riedel rightly concludes that supply rather than demand conditions have principally determined developing country exports of manufactures. This is consistent with the models of comparative advantage and growth with a Ricardo–Marx–Lewis closure applied to developing countries exporting manufactures. The findings for raw materials are consistent with the Nurkse–Cairncross pessimism about changes in the demand for raw materials, presumably because of technical change and synthetic substitutes. Only in the case of food exports is the engine of growth constant.

### 9.3.3 Trade as the handmaiden of growth

The identification of a role for supply-side factors in determining the rate of growth of developing country exports is a first step in a critique of the trade as engine of growth hypothesis. There is a deeper sense in which the metaphor is inappropriate, for the engine which drives the model is not trade alone. Developing the mechanical metaphor a little, the real engine which seems to underline the idea is the surplus labour assumption combined with a lack of any other supply-side constraints; the role of trade is merely to provide the fuel. There is, of course, no need to assume that output and the supply of exports are unconstrained, with the rate of growth governed by the rate of growth of industrial production in the North. The Ricardian growth model set out in Sections 2.2 and 3.5, and the circulating captial models described in Chapters 6 and 7 are all compatible with the presence of surplus labour and supply-side constraints on production. The key role of trade when there is a Ricardo–Marx–Lewis closure is the effect on accumulation and growth operating through the effect of trade on the rate of profit.

There is another set of considerations which undermine the trade as engine of growth thesis. At the very heart of the surplus labour argument as outlined in Section 3.3 is the role of social and institutional factors which govern the supply of surplus labour. The forces which shape and mould the development of capitalist relations of production, which influence and change the social and institutional arrangements in pre-capitalist areas over time, and the role of the state, all crucially affect the potential supply of surplus labour, adding force to the need for close attention to be paid to the supply side in this broader sense. Both neo-classical and analytical Marxian schools can find common ground in the proposition that trade is the handmaiden rather than the engine of growth. Some of these issues will be developed further after a discussion of the empirical evidence on the long-run terms of trade facing developing countries.

## 9.4 THE NET BARTER TERMS OF TRADE[6]

There is a considerable theoretical and empirical literature on the unequal distribution of the gains from trade and technical change between primary commodities and manufactures, giving rise to long-run terms of trade pessimism for both primary commodity producers and developing countries. It is often argued that this persistent bias in the terms of trade against primary commodity producers significantly weakens the role of trade as an 'engine' of growth discussed in the previous section. These two interconnected sets of ideas have dominated much of the discussion of the distribution of the long-run benefits of commodity trade between developed and developing countries in the post-war period.

The main statistical evidence of the long-run decline of the terms of trade between manufactures and primary commodities for the period since 1800 has been re-examined in several recent studies (Grilli and Yang, 1986; Sapsford, 1984, 1985; Sarkar, 1986; Spraos, 1983: the results of these studies are summarised in Table A9.2.3). Taken at face value there is strong evidence of a rising trend in the terms of trade between primary commodities and manufactures from 1800 to 1860, after which there is a declining trend. There are, however, serious difficulties in finding the best equation to summarise the long-run movements, since there may be a very long-run cyclical component in the data, but the time series is not long enough to give much guidance on the strength and significance of such effects. For this reason, the quadratic term used in the Grilli and Yang study should not be taken too seriously (see the last equation reported in Table A9.2.3). This is especially so since the adverse long-run trend had been exacerbated by the adverse short-run decline in the terms of trade for primary commodities in the 1980s. It would therefore seem that, for the whole of the twentieth century, there is evidence of a declining trend in the non-oil primary commodities/ manufactures terms of trade.

There are important discrepancies in the estimated size of the long-run negative trend in the aggregate non-oil primary commodities/manufactures terms of trade (see Table A9.2.3). For example, Sapsford's estimates of the long-run trend are around three times larger than those obtained by Grilli and Yang. There is no obvious reason for preferring one data set to another, but since Grilli and Yang recalculated the unit price indices and the weights from the historical data sources, there may be a case for having more confidence in the lower estimates of the long-run trend implied by their data.

There has been a long debate on the effects of quality improvements and transport costs which may have masked possible improvements in the terms of trade. However, Spraos (1983, Ch. III) convincingly argues that there are important quality changes in both primary and manufactured commodities which are not accounted for, so that there is no strong presumption that the terms of trade index will be biased in either direction on this account. Further, Sarkar (1986, Table 2) makes ingenious use of historical evidence to show that there is either no correlation or a negative correlation between shipping freights and the inverse of Britain's terms of trade over the period 1882 to 1929, providing an opposite valuation bias against the declining primary commodities/manufactures terms of trade on account of transport costs. Thus, there are grounds for believing the Grilli and Yang estimate of the primary commodities/manufactures terms of trade decline of around −0.5 per cent per annum, estimated without a quadratic trend term of quality or transport cost biases. For the future, it would seem that the underlying structural changes now taking place in the world economy make it very difficult to predict the movement of aggregate commodity prices outside of the sample period.

One of the frequent criticisms of the terms of trade pessimists is that the aggregate adverse trend hides a wide diversity of experience for different commodities in different time periods. (Some recent disaggregated estimates of terms of trade movements by commodity and time period put together by the World Bank are summarised in Table A9.2.4.) The disaggregated trends for the period 1900–83 show a considerable diversity of experience. Since 1941 beverages and metals both show significant positive trends, whilst the position of cereals and non-food agricultural products show a negative trend. Overall, the 1950–84 experience of the agricultural commodities and metals and minerals shows a downward trend, but the main falls for agricultural commodities are in the 1950s and for metals in the 1970s. The trends for beverages in the 1970s, for cereals in the 1960s and for metals and minerals in the 1950s and 1960s provide the strongest examples of favourable terms of trade experiences.

Given the diversity of the terms of trade movements for different commodities, it is important that any model used to try and explain the underlying determinants of the terms of trade must be able to encompass a wide range of empirical experience.

An important motivation for the Lewis terms of trade model descibed in Section 3.3 was his desire to square the observed adverse long-run trend in the aggregate terms of trade between primary commodities and manufactures, and the prediction of the open dynamic Ricardian model discussed in Section 3.5 that the long-run terms of trade would move in favour of primary commodities. As already discussed in Section 3.3 in the context of surplus labour in the South and full employment in the North, changes in the commercials/manufactures terms of trade are determined by the degree of hypothesised bias in technical change in the South towards commercials and in the North towards temperate agriculture.

The bare essentials of the Lewis terms of trade argument are strikingly different from those of the other well-known arguments for the long-run decline in the terms of trade of primary commodities produced by developing countries suggested by Prebisch (1950) and Singer (1950). The early Prebisch–Singer (P–S) argument analyses the enclave character of the development of commercials production for export, stressing the role of both specific resources in the production of such commodities and the consequences of having such resources exploited by foreign investors. This body of literature has been re-examined and extended in Singer (1975, 1984, 1987). Singer (1987) summarises the four points in the Prebisch–Singer argument, as follows:

1. Low price elasticities of demand for primary commodities compared with manufactures.
2. Low income elasticities of demand for primary commodities compared with manufactures, partly due to the operation of Engel's Law, and partly due to the technological superiority of industrial countries giving rise to economies in primary commodity usage and the development of synthetic substitutes.
3. The technological superiority of the industrial countries leads to a Schumpeterian rent element for innovation and a monopolistic profit element because of the size and power of the multi-national corporations and trade unions in the North.
4. Differences in the structure of commodity and labour markets, with strong unions in the developed countries and monopolistic market structures which lead to the absorption of the benefits of technical change in the developed countries. On the other hand, with surplus labour in both rural and urban areas, the benefits of technical change are passed on to developed country consumers.

It is not entirely clear how the components listed under point 3 of the P–S argument interact to determine a long-run tendency for the primary commodity terms of trade to deteriorate over time, as distinct from once-and-for-all effects on the terms of trade arising from such factors as the degree of monopoly power. Similarly, there is no analysis of how the degree of factor market monopoly and the effects of strong unions in the North change over time. However the circulating capital model described in Section 7.4 provides a useful framework for disentangling the different effects which may influence the long-run terms of trade.

The diversity of explanation of terms of trade movements is consistent with the empirical evidence (see Tables A9.2.3, A9.2.4 and A9.2.5 for a summary of some of the evidence). For example, the twentieth century experience of the beverages and metals was favourable whilst the experience for other agriculture was unfavourable. There were strong upward movements in the temperate agriculture/manufactures terms of trade in the earlier part of the nineteenth century, followed by a consistent decline as reflected in the movement of the UK's terms of trade. The rise and then fall in the temperate agriculture/manufactures terms of trade is also reflected in the evidence on disaggregated temperate agriculture/wholesale price index for the USA.

Although the evidence is not uniform, it is striking that for both wheat and corn in the USA, there is a long period of an increasing price trend followed by a decreasing trend. For sugar, there is evidence of a decreasing price trend since about 1860, and for rice at least since around 1941. Thus the US experience bears out the declining trend for world food/manufactures and cereals/manufactures terms of trade. Whilst the turning point from a rising to a declining price varies considerably from commodity to commodity in the USA, it is pertinent to ask whether or not there is a common explanation for the historical rise and then fall in the food component of the temperate agriculture/ manufactures terms of trade, hereafter referred to as the temperate food/manufactures terms of trade.

One obvious candidate is the sectoral bias in technical change hypothesis advanced by Lewis, but the data requirements for testing this hypothesis are formidable.[7] Ideally, estimates of total productivity changes in both the North and the South over a long historical period would be required, combined with estimates of all other factors influencing the terms of trade. All that can be considered here is the role of technical change. For the North, the USA plays a pivotal role in world food trade and the US evidence on technical change is probably the most important to consider. (Some rather incomplete and fragmentary evidence on technical change in the USA and some other countries in the North for the period from 1880 is set out in Table A9.2.6.)

The evidence on sectoral bias in technical change in the North in favour of temperate agriculture cited by Lewis (1969) is based on labour productivity comparisons. However, if attention is focused on the estimates of total factor productivity for the USA, it would appear that there is no absolute bias towards agriculture as a whole (see Table A9.2.6). Compared with the late nineteenth and early twentieth centuries, the productivity of labour and capital used in US agriculture simply caught up to but did not surpass that of manufactures. This conclusion is reinforced when the estimates of agricultural output in wheat units per hectare are examined for the USA. Whilst there is also a dramatic improvement in the rate of growth of productivity of land from the 1930s, the inclusion of land in the total productivity comparisons would almost certainly show that manufactures retained an absolute productivity growth advantage over the whole period, albeit dramatically lowered in the post-1930 period. The labour productivity comparisons for the USA and for other countries reinforce this conclusion (see Table A9.2.6). By the post-1950 period, the rate of improvement in labour productivity in agriculture often exceeded that for manufactures, but it is unlikely that this picture would hold true for total productivity comparisons. The evidence also shows a dramatic increase in the rate of growth of the productivity of agricultural land, but in only one case does this exceed the rate of growth of labour productivity in the same countries. What, then, remains of the Lewis hypothesis that sectoral bias in technical change is the central determinant of long-run terms of trade movements?

Whilst the evidence is not consistent with the absolute sectoral bias hypothesis, it does not mean that changes in the relative rate of growth of productivity between temperate agriculture and manufactures will not exert a powerful influence on the terms of trade. The enormous increase in the rate of growth of agricultural productivity compared with manufactures from the 1930s must have exerted a strong downward pressure on the temperate food/ manufactures terms of trade. Thus, broadly speaking, there were three main influences on the temperate food/manufactures terms of trade in the nineteenth century.

First, on the supply side, the rate of growth of the labour supply relative to land was a key determinant of the extent to which diminishing returns to land would lead to a rising temperate food/manufactures terms of trade. Once the frontier effects of agricultural expansion in North America and Australasia worked through, the expansion of labour relative to land would put upward pressure on the temperate food/manufactures terms of trade. Second, a bias in the rate of technical change towards manufactures would work in the same direction. Finally, Engel curve effects imparted a downward pressure on the temperate food/manufactures terms of trade. In the later period, the rise in the growth of productivity in temperate agriculture to similar rates as experienced in manufactures provides an extra downward pressure on the temperate food/manufactures terms of trade. The evidence is consistent with the conjecture that, with the elimination of the sectoral bias in technical change in the temperate North, the final effects on the temperate food/manufactures terms of trade depend on the outcome of the opposing effects of diminishing returns to land and the Engel curve effects. It would seem from the empirical evidence that the latter effect is sufficiently powerful to overcome the effects of diminishing returns to land.

The experience of higher rates of technical change in temperate agriculture was broadly repeated elsewhere in the North, at least judging from a comparison of the rates of improvement in labour and land productivity for some North countries (see the bottom part of Table A9.2.6). However, in the case of both Japan and Western Europe, changes in the degree of protection of agriculture will also have powerful effects which should be taken into account. As already noted in Section 7.4, a rising degree of protection for temperate agriculture acts as technical regress and will therefore tend to improve the internal temperate agriculture/manufactures terms of trade in the protecting country, whilst worsening them in world trade. Therefore an upward shift in the level of agricultural protection would tend to work in the same direction as the elimination of sectoral bias in technical change in the North. As long as there is relatively little bias in technical change and unchanged protection, then the long-run effects of the Engels curve on the demand side and diminishing returns to land are likely to be the dominant influences determining the long-run temperate agriculture/manufacturing terms of trade.

What of the sectoral bias hypothesis in the South? There are no sources of reliable and systematic data on the bias on technical change in the South towards commercials, though there are many case studies which show such a bias. Furthermore, there is no simple reading of the disaggregated terms of trade trends which suggests that there is likely to be a declining aggregate commercials/manufactures terms of trade. The most significant commodity grouping for which the South experiences adverse terms of trade is for non-food agricultural commodities. Another adverse terms of trade case hidden in the aggregate food commodities index is the example of bananas. Ellis (1978) provides very strong evidence of dramatic technological change in the production of bananas produced by vertically-integrated multi-national companies in Central America over the post-war period. His evidence suggests that, over the period from the later 1940s to the early 1970s, output per hectare more than doubled as the producing countries switched to Panama disease-resistant varieties, capital per worker increased by nearly four times whilst the number of workers per hectare decreased by around 20 per cent. With wages approximately constant in real terms (indicating the lack of technical change in subsistence agriculture), the major beneficiaries of this rapid technical change were both the producing companies and consumers, who experienced a fall in the real price of bananas of about 50 per cent. In a different context, de Janvry (1981) shows evidence of systematic bias in technical change in Argentina towards large-scale agriculture arising out of the power of landed elites to command state resources for infrastructure, extension and research and development, thus contributing to the stagnation of subsistence agriculture in Argentina. Important as these effects might be for the individual commodity or country, it is more difficult to find the experience reflected in the more aggregate statistics.

Another source of indirect evidence on biased technical change in the South can be gauged from the pattern of allocation of expenditure for agricultural research (AR), recently surveyed for sub-Saharan Africa by Lipton (1986). Although the overall return on AR expenditure in sub-Saharan Africa is much lower than for other areas of the South, Lipton stresses in his findings that AR expenditure on some of the most important food crops such as cassava have been seriously neglected at the expense of export crops. Yet there are no long-run historical series on the relative price of cassava to either manufactures or other traded agricultural commodities, precisely because it is a non-traded subsistence crop.

The above analysis suggests that it is the change in the pattern of biased technical change which provides a powerful part of the explanation of the observed adverse movements in the price of primary commodities against manufactures. There would seem to be no evidence to support the hypothesis of an absolute sectoral bias in technical change towards temperate agriculture in the North, but there is strong evidence of a dramatic improvement in the rate of technical change in temperate agriculture compared with manufactures. It is this effect, combined with the Engel curve effects which work in the same direction, that has prevented the predictions of classical political economy, that the price of food relative to manufactures would rise in the long run as a result of diminishing returns to land, from coming about. From the perspective of developing countries with still rapidly growing populations, the knowledge that the rate of technical advance in agriculture for the world as a whole continues to offset diminishing returns to land is a mixed blessing, unless net food exporters in the South are also participating in the rapid growth of agricultural productivity. Further, as has been stressed in some of the more conventional literature, adverse aggregate commodity terms of trade do not necessarily translate into deteriorating country terms of trade. This has been confirmed recently by Grilli and Yang (1986, Table 5), who show that a 1 per cent decline in the non-oil primary commodity/manufactures terms of trade estimated on the basis of the simple exponential trend over the period 1953–83 only translates into about a 0.3 per cent decline in the terms of trade of non-oil developing countries. This is quite apart from the well-known argument that it is the income terms of trade which are far more important for developing countries and that a declining net barter terms of trade does not mean that there are no gains from trade.

## 9.5   EXPORT TAXES AND THE FALLACY OF COMPOSITION

One of the key arguments against full exploitation of comparative advantage and the international division of labour in the 1950s and 1960s was export pessimism arising from the long-run secular trends in the terms of trade for primary commodities discussed in the previous section. More recently, the failure of the 'engine of growth' in the industrial North, the shorter-run terms of trade decline in the 1980s, and the rise of protectionism in the 1970s and 1980s, have rekindled these concerns. One form in which the case is put is in terms of the fallacy of composition argument.

The fallacy of composition argument against full participation in the international division of labour arises when a relatively small group of developing country exporters of a particular product face a less than perfectly elastic export demand curve from the industrial North. That is, the case for an optimal export tax outlined in Section 8.2.1 holds for a group of countries. Particular concern with such a possibility arises when international agencies such as the World Bank and the International Monetary Fund (IMF) recommend adjustment policies which would lead to export expansion for several countries which collectively face the fallacy of composition problem.[8] How important is this problem, and what can be done about it?

Karunasekara (1984, page 45) identified eight possible primary commodities where it may be possible to increase export revenue by applying a uniform export tax on all developing countries, namely coffee, cocoa, tea, bananas, bauxite, copper, tin and tropical timber. More recently, Singer (1988) has suggested that the same arguments apply to developing country exports of labour-intensive manufactures. For developing countries facing severe foreign exchange constraints, the chance to raise export revenues by collective export restriction or by a uniform export tax has an immediate attraction. There are, however, two sets of arguments against such policies.

The first set of objections are practical. For as long as any one country has an export elasticity of demand for a particular product which is greater than one, it will have an incentive to break any collective action to impose an export tax or other form of restriction. The experience of commodity agreements in the pre-war period, and in the 1970s and 1980s, strongly suggests that the chance that collective action to impose a uniform export tax will be able to escape such incentive problems is remote (see a summary of these arguments in Evans, 1990). The best that can be hoped for is that, when the major producing countries of the key commodities concerned are in receipt of policy advice from the international agencies as a part of short- and long-run structural adjustment programmes, there is recognition of the fallacy of composition problem. This could be in the form of short-term measures which either restrict the export expansion of the problem commodities in all of the countries undergoing simultaneous trade policy reform, or which provide additional resources to finance the adjustment process in the face of the loss of export revenue because of low export demand elasticities.

The second set of objections against collective export taxes or other similar policy responses to the fallacy composition problem is that it is difficult to argue that the exercise of collective monopoly power is an appropriate general principle for the operation of the international economy. Such policies tend to focus on the redistribution of a given amount of resources rather than focusing on policies which promote efficient and equitable growth and development. The next section examines in an empirical context some aspects of country experience which may have contributed to different growth performance in the post-war experience.

## 9.6   PRICE DISTORTIONS, INSTITUTIONS AND GROWTH

### 9.6.1   Introductory remarks

The initial thrust of developed country commercial policy in the post-war period was a series of negotiated reductions in protection between the countries of the industrial North under the auspices of the General Agreement on Tariffs and Trade (GATT). The major exception to this was the continued protection of agriculture. Policy-making in the developing South was dominated by the idea that import-substituting industrialisation (ISI), fostered through tariff and other forms of commercial policy was an essential component of development strategy so that high levels of protection was the norm in the 1950s in developing countries. In the 1960s, a major shift in commercial policy and development strategy occurred in many developing countries with the introduction of export-oriented industrialisation (EOI). The commercial policy changes were not negotiated as in the industrial North, but took place as a part of a series of major changes in power relationships within the developing countries concerned, between the developing countries and the international agencies such as the IMF and the World Bank, and between the developing countries and the leading nations of the Western part of the industrial North. At the same time, agricultural protection in the North became ever more entrenched in the USA, the EEC and Japan. During the 1970s, many of the changes in the industrial North towards more open economies gave way to the reintroduction of protectionism through the back door. The most important forms of this back-door protectionism were a wide variety of non-tariff barriers to trade and a new form of trade restriction called voluntary export restraints (VERs). In the case of textiles and clothing, the VERs became formalised in the Multi-Fibre Agreement (MFA), preventing the collapse of these activities in the North as the developing country exports of these commodities expanded rapidly during the 1970s (see the discussion of the empirical case against the trade as engine of growth hypothesis in the previous section). The MFA agreement represented an important repudiation of GATT principles in that it institutionalised discriminatory commercial policies. Other industries fell to the VERs and other forms of restriction, so that by the end of the 1970s and the beginning of the 1980s, over half of world trade in activities as diverse as footwear, electronics, steel, motor vehicles, textiles and clothing and agricultural commodities were subject to significant levels of trade restrictions (for an excellent summary of some of these developments in commerical policy, see MacBean, 1988). Whilst a strong argument can be made to support the case that the re-emergence of protectionism has been an important effect of the slow-down in the growth of the world economy from the middle of the 1960s, contributing to the major structural disequilibria and slow or even negative rates of growth which have emerged in the 1980s, it is not so easy to pinpoint the costs and benefits of ISI *versus* EOI as a long-run development strategy when examined from a single-country perspective.

The case for ISI rests on three major sets of assumptions. First, in the presence of surplus labour, there is an in-built bias against industrialisation. This gives rise to the case for intervention in the price mechanism outlined in Sections 3.3 and 8.2.2 to prevent continued specialisation along the lines of historical comparative advantage through protection of an indigenous industrial capacity. Second, there is the assumption that there is a strong infant industry or even infant nation argument for protection along the lines discussed in Section 8.2.3. Finally, the ISI argument rests on the assumption that there is systematic bias in the structure of the North–South trading environment, culminating in long-run terms of trade problems for developing countries such as those discussed in Sections 3.4, 5.2, 7.4 and 9.4, which require diversification away from historical lines of specialisation. Such a perspective suggests a combination of taxation of export commodities, where the optimum export tax argument can be applied individually or collectively, and a policy of direct intervention in the market to foster industrialisation.

In the neo-classical discussion of ISI *versus* EOI, the basic case for a period of ISI has not been entirely destroyed. Rather, as a rule of thumb, most neo-classical authors argue that the amount of effective protection justified by the infant industry argument is around 10–20 per cent for a five- to eight-year time period. Some of the recent criticisms of the neo-classical case against ISI have rested on a set of empirical propositions which disputes these empirical rules of thumb, arguing that the infant industry learning period is likely to be much longer than five to eight years, and that the level of protection justified cannot be reduced to simple rules of thumb (see for example Bell *et al.*, 1984; Kaplinsky, 1984; and Kaplinsky (ed.), 1984). Another line of criticism of the neo-classical case for EOI challenges the primacy of an efficient market mechanism as the most important requirement of a successful development strategy, compared with social, institutional and political determinants, discussed in Section 8.3.

There is no easy set of theoretical or empirical criteria against which such competing hypotheses and policy regimes can be tested. The remainder of this section examines some of the statistical evidence on growth performance as a background to a discussion of the possible effects of trade policy regimes and institutional variables on growth in the post-war period.

### 9.6.2 Patterns of growth and trade orientation

One way of capturing the effect of trade orientation on growth performance is through the statistical analysis of development patterns. As a part of the revision and up-dating of their earlier work on the patterns of development, Chenery and Syrquin (1986), using a sample of over 100 countries over the period 1950–83, attempt to capture the effects of resource endowments and trade policy on growth. They use indices of primary orientation and trade orientation which measure the deviation of the actual primary orientation or trade orientation of a country from that predicted from the regression analysis for a country of a similar income and size. Their findings suggest that small outward- and manufacturing-oriented countries had the highest growth rates in per capita income over the sample period, and that outward orientation led to fast rates of growth for large and small countries, whether oriented to primary or manufacturing activities (see Table A9.2.7 for a summary of these results). Whilst such statistical studies are extremely useful in establishing common patterns and some key differentiating aspects of country experience, they do not directly relate the degree of primary orientation to resource endowments, or the degree of outward orientation to trade policy variables. The next section examines the extent to which trade policy orientation may affect growth performance.

### 9.6.3 Trade policies and inward and outward orientation

Recently, the World Development Report (World Bank, 1987, Ch. 5) divided a sample of forty-one countries into four categories according to the degree of inward and outward orientation. Four quantitative and qualitative variables were used in this classification scheme, namely:

- effective rate of protection
- use of direct controls such as quotas and import licensing schemes
- use of export incentives
- degree of exchange rate overvaluation.

These variables were combined with a large element of judgement when dividing the sample countries into strong and weak outward orientation and strong and weak inward orientation.[9] The growth performance and other macroeconomic indicators for these countries were then compared for the periods 1963–73 and 1973–85. (The countries in the sample and the results of this exercise are summarised in Fig. A9.2.1.)

Taken at face value, the results lend strong support to the idea that the more outward-oriented countries have experienced a higher rate of growth. There is also some evidence that the more outward-oriented countries have lower capital/output ratios, suggesting that outward orientation may also have been more efficient. However, on closer inspection, the case in favour of outward orientation is not so clear-cut.

For example, South Korea has a very low average measured effective rate of protection, but a very high dispersion of rates of protection.[10] Further, there is evidence which suggests that there has been an overestimation of the effective removal of quantitative controls on the import side (Wade, 1989). The combined force of these observations suggests that there has been much more import substitution induced by targeted, made-to-measure protection than is captured by the available indices of protection. Similar observations have been made by Wade (1989) in relation to Taiwan. Although Taiwan is not in the above sample of countries, these observations nevertheless suggest that the successful non-city state East Asian NICs may have been less outward orientated than suggested, to neutralise the direct effects of import substitution on export costs.

The use of evidence on direct controls in the standard ranking of trade policy instruments, discussed in Section 8.2, suggests that tariffs will be better than import controls. However, it is not clear that trade policy instruments can be ranked in terms of their impact on efficiency and growth applied independently of the institutional context within which they were applied. For example, quantitative controls have always been important in the South Korean case, and certainly more important than revealed by the measured change in the use of quantitative controls, as suggested above. To some extent, the potential for rent-seeking behaviour has not materialised, partly because of the role of ideology already remarked on in Section 8.3. More potently, quantitative controls were often tied to crude incentives in the South Korean case, for example, import licenses tied to the export performance of the firm. This gave the state instruments of direct control over firms necessary for their industrial policies. The view of tariffs as a more efficient protective instrument cannot be sustained. Quantitative controls tied to incentives, however crude, may also be superior to tariffs precisely because they provide the instruments for implementing an interventionist industrial strategy.

Other doubts arise from the data used in the country classification. Direct price comparisons often do not correspond with the measures of protection, and the reasons for the discrepancies are little understood. In addition, the criteria by which the exchange rate is deemed 'realistic' are not very clear.

Bearing these doubts in mind, it is not surprising that the World Bank result for the countries with moderate inward to strong outward orientation are ambiguous. It can be readily seen that, in terms of GDP, GDP per capita, domestic savings and inflation, the moderately inward-oriented countries did better than the moderately outward-oriented countries in the period 1973–85. Other factors than those captured by the moderate inward-moderate outward classification have been influencing growth performance since the world economy began to slow down in the 1970s.

In contrast to the above, the World Bank results are more clear-cut in relation to the strongly inward-oriented category. By all criteria, the countries in this group did far worse than the other countries in the sample, particularly when looked at in terms of per capita GDP. Whilst other factors were obviously at work as well, the evidence suggests that strong inward orientation may be associated with a poor growth performance.

There are few studies which attempt systematically to include both institutional and policy variables in the set of independent variables chosen in studies of competitive growth performance. Nor is there a set of broadly-agreed, socio-economic, socio-political or institutional variables which could be drawn on to extend our analysis. Yet there is a growing literature which challenges the primacy of economic determination of relative growth performance, and the primacy of economic processes such as competition and market clearance mechanisms in determining the course of economic variables, as discussed in Section 6.5.3. For example, measures of the extent of labour market distortion by the capacity of a country to keep the growth of real wages in line with productivity growth ascribe such an outcome to the simple result of greater or lesser labour market efficiency, rather than a result of a complex economic, social and political process which may include a high degree of coercion.[11] Similarly, the neo-classical tradition tends to deal with the economic role of the state in terms of its capacity to intervene in the market efficiently, ignoring the social nature of the state, its political-administrative capacity and the specific modes of involvement. These three distinct dimensions of the developmental state tend to be conflated into arguments over parametric versus pervasive forms of involvement of the state. The former implies a certain degree of autonomy of economic agents, with state intervention confined to the provision of infrastructural capacity, whilst the latter involves direct or mediated organisational penetration by the state at every level and a circumscribed autonomy of economic agents (Evans and Alizadeh, 1984, page 25).

Furthermore, there has also been a lively debate over the positive or negative role of the military in the development process (Kaldor, 1978, Kaldor and Eide (eds), 1979; Benoit, 1973, 1978; Deger and Smith, 1983; Smith and Smith, 1983; Faini *et al.*, 1984; Lim, 1983), and a related discussion about the role of authoritarian political structures in promoting growth (Marsh, 1979 and Samuelson, 1981). Three central issues have been addressed in this literature as it affects developing countries. First, there is direct competition between the mobilisation of surplus for unproductive military rather than productive investment activity. Second, there are possible negative effects on growth through bias in technical change which may impede growth. Third, there may be positive benefits via the impact of military effort and expenditure on infrastructural development, mobilisation, industrial development and, perhaps most important, the direct or indirect coercion of both labour and capital in the growth process.

It goes without saying that all of these socio-economic and socio-political dimensions of growth are extremely difficult to conceptualise, let alone measure, in any clear and precise fashion. Yet, given the widespread belief that such variables are important, perhaps even more important than the purely economic variables, it is useful to attempt some quantification of such variables. The remainder of this section reports the results of a cross-section study on growth performance by Aghazadeh and Evans (1988) which extends World Bank research on the relationship between price distortions, economic efficiency and growth (World Bank, 1983, Ch. 6; Agarwala, 1983) to include social and institutional variables.

The main finding of the Agarwala and World Bank study,

based on a simple cross-section regression of the average growth performance over the 1970s and an unweighted average of seven indices of price distortion indexes, was that about one-third of the variance in growth performance between countries was accounted for by the index of price distortion (see Table A9.2.8 for a summary of the results). Thus, World Bank (1983, pages 61 and 63) concludes that the:

> Statistical analysis of the relationship between the price distortion index and growth in the 1970s confirms these earlier findings. The average growth rate of those developing countries with low distortions in the 1970s was about 7% a year — 2% higher than the overall average. Countries with high distortions averaged growth of about 3% a year, 2% lower than the overall average ... However, price distortions alone can explain less than half the variation in growth among countries, the rest is the result of other economic, social, political and economic factors.

There are a number of points which can be made about these results. First, some of the estimates of the distortion indices are highly subjective; for example, one case where a good deal of judgement was required, since there were radical changes in pricing policy, was after the fall of the Allende government in Chile in 1973. Whilst other distortion indices could be recalculated using other information or judgement, the statistical analysis proceeded on the assumption that there were no errors in variables, and should therefore be interpreted with caution. Second, it is not clear how the price distortions as measured correspond to the underlying theoretical requirements of a distortion measure, except in the case of the measures of protection in industry and agriculture. For example, the labour market distortion is measured in terms of an observed outcome, the extent that real wages moved in line with productivity growth. When data was missing, an assessment was made of the extent to which the labour market was free of distortions, but only in a very impressionistic manner. When real wage movements were found to be in line with productivity growth, the outcome is simply attributed to labour market efficiency rather than to some unobserved institutional or other variable relating to the subordination and repression of labour, which produces the same outcome. Similar criticisms can be made of the measure of capital market efficiency based on the observed real rates of interest. The measure of foreign exchange market distortion is also problematic. It relates to the extent of real exchange rate appreciation over the sample period, without measuring the extent of distortion in the first place. Since the possibility of exchange rate appreciation for other reasons, such as favourable terms of trade movements, cannot be ruled out, in spite of Agarwala's attempts to do so, the foreign exchange distortion index must be interpreted with caution. Thus, although the variables may measure something which is relevant to growth performance, the link between the variable and price distortion is by no means clear. This point should be borne in mind when interpreting the results. Similarly, the purely economic variables are not, by common consent, the only determinants of growth variations. The inclusion of other omitted variables, including institutional variables, may disturb the identified price–growth relationship. Thus, a second criticism of the Agarwala and World Development Report study is that it regards political and institutional factors as being relevant only to outliers or extreme observations, and not as endogenous variables.

A third criticism of the study is the use of an aggregate distortion index rather than the individual indices, as calculated. The grounds for such a procedure are that, in spite of the absence of any well-defined aggregation rules, it is better to underestimate the overall explanation of the relationship between price distortion and growth through the use of an unweighted aggregate index. An alternative procedure is simply to relate aggregate GDP growth to the individual distortion indices, and allow the data to speak for itself. Rather than impose an arbitrary set of aggregation weights for the distortion index, the weights are empirically determined. There is a very wide range of structural, economic, socio-economic, socio-political and institutional variables which might be used for such a preliminary exploration of omitted variables. The list chosen was by no means exhaustive, but seventeen additional variables were chosen, divided into a set of additional structural and economic variables, including such variables as energy, self-sufficiency, the rate of growth of agriculture and the rate of growth of industry, and a set of socio-economic, socio-political and institutional variables. The latter set of variables were included in part by direct measurement of such variables as the share of military expenditure in GDP, or through the qualitative assessment of the importance of a particular variable made by three development experts. The resultant non-economic variables can be thought of as slightly more systematically-defined dummy variables than are usually used.

The main non-economic variable which appeared in the aggregate growth equation was a measure of the overall capacity of the state for strategic development planning. Such a capacity depends, amongst other determinants, on the administrative and political capacity of the state and the institutional framework within which the strategic approach to planning is implemented. A necessary, but not a sufficient condition for a high score on the strategic planning variable is the degree to which the evaluation of class interests represented by the state has a strong developmental interest. Class interests taken to be favourable to development were the dominance of industrial and/or agricultural capitalists, rather than rentier, financial or commercial interests.

In a preliminary check of the new equations using single equation estimates, it was found that the major explanatory power from the price distortion variables comes from two variables, labour market distortion and exchange rate distortion. This is supplemented by a negative influence of manufacturing protection in the individual equations for agricultural growth and export growth. The other most important economic variable is the energy self-sufficiency ratio. For the non-economic variables, the variable capturing the state capacity for strategic planning did surprisingly well. Whatever it was that the three wise men thought they were measuring, it seems to carry considerable explanatory power in the regression equations. The failure of the role of manufacturing protection in the overall growth equation is striking, given the emphasis on the negative effects of protectionism in the standard literature. However, before reaching any final interpretations of these results, a more systematic appraisal of the possible interaction of variables affecting the overall growth performance must be considered.

In an extensive series of tests reported by Aghazadeh and Evans (1988), it was found that the single equation estimate of the growth equation did not change this overall result. In all of the simultaneous equation estimates, there was a common set of economic variables in the growth equation which remained statistically significant for a wide variety of specifications of the structural model. Other variables were chosen in order to try and give content to four alternative stories of the growth. The first was used as the benchmark equation, which included as independent variables the state capacity for strategic planning variable, the share of military expenditure in GDP, the degree of distortion in the labour and foreign exchange markets, and the degree of energy self-sufficiency. This was called the 'non-structuralist' equation. The second alternative considered was a structuralist explanation in which the rate of growth of agriculture was included in the growth equation. The third was based on a neo-Keynesian or neo-Marxian perspective, in which investment growth was included in the overall growth equation. Fourth, export-led growth was modelled by including the rate of growth of exports in the overall growth equation. (For a summary of these results see Table A9.2.9.)

Both the structuralist and neo-Keynesian animal spirits equations have a markedly better corrected $R^2$ statistic compared with the non-structuralist equation, and the export-led growth equation. Part of the explanation for the success of the structuralist story is due to the high weight of agricultural growth in overall growth itself. For this reason, the slightly better statistical performance of the structuralist equation should be discounted, so that it would seem that the animal spirits story fits the data best. Further, the very strong significance of investment growth suggests that rapid accumulation does matter, especially when real wages are kept in line with productivity (by whatever means), and that a high rate of growth of investment is more effective in promoting growth when starting from an initial position of a low rate of savings. This finding is quite compatible with the conclusions reached by Sen (1983) regarding the continued importance of accumulation as a determinant of growth. Preference for the animal spirits story is strengthened by the interconnection between three variables – investment growth, military expenditure and state capacity for strategic planning – and the robustness of the labour market distortion variable. The presence of investment growth in the animal spirits growth equation markedly reduces the level of significance of the non-price variables on account of their collinearity. More generally, the claim for the animal spirits story rests on the strength of the investment growth variable in the growth equation, and not on the state capacity for strategic planning variable. This is reassuring since there must always be doubt about the meaning of the state capacity for strategic planning variable because of the subjectivity of the estimating procedure. The three wise men may have believed in the importance of the capacity of the state for strategic planning in explaining growth performance, so that the variable simply identifies their capacity to come up with a dummy variable which measures their knowledge of the growth performance of the sample countries.

The animal spirits story, or investment-led growth assisted by strategic planning and military expenditure, is also consistent with the finding of Marsh (1979) that authoritarian regimes do rather better at growth, and the quip by Samuelson (1981) to the same effect.

The structuralist equation, and the positive but marginally significant indirect effects of military expenditure operating through investment growth in the animal spirits story, confirm the positive direct effects of military expenditure on growth found by Deger and Smith (1983) who also used simultaneous estimating procedures. The difference between the results reported here and those in Deger and Smith lies in the fact that, in their results, there was significant simultaneity in the structural equations with domestic savings included in the growth equation. Since military expenditure had a negative effect on domestic savings and domestic savings had a positive sign in their growth equation, the overall effect of military expenditure was negative. These findings are at variance with the results of Lim (1983) and Faini et al. (1984), both of whom found negative direct effects of military expenditure on growth using single equation estimating techniques. Our results are closer in spirit to the findings of Benoit (1973, 1978), who argued that military expenditure had a positive effect on growth.

It is not easy to reconcile the different results on the effect of military expenditure on growth. All of the other findings are for earlier time periods and for larger samples, so that on this count alone it could be argued that the structural relations could have changed. However, on the basis of Aghazadeh and Evans, it makes a good deal of difference to the results obtained when experiments are carried out with a wide variety of variables and structural formulations, and single equation estimates should be regarded with caution unless checked for simultaneous equation bias. The most that can be said about the relationship between military expenditure and growth from these results is that more work needs be done on this, both in terms of finding other indicators of positive and negative growth effects of military expenditure and the hypothesised effects on repression and control of labour, and in terms of extending the sample to more countries and more time periods.

How seriously should these results be taken? First, results suggest that the additional disaggregation of the price distortions data and more careful evaluation of what the data measure opens the way to a very different interpretation of the 1970–80 cross-section growth data for the sample countries than that offered by Agarwala and the World Development Report for 1983. The regression estimates suggest that the main explanatory power of what is called price distortion is carried by whatever is measured by the real wage, foreign exchange distortion and manufacturing protection distortion variables. Second, the addition of other economic and non-economic data to the price distortion variables reinforce the conclusion that Agarwala and the 1983 World Development Report both misinterpret the role of non-economic factors and overstate the weight which can be given to the role of price distortions in producing a higher rate of growth on the basis of the particular data set analysed. The final conclusion reached on the role of price distortion variables is highly dependent on the choice between the structuralist and animal spirits stories. If, indeed, the structuralist story is believed rather than the animal spirits story for the 1970s, then the single equation results reported suggest that there is an important negative effect of manufacturing protection on the rate of growth of agriculture. Thus, the interpretation of the importance of manufacturing protection lies in its negative effects on agriculture. The third conclusion relates to the failure of the export-led growth hypothesis to explain the 1970s experience. The results suggest that there is little additional effect of faster export growth other than what is already captured by the price efficiency variables which directly affect the trade regime (exchange rate distortion, real wage distortion and manufacturing protection). Thus suggests that it is the trade regime which captures the beneficial effects of a more open economy rather than the growth of exports as such. This failure of the export-led growth hypothesis is also found in McCarthy, Taylor and Talati (1987).

Finally, any conclusions reached on the basis of our extended analysis of the comparative growth performance of a sample of 31 countries in the 1970s must be heavily qualified. There is, of course, no guarantee that the results would hold up if the sample was extended to include more countries, or if the estimation methods were extended to try to include data from earlier time periods. The analysis suggests that it may be useful to try to extend the sample size and time periods considered; there is also considerable scope for more systematic work on comparative typologies of the development state which might lead to further insights into the relative importance of such non-economic variables. Clearly, the task of interpreting comparative growth performance drawing systematically on economic and non-economic variables is complex but under-researched. Such further quantitative research might help deepen our understanding of the processes involved, but should not blind us to the fact that it is unlikely to allow one to discriminate decisively between the alternative stories sketched out.

## 9.7  TRADE AND DEVELOPMENT STRATEGY

Few would argue with the proposition that trade policy implications must derive from an overall development strategy. There is less agreement when this general proposition is made more concrete, both in terms of the appropriate theory of trade policy and empirical rules of thumb and judgements which are made when implementing policy recommendations.

There is nothing intrinsic in the values or policy concerns addressed in the alternative perspectives which cannot be accommodated by the theory of trade policy discussed in Chapter 8. It is unlikely that the appropriate policy intervention to deal with any conflict between private profit and social welfare would involve directly limiting international trade. The general principle that the best forms of policy intervention tackle inefficiency directly applies.

Some of the policy recommendations advocated within the

alternative perspectives discussed derive from a weak or faulty economic analysis. This is evident from the major area of trade policy initiative in the 1970s embodied in the call for a New International Economic Order (NIEO).[12]

The call for a NIEO stems from the United Nations declaration of May 1974, and a number of related policy proposals by the developing countries calling for a reconstruction of the existing international economic system to improve the development prospects for developing countries, narrowing disparities between rich and poor countries and recognising the sovereign rights of nations, and giving them more control over the shape of their development goals and strategies. It seems that there are three basic interrelated reasons why so little came out of the high ideals and hopes of this programme.

First, there was a strong emphasis on redistributive rather than productive strategies for development. Thus, when the OPEC countries radically increased the price of oil in 1973, many countries within the group of seventy-seven nations at UNCTAD saw this as showing the way for other redistributive policies such as the stabilisation and indexing of commodity prices. There was also the feeling amongst many Third World governments that the international equivalent of union threats to strike could bring developed country governments into serious negotiation for a NIEO (see, for example, Green and Singer, 1975, pages 427–8). The group of seventy-seven support for OPEC policies was based on the idea that the benefits both to OPEC countries and the redistribution to other developing countries through OPEC aid would far outweigh the costs to non-oil developing countries through increased energy costs, and the extra strains that OPEC policies would place on the world economy. In effect, it was an attempt by developing countries to form a coalition to redistribute rents from the unequal per capita distribution of world energy resources from the rich to the poor. It was hoped that this could be achieved without offsetting direct costs through higher energy prices or indirect costs such as occurred through the strains in the international financial system which have, in part, been induced by OPEC policies. Judged in these terms, and by the lack of lasting developmental effects of high oil prices on many of the OPEC countries themselves, developing country support for OPEC must surely be judged as misconceived.

Second, one of the key policy instruments designed to give effect to the NIEO and to overcome the adverse long-run terms of trade trends discussed in Section 9.4, the Integrated Programme on Commodities (IPC) and the associated common fund to finance international commodity agreements was inefficient, inequitable and impractical. It was inefficient because the transfers were to be made indirectly between developed country consumers and developing country producers, thus introducing a market distortion, rather than a direct transfer of resources. It was inequitable because some of the benefits of higher commodity prices would go to developed country consumers, and some of the costs would be borne by poor developing country consumers and marginal producers excluded by quota arrangements. It was impractical since the legitimate commodity price stabilisation component was linked with a commodity price indexing proposal with unpredictably large financing arrangements. What hopes remained even for a truncated IPC were scuppered by the collapse of the well-established International Tin Agreement in 1985.[13]

Third, there is a strong tendency within much of the NIEO literature to over-emphasise the importance of the international context and class structure at the expense of national issues. There is much scope for the exploration of policy reform designed to enhance mutually gainful exchange such as advocated by Bhagwati and Ruggie (eds) (1984). Less radical redistributive strategies, such as the Rawlsian theory of justice which holds that economic inequalities are only acceptable if they can be shown to benefit the least advantaged in society, are potentially much more feasible (see, for example, the basic needs approach discussed by Streeten and others, 1981, and the discussion of aid and trade policy by Toye, 1987, Ch. 7). Moreover, a development strategy oriented towards productive rather than redistributive policies leading to the rapid accumulation of productive assets, might achieve both national and international distributive justice, as is often argued in the case of South Korea.

If the theory of policy analysis is on the side of orthodoxy, are the empirical rules of thumb and judgements made in the application of that theory inadequate? To what extent are the values of policy advocates separated from the positive content of the theoretical and empirical components of policy analysis? The final part of this section looks at four aspects of policy application where there may be some doubts on these issues.

First, as argued in Evans and Alizadeh (1984) and Bell *et al.* (1984), the typically applied rules of thumb in evaluating infant industry protection – learning periods of about five years and a maximum effective protection of 10–20 per cent optimally administered through subsidies rather than tariffs or import controls – would seem to be much too conservative, judging at least from the historical experience of South Korea and Taiwan. Yet there is no well-formulated alternative set of rules of thumb or analysis of incentive structures which opponents of neo-classical orthodoxy are able to cite when using the success stories, such as Japan's successful infant industries of the 1950s, particularly automobiles, steel and electronics, as evidence of the failure of orthodox policy prescriptions.

In a similar vein, the empirical link between price distortions or outward orientation and either growth performance or export performance discussed in Section 9.6 is not as clear-cut as argued in the conventional literature. Moreover, since there is no theoretical reason why higher growth necessarily leads to higher social welfare, the link between growth and efficiency is not well established. In the discussion of trade orientation in the previous section, it was not possible to reach any strong conclusions based on the comparison of the moderately outward- and the moderately inward-oriented countries. Whilst such statistical exercises cannot give clear-cut empirical answers about the association of growth or efficiency with greater trade or fewer price distortions, they have been widely used in recent years to support the case for outward orientation.

There is little doubt that a large number of developing countries which would come under the criterion of 'strongly inward oriented' are in urgent need of trade and other policy reform. However, in the present context of an increasingly uncertain and sluggishly growing world economy, it is by no means clear that a shift from moderately inward to moderately outward orientation, or from moderately outward-oriented to strongly outward-oriented policies, would improve economic performance. Furthermore, increased outward orientation of developing countries may have favourable effects on income distribution, as in the case of South Korea, but the very same success stories are likely to have serious implications for the industrial countries if pursued on a large scale, as discussed in Section 7.5.

However, given the interests of the international agencies such as UNCTAD, the IMF and the World Bank in representing the views of the member governments which dominate these institutions, there is too often little space for discussion of the types of coalitions of domestic interest groups and classes which might be able to implement more egalitarian and productively-oriented strategies in a hostile world environment.

Second, the discussion of domination at the point of production in Evans (1989, Section 4.2) suggests the need for a closer examination of what might be called directly profit-seeking control in which the conflict between profit and growth on the one hand, and social welfare and equity on the other is explored. Such a discussion would provide a useful counterpoint to the well-established literature on directly unproductive profit-seeking activity, or DUP, discussed in Section 8.2.4. Whilst the latter emphasises the expenditure of resources for unproductive lobbying and other such activities, the former emphasises the expenditure of resources for increasing profitable activity. In fact, either type of expenditure may be welfare-reducing under existing institutional and organisational arrangements. This has important implications for both technology and industrial policies, where new institutions and forms of organisation of work may be required to overcome market failure discussed in Section 8.3.

In a similar vein, the organisational considerations and the possibilities for radical technical change can have important policy implications. In a recent study of the industrial sector in Cyprus, Murray et al. (1987) argue that new institutional arrangements combined with changes in attitudes and the overall organisation of work will be necessary for a small-firm economy to be able to take advantage of new product and process technology. Many of the policy recommendations follow from standard arguments for market intervention based on imperfect information, scale economies, public goods, learning and externalities. In practice this means finding the appropriate institutional and organisational innovations to enable the functions of the head office of a large firm to be carried out in a small firm environment.

Third, the literature on the developmental state discussed in Section 8.3 suggests a considerably greater complexity of interaction between the command economy of the state and the decentralised institutions of the market than is often reflected in the policy statements of the international agencies, such as the World Bank, or in the neo-classical literature. An example of this is discussed in Section 9.6 in relation to the contribution of price efficiency, and the effectiveness of state institutions, to growth. Whilst there may now be widespread agreement on the general problem identified, there is less agreement on the details of how major price policy (including trade policy) reform should be combined with institutional reform, and the class and interest group coalitions which may be able to implement such a package (for a recent discussion of some of these issues in relation to sub-Saharan Africa, see White, 1986; Bienefeld, 1986; Bates, 1986; Colclough, 1988; and Evans, 1990).

Finally, the literature on the role of the military in development cited in Section 9.6 draws attention to the increasingly close interconnections between strategic interests, arms trade and trade policy in general. However, in the absence of any theory of arms trade in the standard trade literature, it is difficult to move beyond the exogenous treatment of 'national' or 'strategic' interests in the discussion of this aspect of trade policy issues.

## 9.8  CONCLUDING REMARKS

To what extent does this book help answer the questions asked in Chapter 1? The central thrust of the argument of this book is that a circulating capital model in the Ricardo–Ohlin–Lewis tradition, including a role for resource-based trade, provides a useful starting point for the analysis of trade when combined with the standard theory of trade policy. There is considerable scope for the analysis of a number of central issues regarding trade, growth and development, and to a limited extent, issues relating to class and inequality were brought to bear on the analysis of trade and development. Last but not least, there is a great deal more to be gained from productive cross-fertilisation of competing perspectives than from some efforts to deliver a knockout blow. Attempts by proponents of orthodoxy to claim a monopoly of the truth are as unhelpful as the purist versions of alternative perspectives which reject or ignore the lessons which orthodox theory can offer.

## APPENDIX 9.1 EMPIRICAL TESTS OF TRADE THEORIES

### A9.1.1 Nineteenth-century UK trade

Tests of the static and dynamic Ricardian theory of comparative advantage cannot be made with the available data. However, inspection of the composition and pattern of trade is suggestive of some of the influences which may be at work. To this end some historical data on nineteenth-century UK trade is assembled in Table A9.1.1.

### A9.1.2 Factor price equalisation

Establishing the extent to which factor prices differ between countries is very difficult. Further, the available data does not permit a separation of the differences in factor prices into those arising from differences in resource endowments, difference in technical efficiency, and differences in the quality of factors. The data on factor price differences assembled in Table A9.1.2 therefore must be interpreted with care.

### A9.1.3 The 1980 world trade matrix

The world trade matrix for 1980, for six commodity groups and seven regions, is shown in Table A9.1.3. Care must be taken in interpreting the current price valuations of world trade shown in Table A9.1.3. There may be large variations in prices or quantities traded over time. This will mean that the structure of world trade for 1980 will not necessarily reflect the average pattern of trade for the end of the 1970s, which is the sense in which the table is interpreted in the text. For example, the price of oil in 1980 reflects the restoration of the real 1973 prices in 1979, and other primary commodities are subject to wide cyclical variation

**Table A9.1.1**   UK patterns of trade in the nineteenth century.

|  | 1800 | 1825 | 1850 | 1875 | 1900 |
|---|---|---|---|---|---|
| *Import shares (%)* | | | | | |
| 1. Primary intermediate | | | | | |
| foodstuffs, competing | 7.1 | 3.9 | 12 | 28.4 | 35.4 |
| 2. Other primary | | | | | |
| intermediate, competing | 17.9 | 18.9 | 16.2 | 20.3 | 25.5 |
| 3. Primary intermediate and | | | | | |
| final, non-competing | 75.1 | 77.2 | 71.9 | 51.3 | 39.1 |
| Total | 100 | 100 | 100 | 100 | 100 |
| *Export shares (%)* | | | | | |
| 1. Primary, intermediate | 2.9 | 0.5 | 2.5 | 4.7 | 11.1 |
| 2. Manufacturers, mainly | | | | | |
| intermediate and | | | | | |
| investment | 14.2 | 8.4 | 18.2 | 25.2 | 34.0 |
| 3. Manufactures, mainly | | | | | |
| consumer | 82.9 | 91.1 | 79.4 | 70.2 | 55.0 |
| Total | 100 | 100 | 100 | 100 | 100 |

*Key*
*Imports:*   (1) mainly corn, meat, butter; (2) mainly timber, flax, iron, hides and skins, linen and yarns, raw wool; (3) mainly sugar, tea, coffee, wine, tobacco, hemp, oils, dye stuffs, raw cotton. By 1900, (2) includes a significant import of iron and steel, non-ferrous metals and manufactures.
*Exports:*   (1) mainly coal; (2) iron and steel, machinery, non-ferrous metals and manufactures, chemical and electrical commodities, vehicles, ships and boats; (3) mainly hardware and cutlery, hats and haberdashery, manufactures from cotton, wood, linen, silk and leather. All shares are 25-year averages centred on the years shown. The figures may not always add to 100 due to rounding error.
   Note that imports for 1800, 1825 and 1850 are in official values, as current values for 1875 and 1900. Exports are valued at official prices for 1800 and current values for the rest.
*Source:* Mitchell and Deane (1962, Table 4b & c, Table 5g, Table 7a & b, Table 8). Compiled by E. Tsakalotos.

in prices and quantities. To some extent, such variations in price will be compensated for by quantity movements in the opposite direction so that the value shares of world trade are not as sensitive as might be thought at first sight. Also, the high level of aggregation in Table A9.1.3 would tend to eliminate some of the short-run trends which may affect particular commodities. However, given the very depressed market conditions in 1980 for a wide range of primary commodities with low short-run supply

**Table A9.1.2** Some indicators of international wage, profit and rent differentials.

1. GDP per capita, $US 1982

|  | 1960 | % of industrial market GDP | 1982 | % of industrial market GDP |
|---|---|---|---|---|
| low income economies | 146 | 2.7 | 280 | 2.5 |
| middle income economies | 698 | 12.9 | 1,520 | 13.7 |
| high-income oil exporters | 4,469 | 82.5 | 14,820 | 133.9 |
| industrial market economies | 5,419 | 100 | 11,070 | 100 |
| centrally planned economies |  |  |  |  |
| (Hungary) | 592 | 10.9 | 2,270 | 20.5 |
| (Romania) | 857 | 15.9 | 2,560 | 23.1 |

*Source:* World Bank (1984, Table 1, pp. 278–9).

2. Wage differentials, developed market/developing countries

| Average wage differentials unadjusted | 1970 | 1978 | Annual rate of change (%) |
|---|---|---|---|
| food | 4.6 | 5.6 | 2.5 |
| textiles | 4.2 | 6.3 | 5.2 |
| non-metallic minerals | 4.4 | 4.9 | 1.4 |
| iron + steel | 3.5 | 4.6 | 3.5 |
| non-electrical machinery | 4.1 | 5.5 | 3.7 |

*Source:* ILO Yearbook of International Labour Statistics.

3(a) Corporate profitability

|  | Real rates of return (%) 1962–4 | 1965–9 | 1970–3 | 1974–6 |
|---|---|---|---|---|
| Canada | 7.9 | 9.6 | 9.0 | 9.2 |
| France | 9.7 | 10.0 | 11.6 | 8.0 |
| West Germany | 19.3 | 19.5 | 15.0 | 11.4 |
| Italy | 10.4 | 11.4 | 10.3 | – |
| Japan | 28.2 | 27.9 | 21.9 | 13.5 |
| UK | 11.9 | 10.6 | 8.3 | 3.7 |
| USA | 12.0 | 12.2 | 8.6 | 7.1 |

*Source:* World Bank (1984) Table 2.4, p. 17.

3(b)   US private overseas investment

| Developed market economies | Real rates of return average, 1965–70 (%) | |
|---|---|---|
| | Manufacturing | Other industries |
| Australia, NZ and S. Africa | 11.0 | 12.7 |
| Canada | 7.8 | 6.8 |
| EEC | 12.1 | 7.8 |
| Japan | 21.8 | 17.2 |
| UK | 14.4 | 12.6 |
| Developing market economies | | |
| Latin America | 9.9 | 7.7 |
| Other LDCs | 11.5 | 10.9 |

Source: Griffin (1978, Tables 3 and 4, p. 30).

elasticities, the trade shares for food and other primary commodities need to be interpreted with care.

## A9.1.4   Leamer's tests of the H–O theorem

Leamer (1984, page 84) suggests that his study aims to provide vivid and memorable images of the international economy. Whilst he has to a considerable extent achieved this aim, the only way in which his results can be summarised here is to draw on his econometric tests. Whilst Leamer (1984, page 162) cautions against taking the results of his linear model reported in Table A9.1.4 too seriously, these results, in fact, capture the essence of his findings after far more exhaustive econometric tests of his findings.

## A9.1.5   Stock embodiment in trade

As suggested in Section 9.2.3, estimates of the embodiment of factors in trade from the left-hand side of equation (9.2) do not constitute a check of the H–O theorem in the factor embodiment form since there is no independent estimate of the excess supply of factors on the right-hand side of the equation.

However, equation (9.2) can provide useful information on the net flow of factors embodied in trade in a multi-factor world. However, when the left-hand side of the equation (9.2) is

**Table A9.1.3**  World trade matrix (1980). Source: UN (1981). *Yearbook of International Trade Statistics*, compiled by A. Jazayeri, pp. 1124–205, Geneva: United Nations.

| 1980 Billions of US$ f.o.b. Exports from | Imports of | column headings | Developed market economies | | | | | | | Developing Africa | | | | | | | Developing America | | | | | | | Developing Middle-East | | | | | | |
|---|---|---|---|---|---|---|---|---|---|---|---|---|---|---|---|---|---|---|---|---|---|---|---|---|---|---|---|---|---|---|
| | | | 1 | 2 | 3 | 4 | 5 | 6 | 7 | 1 | 2 | 3 | 4 | 5 | 6 | 7 | 1 | 2 | 3 | 4 | 5 | 6 | 7 | 1 | 2 | 3 | 4 | 5 | 6 | 7 |
| Developed market economies | Food | 1 | 107.4 | | | | | | | 12.8 | | | | | | | 13.6 | | | | | | | 9.0 | | | | | | |
| | Mineral fuels | 2 | | 75.0 | | | | | | | 2.6 | | | | | | | 1.6 | | | | | | | 1.2 | | | | | |
| | Other primary | 3 | | | 117.5 | | | | | | | 3.4 | | | | | | | 4.5 | | | | | | | 3.4 | | | | |
| | Textiles & Clothing | 4 | | | | 47.2 | | | | | | | 3.6 | | | | | | | 2.2 | | | | | | | 3.5 | | | |
| | Machinery & Transport | 5 | | | | | 14.1 | | | | | | | 28.0 | | | | | | | 34.8 | | | | | | | 30.6 | | |
| | Other manufacturing | 6 | | | | | | 478.7 | | | | | | | 39.5 | | | | | | | 35.1 | | | | | | | 37.0 | |
| | Total (Trace) | 7 | | | | | | | 839.9 | | | | | | | 89.9 | | | | | | | 91.8 | | | | | | | 84.7 |
| Developed Africa | Food | 1 | 8.0 | | | | | | | 0.7 | | | | | | | 0.3 | | | | | | | 0.5 | | | | | | |
| | Mineral fuels | 2 | | 33.9 | | | | | | | 1.2 | | | | | | | 5.3 | | | | | | | 1.2 | | | | | |
| | As above | 3 | | | 8.8 | | | | | | | 0.4 | | | | | | | 0.3 | | | | | | | 0.1 | | | | |
| | | 4 | | | | 1.6 | | | | | | | 0.1 | | | | | | | 0.1 | | | | | | | 0 | | | |
| | | 5 | | | | | 0.3 | | | | | | | 0.1 | | | | | | | 0 | | | | | | | 0 | | |
| | | 6 | | | | | | 13.1 | | | | | | | 0.5 | | | | | | | 4.2 | | | | | | | 0.1 | |
| | | 7 | | | | | | | 65.7 | | | | | | | 3.0 | | | | | | | 10.2 | | | | | | | 2.0 |
| Developed America | Food | 1 | 3.3 | | | | | | | 1.0 | | | | | | | 3.2 | | | | | | | 1.2 | | | | | | |
| | Mineral fuels | 2 | | 34.0 | | | | | | | 0.9 | | | | | | | 10.6 | | | | | | | 0.4 | | | | | |
| | As above | 3 | | | 16.5 | | | | | | | 0.2 | | | | | | | 2.5 | | | | | | | 0.3 | | | | |
| | | 4 | | | | 2.3 | | | | | | | 0.1 | | | | | | | 0.9 | | | | | | | 0 | | | |
| | | 5 | | | | | 1.9 | | | | | | | 0.4 | | | | | | | 2.6 | | | | | | | 0.1 | | |
| | | 6 | | | | | | 9.7 | | | | | | | 0.3 | | | | | | | 1.8 | | | | | | | 0.3 | |
| | | 7 | | | | | | | 67.7 | | | | | | | 2.9 | | | | | | | 21.6 | | | | | | | 2.3 |
| Developed Middle-East | Food | 1 | 1.1 | | | | | | | 0.1 | | | | | | | 0 | | | | | | | 1.1 | | | | | | |
| | Mineral fuels | 2 | | 147.1 | | | | | | | 3.1 | | | | | | | 11.7 | | | | | | | 6.7 | | | | | |
| | As above | 3 | | | 1.0 | | | | | | | 0.1 | | | | | | | 0 | | | | | | | 0.2 | | | | |
| | | 4 | | | | 1.1 | | | | | | | 0.1 | | | | | | | 0 | | | | | | | 0.2 | | | |
| | | 5 | | | | | 0.3 | | | | | | | 0.1 | | | | | | | 0 | | | | | | | 1.1 | | |
| | | 6 | | | | | | 2.5 | | | | | | | 0.2 | | | | | | | 0 | | | | | | | 2.0 | |
| | | 7 | | | | | | | 153.1 | | | | | | | 3.7 | | | | | | | 11.7 | | | | | | | 11.4 |
| Developed other Asia | Food | 1 | 9.2 | | | | | | | 1.1 | | | | | | | 0.5 | | | | | | | 2.3 | | | | | | |
| | Mineral fuels | 2 | | 20.7 | | | | | | | 0 | | | | | | | 1.0 | | | | | | | 0.3 | | | | | |
| | As above | 3 | | | 15.5 | | | | | | | 0.4 | | | | | | | 0.3 | | | | | | | 0.7 | | | | |
| | | 4 | | | | 6.9 | | | | | | | 0.9 | | | | | | | 0.6 | | | | | | | 1.5 | | | |
| | | 5 | | | | | 11.5 | | | | | | | 1.1 | | | | | | | 0.7 | | | | | | | 0.4 | | |
| | | 6 | | | | | | 38.8 | | | | | | | 2.1 | | | | | | | 1.5 | | | | | | | 5.0 | |
| | | 7 | | | | | | | 102.6 | | | | | | | 5.6 | | | | | | | 4.6 | | | | | | | 10.2 |
| Developed Oceania | Food | 1 | 0.9 | | | | | | | 0 | | | | | | | 0 | | | | | | | 0 | | | | | | |
| | Mineral fuels | 2 | | 1 | | | | | | | 0 | | | | | | | 0 | | | | | | | 0 | | | | | |
| | As above | 3 | | | 0 | | | | | | | 0 | | | | | | | 0 | | | | | | | 0 | | | | |
| | | 4 | | | | 0 | | | | | | | 0 | | | | | | | 0 | | | | | | | 0 | | | |
| | | 5 | | | | | 0 | | | | | | | 0 | | | | | | | 0 | | | | | | | 0 | | |
| | | 6 | | | | | | 0 | | | | | | | 0 | | | | | | | 0 | | | | | | | 0 | |
| | | 7 | | | | | | | 1.9 | | | | | | | 0 | | | | | | | 0 | | | | | | | 0 |
| Centrally planned economy | Food | 1 | 1.9 | | | | | | | 0.9 | | | | | | | 0.8 | | | | | | | 0.9 | | | | | | |
| | Mineral fuels | 2 | | 2.62 | | | | | | | 0.2 | | | | | | | 1.0 | | | | | | | 0.4 | | | | | |
| | As above | 3 | | | 9.2 | | | | | | | 0.4 | | | | | | | 0.4 | | | | | | | 0.2 | | | | |
| | | 4 | | | | 6.3 | | | | | | | 0.5 | | | | | | | 0.1 | | | | | | | 0.5 | | | |
| | | 5 | | | | | 3.6 | | | | | | | 1.8 | | | | | | | 2.0 | | | | | | | 2.4 | | |
| | | 6 | | | | | | 18.2 | | | | | | | 2.2 | | | | | | | 1.5 | | | | | | | 2.8 | |
| | | 7 | | | | | | | 65.4 | | | | | | | 6.0 | | | | | | | 5.8 | | | | | | | 7.2 |
| Total columns | | 1 | 131.8 | | | | | | | 16.6 | | | | | | | 18.4 | | | | | | | 15 | | | | | | |
| | As above | 2 | | 337.9 | | | | | | | 8 | | | | | | | 31.2 | | | | | | | 10.2 | | | | | |
| | | 3 | | | 168.5 | | | | | | | 4.9 | | | | | | | 8.0 | | | | | | | 4.9 | | | | |
| | | 4 | | | | 65.4 | | | | | | | 5.3 | | | | | | | 3.9 | | | | | | | 5.7 | | | |
| | | 5 | | | | | 31.7 | | | | | | | 31.5 | | | | | | | 40.1 | | | | | | | 34.6 | | |
| | | 6 | | | | | | 561 | | | | | | | 44.8 | | | | | | | 44.1 | | | | | | | 47.2 | |
| | | 7 | | | | | | | 1296.3 | | | | | | | 111.1 | | | | | | | 145.7 | | | | | | | 117.8 |

**1980 Billions of US$ f.o.b.**

Imports of / column headings same as rows:
1 = Food, 2 = Mineral fuels, 3 = Other primary, 4 = Textiles & Clothing, 5 = Machinery & Transport, 6 = Other manufacturing, 7 = Total (Trace)

| Exports from | | Developing other-Asia | | | | | | | Developing Oceania | | | | | | | Centrally planned economy | | | | | | | Total rows | | | | | | |
|---|---|---|---|---|---|---|---|---|---|---|---|---|---|---|---|---|---|---|---|---|---|---|---|---|---|---|---|---|---|
| | | 1 | 2 | 3 | 4 | 5 | 6 | 7 | 1 | 2 | 3 | 4 | 5 | 6 | 7 | 1 | 2 | 3 | 4 | 5 | 6 | 7 | 1 | 2 | 3 | 4 | 5 | 6 | 7 |
| Developed market economies | | 10.4 | 1.4 | 8.3 | 4.6 | 33.8 | 43.3 | 101.8 | 0.6 | 0.1 | 0.1 | 0 | 0.7 | 0.5 | 2.0 | 19.2 | 0.7 | 6.9 | 3.4 | 16.9 | 35.5 | 82.6 | 173.0 | 82.6 | 144.1 | 64.5 | 158.9 | 669.6 | 1292.8 |
| Developed Africa | As above | 0.2 | 0.5 | 0.2 | 0.1 | 0 | 0.2 | 1.2 | 0 | 0 | 0 | 0 | 0 | 0 | 0 | 1.2 | 0.9 | 1.0 | 0.4 | 0 | 0.3 | 3.8 | 10.9 | 43 | 10.8 | 2.3 | 0.4 | 18.4 | 85.9 |
| Developed America | As above | 0.6 | 0.1 | 0.7 | 0.1 | 0.1 | 0.4 | 2.0 | 0 | 0 | 0 | 0 | 0 | 0 | 0 | 7.5 | 0 | 1.7 | 0.4 | 0 | 0.6 | 10.2 | 16.8 | 4.6 | 21.9 | 3.8 | 5.1 | 13.1 | 106.7 |
| Developed Middle-East | As above | 0 | 25.1 | 0.2 | 0 | 0 | 0.3 | 25.6 | 0 | 0.1 | 0 | 0 | 0 | 0 | 0.1 | 0.4 | 2.6 | 0.5 | 0.4 | 0 | 0.2 | 4.1 | 2.7 | 196.4 | 2 | 1.8 | 1.5 | 5.2 | 209.7 |
| Developed other Asia | As above | 5.4 | 6.5 | 5.6 | 3.0 | 5.0 | 10.8 | 36.3 | 0 | 0.3 | 0 | 0 | 0 | 0.1 | 0.4 | 1.6 | 0.3 | 2.0 | 0 | 0.5 | 1.9 | 6.3 | 20.1 | 29.1 | 24.5 | 12.9 | 19.2 | 60.2 | 166 |
| Developed Oceania | As above | 0 | 0 | 0 | 0 | 0 | 0 | 0 | 0 | 0 | 0 | 0 | 0 | 0 | 0 | 0 | 0 | 0 | 0 | 0 | 0 | 0 | 0.9 | 0 | 0 | 0 | 0 | 0 | 1.9 |
| Centrally planned economy | As above | 3.1 | 1.5 | 0.6 | 1.5 | 1.2 | 3.5 | 11.4 | 0 | 0 | 0 | 0 | 0 | 0 | 0 | 13.1 | 15.1 | 10.2 | 4.3 | 35.0 | 25.7 | 103.4 | 20.7 | 44.4 | 21.0 | 13.2 | 46.0 | 53.9 | 199.2 |
| Total columns | As above | 19.7 | 35.1 | 15.6 | 9.3 | 40.1 | 58.5 | 178.3 | 0.6 | 0.5 | 0.1 | 0 | 0.7 | 0.6 | 2.5 | 43 | 19.6 | 22.3 | 8.9 | 52.4 | 64.2 | 210.4 | 245.1 | 442.5 | 224.3 | 98.5 | 231.1 | 820.4 | 2062.1 |

**Table A9.1.4** Net exports and endowments: weighted least-squares estimate.

| | Capital | Labour 1 | Labour 2 | Labour 3 | Land 1 | Land 2 | Land 3 | Land 4 | Coal | Minerals | Oil | $R^2$ | wt(0) |
|---|---|---|---|---|---|---|---|---|---|---|---|---|---|
| **1958** | | | | | | | | | | | | | |
| GNPᵃ | 775** | 4,310 | 89 | 54* | 5.2* | -4.5 | 20.7* | -2.3 | 5.6** | -6.1* | 3.3 | 0.998 | 0.13 |
| PETRO | -7.95** | -126* | 2.5 | 1.8* | -0.12* | -0.01 | -0.6* | -0.3** | -0.02 | 0.19* | 0.58** | 0.84 | 0.43 |
| MAT | -3.7* | -403** | 5.0* | 5.2** | 0.11* | -0.00 | -0.1 | 0.9** | 0.04 | 0.89** | 0.43** | 0.90 | 0.81 |
| FOR | 3.9 | 130 | -5.8 | 0.3 | -0.02 | 0.01 | -1.2* | 1.8** | -0.39** | 0.11 | -0.36* | 0.67 | 0.44 |
| TROP | -8.3* | -305* | 18.5* | 2.4 | 1.00** | 0.02 | 0.1 | -0.6** | -0.36** | 0.48* | 0.63** | 0.90 | 0.10 |
| ANL | 0.83 | 169 | -5.8 | -0.9 | -0.12 | 0.10 | 2.3* | 0.3 | -0.56** | -0.01 | -0.05 | 0.55 | 0.19 |
| CER | 1.4 | -520* | -0.8 | 6.5** | 0.08 | 0.60** | 3.8** | 0.4* | -0.31** | 0.29** | 0.90** | 0.89 | 0.36 |
| LAB | 1.2 | 190* | 2.4 | -3.8** | -0.09* | -0.11 | -0.4 | -0.8** | 0.02 | -0.14* | -0.23** | 0.86 | 0.03 |
| CAPᵃ | 3.2 | 671** | -6.1 | -7.3** | -0.25* | 0.10 | -2.5** | -0.9** | 0.07 | -0.89* | -0.76** | 0.80 | 0.17 |
| MACH | -4 | 68 | -2.6 | -5.5* | -0.32* | -0.65* | -2.5** | -1.4** | 1.5** | -0.94** | 0.28* | 0.97 | 0.08 |
| CHEM | 1.3 | 17 | -4.5* | -0.1 | -0.07 | -0.15* | -0.4* | -0.1 | 0.25** | -0.11 | 0.01 | 0.82 | 0.51 |
| **1975** | | | | | | | | | | | | | |
| GNPᵃ | 452.7** | 15,683** | -445* | -479.7** | 30.1** | -49.1** | 80.6* | -26.6* | 9.0** | 2.8* | 2.1** | 0.997 | 0.42 |
| PETRO | -18.4** | -248 | -0.8 | 30.7* | 0.5 | 7.9** | -5.4 | 0.3 | -1.0** | -0.4 | 0.6** | 0.92 | 0.41 |
| MAT | -8.9** | 127 | -31.2* | -2.3 | 0.89 | 0.47 | 1.1 | 3.3** | 0.45** | 0.86** | 0.04* | 0.86 | 0.46 |
| FOR | -1.7 | 34 | -18.8 | 8.4 | -0.45 | -2.7* | 0.3 | 3.3* | -0.17 | 0.53* | 0.08* | 0.53 | 0.34 |
| TROP | -2.9** | -30.1 | 8.9 | 5.6 | 2.0** | -1.1 | 4.5* | -3.9** | -0.30** | 0.44** | 0.05* | 0.72 | 0.39 |
| ANL | -0.5 | -42 | -29.3 | 14.0 | 0.09 | -0.34 | 5.6* | -1.3 | -0.17 | 0.28 | 0.05 | 0.22 | 0.27 |
| CER | -4.5** | 70 | -51.0* | -6.8 | 1.3* | -4.8** | 16.1** | -3.6 | 0.39** | 0.97** | 0.24** | 0.86 | 0.31 |
| LAB | 1.9 | -397 | 41.6* | 7.4 | -0.97 | 0.00 | -0.6 | -1.6 | -0.10 | -0.09 | -0.07 | 0.13 | 0.99 |
| CAPᵃ | 17.9** | -1,900** | 115.9** | 49.0** | -0.89 | 3.2* | -12.4** | -0.63 | -0.12 | -0.46* | -0.17** | 0.86 | 0.26 |
| MACH | 29.1** | -1,471* | 38.2 | 33.3 | -1.6 | -1.5 | -23.5** | -7.9* | 1.0** | -1.1* | -0.27** | 0.76 | 0.59 |
| CHEM | 4.1** | -154 | -16.0 | 3.0 | -0.57 | -0.30 | -6.0* | -1.0 | 0.3** | -0.15 | -0.04* | 0.51 | 0.66 |

ª GNP is scaled in thousands of dollars; capital is in millions. * indicates that $|t| > 1$, ** that $|t| > 2$.

*Source:* Leamer (1984, p. 163).

*Definition of commodity aggregation*

1. Petroleum (PETRO)
2. Raw materials (MAT)
3. Forest products (FOR)
4. Tropical agriculture (TROP)
5. Animal products (ANL)
6. Cereals, etc. (CER)
7. Labour intensive (LAB)
8. Capital intensive (CAP)
9. Machinery (MACH)
10. Chemicals (CHEM)

*Definition of factors*

1. Capital. Accumulated and discounted gross domestic investment flows since 1948, assuming an average life of 15 years.
2. Labour 1. Number of workers classified as professional or technical.
3. Labour 2. Number of literate non-professional workers.
4. Labour 3. Number of illiterate workers.
5. Land 1. Land area in tropical rainy climate zone; comprises 30% of total area.
6. Land 2. Land area in dry climate zone; comprises 30% of total area.
7. Land 3. Land area in humid mesothermal climate zone (for example, California); comprises 15% of total area.
8. Land 4. Land area in humid microthermal climate (for example, Michigan); comprises 17% of total area.
9. Coal. Value of production of primary solid fuels (coal, lignite, and brown coal).
10. Minerals. Value of production of minerals: bauxite, copper, flourspar, iron ore, lead, Manganese, nickel, potash, pyrite, salt, tin, zinc. Copper and iron ore make up about 50% of the value of minerals.
11. Oil. Value of oil and gas production.

disaggregated into export and imports, and the results are reported as the capital/labour ratios in exports and imports, as in Leontief (1953) and Baldwin (1979), it is only possible to make inferences on the net trade in factors when the underlying trade in factor services are of opposite signs (see Leamer, 1984, Section 2.2). Nevertheless, it is of some interest to examine the available data on the factor intensity ratios in trade which use the (incorrect) Leontief form of the test of the H–O theorem. These are set out in Table A9.1.5.

### A9.1.6 Industry characteristics of trade

The most common form of analysis of the determinants of comparative advantage fits regression equations of the form shown in equation (9.5). For the reasons outlined in Section 9.2.3, these regressions cannot be construed as tests of the H–O theorem since some of the variables chosen are not even proxies for factor endowments. Nevertheless, these regression studies provide a useful way to summarise the observed relationships between the patterns of trade and industry characteristics, summarised in Table A9.1.6.

### APPENDIX 9.2   EMPIRICAL EVIDENCE ON THE RELATIONSHIP BETWEEN TRADE AND GROWTH, AND THE TERMS OF TRADE

One of the most useful sources on the historical evidence of the association between trade and growth is Kravis (1970). His results are summarised in Table A9.2.1.

More recently, Riedel (1983) has provided a detailed disaggregated account of the relationship between developing country export volumes and real GDP in the industrial market economies of the North. His results are summarised in Table A9.2.2. Recently there has been a spate of studies on the long-run trend movement in the terms of trade between primary commodities and manufactures in the nineteenth and twentieth centuries. The results of some of these studies are summarised in Table A9.2.3. Such aggregate trend statistics mask a considerable amount of variation in terms of trade movement for different primary commodities of particular interest to developing countries. Some of these trend estimates for the post-war period are summarised in Table A9.2.4.

One of the key issues in the terms of trade literature is the terms of trade experience of temperate and tropical agricultural commodities. Some very long-run trend evidence for three temperate and one tropical agricultural commodity is summarised in Table A9.2.5.

An important determinant of long-run movements in the terms of trade of temperate agricultural commodities is the rate of technical progress in temperate agriculture compared with manufactures in Northern industrial countries. Some of the available estimates of long-run technical change are summarised in Table A9.2.6.

One way of attempting to capture the relationship between trade and growth for countries with primary and manufacturing orientation, and inward and outward trade orientation, is to divide time series country data statistically. The results of such an exercise carried out by Chenery et al. (1986) are reported in Table A9.2.7.

A recent attempt by the World Bank to capture the relationship between trade and growth under different trade policy regimes, when the latter are explicitly identified, is shown in Fig. A9.2.1.

The key variables and statistical results of the cross-section study of the relationship between growth, price distortions and a range of economic and non-economic variables found in Aghazadeh and Evans (1988) are described in Tables A9.2.8 and A9.2.9.

**Table A9.1.5**  Tests of factor content of trade: average capital/labour ratio of imports divided by capital/labour ratio of exports.

| | US coefficients all trade[a] 1964 | $(k/\ell)_M$ EEC coefficients all trade[a] 1964 | $(k/\ell)_E$ Japanese coefficients all trade[a] 1964 | $(k^1/\ell)_M$ Indian coefficients manufactured trade[b] 1973 | $(k^1/\ell)_E$ Indian coefficients manufactured trade[b] 1973 | |
|---|---|---|---|---|---|---|
| *Developed market economies* | | | | | | |
| Australia | 0.79 | 0.83 | 1.34 | – | – | × |
| Austria | 1.15 | 1.02 | 0.96 | – | – | |
| Belgium–Luxembourg | 1.08 | 0.96 | 0.97 | – | – | × |
| Canada | 0.82 | 0.88 | 0.83 | – | – | |
| Denmark | 1.04 | 0.95 | 1.34 | – | – | |
| EEC | 1.08 | 1.07 | – | – | – | |
| Finland | 1.16 | 0.97 | 1.10 | – | – | |
| France | 1.01 | 1.06 | 1.25 | – | – | |
| Greece | 0.85 | 0.76 | 1.59 | 1.40 | 1.30 | × |
| West Germany | 1.24 | 1.19 | 1.02 | – | – | × |
| Ireland | 0.91 | 0.87 | 1.25 | – | – | × |
| Israel | 0.98 | 1.08 | 1.43 | – | – | × |
| Italy | 1.39 | 1.31 | 1.35 | – | – | × |
| Japan | 1.56 | 1.50 | 1.21 | – | – | × |
| Netherlands | 0.98 | 0.91 | 1.08 | – | – | × |
| Norway | 0.95 | 0.85 | 0.76 | – | – | |
| Portugal | 1.23 | 1.15 | 1.08 | 1.60 | 1.40 | |
| Spain | 1.20 | 1.06 | 1.58 | – | – | |
| Sweden | 1.11 | 0.98 | 0.94 | – | – | × |
| Switzerland | 1.14 | 1.14 | 1.02 | – | – | |
| UK | 1.27 | 1.31 | 1.04 | – | – | |
| USA | 1.06 | 0.94 | 1.35 | – | – | × |
| Yugoslavia | 1.08 | 1.03 | – | – | – | |

| | | | | | | |
|---|---|---|---|---|---|---|
| *Developing Africa* | | | | | | |
| Ghana | 0.96 | 0.80 | 0.81 | – | – | |
| Ivory Coast | 0.87 | 0.70 | 1.06 | – | – | × |
| *Developing America* | | | | | | |
| Brazil | 0.96 | 0.90 | 1.54 | 1.73 | 2.50 | × |
| Chile | – | – | – | 0.90 | 1.3 | × |
| Mexico | 0.76 | 0.80 | 1.48 | – | – | × |
| Peru | – | – | – | 1.40 | 2.60 | × |
| *Developing Middle East* | | | | | | |
| Turkey | 0.78 | 0.78 | 2.86 | 1.6 | 2.0 | × |
| UAR | 1.0 | 1.16 | 1.79 | – | – | × |
| *Developing other Asia* | | | | | | |
| Hong Kong | 1.53 | 1.62 | 1.07 | 1.50 | 1.20 | × |
| India | 1.10 | 1.08 | 0.91 | 1.60 | 1.80 | × |
| South Korea | 1.36 | 1.47 | 1.23 | 1.70 | 1.50 | × |
| Malaysia | – | – | – | 1.40 | 2.30 | × |
| Pakistan | – | – | – | 2.00 | 1.80 | × |
| Philippines | 0.88 | 0.77 | 1.31 | 1.80 | 2.40 | × |
| Singapore | 0.83 | 0.94 | 0.86 | 1.1 | 2.40 | × |
| Taiwan | 1.23 | 1.18 | 1.21 | – | 1.1 | × |
| Thailand | 0.84 | 0.86 | 1.89 | 2.3 | 2.9 | × |
| *45 Developing countries* | | | | | | |
| exports to industrial countries | – | – | – | 0.55 | 0.59 | × |
| exports to developing countries | – | – | – | 0.96 | 1.06 | × |

a *Source:* Baldwin (1979).
b *Source:* Havrylyshyn (1983).
× Indicates result consistent with stock endowments description when results with Japanese coefficients excluded for highly developed economies, when the USA and EEC coefficient results are excluded for obviously less developed economies, and where there is a well researched examination of inconsistent results which eliminate the 'paradox', as in the case of the USA.

**Table A9.1.6**  Selected US industry characteristics related to country trade balances by industry; regression results.[a]

Dependent variable in dollars (adjusted exports minus adjusted imports)

| Developed market economies | $k/\ell$ | Engineers and scientists | Rest of I | II | III | IV | V | VI | Unionisation index | Scale index | $R^2$ | |
|---|---|---|---|---|---|---|---|---|---|---|---|---|
| | | | | % of labour force in various skill groups | | | | | | | | |
| Australia | 0.21 | 1,013 | 2,097 | -1,837 | -943 | -158 | -2,046* | 2,119** | 1,667** | -1,314** | 0.70 | |
| Austria | -0.25 | -1,489 | -2,887 | 563 | 642 | -119 | 2,311** | -268 | -267 | 341 | 0.31 | X |
| Belgium–Luxembourg | -0.12 | -3,425 | -3,764* | 1,266 | 224 | -551 | 1,683** | -258 | -205 | 785** | 0.36 | X |
| Canada | 0.63* | 1,239 | -533 | -830 | -623 | 23 | 968 | -30 | 367 | -251 | 0.23[b] | X |
| Denmark | -0.70 | -1,223 | 3,638 | -688 | 65 | -21 | -1,971 | 1,104** | 774 | -938 | 0.14 | |
| Finland | -0.45 | -5,315 | 2,395 | -2,576 | -560 | 264 | 2,121 | -268 | 488 | -169 | 0.41 | |
| Greece | 0.07 | 1,714 | -64 | 486 | 1,719 | 412 | 1,270 | 1,558** | 838** | -796* | 0.44 | |
| West Germany | -0.72* | -4,168 | 901 | -634 | 694 | -448 | -95 | -657** | 75 | 446 | 0.29 | X |
| Ireland | -0.03 | -2,361 | 3,204 | -510 | -1,326 | 202 | -2,058 | 1,269** | 792 | -733 | 0.46 | |
| Italy | -0.89** | -8,120** | 1,409 | -530 | -69 | 339 | -573 | -456* | -203 | 694* | 0.57 | |
| Japan | -1.4** | -11,232 | -2,095 | 653 | 1,331 | -430 | 1,034 | -635* | -872* | 1,835** | 0.19 | X |
| Netherlands | -0.16 | -133 | 191 | 471 | -465 | -344 | -433 | 339* | 317 | -94 | 0.22 | X |
| Portugal | -0.25 | -3,088 | -35 | -34 | -1,147 | 1,043* | 925 | -103 | -144 | -2 | 0.35 | X |
| Spain | -0.79* | -6,932* | 2,111 | -169 | -324 | 229 | -928 | 636** | 243 | -49 | 0.27 | X |
| Sweden | -0.21 | -4,763 | -36 | -1,699 | 977 | -433 | 1,473 | -279 | 202 | 310 | 0.16 | |
| Switzerland | -0.48 | 434 | 2,778 | -720 | 802 | 141 | -1,020 | -181 | -338 | 3 | 0.41 | |
| UK | -0.77** | -4,343 | -252 | -282 | 815 | -300 | 31 | -574** | -126 | 660* | 0.44 | |
| USA | -1.20** | 5789* | -1,145 | -84 | 1603* | -310 | -728 | 854** | 295 | -478[c] | 0.16 | X |
| Yugoslavia | -0.20 | -188 | -265 | -292 | -153 | 495 | 500 | 337 | 32 | -196 | | |

| | $k/\ell$ | I | Rest of I | II | III | IV | V | VI | Unionisation index | Scale index | Coefficient for index of concentration | |
|---|---|---|---|---|---|---|---|---|---|---|---|---|
| *Developing Africa* | | | | | | | | | | | | |
| Ghana | −0.18 | 3,416 | 1,327 | −1,071 | −803 | −161 | 262 | 1,056 | 1,551 | −1,586 | 0.14 | X |
| Ivory Coast | −0.72 | 14,663 | −3,463 | −1,000 | 1,955 | 213 | 3,729 | 2,894** | 279 | −1,564 | 0.32 | |
| Libya | 6.1** | 21,908 | −2,393 | 6,575 | −1,214 | 1,528 | −157 | −1,239 | −3,540** | −588 | 0.53 | |
| Malawi | −0.67 | 11,835 | 2,222 | −2,039 | 1,651 | 287 | −2,540 | 4,711** | 697 | −1,746 | 0.37 | X |
| *Developing America* | | | | | | | | | | | | |
| Brazil | −0.42 | −1,186 | −319 | −789 | 490 | −3 | −839 | 2,998** | 715 | −670 | 0.46 | X |
| *Developing other Asia* | | | | | | | | | | | | |
| Hong Kong | −0.18 | −6,447 | 3,464 | −571 | −2,082 | 2,076** | −2,007 | −927 | −432 | 198 | 0.27 | X |
| South Korea | −0.20 | −3,985 | 1,264 | −598 | −2,386* | 2,026** | −77 | −275 | −467 | 306 | 0.37 | X |
| Philippines | 0.42 | 4,101 | −2,705 | −1,402 | −398 | 206 | 3,773 | 854 | 763 | −913 | 0.28 | X |
| Taiwan | −0.18 | −2,191 | 840 | −32 | −2,394* | 1,237** | 89 | 50 | 46 | −39 | 0.32 | X |
| Thailand | −0.15 | 1,756 | 8,594* | −4,210 | −1,467 | 210 | −326 | 2,028** | 1,142 | −1,560* | 0.50 | X |

[a] *Source:* Baldwin (1971, 1979).

[b] Entry missing in original
[c] Coefficient for index of concentration
* *t*-statistic significant at 5% level (10% level of significance in the case of the USA)
** *t*-statistic significant at 1% level
X consistent with stock endowments description

coefficients with an incorrect sign were ignored if statistically insignificant

Note. The economic characteristics are as follows. $k/\ell$ – capital per person in thousands of dollars; Engineers and scientists – proportion of engineers and scientists in an industry; Rest of I – percentage of professional, technical and managerial employees less percentage of engineers and scientists; II – percentage of clerical and sales workers; III – percentage of craftsmen and foremen; IV – percentage of operatives; V – percentage of non-farm labourers and service workers; VI – percentage of farmers and farm labourers; Unionisation index – percentage of industry's production workers in plants where a majority of workers are covered by collective bargaining contracts; Scale index – percentage of workers in plants of 250 or more employees. The characteristics are for 1960.

Adjusted exports minus imports are a representative per million dollar bundle of total commodity exports less a representative per million dollar bundle of total commodity imports.

**Table A9.2.1** Development of world exports of primary products and manufactures, originating in developed and underdeveloped areas, 1876–80 to 1966.

| | Millions of dollars (current prices) | | | | Rate of growth per decade | | |
|---|---|---|---|---|---|---|---|
| | 1876–80 (1) | 1913 (2) | 1953 (3) | 1966 (4) | 1876–80 to 1913 (5) | 1913 to 1953[b] (6) | 1953 to 1966[b] (7) |
| total trade | | | | | | | |
| all countries | 6,010 | 19,159 | 68,410 | 170,800 | 39 | 43(41) | 102(104) |
| developed | 4,562 | 14,871 | 47,980 | 135,080 | 40 | 40(40) | 122(126) |
| underdeveloped | 1,448 | 4,233 | 20,410 | 35,720 | 36 | 50(42) | 54(37) |
| primary products | | | | | | | |
| all countries | 3,720 | 12,176 | 35,800 | 64,560 | 40 | 39(35) | 57(50) |
| developed | 2,307 | 8,310 | 17,980 | 35,820 | 44 | 32(31) | 70(74) |
| underdeveloped | 1,413 | 3,866 | 17,820 | 28,740 | 33 | 51(41) | 44(20) |
| manufactures | | | | | | | |
| all countries | 2,290 | 6,928 | 31,320 | 103,130 | 37 | 48 | 150 |
| developed | 2,255 | 6,561 | 28,880 | 96,270 | 36 | 48 | 152 |
| underdeveloped | 35 | 367 | 2,450 | 6,870 | 96 | 49 | 121 |
| shares of primary products[a] (%) underdeveloped in | | | | | | | |
| total exports | 24 | 22 | 30 | 21 | | | |
| primary exports | 38 | 32 | 50 | 45 | | | |
| manufactured exports | 2 | 5 | 8 | 7 | | | |

[a] Shares in sum primary and manufactured exports; total exports usually contain small amount that could not be allocated to one or the other of the categories.

[b] Growth rates in parentheses are for exports excluding fuels.

*Notes:* Columns 1 and 2: based on Yates (58, Tables A-19, A-21 and A-23). The developed countries include the USA and Canada, Europe, Oceania and Japan. In 1876–80, however, data for Oceania and Japan were not separated from those of the underdeveloped continents. Columns 3 and 4: based on UN (1954). No attempt has been made to adjust the 1953 figures for developed countries exports upwards for revisions made in the later issue, which did not contain 1953 data; for 1955 the later issue reported developed country exports at a figure that was 3.75% higher than the figure in the earlier issue. The data exclude exports to or from centrally planned economies. Column 5: calculated from columns (1) and (2). Column 6: calculated from data in Yates (*idem*) which excludes centrally planned economies. Column 7: calculated from columns (3) and (4).

*Source:* Kravis (1970).

**Table A9.2.2** Regressions of LDC export volumes on DC real GDP: 1960–78.

| Dependent variable | Independent variables | | | | | |
|---|---|---|---|---|---|---|
| | Constant | log $Y$ | $D$ log $Y$ | $D$ | $R^2$ | $DW$ |
| 1. volume of non-fuel exports LDCs (SITC 0–9 Minus 3) | −0.609 (−2.755) | 0.863 (18.857) | 0.884 (9.260) | −4.441 (−9.019) | 0.996 | 1.876 |
| 2. volume of manufactures exports LDCs (SITC 5–9 less 68) | −4.011 (−6.422) | 1.873 (14.503) | 2.210 (8.201) | −11.111 (−7.966) | 0.993 | 1.753 |
| 3. volume of raw materials LDCs (SITC 2 + 4 + 68) | 0.181 (0.334) | 0.951 (8.490) | −0.883 (−3.776) | 4.573 (3.792) | 0.935 | 1.667 |
| 4. volume of food exports LDCs (SITC 0 + 1) | 2.311 (7.593) | 0.495 (7.868) | 0.152 (1.158) | −0.729 (−1.077) | 0.965 | 2.354 |

*Notes*: $t$ statistics in parentheses; $D = 1$ for observation 1970–8 and zero otherwise; $Y$ = index of real US dollar GDP of OECD 'Northern' countries, i.e. OECD excluding Greece, Portugal, Spain and Turkey.
*Source*: Riedel (1983, Table 4).

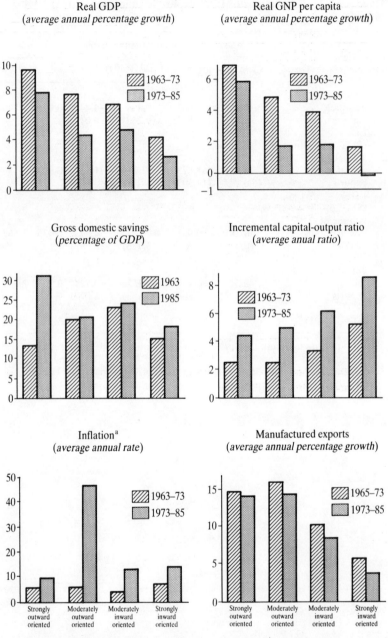

Real GDP
(average annual percentage growth)

Real GNP per capita
(average annual percentage growth)

Gross domestic savings
(percentage of GDP)

Incremental capital-output ratio
(average anual ratio)

Inflation[a]
(average annual rate)

Manufactured exports
(average annual percentage growth)

Note Averages are weighted by each country's share in the group total for each indicator.
[a] Inflation rates are measured by the implicit GDP deflator. Values are group medians

Classification of countries

| | Outward oriented | | Inward oriented | |
|---|---|---|---|---|
| | Strong | Moderate | Moderate | Strong |
| 1963–73 | Hong Kong<br>Republic of Korea<br>Singapore | Brazil<br>Cameroon<br>Columbia<br>Costa Rica<br>Côte d'Ivoire<br>Guatamala<br>Indonesia<br>Israel<br>Malaysia<br>Thailand | Bolivia<br>El Salvador<br>Honduras<br>Kenya<br>Madagascar<br>Mexico<br>Nicaragua<br>Nigeria<br>Philippines<br>Senegal<br>Tunisia<br>Yugoslavia | Argentina<br>Bangladesh<br>Burundi<br>Chile<br>Dominion Republic<br>Ethiopia<br>Ghana<br>India<br>Pakistan<br>Peru<br>Sri Lanka<br>Sudan<br>Tanzania<br>Turkey<br>Uruguay<br>Zambia |
| 1973–85 | Hong Kong<br>Republic of Korea<br>Singapore | Brazil<br>Chile<br>Israel<br>Malaysia<br>Thailand<br>Tunisia<br>Turkey<br>Uraguay | Cameroon<br>Columbia<br>Costa Rica<br>Côte d'Ivoire<br>El Salvador<br>Guatamala<br>Honduras<br>Indonesia<br>Kenya<br>Mexico<br>Nicaragua<br>Pakistan<br>Philippines<br>Senegal<br>Sri Lanka<br>Yugoslavia | Argentina<br>Bangladesh<br>Bolivia<br>Burundi<br>Dominion Republic<br>Ethiopia<br>Ghana<br>India<br>Madagascar<br>Nigeria<br>Peru<br>Sudan<br>Tanzania<br>Zambia |

**Fig. A9.2.1** Macroeconomic performance of 41 developing economies grouped by trade orientation.

**Table A9.2.3**   Terms of trade between primary commodities and manufactures, 1800–1983.

| Period | Data | Study | Type of estimate | Range of estimated time trend[a] and $R^2$ | Average trend (% p.a.) |
|---|---|---|---|---|---|
| 1800–60 | UK | Sarkar (1986, Table 1) | OLS trend | 0.9–1.4% p.a. $R^2$: 0.67–0.86 | 0.6–1.4 |
| 1876–1938 | UK | Sarkar (1986, Table 1) | OLS trend | −0.4–0.8% p.a. $R^2$: 0.62–0.92 | −0.4–0.8 |
| 1900–82 | world excl. oil | Sapsford (1985, Table 1) | OLS trend + dummy | −1.3% p.a. $R^2$: 0.41 | −1.7[b] |
| 1900–83 | world excl. fuel | Grilli and Yang (1986, Table 1) | OLS trend | −0.5% p.a. $R^2$: 0.43 | −0.5 |
| 1900–83 | world excl. fuel | Grilli and Yang (1986, Table 7) | OLS + quadratic trend | −1.2% p.a.[c] $R^2$: 0.50 | −0.1[b] |

[a] All coefficients significant at 5% confidence level or better.
[b] Estimated for 1983.
[c] Coefficient of linear time trend.

**Table A9.2.4**   Some disaggregated estimates of the terms of trade trends between primary commodities and manufactured goods in developing country trade.

(i)   1900–83[a]

|  | Time trend (% p.a.)[b] | $R^2$ |
|---|---|---|
| food commodities | −0.3 | 0.12 |
| cereals | −0.6 | 0.39 |
| tropical beverages | +0.6 | 0.27 |
| non-food agricultural commodities | −0.8 | 0.52 |
| metals   whole period | −0.8 | 0.40 |
| pre-1941 | −1.7 | 0.52 |
| post-1941 | +0.9 | 0.51 |

(ii)   1950–84[c]

|  | Time trend (% p.a.)[c] | | | |
|---|---|---|---|---|
|  | 1950–9 | 1960–9 | 1970–9 | 1950–84 |
| total agriculture | −2.9 | 0.0 | 0.0 | −1.0 |
| beverages | −2.1 | −1.3 | 7.5 | −1.1 |
| cereals | −3.8 | 2.7 | −1.3 | −1.3 |
| fats and oils | −3.7 | −0.7 | −0.8 | −1.3 |
| raw materials | −2.5 | 0.5 | −1.7 | −1.1 |
| metals and minerals | 0.1 | 6.1 | −4.1 | −0.1 |

[a] *Source*: Grilli and Yang (1986, Tables 1 and 6).
[b] Time trends significant at the 5% confidence level or better.
[c] *Source*: World Bank (1986, p. 7). *t*-statistics and $R^2$ not published.

**Table A9.2.5**   Terms of trade of temperate agricultural commodities in the USA.[a]

|  | Change (% p.a.) | |
| --- | --- | --- |
| Crop | Time span | Trend[b] |
| wheat | 1800–55 | 1.0 |
|  | 1855–1980 | −1.0 |
| sugar | 1800–60 | no trend |
|  | 1860–1920 | −1.3 |
|  | 1920–80 | −0.4 |
| corn | 1800–1950 | 0.4 |
|  | 1950–80 | −1.7 |
| rice | 1869–1941 | −1.0[c] |
|  | 1880–1941 | −1.4[c] |

[a] Real price of commodities measured against the US wholesale price index.
[b] Time trends calculated on the basis of five-year averages centred on the years shown, from the worksheets provided by the World Bank for the data used in World Bank (1986, Fig. 1.3).
[c] Time trends calculated roughly on the basis of estimates of the beginning and end points read off from World Bank (1986, Fig. 1.3).
*Source*: World Bank (1986, Fig. 1.3).

**Table A9.2.6** Some evidence on technical change in six North countries, 1880–1970.

| | | Average change (% p.a.) | | | | | |
|---|---|---|---|---|---|---|---|
| | | Japan | Germany | Denmark | France | UK | USA |
| agriculture total factor productivity | 1880–1930 | 1.0[a] | – | – | – | – | 0.2[b] |
| | 1930–60 | 0.6[a] | – | – | – | – | 2.5[c] |
| | 1960–70 | – | – | – | – | – | 3.1[c] |
| manufactures total factor productivity | 1880–1930 | – | – | – | – | – | 2.1[b] |
| | 1930–60 | 6.4[d] | – | – | – | – | 2.4[c] |
| | 1960–70 | – | – | – | – | – | 3.1[c] |
| agriculture output per male worker in wheat units | 1880–1930[e] | 1.8 | 1.4 | 1.7 | 1.2 | 0.4 | 1.1 |
| | 1930–60[e] | 2.0 | 2.7 | 2.3 | 3.1 | 2.7 | 4.7 |
| | 1960–70[e] | 6.5 | 6.3 | 7.1 | 6.0 | 6.8 | 5.9 |
| agriculture output per hectare in wheat units | 1880–1930[e] | 1.1 | 1.4 | 1.8 | 0.7 | 0.1 | 0.2 |
| | 1930–60[e] | 1.3 | 1.6 | 1.5 | 1.7 | 1.7 | 1.3 |
| | 1960–70[e] | 3.0 | 3.0 | 1.3 | 4.1 | 3.0 | 1.9 |
| agriculture output manufactured output per worker | 1950–73[f] | 7.3 | 6.3 | – | 5.6 | 4.7 | 5.5 |
| | 1953–70[f] | 9.5 | 5.6 | – | 5.2 | 2.9 | 2.4 |
| | 1950–60[g] | 11.0 | 4.8 | 3.2[h] | 5.9 | 2.2 | 2.4 |
| | 1960–70[g] | 11.2 | 4.7[i] | 4.7[j] | 5.8 | 3.1 | 4.4 |

[a] Hayami and Yamada (1968, Table 5A-2).
[b] Kendrick (1961, Table 34) for 1899–1929, land excluded.
[c] Kendrick (1973, Tables A-22, A-32) for 1930–60 and 1960–6, land excluded.
[d] Watanabe (1968, Table 4.1) for 1952–62.
[e] Ruttan et al. (1978, Appendix 3.2).
[f] Maddison (1982, Table 5.11).
[g] UN (1963, 1973).
[h] 1953–60.
[i] 1963–70.
[j] 1963–70 for all industry.

**Table A9.2.7**  Annual growth rates in income per capita 1950–83, decomposed by size, primary and trade orientation.

| Strategy | Large No. of countries | $g_y$ | Small No. of countries | $g_y$ | | |
|---|---|---|---|---|---|---|
| primary | | | | | | |
| inward | 10 | 2.56 | 22 | 1.63 | | |
| outward | 4 | *3.48* | 21 | *2.38* | | All primary |
| | (LP) | 2.82 | (SP) | 2.00 | (P) | *2.20* |
| manufacturing | | | | | | |
| inward | 6 | 2.87 | 16 | 3.19 | | |
| outward | 8 | *3.93* | 11 | *4.03* | | All manufacturing |
| | (LM) | 3.47 | (SM) | 3.53 | (M) | *3.51* |
| | (L) | 3.15 | (S) | 2.59 | | |
| *all inward* | | 2.41 | | *all   2.75* | | |
| *all outward* | | 3.18 | | | | |

*Notes*: Simple averages (per cent). Growth rates within countries are OLS estimates. The number of annual observations varies from 14 to 34 (see Table 7). Only countries with positive growth rates are included in the averages. The number of countries with negative growth rate by type: 1 LP, 8 SP, 1 SM.
*Source*: Chenery and Syrquin (1986, Table 8).

**Table A9.2.8**  Some cross-section results on growth performance in the 1970s (*t*-statistics in parentheses).

1.  $G = 11.95 - 3.43DI$            Corrected  $R^2 = 0.31$
         (3.85)                                    $SEE = 2.03$
2.  $G = 9.955 - 1.741ER - 1.169RW$     Corrected  $R^2 = 0.39$
         (−3.80)     (−2.52)                      $SEE = 1.94$
3.  $G = 12.462 - 1.807ER - 0.937RW + 0.214ESSR - 1.607SCADP$
         (−4.36)     (−2.53)     (3.15)     (−2.28)
                                           Corrected  $R^2 = 0.56$
                                           $SEE = 1.96$

Key:  $G$      Rate of growth of real GDP (% p.a.) 1970–80.
       $DI$      Composite index of price distortion.
       $ER$      Distortion level in exchange rate.
       $RW$      Distortion level in real usage.
       $ESSR$    Energy self-sufficiency ratio.
       $SCADP$ Capacity of state for strategic development planning.
*Source*: Aghazadeh and Evans (1988, equation (2.1), equation 1, Table 2.3 and equation 1, Table 3.3).

**Table A9.2.9** Some empirical evidence on four stories about growth in the 1970s.

| Variable | Equation 1 of Table 3.3 | Non-structuralist | Structuralist | Animal spirits | Export-led |
|---|---|---|---|---|---|
| SCADP | −1.61** | −1.34** | −0.78 | −0.56 | −0.76 |
| ME | – | 0.28* | 0.34** | 0.08 | 0.23 |
| RW | −0.94** | −1.04** | −0.75** | −0.67** | −0.78* |
| ER | −1.81** | −1.74** | −0.98** | −1.06** | −1.73** |
| ESSR | 0.21** | 0.19** | 0.18** | 0.04 | 0.18** |
| AGR | – | – | 0.67** | – | – |
| IG | – | – | – | 0.23** | – |
| EG | – | – | – | – | 0.09* |
| SEE | 1.96 | 1.56 | 1.27 | 1.21 | 1.52 |
| $R^2$ | 0.62 | 0.66 | 0.78 | 0.80 | 0.69 |
| $\bar{R}^2_v$ | 0.56 | 0.59 | 0.72 | 0.75 | 0.61 |

\* indicates a $t$-statistic $1.5 < t < 1.7$ or a 5–10% level of significance.
\*\* indicates a $t$-statistic $1.70 < t$ or a 5% level of significance.
Additional variables: *ME* Military expenditure as % of GDP.
                 *AGR* Average rate of growth of agricultural output (% p.a.).
                 *IG* Average rate of growth of investment (% p.a.).
                 *EG* Average rate of growth of exports (% p.a.).

*Source*: Aghazadeh and Evans (1988, Table 4.2).

## NOTES

1. The main tests of the Ricardian theory are summarised in Deardorff (1984).
2. The measured differences in GDP per capita are very much less when measured in terms of approximate purchasing power parity (Kravis et al., 1978). However, using the purchasing-power parity-corrected estimates of GDP would not eliminate the effects of differential endowments of productive stocks on GDP.
3. Some of the discussion in Ohlin (1933, Ch. V) provides a useful reminder of the extent to which these factors are important. The observation that only 17 per cent of private US foreign investment is in the developing market economies – economies which by common consent are capital-scarce – reinforces the point that there is much that is not included in the H–O–S model.
4. For rather different reasons, Stewart (1984) also rejects the factor endowments theory of comparative advantage in her search for more dynamic theories of comparative advantage. However, Stewart rejects only the simple labour and capital-as-land version of the H–O–S model and pays no attention to the role of primary non-produced stocks in her discussion of the H–O–S theory. Similarly, Stewart's interest in the role of skilled labour in determining comparative advantage is quite consistent with the disaggregated H–O–S framework. A proper concern with more dynamic theories of comparative advantage should not be allowed to obscure the very powerful role played by resource and other endowments in explaining comparative advantage and growth.
5. Leamer's method of resolution of the Leontief Paradox is of interest because it shows that the USA was a net exporter of both labour and capital services in 1947. Disaggregation of the labour embodied in the factor flows suggests that the USA was a net exporter of embodied skilled labour and a net importer of embodied unskilled labour. See Leamer (1984, Section 2.2).
6. This section is based on Evans (1987).
7. There are, of course, other historical factors which will influence the relative price changes which have not been discussed here. For example, the opening up of new agricultural land in the nineteenth century increased the supply of land relative to labour, an effect which would tend to counteract a price increase, or accelerate the decline in the temperate agriculture/manufactures terms of trade.
8. See, for example, Stewart (1987).
9. For details, see the background paper by Greenaway (1986).
10. See Greenaway (1986, Table 6).
11. See, for example, Evans and Alizadeh (1984) for a discussion of some of these processes in relation to the NICs and Bowles et al. (1983) for a discussion in relation to the USA. For a theoretical discussion, see Pagano (1985) and Bowles (1985).

12. For an overview of the call for a NIEO, see Green and Singer (1975), Bhagwati (ed.) (1977) and the Reports of the Commonwealth Group of Experts (1975, 1976 and 1977).
13. See Evans (1979) for a discussion of the IPC. For a recent summary of the objections to the IPCs and the current state of the negotiations, see Toye (1987, Ch. 7).

# BIBLIOGRAPHY

Agarwala, R. (1983) *Price Distortions and Growth in Developing Countries*, World Bank Staff Working Paper No. 575, Management & Development Series, Washington DC: International Bank for Reconstruction and Development.

Aghazadeh, E. and Evans, H. D. (1988) 'Price distortions, efficiency and growth', mimeo, Brighton: IDS, University of Sussex.

Amin, S. (1974) *Accumulation on a World Scale: A Critique of the Theory of Underdevelopment*, Hemel Hempstead: Harvester Wheatsheaf.

Anand, S. and Joshi, V. (1979) 'Domestic distortions, income distribution and the theory of optimum study', *Economic Journal*, vol. 89, pp. 336–52.

Baldwin, R. E. (1971) 'Determinants of the commodity structure of US trade', *American Economic Review*, vol. 61 (March), pp. 126–46.

Baldwin, R. E. (1979) 'Determinants of trade and foreign investment: further evidence', *Review of Economics and Statistics*, vol. 61, (February), pp. 40–8.

Baldwin, R. E. (1984) 'Trade policies in developed countries', in: R. W. Jones and P. B. Kenen (eds) *Handbook of International Economics*, vol. 1, Amsterdam: Elsevier.

Barber, C. L. (1955) 'Canadian tariff policy', *Canadian Journal of Economics & Political Science*, vol. 21, pp. 513–30.

Bardhan, P. K. (1965a) 'Optimum accumulation and international trade', *Review of Economic Studies*, vol. 32 (July), pp. 241–4.

Bardhan, P. K. (1965b) 'Equilibrium growth in the international economy', *Quarterly Journal of Economics*, vol. 79, pp. 455–64.

Bardhan, P. K. (1970) *Economic Growth, Development and Foreign Trade: A Study in Pure Theory*, New York: Wiley.

Bardhan, P. K. (1982) 'Unequal exchange in a Lewis-type world' in M. Gersovitz *et al.* (eds), *The Theory and Experience of Economic Development*, London: George Allen and Unwin.

Bardhan, P. K. (1984) *The Political Economy of Development in India*, Oxford: Basil Blackwell.

Bardhan, P. K. (1988) 'Alternative approaches to economics: an evaluation', Chapter 3 in H. Chenery and T. N. Srinivasan (eds), *Handbook of Development Economics*, vol. I, Amsterdam: North-Holland.

Barratt-Brown, M. (1974) *The Economics of Imperialism*, Harmondsworth: Penguin.

Bates, R. H. (1981) *Markets and States in Tropical Africa: The Political Basis of Agricultural Policies*, Berkeley: University of California Press.

Bates, R. H. (1983) *Essays on the Political Economy of Rural Africa*, Cambridge: Cambridge University Press.

Bates, R. H. (1986) 'The politics of agricultural policy–a reply', *IDS Bulletin*, (January) pp. 12–15.

Baumol, W. J. (1977) *Economic Theory and Operations Analysis*, London: Prentice-Hall.

Bell, M. *et al.* (1984) 'Assessing the performance of infant industries', *Journal of Development Economics*, 16, pp. 101–28.

Benoit, E. (1973) *Defense and Economic Growth in Developing Countries*, Boston: Heath (Lexington Books).

Benoit, E. (1978) 'Growth and defense in developing countries', *Economic Development & Cultural Change*, vol. 26, no. 2, pp. 271–80.

Bhagwati, J. N. (1978) 'Anatomy and consequences of exchange control regimes,' in: *Foreign Trade Regimes and Economic Development*, vol. XI, Cambridge, Massachusetts: Ballinger Press (for NBER).

Bhagwati, J. N. (1982) 'Directly unproductive, profit-seeking (DUP) activities', *Journal of Political Economy*, vol. 90, no. 5 (October), pp. 988–1002.

Bhagwati, J. N. (ed.) (1977) *The New International Economic Order: The North–South Dialogue Debate*, Cambridge, MA: MIT Press.

Bhagwati, J. N. and Ruggie, J. G. (eds) (1984) *Power, Passions and Purpose: Prospects for North–South Negotiations*, Cambridge, MA: MIT Press.

Bhagwati, J. N. and Srinivasan, T. N. (1982) 'The welfare consequences of directly-unproductive profit-seeking (DUP) activities: price vs quantity distortions', *Journal of International Economics*, vol. 13, pp. 33–44.

Bickerdyke, C. F. (1906) 'The theory of incipient taxes', *Economic Journal*, vol. 16 (December), pp. 529–35.

Bienefeld, M. (1986) 'Analysing the politics of African state policy: Some thoughts on Robert Bates' work: *IDS Bulletin*, January, pp. 5–11.

Binswanger, H. P. and McIntire, J. (1984) *Behavioural and Material Determinants of Production Relations in Land-Abundant Tropical Agriculture*. Research Unit, Agricultural & Rural Development

340 BIBLIOGRAPHY

Department, Operational Policy Staff, World Bank Report no. ARU 17 (June). Washington DC: International Bank for Reconstruction & Development.

Binswanger, H. P. and Rosenzweig, M. R. (1986) 'Behavioural and material determinants of production relations in agriculture', *Journal of Development Studies*, vol. 22, no. 3, pp. 503–39.

Bliss, C. J. (1973) 'Discussion of J. S. Metcalfe and I. Steedman (1973): heterogeneous capital and the Heckscher–Ohlin–Samuelson theory of trade,' in: J. M. Parkin (ed.) *Essays in Modern Economics*, London: Longman.

Bliss, C. J. (1975) 'Capital theory and the distribution of income', in C. J. Bliss and M. D. Intriligator (eds) *Advanced Textbooks in Economics*, vol. 4, Amsterdam: North-Holland.

Bliss, C. J. (1989) 'Trade and development: Theoretical issues and policy implications', Chapter 24 in H. Chenery and T. N. Srinivasan (eds), *Handbook of Development Economics*, vol. II, Amsterdam: North-Holland.

Bowles, S. (1985) 'The production process in a competitive economy: Walrasian, neo-Hobbesian, and Marxian models', *American Economic Review*, vol. 75, no. 1 (March), pp. 16–36.

Bowles, S., Gordon, D. M. and Weisskopf, T. E. (1983a) *The Social Structure of Accumulation and Profitability in Post-War US Economy*, Department of Economics, University of Massachusetts, Amherst, USA.

Brecher, R. A. (1974) 'Optimal commercial policy for a minimum-wage economy', *Journal of International Economics*, vol. 4, pp. 139–49.

Brecher, R. A. and Choudhuri, E. U. (1982) 'The factor content of international trade without factor price equalisation', *Journal of International Economics*, vol. 12, pp. 277–83.

Brecher, R. A. and Diaz-Alejandro, C. F. (1977) 'Tariffs, foreign capital and immiserizing growth', *Journal of International Economics*, vol. 7, pp. 317–22.

Brett, E. A. (1985) *The World Economy since the War: The Politics of Uneven Development*, London: Macmillan.

Brewer, A. (1980) *Marxist Theories of Imperialism: A Critical Survey*, London: Routledge.

Brigden, J. B. *et al.* (1929) *The Australian Tariff*, Melbourne: Melbourne University Press.

Brody, A. (1970) *Proportions, Prices and Planning*, Amsterdam: North-Holland.

Brody, A. (1985) *Slowdown: Global Economic Maladies*, Institute of Economic Growth, Studies in Economic Development and Planning, No. 36.

Bukharin, N. (1972) *Imperialism and World Economy*, London: Merlin Press.

Burgstaller, A. (1986) 'Unifying Ricardo's theories of growth and comparative advantage', *Economica*, **53**, pp. 467–81.

Cairncross, A. K. (1960) 'International trade and economic development', *Kyklos*, vol. 13, no. 4; pp. 545–58.

Caves, R. E. and Jones, R. W. (1981) *World Trade and Payments: An Introduction*, (3rd edn) Boston: Little, Brown.

Chenery, H. B. and Syrquin, M. (1986) 'Patterns of development: 1950–83', *mimeo* (June).

Chipman, J. S. (1965a) 'A survey of the theory of international trade: Part 1, The classical theory', *Econometrica*, vol. 33, no. 3 (July), pp. 477–519.

Chipman, J. S. (1965b) 'A survey of the theory of international trade: Part 2, The neo-classical theory', *Econometrica*, vol. 33, no. 4 (October), pp. 685–760.

Chipman, J. S. (1966) 'A survey of the theory of international trade: Part 3, The modern theory', *Econometrica*, vol. 34, no. 1 (January), pp. 18–76.

Colclough, C. (1988) 'Zambian adjustment strategy: With and without the IMF'. *IDS Bulletin*, **19**, no. 1, pp. 51–60.

Commonwealth Secretariat (1975) 'Towards a new international economic order', Report by Commonwealth Group of Experts, London. Further report (1976); final report (1977).

Corden, W. M. (1966) 'The structure of a tariff system and the effective protection rate', *Journal of Political Economy*, vol. 74 (June), pp. 221–37.

Corden, W. M. (1974) *Trade Policy and Economic Welfare*, Oxford: Clarendon Press.

Corden, W. M. (1984) 'The normative theory of international trade', in: R. W. Jones and P. B. Kenen (eds) *Handbook of International Economics*, vol. 1, Amsterdam: Elsevier.

Corden, W. M. and Neary, J. P. (1982) 'Booming sector and de-industrialisation in a small open economy', *Economic Journal*, vol. 92 (December), pp. 825–48.

De Janvry, A. (1981) *The Agrarian Question and Reform in Latin America*, Baltimore: Johns Hopkins University Press.

De Janvry, A. (1984) 'Social structure and biased technical change in Argentinian agriculture' in H. P. Binswanger and J. McIntire (1984), *Behavioural and Material Determinants of Production Relations in Land-Abundant Tropical Agriculture*, Research Unit, Agricultural and Rural Development Department, Operational Policy Staff, World Bank Report no. ARU 17 (rev. ed. June), Washington DC: International Bank for Reconstruction and Development.

Deane, P. (1978) 'The evolution of economic ideas', in: P. Deane and J. Robinson (eds) *Modern Cambridge Economics*, Cambridge: Cambridge University Press.

Deane, P. (1978, reprinted 1984) *The Evolution of Economic Ideas*, Cambridge: Cambridge University Press.

Deardorff, A. V. (1974) 'A geometry of growth and trade', *Canadian Journal of Economics*, vol. 7, no. 2 (May), pp. 295–306.

Deardorff, A. V. (1982) 'The general validity of the Heckscher-Ohlin theorem', *American Economic Review*, vol. 72, no. 4 (September), pp. 683–94.

Deardorff, A. V. (1984) 'Testing trade theories and predicting trade flows', in R. W. Jones and P. B. Kenen (eds) *Handbook of International Economics*, vol. 1, Amsterdam: Elsevier.

Deger, S. and Smith, R. (1983) 'Military expenditure and growth in less developed countries', *Journal of Conflict Resolution*, vol. 27, no. 2, pp. 335–53.

Diaz-Alejandro, C. F. and Helleiner, G. K. (1982) *Handmaiden in Distress: World Trade in the 1980s*, Ottowa: North-South Institute, Washington DC: Overseas Development Council, London: Overseas Development Institute.

Dobb, M. (1969) *Welfare Economics and the Economics of Socialism*, Cambridge: Cambridge University Press.

Dorfman, R., Samuelson, P. A. and Solow, R. M. (1958) *Linear Programming and Economic Analysis*, New York: McGraw-Hill.

Dornbusch, R., Fischer, S. and Samuelson, P. A. (1977) 'Comparative advantage, trade and payments in a Ricardian model with a continuum of goods', *American Economic Review*, vol. 67 (December), pp. 823–39.

Edgeworth, F. Y. (1894) 'The theory of international values', *Economic Journal*, no. 4 (March), p. 40.

Ellis, F. (1978) 'The banana export activity in Central America 1967–1976: A case study of plantations by vertically integrated transnational corporations', PhD thesis, Brighton: University of Sussex.

Elson, D. (ed.) (1979) *Value: The Representation of Labour in Capitalism*, London: CSE Books.

Ethier, W. (1979) 'The theorems of international trade in time-phased economies', *Journal of International Economics*, vol. 9, pp. 225–38.

Ethier, W. (1981) 'A reply to Professors Metcalfe and Steedman', *Journal of International Economics*, vol. 11, pp. 273–7.

Evans, H. D. (1979) 'International commodity policy: UNCTAD and NIEO in search of a rationale', *World Development*, 7, no. 3, pp. 259–79.

Evans, H. D. (1987) 'The long-run determinants of the North–South terms of trade and some recent empirical evidence', special issue on commodities of *World Development* (ed. A. Maizels), 15, no. 5, pp. 657–71.

Evans, H. D. (1989) 'Alternative perspectives on trade and development', Chapter 24 in H. B. Chenery and T. N. Srinivasan (eds) *Handbook of*

*Development Economics*, vol. II, Amsterdam: North-Holland.

Evans, H. D. (1990) 'Visible and invisible hands in trade policy reform', in C. Colclough and J. Manor (eds) *Imperfect Market or Imperfect States: Neo-Liberalism and the Development Policy Debate*, Oxford: Oxford University Press, forthcoming.

Evans, M. D. and Alizadeh, P. (1984) 'Trade, industrialisation and the visible hand', *Journal of Development Studies*, vol. 21, no. 1 (October), pp. 22–46.

Faini, R., Annez, P. and Taylor, L. (1984) 'Defense spending, economic structure and growth: evidence among countries and over time', *Economic Development and Cultural Change*, vol. 32, no. 3 (April), pp. 487–98.

Fei, J. C. H. and Ranis, G. (1964) *Development of the Labor Surplus Economy: Theory and Policy*, Homewood, Illinois: Irwin.

Findlay, R. (1974) 'Relative prices, growth and trade in a simple Ricardian system', *Economica*, vol. 41, pp. 1–13.

Findlay, R. (1980) 'The terms of trade and equilibrium growth in the world economy', *American Economic Review*, vol. 70, pp. 291–9.

Findlay, R. (1981) 'Fundamental determinants of the terms of trade', in: S. Grassman and E. Lundberg (eds) *The World Economic Order: Past and Prospects*, London: Macmillan.

Findlay, R. (1984) 'Growth and development in trade models', in: R. W. Jones and P. B. Kenen (eds) *Handbook of International Economics*, vol. 1, Amsterdam: Elsevier.

Findlay, R. and Kierzkowski, H. (1983) 'International trade and human capital: A simple general equilibrium model', *Journal of Political Economy*, vol. 91, no. 6, pp. 957–78.

Fine, B. and Harris, L. (1979) *Rereading Capital*, London: Macmillan.

Fisher, I. (1931) *The Theory of Interest*, Philadelphia: Porcupine Press.

Fitzgerald, E. V. K. (1986) 'The problem of balance in the peripheral socialist economy', in K. Martin, *Readings in Capitalist and Non-Capitalist Development Strategies*, London: Heinemann.

Garegnani, P. (1983) 'The classical theory of wages and the role of demand schedules in the determination of relative prices', *American Economic Review*, vol. 73, no. 2 (May), pp. 309–13.

General Agreement on Tariffs and Trade (GATT) (1986–7) *International Trade YearBook*, Geneva.

Georgescu-Rogen, N. (1950) 'Leontief's system in the light of recent results', *Review of Economics and Statistics*, vol. 22, pp. 214–22.

Gerschenkron, A. (1966) *Economic Backwardness in Historical Perspective: A Book of Essays*, Cambridge, Massachusetts: The Belknap Press of Harvard University Press.

Godfrey, M. (1985) *Global Unemployment: The New Challenge to Economic Theory*, Hemel Hempstead: Harvester Wheatsheaf.

Graham, F. D. (1948) *The Theory of International Values*, Princeton:

Princeton University Press.

Green, R. H. and Singer, H. W. (1975) 'Towards a rational and equitable new international economic order: A case for negotiated structural changes', *World Development*, vol. 3, no. 6, pp. 427–44.

Greenaway, D. (1986) 'Characteristics of industrialization and economic performance under alternative development strategies', *mimeo*, background paper for Chapter 5, World Development Report 1987, Washington DC: World Bank.

Greenaway, D. (ed.) (1988) *Economic Development and International Trade*, Basingstoke: Macmillan.

Greenaway, D. and Milner, C. (1987) 'Trade theory and the LDCs', in N. Glemmell (ed.) *Surveys in Development Economics*, Oxford: Blackwell, pp. 11–55.

Gregory, C. A. (1982) *Gifts and Commodities*, London: Academic Press.

Griffin, K. (1978) *International Inequality and National Poverty*, London: Macmillan.

Grilli, E. R. and Yang, M. C. (1986) 'Long-term movements of non-fuel primary commodity prices: 1900–1983', Economic Analysis and Projections Department, preliminary draft, Washington DC: World Bank.

Hagen, E. E. (1958) 'An economic justification of protectionism', *Quarterly Journal of Economics*, vol. 72 (November), pp. 496–514.

Hahn, F. H. (1973) 'The winter of our discontent', *Economica*, vol. 40 (August), pp. 322–30.

Hahn, F. H. (1982) 'Reflections on the invisible hand', *Lloyds Bank Review*, no. 144 (April), pp. 1–21.

Halevy, E. (1928) *The Growth of Philosophic Radicalism*, translated by M. Morris, reprinted in 1949, London: Faber & Faber.

Hamilton, A. (1791) 'Encouragement of manufacturers', in R. B. Morris (ed.) (1957) *Alexander Hamilton and the Founding of the Nation*, New York: Harper & Row.

Harris, J. R. and Todaro, M. P. (1970) 'Migration, unemployment and development', *American Economic Review*, **60**, pp. 126–42.

Havrylyshyn, O. (1983) 'The directions of developing country trade: Empirical evidence of differences between South–South and South–North trade', paper presented for a Conference on South–South vs South–North Trade: Does the Direction of Developing Country Exports Matter? February 28–March 1, 1983. Université Libre de Bruxelles, Brussels.

Havrylyshyn, O. (1985) 'The directions of developing country trade: Empirical evidence of differences between South–South and South–North trade', *Journal of Development Economics*, **19**, no. 3, pp. 255–81.

Hayami, Y. and Yamada, S. (1968) 'Technical progress in agriculture', in L. Klein and K. Ohkawa (eds), *Economic Growth: The Japanese Experience since the Meiji Era*, Homewood, Illinois: Richard D. Irwin.

Heckscher, E. F. (1934) *Protection*. Encyclopaedia of Social Sciences, vol. 12, pp. 559–67, New York: Macmillan.

Helpman, E. (1984) 'Increasing returns, imperfect markets, and trade theory', in: R. W. Jones and P. B. Kenen (eds) *Handbook of International Economics*, vol. 1, Amsterdam: Elsevier.

Henderson, J. M. and Quandt, R. E. (1958) *Microeconomic Theory: A Mathematical Approach*, (page and chapter refers to the third edition, 1980), New York: McGraw-Hill.

Henderson, J. M. and Quandt, R. E. (1980) *Microeconomic Theory: A Mathematical Approach*, Tokyo: McGraw-Hill Kogakusha, 3rd ed, pp. 48–9.

Hicks, J. R. (1946) *Value and Capital*, 2nd edn, Oxford: Clarendon Press.

Hong, W. (1975) 'Capital accumulation, factor substitution and changing factor intensity of trade: the case of Korea (1966–72)', in: W. Hong and A. O. Krueger (eds) *Trade and Development in Korea*, Seoul: Korea Development Institute.

ILO (1969) *International Standard Classification of Occupations*, revised edition 1968, Geneva: International Labour Organisation.

ILO (1984) *Yearbook of Labour Statistics*, 4th issue, Geneva: International Labour Organisation.

Johansen, L. (1960) *A Multi-Sectoral Study of Economic Growth*, Amsterdam: North-Holland.

Johnson, H. G. (1967) 'The possibility of income losses from increased efficiency in factor accumulation in the presence of tariffs', *Economic Journal*, vol. 77, pp. 151–4.

Jones, H. G. (1975) *An Introduction to Modern Theories of Economic Growth*, Walton-on-Thames, Surrey: Thomas Nelson.

Jones, R. W. (1961) 'Comparative advantage and the theory of tariffs: A multi-country, multi-commodity model', *Review of Economic Studies*, vol. 28 (June), pp. 161–75.

Jones, R. W. (1965) 'The structure of simple general equilibrium models', *Journal of Political Economy*, vol. 73 (December), pp. 557–72, reprinted in R. W. Jones (1979) *International Trade: Essays in Theory*, Amsterdam: Elsevier.

Jones, R. W. (1971) 'A three-factor model in theory, trade, and history', in: J. N. Bhagwati, R. W. Jones, R. A. Mundell and J. Vanek (eds) *Trade, Balance of Payments, and Growth: Essays in Honour of Charles P. Kindleberger*, Amsterdam: North-Holland.

Jones, R. W. and Neary, J. P. (1984) 'The positive theory of international trade' in: R. W. Jones and P. B. Kenen (eds) *Handbook of International Economics*, vol. 1, Amsterdam: Elsevier.

Kaldor, M. (1978) 'The military in third world development', in: R. Jolly (ed.) *Disarmament and World Development*, Oxford: Pergamon Press.

Kaldor, M. and Eide, A. (eds) (1979) *The World Military Order*, London: Macmillan.

Kaldor, M. and Walker, W. (1988) 'Military technology and the loss of industrial dynamism', *mimeo*, Brighton: SPRU, University of Sussex, published as 'Technologie militaire et dynamisme économique', *La Recherche*, no. 23, 1988.

Kaldor, N. (1955) 'Alternative theories of distribution', *Review of Economic Studies*, vol. 23, pp. 83–98.

Kalecki, M. (1960) 'Unemployment in underdeveloped countries', *Indian Journal of Labour Economics*, vol. 3 no. 2 (July), pp. 59–61.

Kalecki, M. (1976) *Essays on Developing Countries*, Hassocks: Harvester Press.

Kanbur, R. and McIntosh, J. (1984) 'Dual economy models: retrospect and prospect', Essex: Department of Economics, University of Essex.

Kaplinsky, R. (1984) 'The international context for industrialisation in the coming decade', *Journal of Development Studies*, vol. 21, no. 1 (October), pp. 75–96.

Kaplinsky, R. (ed.) (1984) 'Third world industrialisation in the 1980s: open economies in a closing world', *Journal of Development Studies*, vol. 21, no. 1 (October).

Karunasekera, M. V. D. J. (1984) 'Export taxes on primary products: A policy instrument in international development', Commonwealth Economic Papers no. 19, London: Commonwealth Secretariat.

Kemp, M. (1969) *The Pure Theory of International Trade and Investment*, Englewood Cliffs: Prentice-Hall.

Kendrick, J. W. (1961) *Productivity Trends in the USA*, New York: National Bureau for Economic Research.

Kendrick, J. W. (1973) *Postwar Production Trends in the US 1948–1969*, New York: NBER and Columbia University Press.

Kindleberger, C. P. (1962) *Foreign Trade and the National Economy*, New Haven: Yale University Press.

Kravis, I. B. (1970) 'Trade as a handmaiden of growth: similarities between the nineteenth and twentieth centuries', *Economic Journal*, vol. 80 (December), pp. 850–72.

Kravis, I. B., Heston, A. W. and Summers, R. (1978) 'Real GDP per capita for more than one hundred countries', *Economic Journal*, vol. 88, no. 350 (June), pp. 215–42.

Krueger, A. O. (1974) 'The political economy of rent seeking society', *American Economic Review*, vol. 64 (June), pp. 291–303.

Krueger, A. O. (1977) 'Growth, distortions and the pattern of trade among many countries', Princeton Studies in International Finance, no. 40, Princeton, New Jersey: Princeton University.

Krueger, A. O. (1978) *Liberalisation Attempts and Consequences*, Foreign Trade Regimes and Economic Development, vol. X, Cambridge, Massachusetts: Ballinger Press (for NBER).

Krueger, A. O. (1984) 'Trade policies in developing countries', in: R. W. Jones and P. B. Kenen (eds) *Handbook of International Economics*, vol. 1, Amsterdam: Elsevier.

Lal, D. (1983) *The Poverty of Development Economics*. London: Institute of Economic Affairs.

Lary, H. B. (1968) *Imports of Manufactures from Less Developed Countries*, New York: National Bureau of Economic Research (NBER).

Lazear, E. (1981) 'Agency, earnings profiles, productivity, and hours restrictions', *American Economic Review*, **71**, pp. 606–20.

Leamer, E. (1980) 'The Leontief paradox, reconsidered', *Journal of Political Economy*, vol. 88 (June), pp. 495–503.

Leamer, E. (1984) *Sources of International Comparative Advantage: Theory and Evidence*, Cambridge, MA: MIT Press.

Leontief, W. (1933) 'The use of indifference curves in the analysis of foreign trade', *Quarterly Journal of Economics*, vol. 47 (May), pp. 493–503. Reprinted in H. S. Ellis and L. A. Metzler (eds) (1949) *The Theory of International Trade*, Philadelphia: Blakiston.

Leontief, W. (1953) 'Domestic production and foreign trade: the American capital position reexamined', *Proceedings of the American Philosophical Society*, vol. 93, pp. 332–49.

Lerner, A. P. (1952) 'Factor prices and international trade', *Economica*, vol. 19, pp. 1–15.

Lewis, W. A. (1954) 'Economic development with unlimited supplies of labour', in: M. Gersovitz (ed.) (1983) *Selected Economic Writings of W. Arthur Lewis*, New York: New York University Press.

Lewis, W. A. (1969) 'Aspects of tropical trade 1883–1965', in: M. Gersovitz (ed.) (1983) *Selected Economic Writings Of W. Arthur Lewis*. New York: New York University Press.

Lewis, W. A. (1972) 'Reflections on unlimited labour', in: M. Gersovitz (ed.) (1983) *Selected Economic Writings of W. Arthur Lewis*, New York: New York University Press.

Lewis, W. A. (1980) 'The slowing down of the engine of growth (the Nobel lecture)', *American Economic Review*, vol. 70, no. 4, pp. 555–64.

Lim, D. (1983) 'Another look at growth and defense in less developed countries', *Economic Development and Cultural Change*, vol. 31, no. 2, pp. 377–84.

Lipsey, R. and Lancaster, K. (1956) 'The general theory of second best', *Review of Economic Studies*, vol. 24 (December), pp. 11–32.

Lipton, M. (1986) 'The place of agricultural research in the development of sub-Saharan Africa', Brighton: Institute of Development Studies, University of Sussex, DP 202 (March).

List, F. (1885) *The National System of Political Economy*, London: Longman.

Little, I. M. D. (1960) *A Critique of Welfare Economics*, Oxford: Oxford University Press.

Little, I. M. D. (1982) *Economic Development: Theory, Policy and International Relations*, New York: Basic Books.

Little, I. M. D., Scitovsky, T. and Scott, M. (1970) *Industry and Trade in Some Developing Countries: A Comparative Study*, London: Oxford University Press (for OECD).

MacBean, A. (1988) 'Uruguay and the developing countries', draft paper, Lancaster: University of Lancaster.

Maddison, A. (1982) *Phases of Capitalist Development*, Oxford: Oxford University Press.

Mainwaring, L. (1976) 'Relative prices and "factor price" equalisation in a heterogeneous capital goods model', *Australian Economic Papers*, vol. 15, no. 26 (June), pp. 109–18. Reprinted in I. Steedman (ed.) (1979).

Mainwaring, L. (1984a) 'The treatment of capital in "classical" theory of international trade', *mimeo*, Cardiff: University College.

Mainwaring, L. (1984b) 'Theory of international transport cost with tradeable intermediate goods', *mimeo*, Cardiff: University College.

Mainwaring, L. (1984c) *Value and Distribution in Capitalist Economics: An Introduction to Sraffan Economics*. Cambridge: Cambridge University Press.

Manoilesco, M. (1931) *The Theory of Protection and International Trade*, London: King.

Marglin, S. A. (1976) *Value and Price in the Labour-Surplus Economy*, Oxford: Clarendon Press.

Marglin, S. A. (1984a) *Growth, Distribution and Prices*, Cambridge, MA: Marvard University Press.

Marglin, S. A. (1984b) 'Growth, distribution, and inflation: a centennial synthesis', *Cambridge Journal of Economics*, vol. 8, pp. 115–44.

Marsh, R. M. (1979) 'Does democracy hinder economic development in the latecomer developing nations?', *Comparative Social Research*, vol. 2., Greenwich, Conn: Jai Press.

Marx, K. (1867) *Capital*, vol. 1, Harmondsworth: Penguin (1976).

McCarthy, F. D., Taylor, L. and Talati, C. (1987) 'Trade patterns in developing countries 1964–1982'. *Journal of Development Economics*, **27**, pp. 5–39.

McKenzie, L. W. (1954a) 'On equilibrium in Graham's model of world trade and other competitive systems', *Econometrica*, vol. 22 (April), pp. 147–61.

McKenzie, L. W. (1954b) 'Specialisation and efficiency in world production', *Review of Economic Studies*, vol. 21 (June), pp. 165–80.

Meade, J. E. (1961) *A Neo-Classical Theory of Economic Growth*, London: Allen and Unwin.

Melvin, J. R. (1968) 'Production and trade with two factors and three goods', *American Economic Review*, vol. 58, no. 5, pp. 1248–68.

Metcalfe, J. S. and Steedman, I. (1972) 'Reswitching and primary input use', *Economic Journal*, vol. 82 (March), pp. 140–57. Pagination refers to reprint in I. Steedman (ed.) (1979).

Metcalfe, J. S. and Steedman, I. (1973) 'Heterogeneous capital and the Heckscher-Ohlin-Samuelson theory of trade', in: J. M. Parkin (ed.) *Essays in Modern Economics*, London: Longman. Reprinted in Steedman (ed.) (1979).

Metcalfe, J. S. and Steedman, I. (1981) 'On the transformation of theorems', *Journal of International Economics*, vol. 11, pp. 267–71.

Michaely, M. (1977) *Theory of Commercial Policy: Trade and Protection*, Oxford: Philip Allan.

Mill, J. S. (1844) *Essays on Some Unsettled Questions of Political Economy*, 2nd edn. of 1874, reprinted 1968 New York: Augustus M. Kelley.

Mitchell, B. R. and Deane, P. (1962) *Abstract of British Historical Statistics*, Cambridge: Cambridge University Press.

Morishima, M. and Catephores, G. (1978) *Value, Exploitation and Growth*, London: McGraw-Hill.

Murray, R. (1975) *Multinational Companies and Nation States*. Nottingham: Spokesman Press.

Murray, R. (1977, 1978), 'Value and theory of rent: Parts I and II', *Capital and Class*, nos. 3 and 4, pp. 100–22, 1–33.

Murray, R. *et al.*, (1987) 'Cyprus industrial strategy: report of the UNDP/ UNIDO mission', Brighton: IDS, University of Sussex.

Myint, H. (1958) 'The "classical theory" of international trade and the underdeveloped countries', *Economic Journal*, vol. 68, no. 270 (June), pp. 317–37.

North, D. (1981) *Structure and Change in Economic History*, New York: Norton.

Nurkse, R. (1959) *Patterns of Trade and Development*, Stockholm: Almquist and Wicksell. Republished (1961) Oxford: Blackwell.

Ohlin, B. (1933) *Interregional and International Trade*. Harvard Economic Studies, vol. 36, Cambridge, Massachusetts: Harvard University Press.

Olsen, M. (1982) *The Rise and Decline of Nations*, New Haven: Yale University Press.

Pack, H. and Westphal, L. E. (1986) 'Industrial strategy and technological change: Theory versus reality', *Journal of Development Economics*, **22**, pp. 87–128.

Pagano, U. (1985) *Work and Welfare in Economic Theory*, Oxford: Basil Blackwell.

Pareto, V. (1971) *Manual of Political Economy*, A. S. Schwier and A. N. Page (eds), translated from the French edition of 1927 by A. S. Schwier, London: Macmillan.

Parrinello, S. (1979) 'Distribution, growth and international trade', in: I. Steedman (ed.) *Fundamental Issues in the Trade Theory*, London: Macmillan.

Pasinetti, L. L. (1960) 'A mathematical formulation of the Ricardian system', *Review of Economic Studies*, vol. 27 (February), pp. 78–98.

Pasinetti, L. L. (1981) *Structural Change and Economic Growth*, Cambridge: Cambridge University Press.

Pearce, I. F. (1952) 'A note on Mr. Lerner's paper', *Economica*, vol. 19, pp. 16–18.

Prebisch, R. (1950) *The Economic Development of Latin America and its Principal Problems*. New York: United Nations.

Prebisch, R. (1959) 'International payments in an era of co-existence: commercial policy in the underdeveloped countries', *American Economic Review*, vol. 49, no. 2, pp. 251–73.

Ramaswamy, V. K. and Srinivasan, T. N. (1971) 'Tariff structure and resource allocation in the presence of factor substitution', in: J. N. Bhagwati, R. W. Jones, R. A. Mundell and J. Vanek (eds) *Trade, Balance of Payments and Growth: Essays in Honour of Charles P. Kindleberger*, Amsterdam: North-Holland.

Ramsey, F. P. (1928) 'A mathematical theory of savings', *Economic Journal*, vol. 38, no. 152, pp. 543–59.

Ranis, G. (1981) 'Employment, income distribution and growth in the East Asian context: A comparative analysis', paper presented at the Conference on Experiences and Lessons of Small Open Economies, Santiago, Chile (November).

Ricardo, D. (1815) 'An essay on the influence of low price of corn on profits of stock', in: P. Sraffa (ed.) with the collaboration of M. H. Dobb, *The Works and Correspondence of David Ricardo*, vol. IV, *Pamphlets and Papers 1815–1823*, Cambridge: Cambridge University Press for Royal Economic Society.

Ricardo, D. (1817) 'The principles of political economy, and taxation', in: P. Sraffa (ed.) with the collaboration of M. H. Dobb, *The Works and Correspondence of David Ricardo*, vol. I, Cambridge: Cambridge University Press for Royal Economic Society.

Ricardo, D. (1822) 'On protection to agriculture', in: P. Sraffa (ed.) with the collaboration of M. H. Dobb, *The Works and Correspondence of David Ricardo*, vol. IV: *Pamphlets and Papers 1815–1823*, Cambridge: Cambridge University Press for Royal Economic Society.

Riedel, J. (1983) *Trade as the Engine of Growth in Developing Countries: A Reappraisal*, World Bank Staff Working Paper No. 555,

Washington DC: International Bank for Reconstruction and Development.

Robinson, J. V. (1951) 'Introduction to R. Luxemburg, *The Accumulation of Capital*', London: Routledge and Kegan Paul.

Robinson, J. V. (1974) *Reflections on the Theory of International Trade*, Manchester: Manchester University Press.

Roemer, J. E. (1981) *Analytical Foundations of Marxian Economic Theory*, New York: Cambridge University Press.

Roemer, J. E. (1982) *A General Theory of Exploitation and Class*, Cambridge, MA: Harvard University Press.

Roemer, J. E. (1984) 'History's effect on the distribution of income', *mimeo*, Department of Economics, University of California, Davis.

Roemer, J. E. (1986) 'Rational choice Marxism: Some issues in methodology', in: J. E. Roemer (ed.) *Analytical Marxism: A Reader*, Cambridge: Cambridge University Press.

Roemer, J. E. (ed.) (1986) *Analytical Marxism*, Cambridge: Cambridge University Press, Paris: Edition de la Maison des Sciences de l'Homme.

Rowthorn, B. (1974) 'Neo-classicism, neo-Ricardianism and Marxism', *New Left Review* (July/August), pp. 63–87.

Rowthorn, B. (1980) *Capitalism, Conflict and Inflation: Essays in Political Economy*, London: Lawrence & Wishart.

Ruffin, R. J. and Jones, R. W. (1977) 'Protection and real wages: The neo-classical ambiguity', *Journal of Economic Theory*, vol. 14, pp. 337–48.

Ruttan, V. W. *et al.* (1978) 'Factor productivity growth: A historical interpretation', in H. P. Binswanger *et al. Induced Innovation: Technology, Institutions and Development*, Baltimore: Johns Hopkins University Press.

Rybczynski, T. M. (1955) 'Factor endowments and relative commodity prices', *Economica*, vol. 22 (November), pp. 336–41.

Samuelson, P. A. (1948) 'International trade and the equalisation of factor prices', *Economic Journal*, vol. 58 (June), pp. 163–84.

Samuelson, P. A. (1949) 'International factor-price equalisation once again', *Economic Journal*, vol. 59 (June), pp. 181–97.

Samuelson, P. A. (1951) 'Abstract of a theorem concerning substitutability in open Leontief models', in: T. C. Koopmans (ed.) *Activity Analysis of Production and Allocation*, New York: Wiley.

Samuelson, P. A. (1971) 'Ohlin was right', *Swedish Journal of Economics*, vol. 73, pp. 365–84.

Samuelson, P. A. (1981) 'The world economy at century's end', *Bulletin of the American Academy of Arts and Sciences*, XXXIV, no. 8 (May) pp. 35–44.

Sapsford, D. (1984) 'The determinants of primary commodity price movements: A long-run analysis', Washington DC: Research Department, IMF, and Norwich: University of East Anglia, School of Economic and Social Studies.

Sapsford, D. (1985), 'The statistical debate on the net barter terms of trade between primary commodities and manufactures: A comment and some additional evidence', *Economic Journal*, **95**, no. 379 (September), pp. 781–8.

Sarkar, P. (1986) 'The terms of trade experience of Britain since the nineteenth century', *Journal of Development Studies*, **23**, no. 1, pp. 20–39.

Seers, D. (1972) 'What are we trying to measure?' *Journal of Development Studies*, vol. 8, no. 3 (April), pp. 21–36.

Seers, D. (1983) *The Political Economy of Nationalism*, Oxford: Oxford University Press.

Sen, A. K. (1963) 'Neo-classical and neo-Keynesian theories of distribution', *Economic Record*, **39**, pp. 46–53.

Sen, A. K. (1981) 'Ethical issues in income distribution: National and international', in S. Grassman and E. Lundberg (eds), *The World Economic Order: Past and prospects*, London: Macmillan, pp. 464–94.

Sen, A. K. (1982) *Choice, Welfare, and Measurement*, Oxford: Blackwell.

Sen, A. K. (1983) 'Development: which way now?', *Economic Journal*, **93**, (December) pp. 745–62.

Sender, J. and Smith, S. (1986) *The Development of Capitalism in Africa*, London: Methuen.

Shackle, G. L. (1972) *Epistemics and Economics: A Critique of Economic Doctrines*, Cambridge: Cambridge University Press.

Shaw, G. K. (1984) *Rational Expectations: An Elementary Exposition*, Hemel Hempstead: Harvester Wheatsheaf.

Sheehan, J. (1987) *Patterns of Development in Latin America: Poverty, Repression and Economic Strategy*, Princeton: Princeton University Press.

Sheehan, J. (1988) 'Liberalization of North–South trade: Consequences for poverty in the South', *mimeo*, conference paper, 'North–South approaches to trade and development', Chapel Hill: University of North Carolina.

Sideri, S. (1970) *Trade and Power: Informal Colonialism in Anglo-Portuguese Relations*, Rotterdam: Rotterdam University Press.

Singer, H. W. (1949) 'Economic progress in underdeveloped countries', *Social Research*, vol. 16, no. 1, pp. 1–11.

Singer, H. W. (1950) 'The distribution of gains between investing and borrowing countries', *American Economic Review*, vol. 40, no. 2, pp. 473–85.

Singer, H. W. (1975) 'The distribution of gains from trade and investment – revisited', *Journal of Development Studies*, vol. 11, no. 4 (July), pp. 377–82.

Singer, H. W. (1984) 'The terms of trade controversy and the evolution of soft financing: The early years in the UN', in G. Meier and D. Seers (eds) *Pioneers in Development*, Oxford: Oxford University Press, for the World Bank.

Singer, H. W. (1987) 'Prebisch–Singer hypothesis', in J. Eatwell, M. Milgate and P. Newman (eds) *The New Palgrave: A Dictionary of Economics*, London: Macmillan.

Singer, H. W. (1988) 'Industrialization and world trade: Ten years after the Brandt Report', paper prepared for the International Symposium 'The crises of the global system: The world ten years after the Brandt Report – crises management for the nineties', Vienna, 29 September– 1 October.

Smith, A. (1776) *An Inquiry into the Nature and Causes of the Wealth of Nations*, reprinted in R. H. Campbell, A. S. Skinner and W. B. Todd (eds) (1976) Oxford: Clarendon Press.

Smith, K. (1977) 'The mercantilist oeconomy: Trading relations and national space in the history of "economic" theory', MPhil Dissertation, University of Sussex, Brighton, UK.

Smith, M. A. M. (1984) 'Capital theory and trade theory', in: R. W. Jones and P. B. Kenen (eds) *Handbook of International Economics*, vol. 1, Amsterdam: Elsevier.

Smith, S. (1976) 'An extension of the vent-for-surplus model in relation to long-run structural change in Nigeria', *Oxford Economic Papers*, vol. 28, no. 3 (November), pp. 426–46.

Smith, D. and Smith, R. (1983) *The Economics of Militarism*, London: Pluto Press.

Solow, R. M. (1956) 'A contribution to the theory of economic growth', *Quarterly Journal of Economics*, vol. 70, no. 1 (February), pp. 65–94.

Spraos, J. (1983) *Inequalising Trade: A Study of Traditional North–South Specialisation in the Context of Terms of Trade Concepts*, Oxford: Clarendon Press in cooperation with UNCTAD.

Sraffa, P. (1960) *Production of Commodities by Means of Commodities: Prelude to a Critique of Economic Theory*, Cambridge: Cambridge University Press.

Sraffa, P. (ed.) (1951–73) *The Works and Correspondence of David Ricardo*, with the collaboration of M. H. Dobb, Cambridge: Cambridge University Press for the Royal Economic Society.

Srinivasan, T. N. (1986) 'Neoclassical political economy, the state and economic development', paper no. 375, New Haven: Economic Growth Center, Yale University.

Srinivasan, T. N. (1987) 'The theory of international trade, steady state analysis and economics of development', *mimeo*, New Haven: Yale University.

Steedman, I. (1977) *Marx after Sraffa*, London: New Left Books.

Steedman, I. (ed.) (1979) *Fundamental Issues in the Trade Theory*, London: Macmillan.

Steedman, I. (1979a) *Trade Amongst Growing Economies*, Cambridge: Cambridge University Press.

Steedman, I. (1979b) 'The von Neumann analysis and the small open economy', in: I. Steedman (ed.) *Fundamental Issues in the Trade Theory*, London: Macmillan.

Steedman, I. (1981a) 'Time preference, the rate of interest and abstinence from accumulation', *Australian Economic Papers*, vol. 20, no. 37 (December), pp. 219–34.

Steedman, I. (ed.) (1981b) *The Value Controversy*, London: Verso.

Steedman, I. (1982) 'Marx on Ricardo', in: I. Bradley and M. Howard (eds) *Classical and Marxian Political Economy*, London: Macmillan.

Steedman, I. and Metcalfe, J. S. (1973) 'On foreign trade', in: I. Steedman (ed.) *Fundamental Issues in the Trade Theory*, London: Macmillan.

Steedman, I. and Metcalfe, J. S. (1977) 'Reswitching, primary inputs and the H-O-S theory of trade', *Journal of International Economics*, vol. 7, pp. 201–8. Reprinted in I. Steedman (ed.) (1979).

Stewart, F. (1984) 'Recent theories of international trade: some implications for the South', in: H. Kierzkowski (ed.) *Monopolistic Competition and International Trade*, Oxford: Clarendon Press.

Stewart, F. (1987) 'Back to Keynesianism', *World Policy Journal*, **IV**, no. 3, pp. 465–83.

Stiglitz, J. E. (1970) 'Factor price equalisation in a dynamic economy', *Journal of Political Economy*, vol. 78, no. 3 (May/June), pp. 456–88.

Stolper, W. F. and Samuelson, P. A. (1941) 'Protection and real wages', *Review of Economic Studies*, vol. 9 (November), pp. 58–73; reprinted in S. Ellis and L. A. Metzler (eds) (1949) *Readings in the Theory of International Trade*, Philadelphia: Blakiston.

Streeten, P. *et al.* (1981) *First Things First: Meeting Basic Human Needs in Developing Countries*, Oxford: World Bank Publication, Oxford University Press.

Swan, T. W. (1956) 'Economic growth and capital accumulation', *Economic Record*, vol. 32, pp. 334–61.

Taylor, L. (1979) *Macro Models for Developing Countries*, New York: McGraw-Hill.

Taylor, L. (1984) 'Social choice theory and the world in which we live', *Cambridge Journal of Economics*, vol. 8, no. 2 (June), pp. 189–96.

Thirlwall, A. P. (1986) 'A general model of growth and development on Kaldorian lines', *Oxford Economic Papers*, **38**, no. 2, pp. 199–219.

Toye, J. (1987) *Dilemmas of Development*, Oxford: Basil Blackwell.

Travis, W. P. (1964) *The Theory of Trade and Protection*, Harvard

Economic Studies, vol. 121, Cambridge, Masachusetts: Harvard University Press.

UN (1963) *The Growth of World Industry 1938–61*, New York: United Nations.

UN (1971) 'Indices to the international standard industrial classification of all economic activities', *Statistical Papers*, Series M, no. 4, rev. 2, add. 1; indexed, New York: United Nations.

UN (1973) *The Growth of World Industry*, I, New York: United Nations.

UN (1975) 'Standard international trade classification', Revision 2, *Statistical Papers*, Series M, no. 34, rev. 2, New York: United Nations.

UNIDO (1986) *International Comparative Advantage in Manufacturing*, Vienna: UNIDO.

Vanek, J. (1959) 'The natural resource content of foreign trade, 1870–1955, and the relative abundance of natural resources in the United States', *Review of Economics and Statistics*, vol. 41 (May), pp. 146–53.

Vanek, J. (1963) 'Variable factor proportions and inter-industry flows in the theory of international trade', *Quarterly Journal of Economics*, vol. 77 (February), no. 1, pp. 129–42.

Vanek, J. (1968) 'The factor proportions theory: The N-factor case', *Kyklos*, vol. 21 (October), pp. 749–56.

Viner, J. (1934) *Tariffs*, Encyclopaedia of Social Sciences, vol. 14, pp. 514–22, New York: Macmillan.

Vines, D. (1984) 'A North–South growth model along Kaldorian lines', Discussion Paper Series no. 26, Centre for Economic Policy Research, London.

Walsh, V. and Gram, H. (1980) *Classical and Neoclassical Theories of General Equilibrium: Historical Origins and Mathematical Structure*, New York: Oxford University Press.

Watanabe, T. (1968) 'Technical progress and dual structure', in L. Klein, and K. Ohkawa (eds) *Economic Growth: The Japanese Experience Since the Meiji Era*, Homewood, Illinois: Richard D. Irwin.

White, G. (1984) 'Developmental states and socialist industrialisation in the Third World', in: R. Kaplinsky (ed.) *Third World Industrialisation in the 1980s: Open Economies in a Closing World*, London: Frank Cass.

White, G. (1986) 'Developmental states and African agriculture: An editorial preface', *IDS Bulletin* (January).

White, G. and Wade, R. (eds) (1988) *Development States and Markets in East Asia*, London: Macmillan.

Whitin, T. M. (1953) 'Classical theory, Graham's theory and linear programming in international trade', *Quarterly Journal of Economics*, vol. 67 (November), pp. 520–44.

Wicksell, K. (1934) *Lectures on Political Economy*, vol. 1, London: Routledge.

Williams, J. H. (1929) 'Theory of international trade reconsidered', *Economic Journal*, vol. 39 (June), pp. 195–209.

Williamson, O. E. (1975) *Markets and Hierarchies: Analysis and Anti-Trust Implications*, New York: The Free Press.

Williamson, O. E. (1985) *The Economic Institutions of Capitalism: Firms, Markets and Rational Contracting*, New York: The Free Press.

Willoughby, J. (1986) *Capitalist Imperialism, Crisis and the State*, Switzerland: Harwood Academic Publishers.

Wood, A. (1986) 'North–South trade: Division of labour or diversion of labour?', *mimeo*, Brighton: IDS, University of Sussex.

Woodland, A. D. (1982) 'International trade and resource allocation', in: C. J. Bliss and M. D. Intriligator (eds) *Advanced Textbooks in Economics*, vol. 19, Amsterdam: Elsevier.

World Bank (1983) *World Development Report 1983*, International Bank for Reconstruction and Development, New York: Oxford University Press.

World Bank (1984) *World Development Report 1984*, International Bank for Reconstruction and Development, New York: Oxford University Press.

World Bank (1985) *World Development Report 1985*, International Bank for Reconstruction and Development, New York: Oxford University Press.

World Bank (1986) *World Development Report 1986*, New York: Oxford University Press.

World Bank (1987) *World Development Report 1987*, New York: Oxford University Press.

# AUTHOR INDEX

# SUBJECT INDEX

accumulation
  as determinant of growth, 303
  Golden Rule of, 134–5, 136, 153
  adjustment, burden of, 239–40
  analytical Marxian theory, 2, 3, 4, 9,
    162–3
  model of trade between England
    and Tropics, 219–22
  magnification effects, 240–3
  see also circulating capital model,
    with labour and resource,
    comparative dynamics
autarky, 2
  circulating capital, with labour,
    196–8
  H–O–S, dynamic model, 136
  H–O–S, static model, 81, 82
  neo-Ricardian model, 173–6
  Ricardian model, 12–16, 161
  see also opening of trade

capital, concepts of, 78–9, 159, 169
circulating capital model
  with labour, 4, 160, 163, 168–78
    neo-Keynesian closure, 171, 176
    Ricardo-Marx-Lewis closure,
      171, 176
    specialisation, 174–5
    steady state equilibrium, 177
  with labour and resource, 163,
    178–83
class, 6–7, 160, 307
  see also interest groups
classical trade theory, 2–3, 46–9, 161
  Williams' critique of, 3, 48–9
  see also Ricardian trade theory

comparative dynamics
  analytical Marxian model, 222–8
comparative statics
  H–O–S model, 114–17
  Lewis term of trade model, 74–6
  Ricardo-Mill model, 56–60, 72–4
  see also magnification effects
composite tradable commodity, 34,
  45n
cone of diversification, 131, 135, 137
  in circulating capital model, 187
  see also specialisation
consumption, optimising conditions
  153–7

development strategies, 309–11
developmental state, 258–61, 311
  role of ideology in, 260
  see also state, role of
diminishing returns in agriculture,
  61–8
  see also Ricardian trade theory,
    economic pessimism
directly profit-seeking control
  (DPC), 257, 310
directly unproductive profit-seeking
  activities (DUP), 255–8
  effects on net benefits of
    protection, 256
distribution closure, 164–7
  neo-Keynesian, 165, 167, 171–2
  Ricardo-Marx, 164–5
  Richardo-Marx-Lewis, 165, 171,
    279, 283
  see also income distribution
Dutch disease, 36, 195, 236–40